Thomas Wentworth Higginson

A larger history of the United States of America : to the close of President Jackson's administration

Thomas Wentworth Higginson

A larger history of the United States of America : to the close of President Jackson's administration

ISBN/EAN: 9783337185534

Printed in Europe, USA, Canada, Australia, Japan

Cover: Foto ©ninafisch / pixelio.de

More available books at **www.hansebooks.com**

GEORGE WASHINGTON.

[Engraved by G. Kruell from the painting by Gilbert Stuart in the Boston Museum of Fine Arts.]

A LARGER HISTORY

OF THE

UNITED STATES OF AMERICA

TO THE CLOSE OF

PRESIDENT JACKSON'S ADMINISTRATION

BY

THOMAS WENTWORTH HIGGINSON
AUTHOR OF
"YOUNG FOLKS' HISTORY OF THE UNITED STATES"

ILLUSTRATED BY MAPS, PLANS, PORTRAITS, AND OTHER ENGRAVINGS

NEW YORK
HARPER & BROTHERS, FRANKLIN SQUARE

Entered according to Act of Congress, in the year 1882, by
HARPER & BROTHERS,
In the Office of the Librarian of Congress, at Washington.

PREFACE.

IT is said by Mr. Conway that Carlyle could never quite forgive Shakespeare for not having written a history of England; and it would seem that every author, great or small, should do his share, first or last, towards elucidating his own country's annals, or at least making them attractive. Ever since my own humble contribution of this kind in the "Young Folks' History of the United States," I have been repeatedly urged by readers, and even by parents and teachers, to tell the story of the nation over again upon a much larger scale, but on the same general principles. This has now been done, after waiting long enough to make sure of a wholly fresh treatment instead of a mere amplification.

If the smaller book has met the popular demand, or if this work is destined to excite any similar interest, it grows mainly out of one fact—that the theme appears, and has always appeared to me more important, more varied, more picturesque, and more absorbingly interesting than any historic subject offered by the world beside. I know that in this I seem to oppose myself to some of the most cultivated minds among my fellow-countrymen. Hawthorne called American history only a scene of "commonplace prosperity;" Lowell pronounced the details of our early annals to be "essentially dry and unpoetic." Yet Hawthorne by his prose and Lowell by his poetry have done much toward refuting their own charges; and it seems to me, at any rate, that an American author can render no better service than to take up just those despised details and see, by a fair test, whether any nation has better material to offer. Our profounder historical students are now adding enormously to the wealth of this kind of knowledge; and it is the lighter but not always easier task of the literary man to reduce these accumulations into compact shape, select what is most characteristic, and make the result readable. If I have failed in doing this, the defect is not in my subject-matter but in my skill.

My thanks are especially due, among those learned masters of whom I have spoken, to my near neighbors and ever kind friends, Justin Winsor and Charles Deane; and also to a young kinsman who is already following in their laborious footsteps— Dr. Edward Channing, of Harvard University. I owe thanks to the Century Company for the liberty of reprinting, with the original illustrations, a chapter of this work which was first published in their magazine. I am also greatly indebted for the opportunity of photographing valuable portraits to Dr. John C. Warren and Mrs. Gardner Brewer, of Boston; to Winslow Warren, Esq., of Dedham, Mass.; to Hon. William C. Endicott, of Salem, Mass.; to Mrs. G. H. Pendleton, of Cincinnati; to J. G. Rosengarten, Esq., of Philadelphia; to Mrs. Fisher, of Alverthorpe, Germantown, Pa.; to J. R. Bryan, Esq., of Fredericksburgh, Va.; and to the city authorities of Boston. To my publishers I am indebted for most of the illustrations of the volume, and especially for what is, if I mistake not, by far the finest series of portraits of statesmen yet seen in any American book.

CONTENTS.

CHAP.		PAGE
I.	THE FIRST AMERICANS	1
II.	THE VISIT OF THE VIKINGS	27
III.	THE SPANISH DISCOVERERS	52
IV.	THE OLD ENGLISH SEAMEN	75
V.	THE FRENCH VOYAGEURS	108
VI.	"AN ENGLISH NATION"	137
VII.	THE HUNDRED YEARS' WAR	169
VIII.	THE SECOND GENERATION OF ENGLISHMEN IN AMERICA	192
IX.	THE BRITISH YOKE	216
X.	THE DAWNING OF INDEPENDENCE	241
XI.	THE GREAT DECLARATION	265
XII.	THE BIRTH OF A NATION	283
XIII.	OUR COUNTRY'S CRADLE	309
XIV.	THE EARLY AMERICAN PRESIDENTS	333
XV.	THE SECOND WAR FOR INDEPENDENCE	360
XVI.	THE ERA OF GOOD FEELING	381
XVII.	THE GREAT WESTERN MARCH	406
XVIII.	"OLD HICKORY"	431
	INDEX	457

ILLUSTRATIONS.

	PAGE
GEORGE WASHINGTON	*Frontispiece*
RUINS OF THE PUEBLO PINTADO	2
PLAN OF THE PUEBLO PINTADO	3
RESTORATION OF THE PUEBLO HUNGO PAVIE	5
PLAN OF HUNGO PAVIE	6
THE NORTH PUEBLO OF TAOS	8
RUINED PUEBLO AND CITADEL	9
HODENOSOTE, OR LONG HOUSE OF THE IROQUOIS	12
PLAN OF IROQUOIS HOUSE	12
PLAN OF NECHECOLEE HOUSE	12
FORTIFIED VILLAGE OF MOUND-BUILDERS, GROUND-PLAN	14
FORTIFIED MANDAN VILLAGE	15
FORTIFIED ONONDAGA VILLAGE	16
MORGAN'S HIGH BANK PUEBLO	17
DIEGO DE LANDA'S MAYA ALPHABET	18
COLOSSAL STATUE OF CHAAC-MOL	20
SCULPTURED HEAD OF YUCATAN	21
INCENSE-BURNERS FROM YUCATAN	22
FEMALE FACE FROM TOPILA	23
INDIAN VASE FOUND IN VERMONT	25
VIKING'S WAR SHIP, ENGRAVED ON ROCK IN NORWAY	27
NORSE BOAT UNEARTHED AT SANDEFJORD	32
OLD NORSE RUINS IN GREENLAND	37
THE OLD MILL AT NEWPORT, R. I.	43
STONE WINDMILL AT CHESTERTON	44
THE DIGHTON ROCK	45
THE MOUNT HOPE BAY INSCRIPTION	46
HIEROGLYPHICS ON ROCK IN NEW MEXICO	46
HIEROGLYPHICS ON INSCRIPTION ROCK, NEW MEXICO	47

ILLUSTRATIONS.

	PAGE
North Atlantic, by the Icelander Sigurd Stephanius, in 1570.	50
Christopher Columbus	53
The Vision of Columbus	57
The Landing at Guanahani	61
Da Vinci's Mappemonde	66
A Chart of the Sixteenth Century	67
Vasco Nuñez de Balboa	68
Ponce de Leon	71
Sebastian Cabot, by Holbein	77
Map of Sebastian Cabot	79
Sir John Hawkins, Kt.	86
The Hawkins Arms	88
Defeat of the British under Sir John Hawkins at San Juan de Ulloa	89
Sir Francis Drake	91
"Thomas Moon began to lay about him with his Sword"	93
Part of Map of Drake's Voyages, published by J. Hondius in Holland towards the close of the Sixteenth Century	95
Drake's Attack on San Domingo	99
Thomas Cavendish	102
Capture of the "Santa Anna," Spanish Flag-ship, by Cavendish	103
Sir Walter Raleigh	105
Jacques Cartier	111
Jacques Cartier setting up a Cross at Gaspé	113
The Landing of Jean Ribaut	115
Indian Dwelling and Canoe	117
Indians Decorating Ribaut's Pillar	118
Dominique de Gourgues Avenging the Murder of the Huguenot Colony	120
"He brought both Catholic Priests and Huguenot Ministers, who disputed heartily on the way"	121
Samuel de Champlain	127
Champlain's Fortified Residence at Quebec	130
"He rested his Musket"	132
Attack on an Iroquois Fort	134
Captain John Smith	142
Powhatan	144
Map of the New England Coast, from Captain John Smith's "Historie of Virginia"	145

ILLUSTRATIONS.

	PAGE
MAP OF JAMESTOWN SETTLEMENT, FROM CAPTAIN JOHN SMITH'S "HISTORIE OF VIRGINIA"	148
ARRIVAL OF THE YOUNG WOMEN AT JAMESTOWN	150
VISIT OF PILGRIMS TO THE SHORE	159
JOHN ENDICOTT	161
JOHN WINTHROP	163
CECIL CALVERT, SECOND LORD BALTIMORE	166
DEATH OF KING PHILIP	179
FAC-SIMILE FROM MS. OF FATHER RASLE'S ABENAKI GLOSSARY	186
SIR WILLIAM PEPPERRELL	188
LOUIS JOSEPH MONTCALM	190
JAMES WOLFE	191
COTTON MATHER	196
A QUAKER EXHORTER IN NEW ENGLAND	205
SAMUEL SEWALL	208
ARRESTING A WITCH	209
PETER STUYVESANT TEARING THE LETTER DEMANDING THE SURRENDER OF NEW YORK	212
GOVERNOR ANDROS AND THE BOSTON PEOPLE	221
JAMES OTIS	223
GENERAL OGLETHORPE, FOUNDER OF GEORGIA	226
LORD CHATHAM	228
THE "BOSTON MASSACRE"	230
BURNING OF THE "GASPEE"	231
REV. EZRA STILES	232
PATRICK HENRY	233
AN OUT-OF-DOOR TEA-PARTY IN COLONIAL NEW ENGLAND	236
PAUL REVERE	243
LEXINGTON GREEN.—"IF THEY WANT A WAR, LET IT BEGIN HERE"	246
DR. JOSEPH WARREN	247
GENERAL WILLIAM HEATH	248
FAC-SIMILE OF WARREN'S ADDRESS	250
SAMUEL ADAMS	255
SERGEANT JASPER AT THE BATTLE OF FORT MOULTRIE	261
TRUMBULL'S "SIGNING OF THE DECLARATION"	266
JOHN DICKINSON	270
HOUSE IN WHICH JEFFERSON WROTE THE DECLARATION, CORNER OF MARKET AND SEVENTH STREETS, PHILADELPHIA	274
VIEW OF INDEPENDENCE HALL, THROUGH THE SQUARE	276
TABLE AND CHAIRS USED AT THE SIGNING OF THE DECLARATION	278

ILLUSTRATIONS.

	PAGE
TEARING DOWN THE KING'S ARMS FROM ABOVE THE DOOR IN THE CHAMBER OF THE SUPREME COURT ROOM IN INDEPENDENCE HALL, JULY 8, 1776	280
GARDEN-HOUSE, OWNED BY DR. ENOCH EDWARDS, WHERE JEFFERSON AND OTHERS CELEBRATED THE PASSAGE OF THE DECLARATION	281
THE FRENCH OFFICERS AT NEWPORT	290
GENERAL SIR GUY CARLETON	292
ELBRIDGE GERRY	299
FISHER AMES	301
SHAYS'S MOB IN POSSESSION OF A COURT-HOUSE	303
THE INAUGURATION OF WASHINGTON	307
AT MRS. WASHINGTON'S RECEPTION	315
ALEXANDER HAMILTON	317
MRS. BINGHAM	323
MRS. THEODORE SEDGWICK	325
COUNT FERSEN	334
JOHN ADAMS	337
ABIGAIL ADAMS	341
THOMAS JEFFERSON	345
WASHINGTON IN 1800	351
MERCY WARREN	353
AARON BURR	357
JAMES MADISON	363
IMPRESSMENT OF AMERICAN SEAMEN	367
FRANCIS SCOTT KEY	378
JAMES MONROE	385
HENRY CLAY	391
JOHN RANDOLPH	397
RUFUS KING	401
JOHN QUINCY ADAMS	409
MAP SHOWING THE MOVEMENT OF THE CENTRE OF POPULATION WESTWARD ON THE THIRTY-NINTH PARALLEL	416
JOHN C. CALHOUN	425
ANDREW JACKSON	435
DANIEL WEBSTER	445

HISTORY OF THE UNITED STATES.

I.

THE FIRST AMERICANS.

IT happened to the writer more than once, during the late civil war, to sail up some great Southern river that was to all appearance unfurrowed by the keel of man. If it was not the entrance to a newly discovered continent, it might as well have been. No light-house threw its hospitable gleam across the dangerous bar, no floating buoys marked the intricacies of the channel; the lights had been extinguished, the buoys removed, and the whole coast seemed to have gone back hundreds of years in time, reverting to its primeval and unexplored condition. There was commonly no sound except the light plash of waves or the ominous roll of heavy surf. Once only, I remember, when at anchor in a dense fog off St. Simon's Island, in Georgia, I heard a low continuous noise from the unseen distance, more wild and desolate than anything else in my memory can parallel. It came from within the vast girdle of mist, and seemed as if it might be the cry of lost souls out of some Inferno of Dante; yet it was but the sound of innumerable sea-fowl at the entrance of the outer bay. Amid such experiences I was for the first time enabled to picture to myself the American Continent as its first European visitor saw it.

Lonely as the land may have seemed, those early voyagers always came upon the traces, ere long, of human occupants. Who were those men and women, what was their origin, what

RUINS OF THE PUEBLO PINTADO.

their mode of life? Every one who explores the mounds of the Ohio Valley, or gazes on the ruins of Yucatan, or looks into the wondrous narratives of the Spanish conquerors, must ask himself this question. Until within a few years there has seemed no answer to it. Facts have come in faster and faster, and every new fact has made the puzzle seem more hopeless, so long as no one could offer the solution. These various prehistoric races, so widely sundered, threw no light upon each other; they only deepened each other's darkness. Indians, Aztecs, Mayas, Mound-builders, seemed to have no common origin, no visible analogy of life or habits. The most skilful student was hardly in advance of the least skilful as to any real comprehension of the facts; nor could this possibly be otherwise, so long as the clew to the labyrinth was not found. It is only some thirty years since it may be said to have been discovered; only some eight or ten years since it has been resolutely and persistently used. Let us see what results it has already yielded.

When in 1852 Lieutenant J. H. Simpson, of the United States army, gave to the world the first detailed description of the vast ruined pueblos of New Mexico, and of the other pueblos still occupied, he did not know that he was providing the means for rewriting all the picturesque tales of the early conquerors. All their legends of cisatlantic emperors and em-

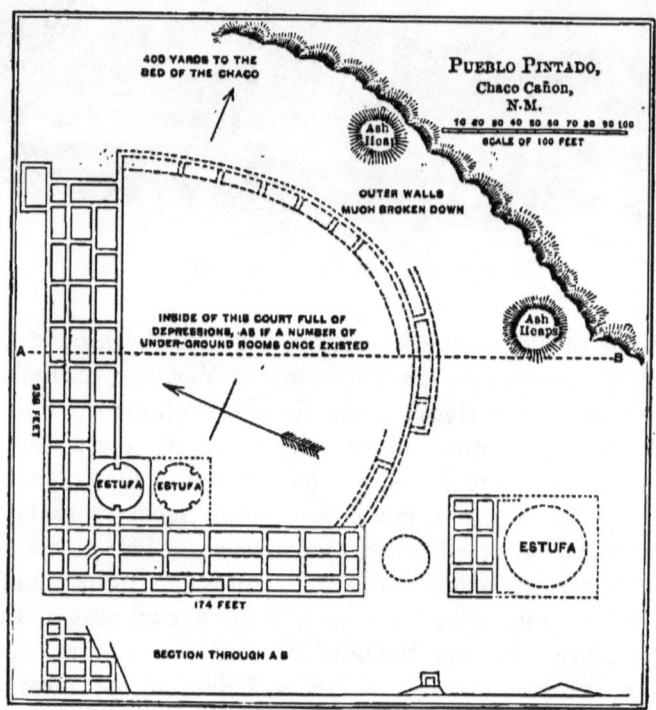

PLAN OF THE PUEBLO PINTADO.

pires were to be read anew in the light of that one discovery. These romances had been told in good faith, or something as near it as the narrator knew, and the tales had passed from one to another, each building on what his predecessor had laid down. The accounts were accepted with little critical revision by modern writers; they filled the attractive pages of Prescott; even Hubert Bancroft did not greatly modify them; but the unshrinking light of a new theory was to raise questions as to them all. And with them were to be linked also Stephens's dreams of vast cities, once occupied by an immense population, and now remaining only as unexplored ruins amid the forests of Central America. The facts he saw were confirmed, but his impressions must be tested by a wholly new interpretation. And, after all, these various wonders were only to be exchanged for new marvels, as interesting as the old ones, and more intelligible and coherent.

From the publication of Lewis H. Morgan's remarkable essay, entitled "Montezuma's Dinner," in the *North American Review* for April, 1876, the new interpretation took a definite form. The vast accumulation of facts in regard to the early American races then began to be classified and simplified; and with whatever difference of opinion as to details, the general opinion of scholars now inclines to the view which, when Morgan first urged it, was called startling and incredible. That view is still a theory, as Darwin's "origin of species" is still a theory; but Morgan's speculations, like Darwin's, have begun a new era for the science to which they relate. He holds that there never was a prehistoric American civilization, properly so called, but only an advanced and wonderfully skilful barbarism, or semi-civilization at the utmost. The aboriginal races, except perhaps the Eskimo, were essentially one in their social structure, he thinks, however varying in development. In his view there never was an Aztec or Maya empire, but only a league of free tribes, appointing their own chiefs, and accepting the same general modes of organization, based on consanguinity, that have prevailed among all the more advanced families of North American Indians. Montezuma was not an emperor, and had no palace, but he lived in the great communal dwelling of his tribe, where he was recognized and served as head. The forests of Yucatan held no vast cities—cities whose palaces remain, while the humble dwellings of the poor have perished—but only pueblo towns, in whose great communal structures the rich and the poor alike dwelt. There are questions enough left unsolved in American archæology, no doubt, but the solution of this part of the problem has now

RESTORATION OF THE PUEBLO HUNGO PAVIE.

been proposed in intelligible terms, at least; and it has been rapidly followed up by the accurate researches of Morgan and Putnam and Bandelier.

I have said that all this new view of the problem dates from our knowledge of the Pueblo or Village Indians of New Mexico. What is a pueblo? It is an Indian town, of organization and aspect so peculiar that it can best be explained by minute descriptions. Let us begin with the older examples, now in ruins. Mr. Bandelier has lately examined for the American Archæological Institute a ruined building at Pecos, in New Mexico, which he claims to be the largest aboriginal structure of stone within the limits of the United States. It has a circuit of 1480 feet, is five stories high, and once included by calculation 500 separate rooms. This is simply a ruined pueblo. This composite dwelling once sheltered the inhabitants of a whole Indian town. Pueblo Bonito, on the Rio Chacos, described by Lieutenant Simpson, and more lately by Dr. W. H. Jackson, is 1716 feet in circuit; it included 641 rooms, and could have housed, it is estimated, 3000 Indians. A stone pueblo on the Animas River, lately visited and described by Mr. L. H. Morgan, had more than 400 rooms—and such instances could easily be multiplied. As a rule, each of these buildings constituted a village—a single vast house built on three sides of a court. The stories rose in successive terraces, each narrower than the one beneath, and each approachable only by ladders, there being no sign of any internal means of ascent from story to story. The outer walls were built usually of thin slabs of gray sandstone, laid with the greatest precision and accuracy, often with no signs of mortar, the intervals being filled with stones of the minutest thinness, so that the whole ruin appears in the distance, according to Simpson, "like a magnificent piece of mosaic-work." These pueblos were practically impregnable to all uncivilized warfare, and they differ only in material, not in the essentials of their structure, from the adobe pueblos occupied by the Village Indians of to-day.

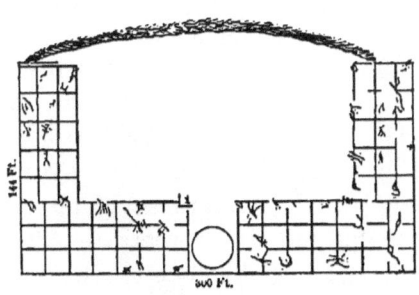

PLAN OF HUNGO PAVIE.

The first impression made by the adobe pueblos now inhabited is quite different from that produced by these great stone structures, yet the internal arrangement is almost precisely the same. As you cross, for instance, the green meadows of the Rio Grande, you see rising abruptly before you, like a colossal ant-hill, a great drab mound, with broken lines that suggest roofs at the top. As you draw nearer, you see before you solid walls or banks of the same drab hue, perforated here and there by small openings. These walls are in tiers—tiers of terraces —each spreading out flat at the top, and a few feet wide, with a higher one behind it, and another behind that, until in some cases they are five stories high. Strips of what seems lattice-work stand on these terraces, slanted, tilted, propped irregularly here and there; they also are of a drab color, "as if walls, roofs, ladders, all had been run, wet mud, into a fretted mould, baked, and turned out like some freaky confectioner's device made of opaque, light brown cough candy." At intervals upon these terraces, or on the ground near the base of the walls, there stand low oval mounds of the same baked drab mud, shaped like the half of an egg-shell, with an aperture left in the small end. Then there are on the roof, lifted a few feet above them, little thatches of brush, ragged and unfinished, like the first rough platform of twigs and mud which the robin constructs for her nest. Closer inspection shows that the tiers and terraces are the stories and roofs of the houses; the holes are doors and windows opening into rooms under the terraced roofs; the strips of lattice-work are ladders, these being the only means of going from one terrace to another; the little oval mounds are ovens; and the bits of thatch are arbors on the roofs. In the pueblo of San Juan—as recently portrayed by Mrs. Helen Jackson, of whose graphic description the above is but an abstract—there are four or five of these large terraced buildings, with a small open plaza or court between. When this lady visited the scene, upon a festal day, this plaza was filled with Indians and Mexicans, and the terraces were all covered with them, dressed for the most part in blankets of the gayest colors, relieved against the drab adobe walls or against a brilliant blue sky. This group of strange structures, thus tenanted and thus adorned, is an inhabited pueblo.

Sometimes, as at Taos, the separate dwellings or cells of the building are so crowded together as to resemble, in the words of Bandelier, "an extraordinarily large honey-comb." The same

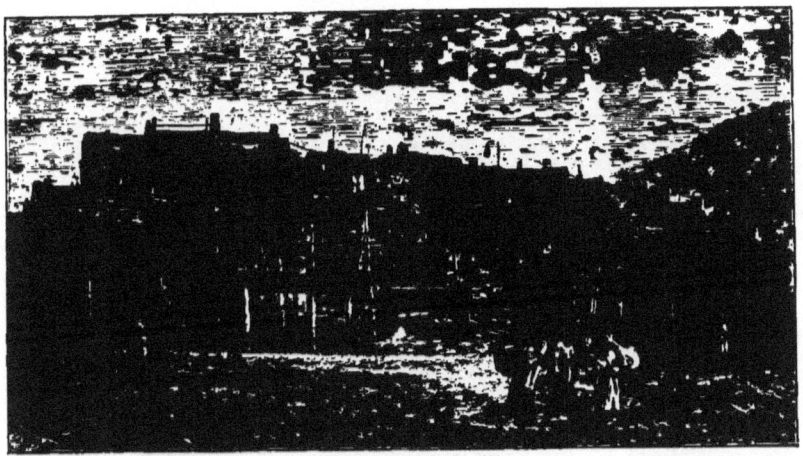

THE NORTH PUEBLO OF TAOS.

is the case with that of Zuñi, both these pueblos being now inhabited, and the latter, which is the larger, giving shelter to fifteen hundred Indians. Others again, like that of Acoma, are so protected by their situation that this close aggregation of cells is not necessary; and the little tenements are simply placed side by side like houses in a block, the whole being perched on a cliff three hundred and fifty feet high, accessible only by a single row of steps cut in the rock. Sometimes the whole structure is in a cleft of a rock, yet even there it is essentially a pueblo, with the same terraces and the same ladders, so far as there is room. Sometimes we find the main pueblo, ruined or inhabited, beneath the cliff, and the citadel of refuge in a position almost inaccessible among the rocks above. Many of these masses of building are now occupied, more are in ruins. Each shelters, or may have sheltered, hundreds of inhabitants, and the existing Village Indians probably represent for us not merely the race, but the mode of living of those who built every one of these great structures. If we wish to know what was the America which Cortez invaded, we must look for it in the light of these recent investigations.

RUINED PUEBLO AND CITADEL.

No trace now remains of the so-called city of Mexico, as Cortez saw it; but we know, in a vague way, how it compared with the pueblos that still exist. The clew to a comparison is as follows: There prevailed in the sixteenth century a legend that seven bishops had once sailed west from Portugal, and founded seven cities in America. Cabeza de Vaca, after his wanderings in the interior of America in 1536, brought back an account of large and semi-civilized communities dwelling in palaces; and it was thought that these might be identified with the cities founded by the bishops. They were seen again by Fray Marco de Niza in 1539, and by Coronado in 1540, and were by them mentioned as "the seven cities of Cibola." Coronado fully describes the "great houses of stone," "with ladders instead of stairs," thus identifying them unmistakably with the still existing pueblos. Whether they were the seven pueblos of the Zuñis, or those of the Moquis in Arizona, is as yet unsettled; but it is pretty certain that they were identical with the one or the other; and as Fray Marco declared them to be in his day "more considerable than Mexico," we have something like a standard of comparison. Such great communal houses, which could shelter a whole Spanish army within their walls, could seem nothing else than palaces to those wholly unused to the social organization which they represented. The explorers reasoned, just as students reasoned for three centuries longer, that structures so vast could only have been erected by despotism. They saw an empire where there was no empire; they supposed themselves in presence of a feudalism like their own; all their descriptions were cast in the mould of this feudalism, and the mould remained unbroken until the civilized world, within thirty years, rediscovered the pueblos.

Again, so long as the Pueblo Indians were unknown to us, there appeared an impassable gap between the roving Indians of the North and the more advanced race that Cortez conquered. Yet writers had long since pointed out the seeming extravagance of the Spanish descriptions, the exaggeration of their statistics. In the celebrated Spanish narrative of Montezuma's banquet, Bernal Diaz, writing thirty years after the event, describes four women as bringing water to their chief—an occurrence not at all improbable. In the account by Herrera, written still later, the four have increased to twenty. According to Diaz, Montezuma had 200 of his nobility on guard in the palace; Cortez expands them to 600, and Herrera to 3000. Zuazo, describing the pueblo or town of Mexico in 1521, attributed to it 60,000 inhabitants, and the "anonymous conqueror" who was with Cortez wrote the same. This estimate Morgan believes to have been twice too large; but Gomara and Peter Martyr transformed the inhabitants into houses—the estimate which Prescott follows—while Torquemada, cited by Clavigero, goes still further, and writes 120,000 houses. Supposing that, as seems probable, the Mexican houses were of the communal type, holding fifty or a hundred persons each, we have an original population of perhaps 30,000 swollen to 6,000,000. These facts illustrate the extravagances of statement to which the study of the New Mexican pueblos has put an end. This study has led us to abate much of the exaggeration with which the ancient Mexican society has been treated, and on the other hand to do justice to the more advanced among the tribes of Northern Indians. The consequence is that the two types appear less unlike each other than was formerly supposed.

Let us compare the habits of the Pueblo Indians with those of more northern tribes. Lewis and Clark thus describe a village of the Chopunish, or Nez Percés, on the Columbia River:

"The village of Tunnachemootoolt is in fact only a single house 150 feet long, built after the Chopunish fashion with sticks, straw, and dried grass. It contains twenty-four fires, about double that number of families, and might perhaps muster one hundred fighting men."

This represents a communal household of nearly five hundred people, and another great house of the same race (Nechecolees) was still larger, being 226 feet in length. The houses of the Iroquois were 100 feet long. The Creeks, the Mandans, the Sacs, the Mohaves, and other tribes lived in a similar communal way, several related families in each house, living and eating in common. All these built their houses of perishable materials; some arranged them for defence, others did not, but all the structures bear a certain analogy to each other, and even, when carefully considered, to the pueblos of New Mexico.

HODENOSOTE, OR LONG HOUSE OF THE IROQUOIS.

Compare, for instance, a ground-plan of one of the Chopunish houses among the Nechecolees with that of an Iroquois house and with a New Mexican pueblo, and one is struck with the resemblance. All these houses seem obviously adapted to a communal life, and traces of this practice, varying in different places, come constantly before us. The Pueblo Indians hold their lands in common. The traveller Stephens saw near the ruins of Uxmal the food of a hundred laboring-men prepared at one hut, and each family sending for its own portion — "a procession of

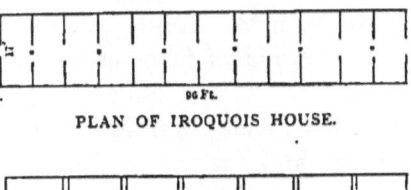

PLAN OF IROQUOIS HOUSE.

PLAN OF NECHECOLEE HOUSE.

women and children, each carrying a smoking bowl of hot broth, all coming down the same path, and dispersing among the huts." But this description might easily be paralleled among Northern tribes. I will not dwell on the complex laws of descent and relationship, which are so elaborately described by Morgan in his "Ancient Society," and which appear to have prevailed among all the aboriginal clans. The essential result of all these various observations is this, that whatever degree of barbarism or semi-civilization was attained by any of the early American races, it was everywhere based on similar ways of living; it never resembled feudalism, but came much nearer to communism; it was the condition of a people substantially free, whose labor was voluntary, and whose chiefs were of their own choosing. After the most laborious investigation ever made into the subject, Bandelier—in the twelfth report of the Peabody Institute—comes to the conclusion that "the social organization and mode of government of the ancient Mexicans was a military democracy, originally based upon communism in living." And if this was true even in the seemingly powerful and highly organized races of Mexico, it was certainly true of every North American tribe.

If we accept this conclusion — and the present tendency of archæologists is to accept it—the greater part of what has been written about prehistoric American civilization proves to have been too hastily said. Tylor, for instance, after visiting the pyramid of Cholula, twenty-five years ago, laid it down as an axiom: "Such buildings as these can only be raised under peculiar social conditions. The ruler must be a despotic sovereign, and the mass of the people slaves, whose subsistence and whose lives are sacrificed without scruple to execute the fancies of the monarch, who is not so much the governor as the unrestricted owner of the country and the people." He did not sufficiently consider that this is the first and easiest way to explain all great structures representing vast labor.

An American writer finds it necessary to explain even the works of the Mound-builders in a similar way. Mr. Foster thinks it clear that "the condition of society among the Mound-builders was not that of freemen, or, in other words,

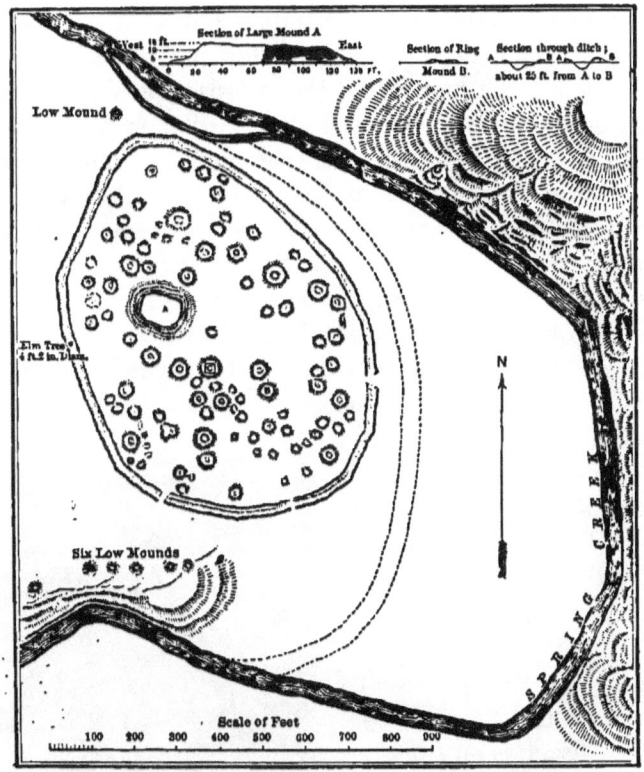

FORTIFIED VILLAGE OF MOUND-BUILDERS, GROUND-PLAN.

that the State possessed absolute power over the lives and fortunes of its subjects." But the theory of despotism is no more needed to explain a mound or a pueblo than to justify the existence of the "Long Houses" of the Iroquois. Even the less civilized types of the aboriginal American race had learned how to unite in erecting their communal dwellings; and surely the higher the grade the greater the power.

The Mound-builders were formerly regarded as a race so remote from the present Indian tribes that there could be nothing in common between them, yet all recent inquiries tend to diminish this distance. Many Indian tribes have built burial mounds for their dead. Squier, after the publication of his great work on the mounds of the Mississippi Valley, made an exploration of those of Western New York, and found, contrary to all his preconceived opinions, that these last must have been made by the Iroquois. Some of the most elaborate series of works, as those at Marietta and Circleville, Ohio, have yielded from their deepest recesses articles of European manufacture, showing an origin not farther back than the historic period. Spanish swords and blue glass beads have been found in the mounds of Georgia and Florida. But we need not go so far as this to observe the analogies of structure. If we look at Professor Putnam's ground-plan of a fortified village of the Mound-builders on Spring Creek, in Tennessee, and compare it with a similar plan of a Mandan village as given by Prince Maximilian of Neuwied in 1843, we find their arrangement to be essentially the same. Each is on a promontory protected by the bend of a stream; each is surrounded by an embankment which was once, in all prob-

FORTIFIED MANDAN VILLAGE.

ability, surmounted by a palisade. Within this embankment were the houses, distributed more irregularly in Putnam's plan, more formally and conventionally in that of the Prince of Neuwied; in other respects the two villages are almost duplicates. To see how they may have looked when occupied, we may compare them with a representation of a village of the Onondagas, attacked by Champlain in 1615. This

FORTIFIED ONONDAGA VILLAGE.

wood-cut is reproduced from one in the "Documentary History of New York." It is clear that the Mound-builders had much in common with those well-known tribes of Indians the Mandans and Onondagas, in their way of placing and protecting their houses; and another comparison has lately been made which links their works on the other side with the New Mexican pueblos. Mr. Morgan has caused to be prepared a conjectural restoration of the High Bank mounds in Ross County, Ohio, on the theory that in that instance the houses of the inhabitants were "Long Houses" in structure, and were built for defensive purposes on top of the embankment. This makes the villages into pueblos, and Mr. Morgan therefore baptizes the settlement anew with the name of "High Bank Pueblo." A mere glance at his restoration will show how

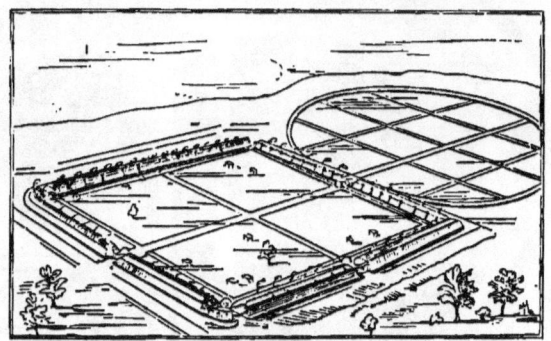

MORGAN'S HIGH BANK PUEBLO.

much there was in common between the various types of what he calls the aboriginal American race.

It remains to be considered whether the very highest forms of this race—the Aztecs and the Mayas—were properly to be called civilized. It is a matter of definitions; it depends upon what we regard as constituting civilization. Here was a people whose development showed strange contradictions. The ancient Mexicans were skilled in horticulture, yet had no beasts of burden and no milk, although the ox and buffalo were within easy reach. They were a trading people, and used money, but had apparently no system of weighing. They used stone tools so sharp that Cortez found barbers shaving with razors of obsidian in the public squares; they worked in gold and copper, yet they had not learned to make iron tools from the masses of that metal which lay, almost pure, in the form of aerolites, in their midst. They could observe eclipses and make a calendar, yet it is still doubtful whether they had what is properly to be

	Signs.	Phonetic value.		Signs.	Phonetic value.		Signs.	Phonetic value.
1.		a	10.		i	19.		p
2.		a	11.		ca	20.		pp
3.		a	12.		k	21.		cu
4.		b	13.		l	22.		ku
5.		b	14.		l	23.		x#
6.		e	15.		m	24.		x
7.		t	16.		n	25.		u
8.		ć	17.		o;	26.		u
9.		h	18.		o.	27.		z

DIEGO DE LANDA'S MAYA ALPHABET.

called an alphabet. It is certain that they had a method of picture-writing, not apparently removed in kind from the sort of pictorial mnemonics practised by many tribes of Indians at the present day; and all definite efforts to extract more than this from it have thus far failed. Brasseur de Bourbourg believed that he had found in 1863, in the library of the Royal Academy of History at Madrid, a manuscript key to the phonetic alphabet of the Mayas. It was attached to an unpublished description of Yucatan ("Relacion de las Cosas de Yucatan"), written by Diego de Landa, one of the early Spanish bishops of that country. Amid the general attention of "Americanists," Brasseur de Bourbourg tried his skill upon one of the few Maya manuscripts, but with little success; and Dr. Valentini, with labored analysis, has lately given his reasons for thinking the whole so-called alphabet a Spanish fabrication. The very question of the alphabet remains, therefore, still unproved, while Tylor, the highest living authority on anthropology, considers it essential to the claim of civilization that a nation should have a written language. Tried by this highest standard, therefore, we cannot yet say that either the Aztecs or the Mayas were civilized.

To sum up the modern theory, the key to the whole aboriginal American society is given in the pueblos of New Mexico, representing the communal household. This household is still to be seen at its lowest point in the lodges of the roving Indians of the North, and it produced, when carried to its highest point, all the art and architecture of Uxmal, and all the so-called civilization which the Spanish conquerors admired, exaggerated, and overthrew. The mysterious mounds of the Ohio Valley were erected only that they might give to their builders the advantages possessed without labor by those who dwelt upon the high table-lands of New Mexico. The great ruined edifices in the valley of the Chacos are the same in kind with the ruined "palaces" of Yucatan. All these — lodges, palaces, and pueblos alike — are but the communal dwellings of one great aboriginal race, of uncertain origin and history, varying greatly in grade of development, but one in institutions, in society, and in blood. This is the modern theory, a theory which has given a new impulse to all investigation and all thought upon this subject, but one which the lamented death of its originator leaves only half developed, after' all, so that it must be mentioned as a theory still.

What is now its strength, at this moment, and what its weakness? Its strength is that of a strong, simple, intelli-

COLOSSAL STATUE OF CHAAC-MOL.

gible working hypothesis — not merely the best that has been offered, but the first. What is its weakness? This only, that, like many a promising theory in the natural sciences, it may prove to be only too simple, after all, and not quite adequate to account for the facts.

Mr. Morgan, with all his great merits, had not always the moderation which gives such peculiar value to the works of Darwin; he was not always willing to distinguish between what was firm ground and what was only tentative. In order to make his theory appear consistent he had to ignore many difficulties, and settle many points in an off-hand manner, and there is something almost exasperating in the positiveness with which he sometimes assumes as proved that which is only probable. Grant all his analogies of the *gens* and the communal dwelling, the fact still is that in studying the Central

American remains we are dealing with a race who had got beyond mere household architecture, and were rising to the sphere of art, so that their attempts in this respect must enter into our estimate. In studying them from this point of view, we encounter new difficulties which Mr. Morgan wholly ignores. The tales of the Spanish conquerors are scarcely harder to accept than the assumption that all the artistic decoration of the Yucatan edifices was lavished upon communal houses, built only to be densely packed with Indians "in the Middle Status of Barbarism," as Morgan calls them. That a

SCULPTURED HEAD OF YUCATAN.

statue like that of Chaac-Mol, discovered by Dr. Le Plongeon at Chichen-Itza, should have been produced by a race not differing in descent or essential habits from the Northern Iroquois, seems simply incredible.

Consider the difference. In Central America we find the remains of a race which had begun to busy itself with the very highest department of art, the delineation of the human figure; and which had attained to grace and vigor, if not yet to beauty, in this direction. The stately stone heads of Yucatan; the arch and spirited features depicted on the Maya incense-burners; the fine face carved in sandstone, brought from Topila, and now in possession of the New York Historical Society—these indicate a sphere of development utterly beyond that of those Northern Indians whose utmost achievement consists in some graceful vase like that found in Burlington, Vermont, and now preserved by the Vermont University.

INCENSE-BURNERS FROM YUCATAN.

It is safer to leave the question where it is left by another deceased American archæologist scarcely less eminent than Mr. Morgan, and not less courageous, but far more gentle and more guarded, the late Samuel Foster Haven, of Worcester, Massachusetts, the accomplished librarian of the American

Antiquarian Society: "Mr. Morgan has grasped some of the problems of aboriginal character and habits with a firm and vigorous hand, but is far from being entitled to claim that he has discovered the entire secret of prehistoric life on this continent."

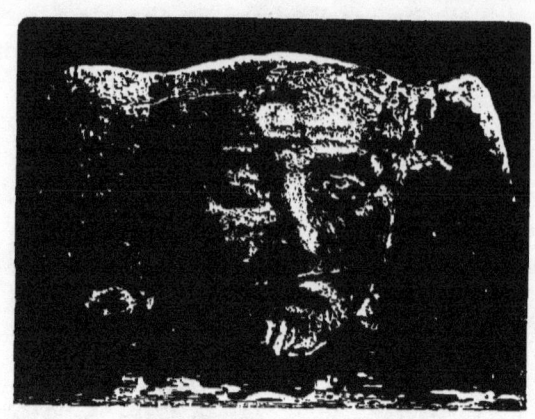

FEMALE FACE FROM TOPILA.

But now suppose the modern theory to be accepted in its fulness. Let us agree, for the moment, with Morgan, that there was in America, when discovered, but one race of Indians besides the Eskimo — the Red Race. Still there lies behind us the problem, in whose solution science has hardly yet gained even a foothold, Whence did this race originate? Here we deliberately confuse ourselves a little by the word "discovery." When we speak of the discovery of America we always mean the arrival of Europeans, forgetting that there was probably a time when Europe itself was first discovered by Asiatics, and that for those Asiatics it was almost as easy to discover America. All that is necessary, even at this day, to bring a Japanese junk to the Pacific coast of North America is that it should be blown out to sea and then lose its rudder; the first mishap has often happened, the second casualty has almost always followed, and the Gulf Stream of the Pacific, the Kuro Siwo, or "black stream," or "Japan current," has done the rest. Mr. Charles W. Brooks, of San Francisco, has a record of no less than a hundred such instances, and there is no reason why similar events should not have been occurring for centuries. Nor is it, indeed, needful to go so far as this for a means of communication. Behring Strait is but little wider than the English Channel, and it is as easy to make the passage from Asia to America as from France to England; and indeed easier for half the year, when Behring Strait is frozen. Besides all this, both geology and botany indicate that the separation between the two continents did not always exist. Dr. Asa Gray, our highest botanical authority, long since pointed out the extraordinary identity between the Japanese flora and that of the Northern United States, as indicating a period when the two continents were one. It is an argument difficult to resist, for surely flowers do not cross the ocean in junks, or traverse the frozen straits upon the ice. The colonization of America from Asia was thus practicable, at any rate, and that far more easily than any approach from the European side. The simple races on each side of Behring Strait, which now communicate with each other freely, must have done the same from very early times. They needed no consent of sovereigns to do it: they were not obliged to wait humbly in the antechamber of some king, suing for permission to discover for him another world. This we must recognize at the outset; but when it is granted, we are still upon the threshold. Concede that America is but an outlying Asia, it does not follow that America was peopled from Asia; the course of population may first have gone the other way. Or it may be that the human race had upon each continent an autochthonous or indigenous place, according as we prefer a hard Greek word or a hard Latin word to express the simple fact that a race comes into existence on a certain soil, instead of migrating thither. Migrations, too, in plenty may in this case have come afterwards, and modified the type, giving to it that Asiatic or Mongoloid cast which is now acknowledged by almost all ethnologists.

INDIAN VASE FOUND IN VERMONT.

How long may this process of migration and mingling have gone on upon the American continent? Who can tell? Sir John Lubbock, a high authority, says "not more than three thousand years;" but it is not so easy to fix a limit. To be sure, some evidences of antiquity that are well established in Europe are as yet wanting in America, or at least imperfectly proved. In the French bone-caves there have been found unquestionable representations of the mammoth scratched on pieces of its own ivory, and exhibiting the shaggy hair and curved tusks that distinguish it from all other elephants. There is as yet no such direct and unequivocal evidence in America of the existence of man during the interglacial period.

The alleged evidence, as given in the books up to the present time, fails to satisfy the more cautious archæologists. The so-called "elephants' trunks" used in ornamentation on the Central American buildings offer only a vague and remote resemblance to the supposed originals. The "elephant pipe" dug up in Iowa, and now preserved by the Davenport Academy of Sciences, does not quite command confidence as to its genuineness. The "Elephant Mound," described and figured in the Smithsonian Report for 1872, has a merely suggestive resemblance, like most of the mounds, to the objects whose name it bears. Lapham long since pointed out that the names of "Lizard Mound," "Serpent Mound," and the like, are usually based on very remote similarities; and Squier tells us of one mound which has been likened successively to a bird, a bow and arrow, and a man.

Other sources of evidences are scarcely more satisfactory. There is no doubt that mammoth bones have been found mingled with arrow-heads in some places, and with matting or pottery in others; but unhappily some doubt rests as yet on all these discoveries. It is in no case quite sure that the deposits had remained undisturbed as found, or that they had not been washed together by floods of water. Up to the present time the strongest argument in favor of the very early existence of man upon this continent is not to be found in such comparatively simple lines of evidence, but in the investigations of Dr. Abbott among primeval implements in New Jersey, or those of Professor J. D. Whitney among human remains in California. Their inquiries may yet conclusively establish the fact that the aboriginal American man was contemporary with the mammoth; in the mean time it is only probable, not quite proved.

Must we not admit that in our efforts to explain the origin of the first American man, it is necessary to end, after all, with an interrogation mark?

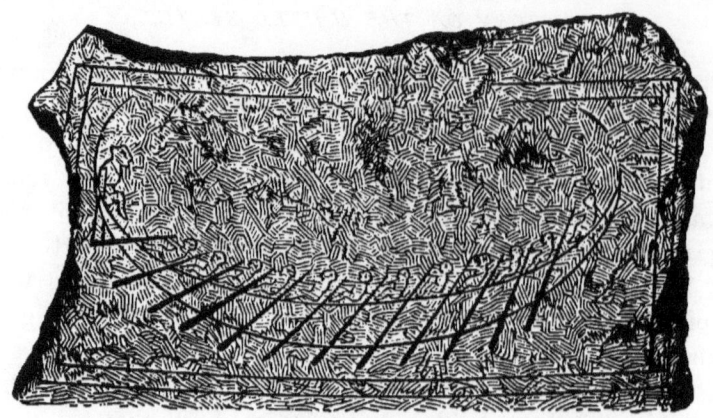

VIKING'S WAR SHIP, ENGRAVED ON ROCK IN NORWAY.

II.

THE VISIT OF THE VIKINGS.

THE American antiquarians of the last generation had a great dislike to anything vague or legendary, and they used to rejoice that there was nothing of that sort about the discovery of America. The history of other parts of the world, they said, might begin in myth and tradition, but here at least was firm ground, a definite starting-point, plain outlines, and no vague and shadowy romance. Yet they were destined to be disappointed, and it may be that nothing has been lost, after all. Our low American shores would look tame and uninteresting but for the cloud and mist which are perpetually trailing in varied beauty above them, giving a constant play of purple light and pale shadow, and making them deserve the name given to such shores by the old Norse legends, " Wonderstrands." It is the same, perhaps, with our early history. It may be fitting that the legends of the Northmen should come in, despite all the resistance of antiquarians, to supply just that indistinct and vague element which is needed for picturesqueness. At any rate, whether we like it or not, the legends are here.

I can well remember, as a boy, the excitement produced among Harvard College professors when the ponderous volume called "Antiquitates Americanæ," containing the Norse legends of "Vinland," with the translations of Professor Rafn, made its appearance on the library table. For the first time the claim was openly made that there had been European visitors to this continent before Columbus. The historians shrank from the innovation: it spoiled their comfort. Indeed, Mr. George Bancroft to this day will hardly allude to the subject, and sets aside the legends, using a most inappropriate phrase, as "mythological." And it so happened, as will appear by-and-by, that when the claim was first made it was encumbered with some very poor arguments. Nevertheless, the main story was not permanently hurt by these weak points. Its truth has never been successfully impeached; at any rate, we cannot deal with American history unless we give some place to the Norse legends. Picturesque and romantic in themselves, they concern men in whom we have every reason to be interested. These Northmen, or Vikings, were not merely a far-away people with whom we have nothing in common, but they really belonged to the self-same race of men with most of ourselves. They were, perhaps, the actual ancestors of some living Americans, and kinsfolk to the majority. Men of the same race conquered England, and were known as Saxons; then conquered France, and were known as Normans; and finally crossed over from France and conquered England again. These Norse Vikings were, like most of us, Scandinavians, and so were really closer to us in blood and in language than was the great Columbus.

What were the ways and manners of these Vikings? We

must remember at the outset that their name implies nothing of royalty. They were simply the dwellers on a *vik*, or bay. They were, in other words, the sea-side population of the Scandinavian peninsula, the only part of Europe which then sent forth a race of sea-rovers. They resembled in some respects the Algerine corsairs of a later period, but, unlike the Algerines, they were conquerors as well as pirates, and were ready to found settlements wherever they went. Nor were the Vikings yet Christians, for their life became more peaceful from the time when Christianity came among them. In the prime of their heathenism they were the terror of Europe. They carried their forays along the whole continent. They entered every port in England, and touched at every island on the Scottish coast. They sailed up French rivers, and Charlemagne, the ruler of Western Europe, wept at seeing their dark ships. They reached the Mediterranean, and formed out of their own number the famous Varangian guard of the later Greek emperors, the guard which is described by Walter Scott in "Count Robert of Paris." They reached Africa, which they called "Saracens' Land," and there took eighty castles. All their booty they sent back to Norway, and this wealth included not only what they took from enemies, but what they had from the very courts they served; for it was the practice at Constantinople, when an emperor died, for the Norse guard to go through the palaces and take whatever they could hold in their hands. To this day Greek and Arabic gold coins and chains are found in the houses of the Norwegian peasants, and may be seen in the museums of Christiania and Copenhagen.

Such were the Vikings, and it is needless to say that with such practices they were in perpetual turmoil at home, and needed a strong hand to keep the peace among them. Sometimes a king would make a foray among his own people, as recorded in this extract from the "Heimskringla," or "Kings of Norway," written by Snorri Sturleson, and translated by Laing:

> "King Harald heard that the Vikings, who were in the West Sea in winter, plundered far and wide in the middle part of Norway, and therefore every summer he made an expedition to search the isles and outskerries [outlying rocks] on the coast. Wheresoever the Vikings heard of him they all took to flight, and most of them out into the open ocean. At last the king grew weary of this work, and therefore one summer he sailed with his fleet right out into the West Sea. First he came to Shetland, and he slew all the Vikings who could not save themselves by flight. Then King Harald sailed southward to the Orkney Islands, and cleared them all of Vikings. Thereafter he proceeded to the Hebrides, plundered there, and slew many Vikings who formerly had had men-at-arms under them. Many a battle was fought, and King Harald was always victorious. He then plundered far and wide in Scotland itself, and had a battle there."

We see from the last sentence that King Harald himself was but a stronger Viking, and that, after driving away other plunderers, he did their work for himself. Such were all the Norsemen of the period; they were daring, generous, open-handed. They called gold in their mythology "the serpent's bed," and called a man who was liberal in giving "a hater of the serpent's bed," because such a man parts with gold as with a thing he hates. But they were cruel, treacherous, unscrupulous. Harald, when he commanded the emperor's body-guard at Constantinople, and was associated with Greek troops, always left his allies to fight for themselves and be defeated, and only fought where his Northmen could fight alone and get all the glory. While seeming to defend the Emperor Michael, he enticed him into his power and put out his eyes. The Norse chronicles never condemn such things; there is never a voice in favor of peace or mercy; but they assume, as a matter of course, that a leader shall be foremost in attack and last in retreat. In case of need he must give his life for his men. There is no finer touch in Homer than is found in one of the sagas which purport to describe the Norse voyages to Vinland. It must be remembered, in order to understand it, that the Northmen believed that certain seas were infested with the teredo, or ship-worm, and that vessels in those seas were in the very greatest danger.

> "Bjarni Grimalfson was driven with his ship into the Irish Ocean, and they came into a worm-sea, and straightway began the ship to sink under them. They had a boat which was smeared with seal oil, for the sea-worms do not attack that. They went into the boat, and then saw that it could not hold them all. Then said Bjarni: 'Since the boat cannot give room to more than the half of our men, it is my counsel that lots should be drawn for those to go in the boat, for it shall not be according to rank.' This thought they all so high-minded an offer that no one would speak against it. They then did so that lots were drawn, and it fell upon Bjarni to go in the boat, and the half of the men with him, for the boat had not room for more. But when they had gotten into the boat, then said an Icelandic man who was in the ship, and had come with Bjarni from Iceland, 'Dost thou intend, Bjarni, to separate from me here?' Bjarni answered, 'So it turns out.' Then said the other, 'Very different was thy promise to my father when I went with thee from Iceland than thus to abandon me, for thou saidst that we should both share the same fate.' Bjarni replied: 'It shall not be thus. Go thou down into the boat, and I will go up into the ship, since I see that thou art so desirous to live.' Then went Bjarni up into the ship, but this man down into the boat, and after that continued they their voyage until they came to Dublin, in Ireland, and told there these things. But it is most people's belief that Bjarni and his companions were lost in the worm-sea, for nothing was heard of them since that time."

Centuries have passed since the ships of the Vikings floated on the water, and yet we know, almost as if they had been launched yesterday, their model and their build. They are found delineated on rocks in Norway, and their remains are still dug up from beneath the ground. One of them was unearthed lately from a mound of blue clay at Gokstad or Sandefjord, in Norway, at a point now half a mile from the sea; and it had plainly been used as the burial-place of its owner. The sepulchral chamber in which the body of the Viking had been deposited was built amidships, being tent-like in shape, and made of logs placed side by side, leaning against a ridge-pole. In this chamber were found human bones, the bones of a little dog, the bones and feathers of a peacock, some fish-hooks, and several bronze and lead ornaments for belts and harness. Round about the ship were found the bones of nine or ten horses and dogs, which had probably been sacrificed at the time of the burial. The vessel was seventy-seven feet eleven inches at the greatest length, and sixteen feet eleven inches at the greatest width, and from the top of the keel to the gunwale amidships she was five feet nine inches deep. She had twenty ribs, and would draw less than four feet of water. She was clinker-built; that is, had plates slightly overlapped, like the shingles on the side of a house. The planks and timbers of the frame were fast-

NORSE BOAT UNEARTHED AT SANDEFJORD.

ened together with withes made of roots, but the oaken boards of the side were united by iron rivets firmly clinched. The bow and stern were similar in shape, and must have risen high out of water, but were so broken that it was impossible to tell how they originally ended. The keel was deep, and made of thick oak beams, and there was no trace of any metallic sheathing; but an iron anchor was found almost rusted to pieces. There was no deck, and the seats for rowers had been taken out. The oars were twenty feet long, and the oar-holes, sixteen on each side, had slits sloping towards the stern to allow the blades of the oars to be put through from inside.

The most peculiar thing about the ship was the rudder, which was on the starboard or right side, this side being originally called "steerboard" from this circumstance. The rudder was like a large oar, with long blade and short handle, and was attached, not to the side of the boat, but to the end of a conical piece of wood which projected almost a foot from the side of the vessel, and almost two feet from the stern. This piece of wood was bored down its length, and no doubt a rope passing through it secured the rudder to the ship's side. It was steered by a tiller attached to the handle, and perhaps also by a rope fastened to the blade. As a whole, this disinterred vessel proved to be anything but the rude and primitive craft which might have been expected; it was neatly built and well preserved, constructed on what a sailor would call beautiful lines, and eminently fitted for sea service. Many such vessels may be found depicted on the celebrated Bayeux tapestry; and the peculiar position of the rudder explains the treaty mentioned in the *Heimskringla*, giving to Norway all lands lying west of Scotland between which and the mainland a vessel could pass with her rudder shipped.

The vessel thus described is preserved at Christiania, and is here represented from an engraving, for which I am indebted to Professor R. B. Anderson, of Madison, Wisconsin. A full account of it, with many illustrations, was published in a quarto volume by N. Nicolayson, at Christiania, in 1882. This was not one of the very largest ships, for some of them had thirty oars on each side, and vessels carrying from twenty to twenty-five were not uncommon. The largest of these were called Dragons, and other sizes were known as Serpents or Cranes. The ship itself was often so built as to represent the name it bore: the dragon, for instance, was a long low vessel, with the gilded head of a dragon at the bow, and the gilded tail at the stern; the moving oars at the side might represent the legs of the imaginary creature, the row of shining red and white shields that were hung over the gunwale looked like the monster's scales, and the sails striped with red and blue might suggest his wings. The ship preserved at Christiania is described as having had but a single mast, set into a block of wood so large that it is said no such block could now be cut in Norway. Probably the sail was much like those still carried by large open boats in that country — a single square sail on a mast forty feet long. These masts have no standing rigging, and are taken down when not in use; and this was probably the practice of the Vikings.

In case of danger these sea-rovers trusted chiefly to their oars. Once, when King Harald's fleet was on its way back to Norway with plunder from Denmark, the vessels lay all night at anchor in the fog, and when the sun pierced the fog in the morning it seemed as if many lights were burning in the sea. Then Harald said: "It is a fleet of Danish ships, and the sun strikes on the gilded dragon-heads: furl the sail, and take to the oars." The Norse ships were heavy with plunder, while the Danish ships were light. Harald first threw overboard light wood, and placed upon it clothing and goods of the Danes, that they might see it and pick it up; then he threw overboard his provisions, and lastly his prisoners. The Danes stopped for these, and the Norwegians got off with the rest. It was only the chance of war that saved the fugitives; had they risked a battle and lost it, they would have been captured, killed, or drowned. Yet it was not easy to drown them; they rarely went far from shore, and they were, moreover, swimmers from childhood, even in the icy waters of the North, and they had the art, in swimming, of hiding their heads beneath their floating shields, so that it was hard to find them. They were full of devices. It is recorded of one of them, for instance, that he always carried tinder in a walnut shell, enclosed in a ball of wax, so that, no matter how long submerged, he could make a fire on reaching shore.

How were these rovers armed and dressed? They fought with stones, arrows, and spears; they had grappling-irons on board, with which to draw other vessels to them; and the fighting men were posted on the high bows and sterns, which sometimes had scaffoldings or even castles on them, so that missiles could be thrown down on other vessels. As to their appearance on land, it is recorded that when Sweinke and his five hundred men came to a "thing," or council, in Norway, all were clad in iron, with their weapons bright, and they were so well armed that they looked like pieces of shining ice. Other men present were clad in leather cloaks, with halberds on their shoulders and steel caps on their heads. Sigurd, the king's messenger, wore a scarlet coat and a blue coat over it, and he rose and told Sweinke that unless he obeyed the king's orders he should be driven out of the country. Then Sweinke rose, threw off his steel helmet, and retorted on him:

> "Thou useless fellow, with a coat without arms and a kirtle with skirts, wilt thou drive me out of the country? Formerly thou wast not so mighty, and thy pride was less when King Hakon, my foster-son, was in life. Then thou wast as frightened as a mouse in a mouse-trap, and hid thyself under a heap of clothes, like a dog on board of a ship. Thou wast thrust into a leather bag like corn into a sack, and driven from house to farm like a year-old colt; and dost thou dare to drive me from the land? Let us stand up and attack him!"

Then they attacked, and Sigurd escaped with great difficulty.

The leaders and kings wore often rich and costly garments. When King Magnus landed in Ireland, with his marshal Eyvind, to carry away cattle, he had a helmet on his head, a red shield in which was inlaid a gilded lion, and was girt with the sword "Legbiter," of which the hilt was of tooth (ivory), and the hand-grip wound about with gold thread, and the sword was extremely sharp. "In his hand he had a short spear, and a red silk short cloak over his coat, on which, both before and behind, was embroidered a lion in yellow silk, and all men acknowledged that they had never seen a brisker, statelier man. Eyvind had also a red silk coat like the king's, and he also was a stout, handsome, warlike man." But the ascendency of the chief did not come from his garments; it consisted in personal power of mind and prowess of body, and when these decayed, the command was gone. Such were the fierce, frank men who, as is claimed, stretched their wanderings over the western sea, and at last reached Vinland—that is to say, the continent of North America.

What led the Northmen to this continent? A trivial circumstance first drew them westward, after they had already colonized Iceland and made it their home. Those who have visited the Smithsonian Institution at Washington will remember the great carved door-posts, ornamented with heads, which are used by the Indians of the north-west coasts. It is to a pair of posts somewhat like these, called by the Northmen *setstokka*, or seat-posts, that we owe the discovery of Greenland, and afterwards of Vinland. When the Northmen removed from one place to another, they threw these seat-posts into the sea on approaching the shore, and wherever the posts went aground there they dwelt. Erik the Red, a wandering Norseman who was dwelling in Iceland, had lent his posts to a friend, and could not get them back. This led to a quarrel, and Erik was declared an outlaw. He went to sea, and discovered Greenland, which he thus called because, he said, "people will be attracted thither if the land has a good name." There he took up his abode, leading a colony with him, about A.D. 986, fifteen years before Christianity was established by law in Iceland. The colony prospered, and there is much evidence that the climate of Greenland was then milder, and that it supported a far larger population than now. The ruined churches of Greenland still testify to a period of civilization quite beyond the present.

With Erik the Red went a man named Heriulf Bardson. Biorni, or Bjarni, this Heriulf's son, was absent from home when they left; he was himself a rover, but had always spent his winters with his father, and resolved to follow him to Greenland, though he warned his men that the voyage was imprudent, since none of them had sailed in those seas. He

OLD NORSE RUINS IN GREENLAND.

sailed westward, was lost in fogs, and at last came to a land with small hills covered with wood. This could not, he thought, be Greenland; so he turned about, and leaving this land to larboard, "let the foot of the sail look towards land," that is, sailed away from land. He came to another land, flat and still wooded. Then he sailed seaward with a south-west wind for two days, when they saw another land, but thought it could not be Greenland because there were no glaciers. The sailors wished to land for wood and water, but Bjarni would not—"but he got some hard speeches for that from his sailors," the saga, or legend, says. Then they sailed out to sea with a south-west wind for three days, and saw a third land, mountainous and with glaciers, and seeming to be an island; and after this they sailed four days more, and reached Greenland, where Bjarni found his father, and lived with him ever after.

But it seems that the adventurous countrymen of Bjarni were quite displeased with him for not exploring farther; and at last a daring man named Leif bought Bjarni's ship, and set sail, with thirty-five companions, to explore southward and westward. First they reached the land which Bjarni had last seen, the high island with the glaciers, and this they called Helluland, or "Flat-stone Land." Then they came to another land which they called Marckland, or "Woodland." Then they sailed two days with a north-east wind, and came to a land with an island north of it; and landing on this island, they found sweet dew on the grass, which has been explained as the honey-dew sometimes left by an insect called *aphis*. This pleased them, like great boys, as they were; then they sailed between the island and the land; then the ship ran aground, but was at last lifted by the tide, when they sailed up a river and into a lake; and there they cast anchor, and brought their sleeping-cots on shore, and remained a long time.

They built houses there and spent the winter; there were salmon in the lake, the winter was very mild, and day and night were more equal than in Greenland. They explored the land, and one day a man of their number, Leif's foster-brother, named Tyrker, came from a long expedition and told Leif, in great excitement, that he had some news for him; he had found grape-vines and grapes. "Can that be true, my foster-brother?" said Leif. "Surely it is true," he said, "for I was brought up where there is no want of grape-vines and grapes"—he being a German. The next day they filled their long-boat with grapes, and in the spring they sailed back to Greenland with a ship's load of tree-trunks—much needed there—and with the news of the newly discovered land, called Vinland, or "Wine-land." Leif was ever after known as "Leif the Lucky," from this success.

But still the Norsemen in Greenland thought the new region had been too little explored, so Thorwald, Leif's brother, took the same ship, and made a third trip, with thirty men. He reached the huts the other party had built, called in the legends Leifsbudir, or "Leif's booths." They spent two winters there, fishing and exploring, and in the second summer their ship was aground under a ness, or cape, to the northward, and they had to repair it. The broken keel they set up on the ness as a memorial, and called it Kialarness. Afterwards they saw some of the natives for the first time, and killed all but one, in their savage way. Soon after there came forth from a bay "innumerable skin-boats," and attacked them. The men on board were what they called "Skraelings," or dwarfs, and they fought with arrows, one of which killed Thorwald, and he was buried, with a cross at the head of his grave, on a cape which they called Krossaness, or "Cross Cape." The saga reminds us that "Greenland was then Christianized, but Erik the Red had died before Christianity came thither."

Thorwald's men went back to Greenland without him, their ship being loaded with grape-vines and grapes. The next expedition to Vinland was a much larger one, headed by a rich man from Norway named Karlsefne, who had dwelt with Leif in Greenland, and had been persuaded to come on this enterprise. He brought a colony of sixty men and five women, and they had cattle and provisions. They found a place where a river ran out from the land, and through a lake into the sea; one could not enter from the sea except at highwater. They found vines growing, and fields of wild wheat; there were fish in the lake, and wild beasts in the woods. Here they established themselves at a place called Hóp, from the Icelandic word *hópa*, to recede, meaning an inlet from the ocean. Here they dwelt, and during the first summer the natives came in skin boats to trade with them — a race described as black and ill-favored, with large eyes and broad cheeks, and with coarse hair on their heads. On their first visit these visitors passed near the cattle, and were so frightened by the bellowing of the bull that they ran away again.

The natives brought all sorts of furs to sell, and wished for weapons, but those were refused by Karlsefne, who had a more profitable project, which the legends thus describe: "He took this plan — he bade the women bring out their dairy stuff for them [milk, butter, and the like], and so soon as the Skraelings saw this they would have that and nothing more. Now this was the way the Skraelings traded: they bore off their wares in their stomachs, but Karlsefne and his companions had their bags and skin wares, and so they parted." This happened again, and then one of the Norsemen killed a native, so that the next time they came as enemies, armed with slings, and raising upon a pole a great blue ball, which they swung at the Norsemen with great noise. It may have been only an Eskimo harpoon with a bladder attached, but it had its effect; the Norsemen were terrified, and were running away, when a woman named Freydis, daughter of Erik the Red, stopped them by her reproaches, and urged them on. "Why do ye run," she said, "stout men as ye are, before these miserable wretches, whom I thought ye would knock down like cattle? If I had weapons, methinks I could fight better than any of you." With this she took up a sword that lay beside a dead man, the fight was renewed, and the Skraelings were beaten off.

There is a curious account of one "large and handsome man," who seemed to be the leader of the Skraelings. One of the natives took up an axe, a thing which he had apparently never seen before, and struck at one of his companions and killed him. Upon which this leader took the axe and threw it into the sea in terror, and after this they all retreated, and came no more. Karlsefne's wife had a child that winter who was called Snorri, and the child is believed to have been the ancestor of some famous Scandinavians, including Thorwaldsen the sculptor. But in spring they all returned to Greenland with a load of valuable timber, and thence went to Iceland, so that Snorri grew up there, and his children after him. One more attempt was made to colonize Vinland, but it failed through the selfishness of a woman who had organized it—the same Freydis who had shown so much courage, but who was also cruel and grasping; and after her return to Greenland, perhaps in 1013, we hear no more of Vinland, except as a thing of the past.

There are full accounts of all these events, from manuscripts of good authority, preserved in Iceland; the chief narratives being the saga of Erik the Red and the Karlsefne saga, the one having been written in Greenland, the other in Iceland. These have been repeatedly translated into various languages, and their most accessible form in English is in Beamish's translation, which first appeared in London in 1841, and has lately been reprinted by the Prince Society of Boston, under the editorship of Rev. E. F. Slafter. This version is, however, incomplete, and is also less vivid and graphic than a partial one which appeared in the *Massachusetts Quarterly Review* for March, 1849, by James Elliot Cabot, of Brookline, Massachusetts. There are half a dozen other references of undoubted authority in later Norse manuscripts to "Vinland the Good" as a region well authenticated. Mingled with these are other allusions to a still dimmer and more shadowy land beyond Vinland, and called "Whiteman's Land," or "Ireland the Mickle," a land said to be inhabited by men in white garments, who raised flags or poles. But this is too remote and uncertain to be seriously described.

Such is the Norse legend of the visit of the Vikings. But to tell the tale in its present form gives very little impression of the startling surprise with which it came before the community of scholars nearly half a century ago. It was not a new story to the Scandinavian scholars: the learned antiquary Torfæus knew almost as much about it in 1707 as we know to-day. But when Professor Rafn published, in 1837, his great folio volume in half a dozen different languages, he thought he knew a great deal more about the whole affair than was actually the case, for he mingled the Norse legend with the Dighton Rock, and the Old Mill at Newport, and with other possible memorials of the Northmen in America —matters which have since turned out to be no memorials at all. The great volume of "Antiquitates Americanæ" contains no less than twelve separate engravings of the Dighton Rock, some of them so unlike one another that it seems impossible that they can have been taken from the same inscription. Out of some of them Dr. Rafn found no difficulty in deciphering the name of Thorfinn and the figures CXXXI., being the number of Thorwald's party. Dr. T. A. Webb, then secretary of the Rhode Island Historical Society, supplied also half a dozen other inscriptions from rocks in Massachusetts and Rhode Island, which are duly figured in the great folio; and another member of the Danish Historical Society, taking Dr. Webb's statements as a basis, expanded them with what seems like deliberate ingenuity, but was more likely simple blundering. Dr. Webb stated, for instance, that there were "in the western part of our country numerous and extensive mounds, similar to the tumuli that are so often met with in Scandinavia, Russia, and Tartary, also the remains of fortifications, etc." Mr. Beamish, with the usual vague notion of Europeans as to American geography, first reads "county" for "country," and then assigns all these vast remains to "the western part of the county of Bristol, in the State of Massachusetts." And the same writer, with still bolder enterprise, carrying his imaginary traces of the Northmen into South America, gives a report of a huge column discovered near Bahia, in Brazil, bearing a colossal figure with the hand pointing to the Northpole. It was more than suspected from certain inscriptions, according to Mr. Beamish, that this also bore a Scandinavian origin. Such was the eager temper of that period that it is a wonder they did not attribute a Scandinavian origin to Trenton Falls or the Mammoth Cave of Kentucky.

For some reason or other the Old Mill at Newport did not play a prominent part in the great volume of Professor Rafn, but he published a pamphlet at Copenhagen in 1841, under the name of "Americas Opdagelse," containing a briefer account of the discoveries, and this contains no less than seven full-page engravings of the Newport structure, all intended to prove its Norse origin. But all these fancies are now pretty thoroughly swept away.

THE OLD MILL AT NEWPORT, R. I.

The Norse origin of the Old Mill has found no scientific supporters since Rev. C. T. Brooks and Dr. Palfrey showed that there was just such a mill at Chesterton, England, the very region from which Governor Benedict Arnold came, who, in his will, made in 1678, spoke of it as "my stone-built windmill," and who undoubtedly copied its structure from the building remembered from his boyhood. A mere glance at two recent photographs of the two buildings will be enough to settle the question for most readers.

And in a much similar way the Norse origin claimed for the Dighton Rock has been set aside. So long as men believed with Dr. Webb that "nowhere throughout our widespread domain is a single instance of their [the Indians] having recorded their deeds or history on stone," it was quite natural to look to some unknown race for the origin of this single inscription. But now when the volumes of Western exploration are full of inscriptions whose Indian origin is undoubted, this view has fallen wholly into disuse. If we put side by side a representation of the Dighton Rock as it now appears, and one of the Indian inscriptions tran-

STONE WINDMILL AT CHESTERTON.

scribed in New Mexico by Lieutenant Simpson, we can hardly doubt that the two had essentially a common origin. There are the same crudely executed and elongated human figures, and the same series of crosses, easily interpreted, when horizontal, into letters and figures.

Another rock, supposed by some to be a memorial of the Northmen, has lately been described and figured. It lies upon the shore, on the farm of Dr. C. H. R. Doringh, within the township of Bristol, Rhode Island. Mr. W. J. Miller, of Bristol, a well-known antiquarian, gives a representation of it in his little book entitled "The Wampanoag Indians." The rock is of graywacke, and is ten and a half by six and a half feet in length, and twenty-one inches thick. It is only bare at low tide, and the surface is much worn by the waves. There is inscribed on it a boat, with a series of lines and angles, the whole being claimed as an inscription, and the theory of Mr. Miller being that it was carved by some sailor left in charge of a boat and awaiting his companions. Had the account been printed in 1840, it would have furnished the whole Danish Society of Antiquarians with a great argument, and even now it well deserves attention. Yet whoever will compare the outline of the boat with the Norse ship already figured will see that they have little in common; and almost

THE DIGHTON ROCK.

any New Mexican inscription will show in different places very much the same idle combination of lines and angles.

All these supposed Norse remains being ruled out of the question, we must draw our whole evidence from the Norse sagas themselves. On this part of the subject, also, there is now a general consent of experts. There can scarcely be a doubt that the Norsemen at an early period not only set-

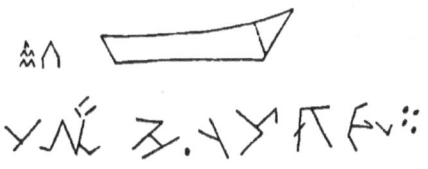

THE MOUNT HOPE BAY INSCRIPTION.

tled in Greenland, but visited lands beyond Greenland, which lands could only have been a part of the continent of North America. This Mr. Bancroft himself concedes as probable. It is true that this rests on the sagas alone, and that these were simply oral traditions, written down perhaps two centuries after the events, while the oldest existing manuscripts are dated two centuries later still. Most of the early history of Northern Europe, however, and of England itself, rests upon very similar authority; and there is no reason to set this kind of testimony aside merely because it relates to America. But when we come to fix the precise topography of their explorations, we have very few data left after the Dighton Rock and the Newport Mill are struck out of the evidence.

HIEROGLYPHICS ON ROCK IN NEW MEXICO.

We can argue nothing from their rate of sailing, for we do not know how often they sailed all night, and how often they followed the usual Norse method of anchoring at dark. Little weight is now attached to the alleged astronomical calculation in the sagas, to the effect that in Vinland, on the shortest day, the sun rose at half-past seven and set at half-past four, which would show the place to have been somewhere in the neighborhood of Mount Hope Bay. Closer observation has shown that no such assertion as that here made is to be found in the Norse narrative. The Norsemen did not divide their time into days and hours, but, like sailors, into "watches." A watch included three hours, and the le-

HIEROGLYPHICS ON INSCRIPTION ROCK, NEW MEXICO.

gends only say that the sun rose, on that day, within the watch called "Dagmalastad," and set in that called "Eyktarstad" (*Sol hovdi thar Eyktarstad ok Dagmalastad um Skamdegi*). This fact greatly impressed the Norse imagination, as in Iceland it rose and set within one and the same watch. But this gives no means for any precise calculation, inasmuch as there is a range of six hours between the longest and the shortest estimate that might be founded upon it. As a consequence, Rafn's calculation puts Vinland about the latitude of 41°, or Mount Hope Bay, while Torfaeus places it about 49°, or near Newfoundland. It is, after all, as has been remarked by Dr. William Everett, about as definite as if the sagas had told us that in Vinland daylight lasted from breakfast-time till the middle of the afternoon.

The argument founded on climate is inconclusive. Wild grapes grow in Rhode Island, and they also grow in Canada and Nova Scotia. The Northmen found no frost during their first winter in Vinland; but it is also recorded that in Iceland during a certain winter there was no snow. If the climate of Greenland was milder in those days, so it may have been with Labrador. Coincidences of name amount to almost as little. The name of Wood's Hole, on the coast of Massachusetts, has been lately altered to Wood's Holl, to correspond to the Norse name for hill. Mount Hope Bay, commonly derived from the Indian *Montaup*, has been carried farther back, and has been claimed to represent the Hóp where Leif's booths were built, although the same Indian word occurs in many other places. All history shows that nothing is less to be relied upon than these analogies. How unanswerable seemed the suggestion of the old traveller Howell, that the words "elf" and "goblin" represented the long strife between Guelf and Ghibelline in Italy, until it turned out that "elf" and "goblin" were much the older words!

There are scarcely two interpreters who precisely agree as to the places visited by the Northmen, and those who are surest in their opinions are usually those who live farthest from the points described. Professor Rafn found Vinland along the coast of New England; Professor Rask, his contemporary, found it in Nova Scotia, Newfoundland, or Labrador. The latter urged, with much reason, that it was far easier to discover wild grapes in Nova Scotia than to meet Eskimo in what is now Rhode Island; and that the whole story of the terror of the Skraelings before the bull indicates an island people like those of Newfoundland or Prince Edward Island, and certainly not the New England Indians, who were familiar with the moose, and might have seen the buffalo. He might also have added, what was first pointed out by Mr. J. Elliot Cabot, that the repeated voyages from Greenland to Vinland, and the perfect facility with which successive explorers found the newly discovered region, indicate some spot much nearer Greenland than Mount Hope Bay, which would have required six hundred miles of intricate and dangerous coast navigation, without chart or compass, in order to reach it. Again, Rafn finds it easy to place the site of Leif's booths at Bristol, Rhode Island, and M. Gravier, a Frenchman, writing so lately as 1874, has not a doubt upon the subject. But a sail from Fall River to Newport, or indeed a mere study of the map, will show any dispassionate man that the description given by the sagas has hardly anything in common with the Rhode Island locality. The sagas describe an inland lake communicating with the sea by a shallow river only accessible at high tide, whereas Mount Hope Bay is a broad expanse of salt water opening into the still wider gulf of Narraganset Bay, and communicating with the sea by a passage wide and deep enough for the navies of the world to enter. Even supposing the Northmen to have found their way in through what is called the Seaconnet passage, the description does not apply much better to that. Even if it did, these hardy sailors must have recognized, the moment they reached the bay itself, that they had come in at the back door, not at the front; and the main access to the ocean must instantly have revealed itself. It suffices to say that the whole interpretation, which seems so easy to transatlantic writers, is utterly rejected by Professor Henry Mitchell, of the Coast Survey, in a manuscript report which lies before me. And the same vagueness and indefiniteness mark all the descriptions of the Northmen. Nothing is more difficult than to depict in words with any accuracy in an unscientific age the features of a low and monotonous sea-shore; and this, with the changes undergone by the coast of southern New England during nine hundred years, renders the identification of any spot visited by the Northmen practically impossible.

The Maine Historical Society has reprinted a map of the North Atlantic, made by the Icelander Sigurd Stephanius in the year 1570, and preserved by the Scandinavian historian Torfaeus in his " Gronlandia Antiqua " (1706). In this map all that is south of Greenland, including Vinland, is a part of one continent. Helluland and Marckland appear upon it, and Vinland is a promontory extending forth from the land of the Skraelings. But whether this abrupt cape is meant to represent Cape Cod, as some would urge, or the far more conspicuous headlands of Newfoundland or Nova Scotia, must be left to conjecture. The fact that it is in the same latitude with the southern part of England would indicate the more northern situation; and it is to be noted that all these promontories are depicted as mountainous—a character which the Northmen, accustomed to the heights of Iceland and Greenland, could hardly have applied to what must have seemed to them the trivial elevations of Cape Cod or Mount Hope Bay. A sand-hill two hundred feet high would hardly have done duty for a mountain on a map made in Iceland. But the cha-

NORTH ATLANTIC, BY THE ICELANDER SIGURD STEPHANIUS, IN 1570.

otic geography of the whole map—in which England is thrown out into mid-ocean, Iceland appears nearly as large as England, one of the Shetland Islands is as large as Ireland, and the imaginary island of Frisland is fully displayed—affords a sufficient warning against taking too literally any details contained in the sagas. If learned Icelanders were so utterly unable, five centuries later, to depict the Europe which they knew so well, how could their less learned ancestors have given any accurate topography of the America which they knew so little? They did not give it; but the same activity of imagination which enabled Professor Rafn to find the name of Thorwald in an Indian inscription might well permit him to identify Krossaness with Sound Point, and Vinland with Nantucket.

Unless authentic Norse remains are hereafter unearthed, there is very little hope of ever identifying a single spot where the Vikings landed, or a single inlet ever furrowed by their keels. But that these bold rovers in sailing westward discovered lands beyond Greenland is as sure as anything can be that rests on sagas and traditions only — as sure, that is, as most things in the earliest annals of Europe. They discovered America; what part of America is of little consequence. They discovered it without clear intention, and by a series of what might almost be called coasting voyages, stretching from Norway to Scotland, from Scotland to Iceland, and thence to Greenland, and at last to the North American continent, each passage extending but a few hundred miles, though those miles lay through stormy and icy seas. They made these discoveries simply as adventurers. There is nothing in their achievement worthy to be compared with the great deed of Columbus, when he formed with deliberate dignity a heroic purpose, and set sail across an unknown sea upon the faith of a conviction. As compared with him and his companions, the Vikings seem but boys beside men.

III.

THE SPANISH DISCOVERERS.

TWENTY-FIVE years ago the American minister at the court of Turin was conversing with a young Italian of high rank from the island of Sardinia, who had come to Turin for education. This young man remarked to the American minister, Mr. Kinney, that he had lately heard about a great Spanish or Italian navigator who had sailed westward from Spain, in the latter part of the fifteenth century, with the hope of making discoveries. Did Mr. Kinney know what had become of that adventurer; had he been heard of again, and if so, what had he accomplished? This, it seemed, was all that was known in Sardinia respecting the fame and deeds of Columbus. The world at large is a little better off, and can at least tell what Columbus found. But whether he really first found it, and is entitled to the name of discoverer, has of late been treated as an unsettled question. He long since lost the opportunity of giving his name to the new continent; there have been hot disputes as to whether he really first reached it. Who knows but that the world will end by doubting if there ever was such a person as Columbus at all?

What does discovery mean? in what does it consist? If the Vikings had already visited the American shore, could it be rediscovered? Was it not easy for Columbus to visit Iceland, to hear the legends of the Vikings, and to follow in their path? These are questions that have lately been often asked.

The answer is that Columbus probably visited Iceland, possibly heard the Viking legends, but certainly did not follow in

CHRISTOPHER COLUMBUS.

the path they indicated. To follow them would have been to make a series of successive voyages, as they did, each a sort of coasting trip, from Norway to Iceland, from Iceland to Greenland, from Greenland to Vinland. To follow them would have been to steer north-northwest, whereas his glory lies in the fact that he sailed due west into the open sea, and found America. His will begins, "In the name of the Most Holy Trinity who inspired me with the idea, and afterwards confirmed me in it, that by traversing the ocean *westwardly*," etc. Thus accurately did he state his own title to fame. So far as climate and weather were concerned, he actually incurred less risk than the Northmen; but when we consider that he sailed directly out across an unknown ocean on the faith of a theory, his deed was incomparably greater.

There is one strong reason for believing that Columbus knew but vaguely of their voyage, or did not know of it at all, or did not connect the Vinland they found with the India he sought. This is the fact, that he never, so far as we know, used their success as an argument in trying to persuade other people. For eight years, by his own statement, he was endeavoring to convert men to his project. "For eight years," he says, "I was torn with disputes, and my project was matter of mockery" (*cosa de burla*). During this time he never made one convert among those best qualified, either through theory or practice, to form an opinion—"not a pilot, nor a sailor, nor a philosopher, nor any kind of scientific man," he says, "put any faith in it." Now these were precisely the men whom the story of Vinland, if he had been able to quote it, would have convinced. The fact that they were not convinced shows that they were not told the story; and if Columbus did not tell it, the reason must have been either that he did not know it, or did not attach much weight to it. He would have told it if only to shorten his own labor in argument; for in converting practical men an ounce of Vinland would have been worth a pound of cosmography. Certainly he knew how to deal with individual minds, and he could well adapt his arguments to each one. The way in which he managed his sailors on his voyage shows that he sought all sorts of means to command confidence. He would have treated his hearers to all the tales in the sagas if that would have helped the matter; the Skraelings and the unipeds, or one-legged men, of the Norse legends, would have been discussed by many a Genoese or Portuguese fireside; and Columbus might never have needed to trouble Ferdinand and Isabella with his tale. We may safely assume that if he knew the traditions about Vinland, they made no great impression on his mind.

Why should they have made much impression? The Northmen themselves had had five hundred years to forget Vinland, and had employed the time pretty effectually for that purpose. None of them had continued to go there. As it met the ears of Columbus, Vinland may have seemed but one more island in the northern seas, and very remote indeed from that gorgeous India which Marco Polo had described, and which was the subject of so many dreams. More than all, Columbus was a man of abstract thought, whose nature it was to proceed upon theories, and he fortified himself with the traditions of philosophers, authorities of whom the Northmen had never heard. That one saying of the cosmographer Aliaco, quoting Aristotle, had more weight with one like Columbus than a ship's crew of Vikings would have had: "Aristotle holds that there is but a narrow sea [*parvum mare*] between the western points of Spain and the eastern border of India." Ferdinand Columbus tells us how much influence that sentence had with his father; but we should have known it at any rate.

When he finally set sail (August 3, 1492), it was with the distinct knowledge that he should have a hard time of it unless Aristotle's "narrow sea" proved very narrow indeed. Instead of extending his knowledge to the sailors and to the young adventurers who sailed with him, he must keep them in the dark, must mislead them about the variations of the magnetic needle, and must keep a double log-book of his daily progress, putting down the actual distance sailed, and then a smaller distance to tell the men, in order to prevent them from being more homesick than the day before. It was hard enough, at any rate. The sea into which they sailed was known as the Sea of Darkness—*Mare Tenebrosum*, the *Bahr-al-Zulmat* of the Arabians. It had been described by an Arab geographer a century before as "a vast and boundless ocean, on which ships dare not venture out of sight of land, for even if they knew the direction of the winds, they would not know whither those winds would carry them, and as there is no inhabited country beyond, they would run great risk of being lost in mist and vapor." We must remember that at that period the telescope and quadrant were not yet invented, and the Copernican system was undiscovered. It was a time when the compass itself was so imperfectly known that its variations were not recognized; when Mercator's system of charts, now held so essential to the use even of the compass, was not devised. The instrument was of itself an object of dread among the ignorant, as being connected with enchantment. One of its Spanish names, *bruxula*, was derived from *bruxo*, a sorcerer.

No one knew the exact shape of the earth; Columbus believed in his third voyage that it was pear-shaped. Somewhere near the stalk of the pear, he thought, was the Earthly Paradise; somewhere else there was Chaos or Erebus. In sailing over those waters, no one knew what a day might bring forth. Above them, it was thought by some, hovered the gigantic bird known as the roc—familiar to the readers of "Sindbad the Sailor"—which was large enough to grasp a ship with all its crew and fly away with it into upper air. Columbus himself described three mermaids, and reported men with tails, men with dogs' heads, and one-eyed men. In the history of Peter Martyr, one of those who first recorded the discoveries of Columbus, the innocent cetacean called the manatee became a half-mythological monster covered with knobbed scales, and with a head like an ox; it could carry a dozen men on its back, and was kind and gentle to all but Christians, to whom it had an especial aversion. Philo-

THE VISION OF COLUMBUS.
[From De Bry.]

ponus has delineated the manatee, and De Bry has pictured the imaginary beings that Columbus saw.

The old maps peopled the ocean depths with yet more frightful and mysterious figures; and the Arab geographers, prohibited by their religion from portraying animals real or imaginary, supplied their place by images even more terrific, as that of the black and clinched hand of Satan rising above the waves in the guise of an overhanging rock, and ready to grasp the daring sailors who profaned the Sea of Darkness with their presence. When we think how superstition, gradually retiring from the world, still keeps its grasp upon the sailors of to-day, we can imagine how it must have ruled the ignorant seamen of Columbus. The thoughtful, lonely ways of their admiral made him only an object of terror; they yielded to him with wonderful submission, but it was the homage of fear. The terror reached its climax when they entered the vast "Sargasso Sea," a region of Gulf-weed — a tract of ocean as large as France, Humboldt says — through which they sailed. Here at last, they thought, was the home of all the monsters depicted in the charts, who might at any moment rear their distorted forms from the snaky sea-weed,

"Like demons' endlong tresses, they sailed through."

At the very best, they said, it was an inundated land (*tierras anegadas*)—probably the fabled sunken island Atlantis, of which they had heard; whose slime, tradition said, made it impossible to explore that sea, and on whose submerged shallows they might at any time be hopelessly swamped or entangled. "Are there no graves at home," they asked each other, according to Herrera, "that we should be brought here to die?" The trade-winds, afterwards called by the friars "winds of mercy," because they aided in the discovery of the New World, were only winds of despair to the sailors. They believed that the ships were sailing down an inclined slope, and that to return would be impossible, since it blew always from home. There was little to do in the way of trimming sails, for they sailed almost on a parallel of latitude from the Canaries to the Bahamas. Their severest labor was in pumping out the leaky ships. The young adventurers remained listlessly on deck, or played the then fashionable game of *primero*, and heard incredulously the daily reports told by Columbus of the rate of sailing. They would have been still more incredulous had they known the truth. "They sighed and wept," Herrera says, "and every hour seemed like a year."

The same Spanish annalist compares Columbus to St. Christopher in the legend bearing the infant Christ across the stream on his shoulders; and the explorer was often painted in that character in those days. But the weight that Columbus had to bear up was a wearisome and unworthy load. Sometimes they plotted to throw him overboard by a manœuvre (*con disimulacion*, Herrera says), intending to say that he fell in while star-gazing. But he, according to Peter Martyr, dealt with them now by winning words, now by encouraging their hopes (*blandis modo verbis, amplâ spe modo*). If they thought they saw land, he encouraged them to sing an anthem; when it proved to be but cloud, he held out the hope of land to-morrow. They had sailed August 3, 1492, and when they had been out two months (October 3d), he refused to beat about in search of land, though he thought they were near it, but he would press straight through to the Indies. Sometimes there came a contrary wind, and Columbus was cheered by it, for it would convince his men that the wind did not always blow one way, and that by patient waiting they could yet return to Spain.

As the days went on, the signs of land increased, but very slowly. When we think of the intense impatience of the passengers on an ocean steamer after they have been ten long days on the water, even though they know precisely where they are, and where they are going, and that they are driven by mechanical forces stronger than winds or waves, we can imagine something of the feelings of Columbus and his crew as the third month wore on. Still there was no sign of hope but a pelican to-day and a crab to-morrow; or a drizzling rain without wind—a combination which was supposed to indicate nearness to the shore. There has scarcely been a moment in the history of the race more full of solemn consequences than that evening hour when, after finding a carved stick and a hawthorn branch, Columbus watched from the deck in the momentary expectation of some glimpse of land. The first shore light is a signal of success and triumph to sailors who cross the Atlantic every three weeks. What then was it to the patient commander who was looking for the first gleam from an unknown world?

The picturesque old tale can never be told in better words than those in which the chronicler Herrera narrates it: "And Christopher Columbus, being now sure that he was not far off, as the night came on, after singing the 'Salve Regina,' as is usual with mariners, addressed them all and said that since God had given them grace to make so long a voyage in safety, and since the signs of land were becoming steadily more frequent, he would beg them to keep watch all night. And they knew well that the first chapter of the orders that he had issued to them on leaving Castile provided that after sailing seven hundred leagues without making land, they should only sail thenceforth from the following midnight to the next day; and that they should pass that time in prayer, because he trusted in God that during that night they should discover land. And that besides the ten thousand maravedis that their Highnesses had promised to him who should make the first discovery, he would give, for his part, a velvet jerkin."

It seems like putting some confusion into men's minds to set them thinking at one and the same time of a new world and a velvet jerkin; but, after all, the prize was never awarded, for Columbus himself was the victor. The vessels of those days had often a high structure like a castle at bow and stern —whence our word forecastle for the forward part of the ship —and we can fancy the sailors and young adventurers watching from one of these while Columbus watched from the other.

The admiral had the sharpest eyes or the highest outlook, and that night he saw a light which seemed to move on the dim horizon. He called to him Pedro Gutierrez, who saw it at once; he called Roderigo Sanchez, who could not see it for some time; but at last all three perceived it beyond doubt. "It appeared like a candle that was raised and lowered. The

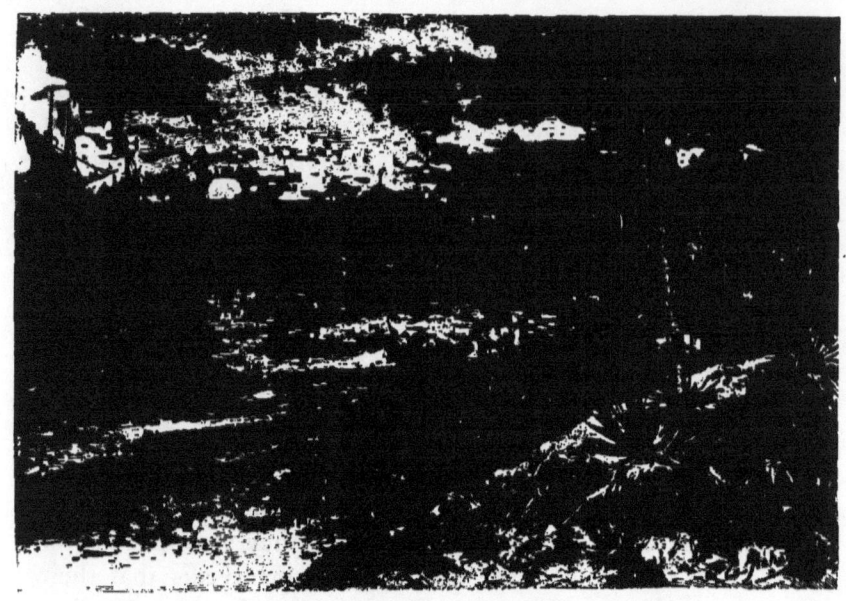

THE LANDING AT GUANAHANI.

admiral did not doubt its being a real light or its being on land; and so it was: it was borne by people who were going from one cottage to another." "He saw that light in the midst of darkness," adds the devout Herrera, "which symbolized the spirit and light which were to be introduced among these savages." This sight was seen at about ten o'clock in the evening; and at two o'clock in the morning land was actually seen from the *Pinta*, the foremost vessel, by a sailor,

Rodrigo de Triana, who, poor fellow, never got the promised reward, and, as tradition says, went to Africa and became a Mohammedan in despair.

The landing of Columbus has been commemorated by the fine design of Turner, engraved in Rogers's poems. Columbus wore complete armor, with crimson over it, and carried in his hand the Spanish flag, with its ominous hues of gold and blood; his captains bore each a banner with a green cross, and the initials F. and Y. for "Ferdinand" and "Ysabel," surmounted by their respective crowns. They fell upon their knees; they chanted the "Te Deum," and then with due legal formalities took possession of the island in behalf of the Spanish sovereigns. It was the island Guanahani, which Columbus rechristened San Salvador, but whose precise identity has always been a little doubtful. Navarrete identified it with Turk's Island; Humboldt and Irving with Cat Island; Captain Becher, of the English Hydrographic Office, wrote a book to prove that it was Gatling Island; while Captain Fox and Harrisse—the latest authority—believe it to have been Acklin's Key. It is a curious fact that the island which made the New World a certainty should itself remain uncertain of identification for four hundred years.

With the glory and beauty of that entrance of European civilization on the American continent there came also the shame. Columbus saw and described the innocent happiness of the natives. They were no wild savages, no cruel barbarians. They had good faces, he says; they neither carried nor understood weapons, not even swords; they were generous and courteous; "very gentle, without knowing what evil is, without killing, without stealing" (*muy mansos, y sin saber que sea mal, ni matar á otros, ni prender*). They were poor, but their houses were clean; and they had in them certain statues in female form, and certain heads in the shape of masks well executed. "I do not know," he says, in Navarrete's account, "whether these are employed for adornment or worship" (*per hermosura ó adoran*). The remains of Aztec and Maya civilization seem less exceptional, when we find among these first-seen aborigines the traces of a feeling for art.

Columbus seems to have begun with that peculiar mixture of kindness and contempt which the best among civilized men are apt to show towards savages. "Because," he said, "they showed much kindliness for us, and because I knew that they would be more easily made Christians through love than fear, I gave to some of them some colored caps, and some strings of glass beads for their necks, and many other trifles, with which they were delighted, and were so entirely ours that it was a marvel to see." There is a certain disproportion here between the motive and the action. These innocent savages gave him a new world for Castile and Leon, and he gave them some glass beads and little red caps. If this had been the worst of the bargain it would have been no great matter. The tragedy begins when we find this same high-minded admiral writing home to their Spanish Majesties in his very first letter that he shall be able to supply them with all the gold they need, with spices, cotton, mastic, aloes, rhubarb, cinnamon, and slaves; "slaves, as many of these idolators as their Highnesses shall command to be shipped" (*esclavos quanto mandaran cargar y seran de los ydolatres*). Thus ended the visions of those simple natives who, when the Europeans first arrived, had run from house to house, crying aloud, "Come, come and see the people from heaven" (*la gente del cielo*). Some of them lived to suspect that the bearded visitors had quite a different origin.

But Columbus shared the cruel prejudices of his age; he only rose above its scientific ignorance. That was a fine answer made by him when asked, in the council called by King Ferdinand, how he knew that the western limit of the Atlantic was formed by the coasts of Asia. "If indeed," said he, "the Atlantic has other limits in that direction than the lands of Asia, it is no less necessary that they should be discovered, and I will discover them." He probably died without the knowledge that he had found a new continent, but this answer shows the true spirit of the great captain. Columbus has been the subject of much discussion. He has been glorified into something like sainthood by such Roman Catholic eulogists as Roselly de Lorges, and has been attacked with merciless vituperation by such writers as Goodrich; but time does not easily dim the essential greatness of the man. Through him the Old and New worlds were linked together for good or for evil, and once united, they never could be separated.

There was another Spanish voyager whose name will always be closely joined with that of Columbus, and who is still regarded by many persons as having unjustly defrauded his greater predecessor, inasmuch as it was he, not Columbus, who gave his name to the New World. Unlike Columbus, Amerigo Vespucci was never imprisoned, enchained, or impoverished, and was thus perhaps the happier of the two during his life, though Columbus himself wrote of him: "Fortune has been adverse to him as she has to many others." Since his death his fate has been reversed, and he has suffered far more than Columbus at the hands of posterity. The very fact that his name was applied to the American continent caused many to regard him as but a base and malignant man. It was believed, moreover, down to the time when Irving wrote, that Vespucci's alleged voyage of 1497 was a fabrication, and that he did not really reach the mainland of South America until 1499, whereas Columbus reached it the year before. But the elaborate works of Varnhagen have changed the opinion of scholars on this point, and it is now believed that Vespucci reached the southern half of the continent in the same year when Cabot first reached the northern. If this be so, it turns out not to be quite so unjust, after all, that his name should have been given to the continent, for he really was the first to attain and describe it definitely, although it may justly be said that after Columbus had reached the outlying islands all else was but a question of time.

The works of Varnhagen, published partly at Lima and partly at Vienna and Paris, are costly and elaborate; they include the minutest investigations as to the text of all the letters, proved or reported, of Vespucci, and the most careful investigation of all internal evidence bearing on the authenticity of those documents. His conclusion is that Vespucci's first voyage was made in 1497–8, as he claimed; that he reached Honduras, and coasted all along the shores of Yucatan, of the Gulf of Mexico, and of Florida, thus proving Cuba to be an island, when Columbus still held it to be part of the mainland; and that he had reached Cape Canaveral before he quitted the shores and set sail for Portugal. The land which he discovered he called "The Land of the Holy Cross," and he believed it to be a promontory of Asia.

His discoveries attracted much attention in Germany, and it was a geographer named Waldsee-Müller who first printed, in 1507, one of his letters at the little town of St. Dié, in Lorraine. This same author, believing the "Land of the Holy Cross" to be a new quarter of the globe discovered by Vespucci (*alia quarta pars per Americanum Vespucium . . . inventa*), suggested, in a book called "Cosmographiæ Introductio," and published in 1507, the year after the death of Columbus, that this new land should be named for Americus, since Europe and Asia had women's names (*Amerigen quasi Americi terram sive Americam dicendam cum et Europa et Asia a mulieribus sua sortita sint nomina*). It is curious to read this sentence in the quaint clear type of that little book, copies of which may be found in the Harvard College library, and in other American collections, and to think that every corner of this vast double continent now owes its name to what was perhaps a random suggestion of one obscure German. The use of the title gradually spread, after this suggestion, and apparently because it pleased the public ear; but no two geographers agreed

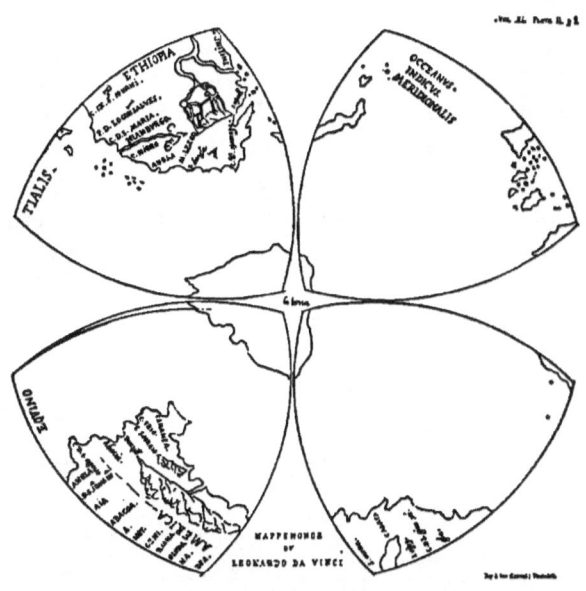

DA VINCI'S MAPPEMONDE.
[By permission of the Society of Antiquaries.]

as to the shape of the land it represented. Indeed, Waldsee-Müller, a man who was not content with one hard name for himself, but must needs have two—being called in Latin Hylacomylus—seems not to have been quite sure what name the newly discovered lands should have, after all. Six years after he had suggested the name America, he printed (in 1513) for an edition of Ptolemy a chart called "Tabula Terre Nove," on which the name of America does not appear, but there is represented a southern continent called "Terra Incognita," with an express inscription saying that it was discovered by Columbus. This shows in what an uncertain way the baptism was given. The earliest manuscript map yet known to bear the name "America" is in a collection of drawings by Leonardo da Vinci, now preserved in England, this being probably made in 1513–14. It was published in the London *Archæologia*, and a portion of it is here reproduced. The earliest engraved map bearing the name was made at Vienna in 1520. The globe of Johann Schoner, also made in 1520, and still preserved at Nuremberg, calls what is now Brazil, "America sive [or] Brazilia," thus doubtfully recognizing the new name; and it gives what is now known to be the northern half of the continent as a separate island under the name of Cuba. It was many years before the whole was correctly figured and comprehended under one name. Every geographer of those days distributed the supposed islands or continents of the New World as if he had thrown them from a dice-box; and the

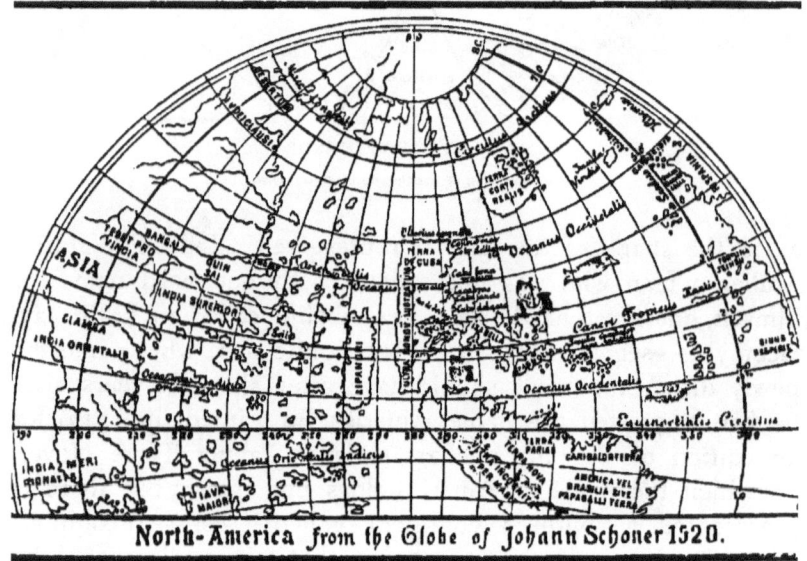

North-America from the Globe of Johann Schoner 1520.

A CHART OF THE SIXTEENTH CENTURY.

royal personages who received gold and slaves from these new regions generally cared very little to know the particulars about them. The young, the ardent, and the reckless sought them for adventure; but their vague and barbarous wonders seemed to princes and statesmen very secondary matters compared with their own intrigues and treaties and royal marriages and endless wars. Vespucci himself may not have

VASCO NUÑEZ DE BALBOA.

known when his name was first used for the baptism of his supposed discoveries. He was evidently one of those who have more greatness thrust upon them than they have ever claimed for themselves.

Another of the great Spanish explorers was one who left Hispaniola, it is said, to avoid his creditors, and then left the world his debtor in Darien. Vasco Nuñez de Balboa deserves to be remembered as one who at least tried to govern the

Indians with humanity; yet even he could not resist putting them to the torture, by his own confession (*dando á unos tormento*), in order to discover gold. But he will be better remembered as the first civilized discoverer of the ocean that covers one-half the surface of the globe. Going forty leagues from Darien to visit an Indian chief named Comogre, the Spaniards received a sumptuous present of gold, and as they were quarrelling about it, the eldest son of the chief grew indignant at what he thought their childishness. Dashing the scales, gold and all, to the ground, he told them that he could show them a country rich enough in gold to satisfy all their greediness; that it lay by a sea on which there were ships almost as large as theirs, and that he could guide them thither if they had the courage. "Our captains," says Peter Martyr, "marvelling at the oration of this naked young man, pondered in their minds, and earnestly considered these things."

At a later time Balboa not only considered, but acted, and with one hundred and ninety Spaniards, besides slaves and hounds, he fought his way through forests and over mountains southward. Coming near the mountain-top whence he might expect, as the Indians had assured him, to behold the sea, he bade his men sit upon the ground, that he alone might see it first. Then he looked upon it,

"Silent upon a peak in Darien."

Before him rolled "the Sea of the South," as it was then called (*la Mar del Sur*), it lying southward of the isthmus where he stood—as any map will show—and its vast northern sweep not yet being known. This was on September 25, 1513. On his knees Balboa thanked God for the glory of that moment; then called his men, and after they also had given thanks, he addressed them, reminding them of what the naked prince had said, and pointing out that as the promise of the southern sea had been fulfilled, so might also that of the kingdom of gold—as it was, indeed, fulfilled long after in the discovery of Peru by Pizarro, who was one of his companions. Then they sang the "Te Deum Laudamus," and a notary drew up a list of all those who were present, sixty-seven in all, that it might be known who had joined in the great achievement. Then he took formal possession of the sea and all that was in it in behalf of Spain; he cut down trees, made crosses, and carved upon the tree trunks the names of Spanish kings. Descending to the sea, some days later, with his men, he entered it, with his sword on, and standing up to his thighs in the water, declared that he would defend it against all comers as a possession of the throne of Spain. Meanwhile some of his men found two Indian canoes, and for the first time floated on that unknown sea. To Balboa and his companions it was but a new avenue of conquest; and Peter Martyr compares him to Hannibal showing Italy to his soldiers (*ingentes opes sociis pollicetur*). But to us, who think of what that discovery was, it has a grandeur second only to the moment when Columbus saw the light upon the shore. Columbus discovered what he thought was India, but Balboa proved that half the width of the globe still separated him from India. Columbus discovered a new land, but Balboa a new sea. Seven years later (1520), Magellan also reached it by sailing southward and passing through the straits that bear his name, giving to the great ocean the name of Pacific, from the serene weather which met him on his voyage.

I must not omit to mention one who was the first European visitor of Florida, except as Vespucci and others had traced the outline of its shores. Yet Ponce de Leon made himself immortal, not, like Columbus, by what he dreamed and discovered, but by what he dreamed and never found. Even to have gone in search of the Fountain of Youth was an event that so arrested the human imagination as to have thrown a sort of halo around a man who certainly never reached that goal. The story was first heard among the Indians of Cuba and Hispaniola, that on the island of Bimini, one of the Lucayos, there was a fountain in which aged men by bathing could renew their youth. The old English translation of Peter Martyr describes this island as one "in the which there is a continual spring of running water of such marvellous virtue that, the water thereof being drunk, perhaps with some diet, maketh old men young." Others added that on a neighboring shore there was a river of the same magical powers — a river believed by many to be the Jordan. With these visions in his mind, Ponce

PONCE DE LEON.

de Leon, sailing in command of three brigantines from Porto Rico, where he had been Governor, touched the mainland, in the year 1512, without knowing that he had arrived at it. First seeing it on Easter Sunday—a day which the Spaniards called Pascua Florida, or "Flowery Easter"— he gave this name to the newly discovered shore. He fancied it to be an island whose luxuriant beauty seemed to merit this glowing name—the Indian name having been Cantio. He explored its coast, landed near what is now called St. Augustine, then returned home, and on the way delegated one of his captains, Juan Perez, to seek the island of Bimini, and to search for the Fountain of Youth upon it. He reached the island, but achieved nothing more.

Long after these days, Herrera tells us, both Indians and Spaniards used to bathe themselves in the rivers and lakes of all that region, hoping to find the enchanted waters. Ponce de Leon once again visited his supposed island, and was mortally wounded by Indians on its shores. He never found the Fountain of Youth, but he found Florida; and for the multitudes who now retreat from the Northern winter to that blossoming region, it may seem that his early dreams were not so unfounded after all.

The conquest of Mexico by Cortez revived anew the zeal of Spanish adventure, and a new expedition to Florida was organized, which led ultimately to a new discovery—that of the first land route across the width, though not across the largest width, of North America. Alvar Nuñez, commonly called Cabeza de Vaca, sailed from Spain to Florida, in 1527, as treasurer of an armada, or armed fleet. They probably landed at what is now called Charlotte Harbor, in Florida, where Cabeza de Vaca and others left their ships and went into the interior as far as what is now Alabama. Then they were driven back in confusion, and reached the sea in utter destitution and helplessness. They wished to build ships and to get away; but they had neither knowledge nor tools nor iron nor forge nor tow nor resin nor rigging. Yet they made a bellows out of deer-skins, and saws out of stirrups, resin from pine-trees, sails from their shirts, and ropes from palmetto leaves and from the hair of their horses' tails. Out of the skins of the legs of horses, taken off whole, and tanned, they made bottles to carry water. At last they made three boats, living on horse-meat until these were ready. Then they set sail, were shipwrecked again and again, went through all sorts of sorrows, lived on half a handful of raw maize a day for each person, and were so exhausted that at one time all but Cabeza de Vaca became unconscious, and were restored to life by being thrown into the water on the capsizing of the boat—a tale which, it is thought, may have suggested to Coleridge his picture of the dead sailors coming to life in the "Ancient Mariner."

During this voyage of thirty days along the coast they passed a place where a great fresh-water river ran into the sea, and they dipped up fresh water to drink; this has been supposed to be the Mississippi, and this to have been its first discovery by white men. Cabeza de Vaca must at any rate have reached the Lower Mississippi before De Soto, and have penetrated the northern part of Mexico before Cortez, for he traversed the continent; and after eight years of wandering, during which he saw many novel wonders, including the buffalo, he found himself with three surviving companions at the Spanish settlements on the Gulf of California, near the river Culiacan. The narrative of Cabeza de Vaca has been translated in full by Buckingham Smith, and no single account of Spanish adventure combines so many amazing incidents. His pictures of the country traversed are accurate and complete; and he had every conceivable experience with the Indians. He was a slave to tribes which kept white captives in the most abject bondage, and every day put arrows to their breasts by way of threat for the morrow. And he encountered other tribes which brought all their food to the white men to be breathed upon before they ate it; tribes which accompanied their visitors by thousands as a guard of honor in their march through the country; and tribes where the people fetched all the goods from their houses, and laid them before the strangers passing by, praying them, as visitors from heaven, to accept their choicest possessions. Yet all these tales are combined with descriptions so minute and occurrences so probable that the main narrative must be accepted for truth, though it is impossible to tell precisely where belief should begin or end.

Such were some of the early Spanish discoveries. I pass by the romantic adventures of Cortez and Pizarro; they were not discoveries, but rather conquests, and their conquests lay almost wholly beyond the borders of the region now known as the United States of America. There is nothing more picturesque in the early history of any country than the period of Spanish adventure; nor is there anything sadder than the reverse of the picture, when we consider the wrongs endured by the native population. Those gentle races whom Columbus found so hospitable and so harmless were soon crushed by the invaders, and the more powerful tribes of the mainland fared no better. Weapons, tortures, fire, and even bloodhounds fiercer than wild beasts were used against them. Spanish writers delight to describe the scars and wounds of these powerful animals, some of which were so highly esteemed as to be rated as soldiers under their own names, receiving their full allowance of food as such, the brute being almost as cruel and formidable as a man. For the credit of civilization and Christianity it is to be remembered that the same nation and faith which furnished the persecutors supplied also the defenders and the narrators; and most of what we know of the wrongs of the natives comes through the protests, not always unavailing, of the noble Las Casas. This good bishop unceasingly urged upon the Spanish rulers a policy of mercy. He secured milder laws, and, as bishop, even refused the sacraments at one time to those who reduced the Indians to slavery. But it was soon plain that to carry out this policy would be practically to abolish the sacraments, and so neither Church nor State sustained him. He has left us the imperishable record of the atrocities he could not repress. "With mine own eyes," he says, "I saw kingdoms as full of people as hives are of bees, and now where are they? . . . Almost all have perished. The innocent blood which they had shed cried out for vengeance; the sighs, the tears, of so many victims went up to God."

IV.

THE OLD ENGLISH SEAMEN.

PROBABLY no single class of men ever made a greater change in the fortunes of mankind than was brought about by the great English seamen of the sixteenth century. Some of them were slave-traders, others were smugglers, almost all were lawless men in a lawless age; but the result of their daring expeditions was to alter the destiny of the American continent, and therefore the career of the human race.

In the year 1500, Spain, with Portugal, was the undisputed master of the New World. At the present time neither Spain nor Portugal owns a foot of land upon the main continent of North or South America. The destiny of the whole Western world has been changed; and throughout almost all the northern half of it the language, the institutions, the habits have been utterly transformed. At the time when Europe was first stirred by the gold and the glory brought from the newly discovered America, it was only Spain, and in a small degree Portugal, that reaped the harvest. These were then the two great maritime and colonizing powers of Europe; and two bulls from Pope Alexander VI., in 1493, had permitted them to divide between them any newly discovered portions of the globe. Under this authority Portugal was finally permitted to keep Brazil—which had been first colonized by Portuguese —while Spain claimed all the rest of the continent. To this day the results of that mutual distribution are plainly to be seen in South America. Brazil speaks Portuguese, while almost all the rest of South America, with Mexico, speaks Spanish. But beyond Mexico, through all the vast length and breadth of North America, English is the prevailing and official language. Throughout that region, instead of the Latin race, the Germanic prevails; instead of the Roman Catholic faith, the Protestant preponderates. There has not been in the history of the world a profounder change in the current of human events. The most remarkable circumstance of all is, that this change was substantially made in a single century (the sixteenth), and was made mainly through a single class of men—the old English seamen. They it was who broke the power of Spain, and changed the future destinies of America.

Other nations doubtless co-operated. Italy, especially, contained the great intellectual and cultivated race in that age, and furnished both Spain and Portugal again and again with ships, mathematical instruments, captains, crews, and even bankers' credits. Spain sent across the Atlantic ocean Columbus and Amerigo Vespucci, both Italians; France sent Verrazzano, an Italian; England sent Cabot, an Italian by citizenship and probably by birth and blood. For centuries the descendants of the Northmen confined their voyages to the shores of Western Europe; they knew less even of the Mediterranean than their Viking ancestors; but London had Italian merchants, and Bristol had Italian sailors, and it is to these that we owe the pioneer explorations of the Cabots. We must begin with these, for on these rested, in the first place, all the claims of England to the North American coast.

There is a great contrast between the ample knowledge that we have about the career of Columbus and the scanty and contradictory information left to us in regard to the Cabots. There is scarcely a fact about them or their voyages which is known with complete accuracy. We do not know past question their nationality or their birthdays, or the dates of their voyages; nor do we always know by which of the family those expeditions were made. John Cabot was long regarded as a Genoese who came to England to reside; yet it has been thought possible that he was an Englishman who was merely naturalized in Venice in 1476. Sebastian Cabot is now pretty well known to have been born in Venice, yet some contemporary authorities describe him as a native of Bristol. He received a patent from the King in 1496—he and his father and brothers— to make discoveries; but the only engraved map bearing his name claims that he had already found North America two years before that date. "John Cabot, a Venetian, and Sebastian Cabot, his son, discovered this region, formerly unknown, in the year 1494, on the 24th day of June, at the fifth hour." This date appears

SEBASTIAN CABOT, BY HOLBEIN.

both in the Latin and Spanish inscriptions on the unique copy of this map in the National Library at Paris; the map itself having been engraved in 1544, but only having come to light in 1843. Its authenticity has been fully discussed by M. D'Avezac, who believes in it, and by Dr. J. G. Kohl and Mr. Charles Deane, who reject it. Mr. R. H. Major, of the British Museum, has made the ingenious suggestion that the date, which is in Roman letters, was originally written by Cabot thus, MCCCCXCVII., and that the V, being carelessly written, passed for II, so that the transcriber wrote 1494 instead of 1497. To add to the confusion, there is evidence in the Spanish State papers that would, if credited, carry back the first voyages of the Cabots to an earlier date than even that of Columbus. The Spanish envoy in England wrote to the sovereigns Ferdinand and Isabella (July 25, 1498), that the people of Bristol had been annually sending ships for seven years "in search of the island Brazil and the seven cities, according to the fancy of that Italian Cabot." This would imply that his first expedition took place in 1491.

But it is quite certain that this carries back the date too far; it is almost certain, also, that it was the example of Columbus which aroused Sebastian Cabot to action. In one of the few sentences positively attributed to him, though by an unknown witness, he says of the first voyage of Columbus: "In that time when news was brought that Don Christopher Colonus, Genoese, had discovered the coasts of Indies, whereof was great talk in all the court of King Henry VII., who then reigned, insomuch that all men, with great admiration, affirmed it to be a thing more divine than human to sail by the West unto the East, where spices grow, by a way that was never known before; by this fame and report there increased in my heart a great flame of desire to attempt some notable thing; and understanding by the sphere (globe) that if I should sail by way of the north-west I should by a shorter track come into India, I imparted my ideas to the King."

It is altogether probable that the map of Sebastian Cabot gives us an authentic basis of knowledge in regard to the points visited by him, even if the date assigned is not quite trustworthy. His "Prima Vista," or point first seen — what sailors call landfall — was in that case Cape Breton. He sailed along Prince Edward Island, then known as the Isle of St. John, and along the Gulf of St. Lawrence, perhaps beyond the site where Quebec now stands. He then sailed eastward to Newfoundland, which he described as consisting of many islands; then southward to the Chesapeake River, and then homeward. He saw first the bleakest and most rugged part of the North American coast. If he saw it in 1494, he was its first known civilized discoverer; if he saw it in 1497, it is possible that Amerigo Vespucci saw Florida in that same year, but very likely at a later period of the year.

At any rate, it is probable that in 1497 Sebastian Cabot and his father sailed with five ships, furnished at their own cost, but upon the condition that they should pay the King one-fifth of all profits. They were authorized by the King to

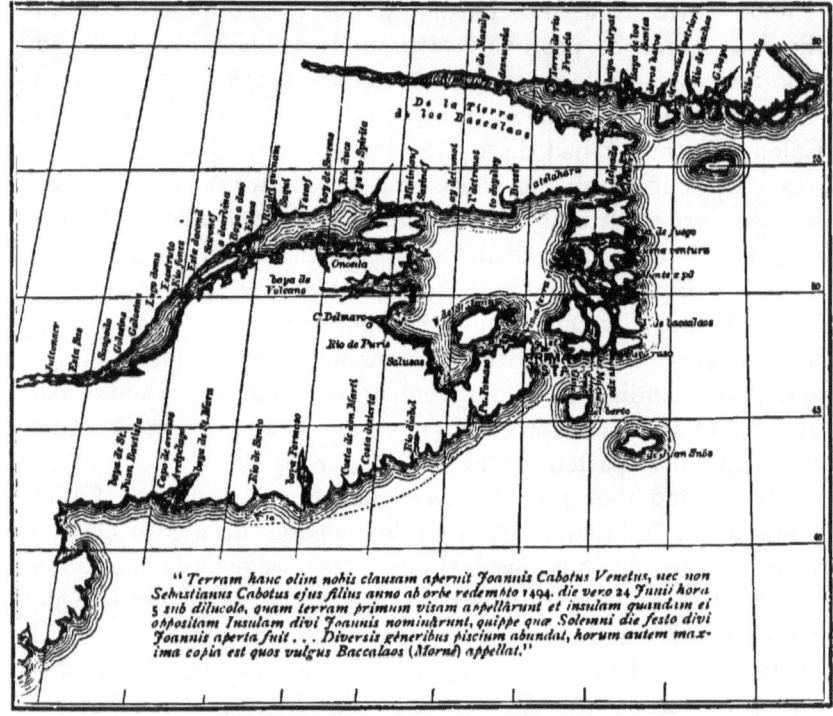

"Sebastian Cabot, Captain and Pilot Major of His Sacred Imperial Majesty, the Emperor Don Carlos the 5th of this name, and King our Lord, made this figure extended in plane in the year of the birth of our Saviour Jesus Christ, 1544."

sail "to all parts, countries, and seas of the East, of the West, and of the North, under our banners and ensigns . . . upon their own proper costs and charges, to seek out, discover, and find whatsoever Isles, Countries, Regions, or Provinces of the Heathen and Infidels whatsoever they be, and in whatsoever part of the world, which before this time have been unknown to Christians." They were also permitted, in the royal phrase, "to set up our banners and ensigns in every village, town, castle, isle, or mainland of them newly found, and to subdue, occupy, and possess them." In addition to all other uncertainties, the authorities differ greatly as to whether it was John or Sebastian who should have the honor of the great discoveries made by this expedition. Hakluyt, who compiled the well-known collection of voyages, and who was born a few years before Sebastian Cabot's death, and was the best-informed Englishman of his time as to nautical matters, declares that "a great part of this continent as well as of the islands was first discovered for the King of England by Sebastian Gabote, an Englishman, born in Bristow, son of John Gabote, in 1496." Elsewhere he says: "Columbus first saw the firme land August 1, 1498, but Gabote made his great discovery in 1496." On the other hand, there is an entry in the Milan archives (August, 1497): "Some months ago his Majesty Henry VII. sent out a Venetian, who is a very good mariner, has good skill in discovering new islands, and he has returned safe, and has found two very large and fertile new islands, having likewise discovered the seven cities, 400 leagues from England, on the western passage." This names neither John nor Sebastian. But there is another letter in the Milan archives, from Lorenzo Pasqualigo to his brother (dated August 23, 1497), which might seem to settle the matter:

"This Venetian of ours, who went with a ship from Bristol in quest of new islands, is returned, and says that seven hundred leagues hence he discovered 'terra firma,' which is the territory of the Grand Cham. He coasted for three hundred leagues, and landed. He saw no human being whatsoever; but he has brought hither to the King certain snares which had been set to catch game, and a needle for making nets; he also found some felled trees; wherefore he supposed there were inhabitants, and returned to his ship in alarm.

"He was three months on the voyage, it is quite certain; and coming back, he saw two islands to starboard, but would not land, time being precious, as he was short of provisions. The King is much pleased with this intelligence. He says that the tides are slack, and do not flow as they do here. The King has promised that in the spring he shall have ten ships, armed according to his own fancy; and at his request he has conceded to him all the prisoners, except such as are confined for high-treason, to man them with. He has also given him money wherewith to amuse himself till then; and he is now at Bristol with his wife, who is a Venetian woman, and with his sons. His name is Zuan Cabot, and they call him the great admiral. Vast honor is paid him, and he dresses in silk; and these English run after him like mad people, so that he can enlist as many of them as he pleases, and a number of our own rogues besides.

"The discoverer of these places planted on his new-found land a large cross, with one flag of England, and another of St. Mark, by reason of his being a Venetian, so that our banner has floated very far afield."

But the librarian of the Bristol public library, Mr. Nicholls, who has compiled a biography of Sebastian Cabot, points out that we have among the privy purse expenses of Henry VII. some entries that quite change this story. We have there recorded the very sum paid to John Cabot (August 10, 1497): "To him who found the new isle, £10." Fifty dollars was certainly a moderate price to pay for the whole continent of North America, and certainly not sufficient to keep "the great admiral" and his Venetian wife in silk dresses from August to the following spring. This evident exaggeration throws some doubt over the whole tone of Signor Pasqualigo's narrative; yet it leaves the main facts untouched. The most probable explanation of the whole contradiction would seem to be that John Cabot, the father, was the leader in the "great voyage," and won most fame at the time, but that his death, which happened soon after, left his son Sebastian in possession of the field, after which time Sebastian's later voyages gave most of the laurels to his name. At any rate, they belonged to the name of Cabot, and this will probably always rank next to that of Columbus in popular renown.

On the death of his father, in 1498, Sebastian Cabot was left, according to Peter Martyr, very rich and full of ambition (*ricchissimo et di grande animo*). A patent for another voyage had just been given to the father, and the son made use of it, though some doubt still exists about the leadership of this expedition, and Mr. Deane thinks that John Cabot had not yet died, but went in command of it. Cabot went expressly, Gomara says, "to know what manner of lands these Indies were to inhabit." The King's privy purse account shows that bounties were given to those who enlisted under Cabot. "A reward of £2 to Jas. Carter for going to the new Isle, also to Thos. Bradley and Launcelot Thirkill, going to the new Isle £30." It would be curious to know if these sums represent the comparative value of the recruits; at any rate, besides two pounds' worth of Carters and thirty pounds' worth of Bradleys and Thirkills—these being respectable merchants—Cabot had a liberal supply of men upon whose heads no bounty was set, unless to pay him for removing them. Perkin Warbeck's insurrection had lately been suppressed, and had filled the jails; and the Venetian calendar tells us that "the King gave Cabot the sweepings of the prisons." It was poor material out of which to make colonists, as Captain John Smith discovered more than a century later.

What with jail-birds and others, Cabot took with him in 1498 three hundred men, and sailed past Iceland, or Island, as it was then called, a region well known to Bristol (or Bristow) men, and not likely to frighten his rather untrustworthy ship's company. Then he sailed for Labrador, which he called "La Tierra de los Baccalaos," or, briefly, "The Baccalaos"—this word meaning simply cod-fish. He said that he found such abundance of this fish as to hinder the sailing of his ships; that he found seals and salmon abundant in the rivers and bays, and bears which plunged into the water and caught these fish. He described herds of reindeer, and men like Eskimo, but he could find no passage to India among the "islands." This is what they were habitually called in those days, though the King more guardedly described the new region in his patent as "the said Londe [land] or Isles." Cabot left some colonists on the bleak shores of Labrador or Newfoundland, then returned and took the poor fellows on board again; he sailed south, following the coast as far as Florida, but not a man would go ashore to found another colony, and he returned to England with increased fame but little profit. Later he explored Hudson Bay, looking vainly for a passage, while the King was still giving bounties to those who went to "the new island," or sometimes to "the Newfounded island," which shows how easily the name Newfoundland came to be fixed upon one part of the region explored.

Sebastian Cabot was certainly in one sense the discoverer of America: it was he who first made sure that it was a wholly new and unknown continent. In his early voyages he had no doubt that he had visited India, but after his voyage of 1498 he expressed openly his disappointment that a "New Found Land" of most inhospitable aspect lay as a barrier between Europe and the desired Asia. As the German writer, Dr. Asher, has well said, "Cabot's displeasure involves the scientific discovery of a new world." In his charts North America stands as a separate and continuous continent, though doubtless long after his time the separate islands were delineated, as of old, by others, and all were still supposed to be outlying parts of Asia. In this, as in other respects, Cabot was better appreciated fifty years later than in his own day. His truthful accounts for the time discouraged further enterprise in the same direction. "They that seek riches," said Peter Martyr, "must not go to the frozen North." And after one or two ineffectual undertakings he found no encouragement to repeat his voyages to the North American coast, but was sought for both by Spain and England to conduct other enterprises. He was employed in organizing expeditions to the Brazils, or to the North-pole by way of Russia, but the continent he had discovered was left unexplored. He was esteemed as a skilful mariner and one who had held high official station; he died dreaming of a new and infallible mode of discovering the longitude which he thought had been revealed to him from Heaven, and which he must not disclose. The date of his death, like that of his birth, is unknown, and his burial-place is forgotten. But fifty years later, when Englishmen turned again for a different object towards the American continent, they remembered his early achievements, and based on them a claim of ownership by right of discovery. Even then they were so little appreciated that Lord Bacon, writing his "Reign of Henry VII.," gives but three or four sentences to the explorations which perhaps exceed in real importance all else that happened under that reign.

For about half a century the English seamen hardly crossed the Atlantic. When they began again it was because they had learned from Spain to engage in the slave-trade. In that base path the maritime glory of England found its revival. For fifty years Englishmen thought of the New World only as a possession of Spain, with which England was in more or less friendly alliance. It was France, not England, which showed at that time some symptoms of a wish to dispute the rich possession with Spain; and after the voyage of Verrazzano, in 1521, the name New France covered much of North America on certain maps and globes. It was little more than a name; but the Breton and Gascon fishermen began to make trips to the West Indies, mingling more or less of smuggling and piracy with their avowed pursuit, and the English followed them—learned the way of them, in fact. Under the sway of Queen Elizabeth, England was again Protestant, not Catholic;

the bigotry of Philip II. had aroused all the Protestant nations against him, and the hereditary hostility of France made the French sailors only too ready to act as pilots and seamen for the English. Between the two the most powerful band of buccaneers and adventurers in the world was soon let loose upon the Spanish settlements.

It is a melancholy fact that the voyage which first opened the West Indian seas to the English ships was a slave-trading voyage. The discreditable promise made by Columbus that America should supply Europe with slaves had not been fulfilled; on the contrary, the demand for slaves in the Spanish mines and the Portuguese plantations was greater than America could supply, and it was necessary to look across the Atlantic for it. John Hawkins, an experienced seaman, whose father had been a Guinea trader before him, took a cargo of slaves from Guinea in 1562, and sold them in the ports of Hispaniola. "Worshipful friends in London," it appears, shared his venture — Sir Lionel Ducket, Sir Thomas Lodge, and the like. He took three ships, the largest only 120 tons; he had but a hundred men in all. In Guinea, Hakluyt frankly tells us in the brief note which gives all that is known of this expedition, "he got into his possession, partly by the sword and partly by other meanes, to the number of three hundred negroes at the least, besides other merchandises which that country yeeldeth." With this miserable cargo he sailed for Hispaniola, and in three ports left all his goods behind him, loaded his own ship with hides, ginger, sugar, and pearls, and had enough to freight two other ships besides. This is almost all we know of the first voyage; but the second, in 1564, was fully described by John Sparke, one of his companions—and a very racy record it is. This was the first English narrative of American adventure; for though Cabot left manuscripts behind him, they were never printed.

When we consider that the slave-trade is now treated as

piracy throughout the civilized world, it is curious to find that these courageous early navigators were not only slave-traders, but of a most pious description. When Hawkins tried to

SIR JOHN HAWKINS, KT.

capture and enslave a whole town near Sierra Leone, and when he narrowly escaped being captured himself, and meeting the fate he richly deserved, his historian says, " God, who worketh all things for the best, would not have it so, and by Him wee escaped without danger; His name be praysed for it." When the little fleet is becalmed, and suffers for want of water, the author says, "But Almightie God, who never suffereth His elect to perish, sent vs the sixteene of Februarie the ordinarie Brieze, which is the north-west winde." With these religious sentiments Hawkins carried his negroes to the Spanish settlements in Venezuela and elsewhere. The news of his former voyage had reached Philip of Spain, who had expressly prohibited the colonists from trading with Hawkins. But they wished for his slaves, and he had the skill to begin his traffic by explaining that he only wished to sell "certaine lean and sicke negroes, which he had in his shippe, like to die upon his hands," but which, if taken on shore, might yet recover. It was thought that it might be a kindness to the poor to let them buy lean negroes at a low price, and so the bargain was permitted. If a town gave him a license to trade in slaves, and charged money for it, he put the prices high enough to cover the charges. If the prices were thought too high, and the town authorities objected, he would go on shore with a hundred men in armor, and "hauing in his great boate two falcons of brasse, and in the other boates double bases in their noses;" and with these cannon would so frighten the people that they would send the town treasurer to negotiate. The treasurer would perhaps come on horseback, with a javelin, but would be so afraid of the captain on foot with his armor that he would keep at a safe distance, and do the bargaining at the top of his voice.

Hawkins and his men seem to have feared nothing seriously except the alligators, which they called crocodiles, and of which they asserted that they drew people to them by their lamentations. "His nature is euer, when he would haue his praie, to crie and sobbe like a Christian bodie to prouoke them to come to him, and then he snatcheth at them; and thereupon came this prouerbe that is applied vnto women when they weepe, *Lachrymæ Crocodili*, the meaning whereof is that as the crocodile when he crieth goeth then about most to deceive, so doth a woman most commonly when she weepeth." Shakespeare, who was about this time writing his play of "King Henry VI.," apparently borrowed from Sir John Hawkins this story, and introduced it in his lines:

> "As the mournful crocodile
> With sorrow snares relenting passengers."
> *2 Henry VI.*, iii. 1.

Hawkins and his men visited Cuba, Hispaniola, the Tortugas, and other places; supplied food to Laudonnière's French settlements in what was then called Florida, and ultimately sailed along the coast of North America to Newfoundland, and thence to Europe. By this voyage Hawkins obtained fame and honor; he became Sir John Hawkins, and was authorized to have on his crest the half-length figure of a negro prisoner, called technically "a demie-Moor bound and captive." Later, when Queen Elizabeth had definitely taken sides against Spain, and withdrawn all obstacles to Hawkins's plans, he established a regular settlement, or "factory," in Guinea as the head-quarters for his slave-trade; sailed with slaves once more for a third voyage across the Atlantic (1568); traded in some places openly, in others secretly and by night, in spite of King Philip's prohibition, and prospered well until

THE HAWKINS ARMS.

DEFEAT OF THE BRITISH UNDER SIR JOHN HAWKINS AT SAN JUAN DE ULLOA.

he met in the port of San Juan de Ulloa a Spanish fleet stronger than his own. Hawkins had already put into the port with disabled ships, when he saw a fleet of thirteen Spanish treasure-ships outside. He might, perhaps, have kept them from entering, or have captured or sunk them, had he dared; but he let them in with a solemn compact of mutual forbearance, was then treacherously attacked by the Spaniards, and an engagement was brought on. The English were at first successful, but the Spaniards used fire-ships against them, and Hawkins was utterly defeated. Some of his vessels were sunk; others were driven to sea without provisions.

Hawkins himself thus plaintively describes their sorrows: "With manie sorrowfull hearts wee wandred in an unknowen Sea by the space of fourteene dayes, tyll hunger enforced vs to seeke the lande, for birdes were thought very good meate, rattes, cattes, mise, and dogges, none escaped that might be gotten, parrotes and monkayes that were had in great prize were thought then very profitable if they served the tourne [turn] one dinner." A poor remnant of the crews reached England at last in a condition as wretched as that of the negroes they had kidnapped; and Hawkins thus sums up their adventures: "If all the miseries and troublesome affaires of this sorrowfull voyage should be perfectly and thoroughly written, there should need a paynfull [painstaking] man with his penne, and as great a time as hee had that wrote the lives and deathes of the martirs." Nothing is more probable than that Hawkins regarded himself as entitled to a place upon the catalogue of saints. But darkened as were these voyages by wrong and by disaster, they nevertheless were the beginning of the long sea-fight between Spain and England for the possession of the New World.

The contest was followed up by the greatest of the English sailors, Francis Drake, first known as commanding a vessel under Hawkins in the ill-fated expedition just described. From the time of that disaster Drake took up almost as a profession the work of plundering the Spaniards; and he might well be called a buccaneer, had he not concentrated his piracy on one particular nation. He was the son of a Protestant chaplain who had suffered for his opinions; and though the policy of Elizabeth was long uncertain, the public sentiment of England was with the United Netherlands in their desperate war against Philip II. The English seamen had found out that the way to reach Spain was through her rich possessions in West India and South America, or by plundering the treasure-ships to which she could afford but meagre escort. Drake made one trip after another to the

SIR FRANCIS DRAKE.

American coast, and on February 11, 1573, he looked for the first time on the Pacific from the top of a tree in Panama. He resolved to become the pioneer of England on that ocean, where the English flag had never yet floated, and he asked the blessing of God on this enterprise. In November,

1577, he embarked for the fulfilment of this purpose, being resolved to take Peru itself from the Spaniards. His enterprise was known at the time as "the famous voyage," and ended in the first English circumnavigation of the globe.

Such novels as Kingsley's "Westward Ho! or, Sir Amyas Leigh" give a picture, hardly exaggerated, of the exciting achievements of these early seamen. Drake sailed from Plymouth, November 15, 1577, with one hundred and sixty-four sailors and adventurers in a fleet of five ships and barks, and after making some captures of Spanish vessels about the Cape de Verd Islands, he steered for the open sea. He was fifty-four days out of sight of land—time enough to have made six ocean voyages in a Liverpool steamer—before he came in sight of the Brazils. There he cruised awhile and victualled his ships with seals, which are not now considered good eating. Following down the coast in the track of Magellan, he reached at last the strait which bears the name of this Portuguese explorer, but which no Englishman had yet traversed. Drake's object was to come by this unexpected ocean route to Peru, and there ravage the Spanish settlements.

Reaching the coast of Chili, he heard from an Indian in a canoe that there was a great Spanish ship at Santiago laden with treasure from Peru. Approaching the port, the Englishmen found the ship riding at anchor, having on board but six Spaniards and three negroes. These poor fellows, never dreaming that any but their own countrymen could have found their way there, welcomed the visitors, beating a drum in their honor, and setting forth a jar of Chilian wine for their entertainment. But as soon as the strangers entered, one of them, named Thomas Moon, began to lay about him with his sword in a most uncivil manner, striking one Spaniard, and shouting, "Go down, dog!" (*Abaxo, perro!*) All the Spaniards and negroes were at once driven below, except one, who jumped overboard and alarmed the town. The people of Santiago fled to the woods, and the Englishmen landed and robbed the town, including a little chapel, from which they took "a silver chalice, two cruets, and one altar-cloth, the spoyle whereof our Generall gave to M. Fletcher, his minister." On board the captured ship they found abundance of wine and treasure, amounting to 37,000 ducats of Spanish money—a ducat being worth five and a half shillings English.

They sailed away, leaving their prisoners on shore. Landing at Tarapaca, they found a Spaniard lying asleep, with thirteen bars of silver beside him, these being worth 4000 ducats.

"THOMAS MOON BEGAN TO LAY ABOUT HIM WITH HIS SWORD."

"We tooke the siluer," says the narrator, briefly, "and left the man." Landing for water at another place, they met a Spaniard and an Indian boy driving eight "*Llamas* or sheepe of Peru, which are as bigge as asses;" each of these having two bags of leather on his back, each bag holding fifty pounds of fine silver—800 pounds weight in all. Soon after they captured three small barks, one of them laden with silver, and another with a quantity of linen cloth. At Lima they found twelve ships at anchor, robbed them, and cut their cables; and afterwards they came up with a bark yielding eighty pounds of gold and a crucifix of gold and emeralds. Everywhere they took people wholly by surprise, such a thing as an English ship being a sight wholly new on the Pacific Ocean, altogether unexpected, and particularly unwelcome.

Everywhere they heard of a great Spanish treasure-ship, the *Cacafuego*, which had sailed before their arrival; they followed her to Payta and to Panama, and the "General" promised his chain of gold to any lookout who should spy her. Coming up with her at last, they fired three shots, striking down her mizzen-mast, and then captured her without resistance. They found in her "great riches, as iewels and precious stones, thirteene chests full of royals [reals] of plate, fourscore pounds weight of golde and sixe and twentie tunne of siluer." To show how thoroughly Drake did his work, piratical as it was, the narrator of the voyage says that there were found on board two silver cups, which were the pilot's, to whom the General said, "Senior [Señor] Pilot, you haue here two siluer cups; but I must needes haue one of them;" and the pilot gave him one "because hee could not otherwise chuse," and gave the other to the ship's steward, perhaps for as good a reason. Thus went the voyage; now rifling a town, now plundering a captive, now capturing a vessel and taking "a fawlcon [breastplate] of golde with a great emeraud in the breast thereof," from the owner in person. Never once did they encounter an armed opponent, or engage in a fair fight; on the other hand, they were never guilty, as the Spaniards often were, of wanton cruelty, judging both sides by the testimony of their own witnesses. It was an ignoble warfare in one sense; but when we consider that these Englishmen were in an unknown sea, with none but unwilling pilots, and that there was not a man along the shore who was not their enemy, there was surely an element of daring in the whole affair.

They repaired their ships at the island of Sanno; and there the attacks upon the Spaniards ended. The narrator thus sums up the situation: "Our General at this place and time, thinking himselfe both in respect of his priuate iniuries receiued from the Spaniards, as also of their contempts and in-

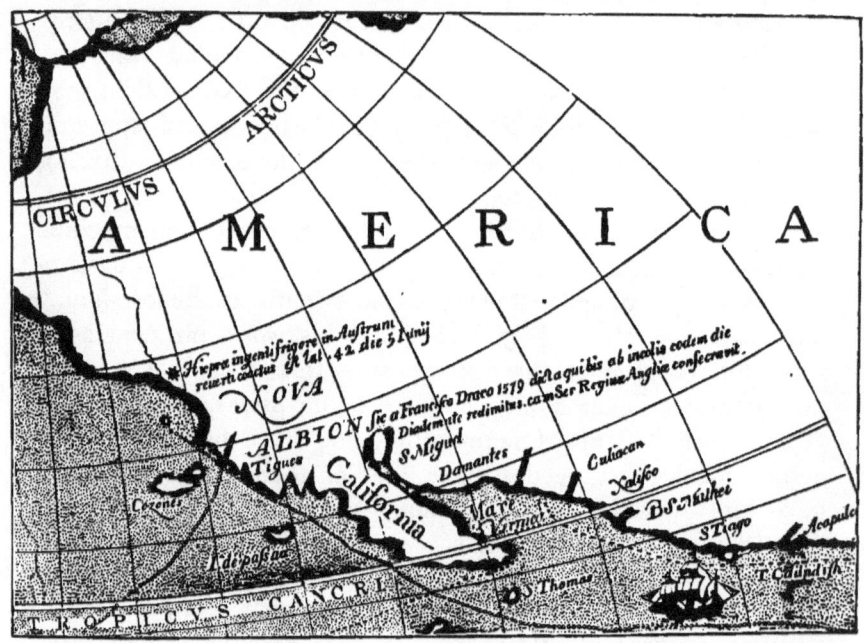

PART OF MAP OF DRAKE'S VOYAGES, PUBLISHED BY J. HONDIUS IN HOLLAND TOWARDS THE CLOSE OF THE SIXTEENTH CENTURY.

dignities offered to our countrey and Prince in generall, sufficiently satisfied and reuenged, and supposing that her Maiestie at his returne would rest contented with this seruice, purposed to continue no longer upon the Spanish coastes, but began to consider and to consult of the best way for his countrey."

He resolved at last to avoid the Strait of Magellan, which he had found dangerous, and the Atlantic Ocean, where he was too well known, and to go northward along the coast, and sail across the Pacific as he had already crossed the Atlantic. He sailed as far north as California, which he called New Albion; he entered "a faire and good bay," which may have been that of San Francisco; he took possession of the country in the name of Queen Elizabeth, setting up a post with that announcement. He then supposed, but erroneously, that the Spaniards had never visited that region, and his recorder says of it: "There is no part of earth here to bee taken up wherein there is not some speciall likelihood of gold and silver." Then he sailed across the Pacific, this passage lasting from midsummer until October 18 (1579), when he and his men came among the islands off the coast of Africa, and so rounded the Cape of Good Hope, and reached England at last, after three years' absence. They were the first Englishmen to sail round the world, and the first of their countrymen to visit those islands of "the gorgeous East" which Portugal had first reached, and Spain had now wrested from Portugal.

The feats of Hawkins and Drake, clouded as they were by the slave-trade in one case, and by what seemed much like piracy in the other, produced a great stir in England. "The nakednesse of the Spaniards and their long-hidden secrets are now at length espied." Thus wrote Hakluyt three years after Drake's return, and urged "the deducting of some colonies of our superfluous people into those temperate and fertile partes of America which, being within six weekes sailing of England, are yet unpossessed by any Christians, and seeme to offer themselves unto us, and stretching nearer unto her Majesty's dominions than to any other part of Europe." The forgotten explorations of Cabot were now remembered. Here was a vast country to which Spain and France had laid claim, but which neither had colonized. The fishermen of four or five nations were constantly resorting thither, but it belonged, by right of prior discovery, to England alone. Why should not England occupy it? "It seems probable," wrote the historian of Sir Humphrey Gilbert in 1583, "by event of precedent attempts made by the Spanyards and French sundry times" (*i. e.*, by their uniform failure) "that the countries lying north of Florida God hath reserued the same to be reduced unto Christian civility by the English nation. For not long after that Christopher Columbus had discouered the islands and continents of the West Indies for Spayne, John and Sebastian Cabot made discovery also of the West from Florida northwards to the behoofe of England." Frobisher had already attempted the North-west passage; Sir Humphrey Gilbert, the first English colonizer, took possession of Newfoundland in the name of the Queen, and tried in vain to settle a colony there; and he died at sea at last, as described in Longfellow's ballad:

> "Beside the helm he sat,
> The Book was in his hand,
> 'Do not fear; Heaven is as near,'
> He said, 'by water as by land.'"

He had obtained a commission from the Queen "to inhabit and possess at his choice all remote and heathen lands not in the actual possession of any Christian prince." He himself obtained for his body but the unquiet possession of a grave in the deep sea; but his attempt was one event more in the great series of English enterprises. After him his half-brother Raleigh sent Amidas and Barlow (1584) to explore what was then first called Virginia in honor of the Queen; and the year after, Raleigh sent an ineffectual colony to establish itself within what is now North Carolina. Then the tumults of war arose again; and Sir Francis Drake was summoned to lead a great naval expedition, a real "armada," to the attack on Spanish America.

He sailed from Plymouth, England, September 17, 1585, with twenty-five vessels carrying 2300 men, and he had under him, as Vice-admiral, Captain Martin Frobisher, famous by his endeavor after the North-west passage. I must pass lightly over the details of Drake's enterprise. It was full of daring, though it must be remembered that the Spanish forts in the West Indies were weak, their ordnance poor, and their garrisons small. At the city of San Domingo, which is described as "the antientest and chief inhabited place in all the tract of country hereabout," Drake landed a thousand or twelve hundred men. A hundred cavalrymen hovered near them, but quickly retreated; the thousand Englishmen divided in two portions, assaulted the two city gates, carried them easily, and then reunited in the market-place. Towards midnight they tried the gates of the castle; it was at once abandoned, and by degrees, street by street, the invaders got possession of half the town. The Spanish commissioners held the other half, and there were constant negotiations for ransom; "but upon disagreement," says the English narrator, "we still spent the early mornings in firing the outmost houses; but they being built very magnificently of stone, with high lofts, gave us no small travail to ruin them." They kept two hundred sailors busy at this work of firing houses, while as many soldiers stood guard over them; and yet had not destroyed more than a third part of the town when they consented to accept 25,000 ducats for the ransom of the rest.

It is hard to distinguish this from the career of a buccaneer; but, after all, Drake was a mild-mannered gentleman,

DRAKE'S ATTACK ON SAN DOMINGO.

and kept a chaplain. There are, to be sure, in the anonymous "short abstract" of this voyage "in the handwriting of the time," published by the Hakluyt Society, some ugly hints as to the private morals of the officers of Drake's ship, including the captain himself. And there is something very grotesque in the final fall from grace of the chaplain, Francis Fletcher, himself, as described in a memorandum among the Harleian MSS. This is the same chaplain who had the chalice and the altar-cloth as his share of the plunder of a church at Santiago. Drake afterwards found him guilty of mutiny, and apparently felt himself free to pronounce both temporal and spiritual penalties, as given in the following narrative by an eye-witness:

"Drake excommunicated Fletcher shortly after. . . . He called all the company together, and then put a lock about one of his legs, and Drake sytting cros legged on a chest, and a paire of pantoffles [slippers] in his hand, he said, Francis Fletcher, I doo heere excomunicate the out of ye Church of God, and from all benefites and graces thereof, and I denounce the to the divell and all his angells; and then he charged him vppon payne of death not once to come before the mast, for if hee did, he swore he should be hanged; and Drake cawsed a posy [inscription] to be written and boñd about Fletcher's arme, with chardge that if hee took it of hee should then be hanged. The poes [posy or inscription] was, Francis fletcher, ye falsest knave that liveth."

Carthagena was next attacked by Drake, and far more stoutly defended, the inhabitants having had twenty days' notice because of the attack on San Domingo. Carthagena was smaller, but for various reasons more important; there had been preparations for attack, the women and children had been sent away, with much valuable property; a few old-fashioned cannon had been brought together; there were barricades made of earth and water-pipes across the principal streets; there were pointed sticks tipped with Indian poisons, and stuck in the ground, points upward. There were also Indian allies armed with bows and poisoned arrows. Against all these obstacles the Englishmen charged pell-mell with pikes and swords, relying little upon fire-arms. They had longer pikes than the Spaniards, and more of the Englishmen were armed. "Every man came so willingly on to the service, as the enemy was not able to endure the fury of such hot assault." It ended in the ransoming of the town for 110,000 ducats, or about £30,000. It seems, by the report of the council of captains, that £100,000 had been the original demand, but these officers say that they can "with much honor and reputation," accept the smaller sum after all, "inasmuch," they add, "as we have taken our full pleasure, both in the uttermost sacking and spoiling of all their household goods and merchandise, as also in that we have consumed and ruined a great part of the town by fire." After all, the Englishmen insisted that this ransom did not include the abbey and the block-house or castle, and they forced the Spaniards to give "a thousand crowns" more for the abbey, and because there was no money left with which to redeem the castle, it was blown up by the English. Drake afterwards took St. Augustine, already settled by the Spaniards, and after sailing northward, and taking on board the survivors of Raleigh's unsuccessful colony in what is now North Carolina, he sailed for England.

What a lawless and even barbarous life was this which Drake led upon the American coast and among the Spanish settlements! Yet he was not held to have dishonored his nation, but the contrary. His Queen rewarded him, poets sang of him, and Sir Philip Sidney, the mirror of all chivalry at that day, would have joined one of his expeditions had not his royal mistress kept him at home. The Spaniards would have done no better, to be sure, and would have brought to bear all the horrors of the Inquisition besides. Yet the English were apt pupils in all the atrocities of personal torture. Cavendish, who afterwards sailed in the track of Drake, circumnavigating the globe like him, took a small bark on the coast of Chili, which vessel had on board three Spaniards and a Fleming. These men were bound to Lima with letters warning the inhabitants of the approach of the English, and they had sworn before their priests that in case of danger the letters should be thrown overboard. "Yet our General," says

THOMAS CAVENDISH.

the narrator, "wrought so with them that they did confess it; but he was fain to cause them to be tormented with their thumbs in a wrench, and to continue three several times with extreme pain. Also he made the old Fleming believe that he would hang him, and the rope being about his neck, he was pulled up a little from the hatches, and yet he would not confess, choosing rather to die than to be perjured. In the end it was confessed by one of the Spaniards." Who can help feeling more respect for the fidelity of this old man, who would die but not break his oath, than for the men who tortured him?

Yet it is just to say that the expeditions of Cavendish, like the later enterprises of Drake, were a school for personal courage, and were not aimed merely against the defenceless. Cavendish gave battle off California to the great Spanish flagship of the Pacific, the *Santa Anna*, of 700 tons burden, bound home from the Philippine Islands. They fought for five or six hours with heavy ordnance and with small-arms, and the Spaniards at last surrendered. There were on board 122,000 *pesos* of gold, besides silks and satins and other merchandise, with provisions and wines. These Cavendish seized, put the crew and passengers — nearly 200 in all — on shore, with tents, provisions, and planks, and burned the *Santa Anna* to the water's edge. Then he sailed for England with his treasures, across the Pacific Ocean, and thus became the second English circumnavigator of the globe. This sort of privateering was an advance on the slave-trading of Hawkins

CAPTURE OF THE "SANTA ANNA," SPANISH FLAG-SHIP, BY CAVENDISH.

and on Drake's early assaults upon almost defenceless towns; but it was often very remote from all honorable warfare. Yet it was by such means that the power of Spain was broken, and that the name of England and England's queen became mighty upon the seas.

As the sixteenth century began with the fame of the Cabots, so it ended with the dreams of Raleigh. It is to be observed that none of these great buccaneers had done anything with a view to colonizing, nor would it have been possible, by armed force, to have held the conquered Spanish towns. Had England only been strong enough for this, South America as well as North America might have spoken the English tongue to-day. But it was the British naval strength only that was established, and after the dispersal of the great Spanish Armada sent by Philip II. against England in 1588, the power of Spain upon the water was forever broken. This opened the way for England to colonize unmolested the northern half of the New World; and the great promoter of this work, Sir Walter Raleigh, was the connecting link between two generations of Englishmen. He was at once the last of the buccaneers and the first of the colonizers.

He himself had made a voyage, led by as wild a dream as any which, in that age of dreams, bewildered an explorer. We must remember that, though the terrors of the ocean were partly dispelled, their mysteries still held their sway over men. Job Hartop, in the region of the Bermudas, describes a merman: "We discovered a monster in the sea, who showed himself three times unto us from the middle upward, in which part he was proportioned like a man, of the complexion of a mulatto or tawny Indian." But especially the accounts were multiplied of cities or islands which now appeared, now disappeared, and must be patiently sought out. Sir John Hawkins reported "certain flitting islands" about the Canaries "which have been oftentimes seene, and when men approached them neere, they vanished . . . and therefore it should seeme he is not yet born to whom God hath appointed the finding of them." Henry Hawkes, speaking of that standing mystery, the Seven Cities of Mexico, says that the Spaniards believed the Indians to cast a mist over these cities, through witchcraft,

SIR WALTER RALEIGH.

so that none could find them. Is it strange that under these influences Sir Walter Raleigh went in search of the fabled empire of Guiana?

Guiana was supposed in those days to be a third great American treasure-house, surpassing those of Peru and Mexico. Its capital was named El Dorado—"the gilded." Spanish adventurers claimed to have seen it from afar, and described its houses as roofed with gold and silver, and its temples as filled with statues of pure gold. Milton links it with Peru and Mexico:

> "Rich Mexico, the seat of Montezuma,
> And Cuzco, in Peru, the richer seat
> Of Atabalipa, and yet unspoiled
> Guiana, whose great city Geryon's sons
> Call El Dorado."

Raleigh himself went in search of this El Dorado, sailing up the Orinoco to find the kingdom, which was said to lie upon an island in a salt-water lake, like the Caspian Sea. He brought home report of many wonders, including a race called Ewaiponima, of whom he says that they have eyes in their shoulders, and mouths in the middle of their breasts, with a long train of hair growing backward between their shoulders. He admits that he never saw them, but says that every child in the provinces he visited affirmed of their existence. It was of these imaginary beings that Shakespeare describes Othello as discoursing:

> "The cannibals that each other eat,
> The anthropophagi, and men whose heads
> Do grow beneath their shoulders."

Raleigh also reports a description he had heard of the inhabitants of this wondrous empire, sitting with the Emperor at their carousals, their bodies stripped naked, and covered with a white balsam, on which powdered gold was blown by servants through hollow canes "until they be all shining from the foot to the head, and in this sort they sit drinking by twenties and hundreds, and continue in drunkenness sometimes six or seven days together."

Raleigh brought home few trophies; but his descriptions of nature were so beautiful, and his treatment of the natives so generous that, in spite of his having a touch of the buccaneer quality about him, we can well accept the phrase that in him "chivalry left the land, and launched upon the deep." But that which makes his memory dear to later generations is that he, beyond any man of his time, saw the vast field open for American colonization, and persistently urged upon Queen Elizabeth to undertake it. "Whatsoever prince shall possesse it," he wrote of his fabled Guiana, "shall be greatest; and if the King of Spayne enjoy it, he will become unresistable." Then he closes with this high strain of appeal, which might well come with irresistible force from the courtier-warrior who had taught the American Indians to call his queen "Ezrabeta Cassipuna Aquerewana," which means, he says, "Elizabeth, the great princess, or greatest commander:"

"To speake more at this time I feare would be but troublesome. I trust in God, this being true, will suffice, and that He which is King of al Kings and Lorde of Lords will put it into thy heart which is Lady of Ladies to possesse it. If not, I will judge those men worthy to be kings thereof, that by her grace and leaue will undertake it of themselues."

V.

THE FRENCH VOYAGEURS.

WHEN Spain and Portugal undertook, in 1494, to divide the unexplored portions of the globe between them, under the Pope's two edicts of the previous year, that impertinent proposal was received by England and France in very characteristic ways. England met it with blunt contempt, and France with an epigram. "The King of France sent word to our great Emperor," says Bernal Diaz, describing the capture of some Spanish treasure ships by a French pirate, "that as he and the King of Portugal had divided the earth between themselves, without giving him a share of it, he should like them to show him our father Adam's will, in order to know if he had made them his sole heirs." (*Que mostrassen el testamento de nuestro padre Adan, si les dexò à ellos solamente por herederos.*) In the meanwhile he warned them that he should feel quite free to take all he could, upon the ocean.

France was not long content with laying claim to the sea, but wished to have the land also. The name of "New France" may still be seen on early maps and globes, sometimes covering all that part of the Atlantic coast north of Florida, and sometimes — as in the map of Ortelius, made in 1574—the whole of North and South America. All this claim was based upon the explorations, first of Verrazzano (1524), and then of Cartier (1534-6). The first of these two voyagers sailed along the coast; the second penetrated into the interior, and the great river St. Lawrence was earliest known to

Europeans through the graphic narrative of its original French explorer. Perhaps no two expeditions since Columbus have added more to the geographical knowledge of the world—or would have added it but for the doubt that still rests in some minds over the authenticity of Verrazzano's narrative. To such extremes has this doubt been carried that Mr. Bancroft, in the revised edition of his history, does not so much as mention the name of Verrazzano, though the general opinion of authorities now accepts his narrative as genuine.

Like many Italian navigators of that age, he served other nations than his own, and sailed by order of Francis I., whose attention had just been called from royal festivals and combats of lions to take part in the exploration of the world. For this purpose he sent out Verrazzano with four ships "to discover new lands" (*a discoprir nuove terre*), and it was to describe these same regions that a letter was written by the explorer from Dieppe to the king, July 8, 1524. This letter was published by Ramusio about forty years later, and an English translation of it appeared in Hakluyt's famous collection. A manuscript copy of the letter was discovered by Professor George W. Greene at Florence about 1840, and the letter itself was reprinted from this copy by the New York Historical Society. If authentic, it is the earliest original account of the Atlantic coast of the United States. Verrazzano saw land first at what is now North Carolina—"a newe land never before seen by any man, either aunciect or moderne"— and afterwards sailed northward, putting in at many harbors. The natives everywhere received him kindly at first, and saved the life of a young sailor who was sent ashore with presents for them, and became exhausted with swimming. In return, the Frenchmen carried off a child, and attempted to carry off a young girl, tall and very beautiful (*di molta bellezza e d' alta statura*), whom they found hidden with an older woman near the shore, and whom they vainly tried to tempt by presents.

Everything which they offered was thrown down by the Indian girl in great anger (*e con ira a terra gittava*), and when they attempted to seize her, she shrieked so loudly that they let her alone. After such a transaction, we can understand why Verrazzano, in the latter part of his voyage, found it impossible to command the confidence of the natives, so that on the northern coast of New England the Indians would not suffer him to land, but would only let down their furs and provisions into the boats from the rocks, insisting on instant payment, and making signs of disdain and contempt (*dispregio e verecondia*). In accordance with the usual logic of adventurers at that day, Verrazzano made up his mind that these poor creatures had no sense of religion.

This early explorer's observations on the natives have little value; but his descriptions of the coast, especially of the harbors of New York and Newport, have peculiar interest, and his charts, although not now preserved, had much influence upon contemporary geography. He sailed northward as far as Newfoundland, having explored the coast from 34° to 50° of north latitude, and left on record the earliest description of the whole region. As to the ultimate fate of Verrazzano reports differ, some asserting that he was killed and eaten by savages, and others that he was hanged by the Spaniards as a pirate. Somewhat the same shadowy uncertainty still attaches to his reputation.

A greater than Verrazzano followed him, aroused and stimulated by what he had done. The first explorer of the St. Lawrence was Jacques Cartier, who had sailed for years on fishing voyages from St. Malo, which was and is the nursery of the hardiest sailors of France. Having visited Labrador, he longed to penetrate farther; and sailing in April, 1534, he visited Newfoundland and the Bay of Chaleur, and set up a cross at Gaspé, telling the natives with pious fraud that it was only intended for a beacon. He then sailed up the St. Lawrence nearly to Anticosti, supposing that this great stream was the long-sought passage to Cathay and the Indies. The next year he sailed again, with three vessels, and for the first time described to the world what he calls "the river of Hochelaga." He applied the name of Canada to a certain part of

JACQUES CARTIER.

the banks of the St. Lawrence, calling all below Saguenay, and all above Hochelaga, these being Indian names. There has been, however, much discussion about the word "Canada," which means "a village" in certain Indian dialects, and also signifies, curiously enough, "a ravine" in Spanish, and "a lane" in Portuguese.

In the greatest delight over the beauty of the river, the Frenchmen sailed onward. They visited Stadaconé, the site of Quebec, and Hochelaga, the site of Montreal, Cartier being the first to give the name of Mont Royal to the neighboring mountain. At Hochelaga they found the carefully built forts of the Indians, which Cartier minutely describes, and the large communal houses already mentioned. They met everywhere with a cordial reception, except that the Indians brought to bear strange pretences to keep them from ascending the river too far. The chief device was the following.

While the Frenchmen lay at Stadaconé they saw one morning a boat come forth from the woods bearing three men "dressed like devils, wrapped in dogs' skins, white and black, their faces besmeared as black as any coals, with horns on their heads more than a yard long," and as this passed the ships, one of the men made a long oration, neither of them looking towards the ships; then they all three fell flat in the boat, when the Indians came out to meet them, and guided them to the shore. It was afterwards explained that these were messengers from the god Cudraigny, to tell the Frenchmen to go no farther lest they should perish with cold. The Frenchmen answered that the alleged god was but a fool—that Jesus Christ would protect his followers from cold. Then the Indians, dancing and shouting, accepted this interpretation, and made no further objection. But when at a later period Cartier and his companions passed the dreary winter, first of all Europeans, in what he called the Harbor of the Holy Cross—somewhere on the banks of the St. Charles River—he learned by suffering that the threats of the god Cudraigny had some terror in them, after all. He returned to France the following summer, leaving no colony in the New World.

For the first French efforts at actual colonization we must look southward on the map of America again, and trace the

JACQUES CARTIER SETTING UP A CROSS AT GASPÉ.

career of a different class of Frenchmen. It would have needed but a few minor changes in the shifting scenes of history to have caused North America to have been colonized by French Protestants, instead of French Catholics. After Villegagnon and his Huguenots had vainly attempted a colony at Rio Janeiro in 1555, Jean Ribaut, with other Huguenots,

THE LANDING OF JEAN RIBAUT.

made an actual settlement seven years later, upon what is now the South Carolina coast. At his first approach to land, the Indians assembled on the shore, offering their own garments to the French officers, and pointing out their chief, who remained sitting on boughs of laurel and palm. All the early experience of the Frenchmen with the natives was marked by this gentleness, and by a very ill-requited hospitality. Then sailing to what is now the St. John's River, and arriving on May-day, they called it "River of May," and found in it that charm which it has held for all explorers, down to the successive military expeditions that occupied and abandoned it during our own civil war. Here they were again received by a picturesque crowd of savages, wading into the water up to their shoulders, and bringing little baskets of maize and of white and red mulberries, while others offered to help their visitors ashore. Other rivers also the Frenchmen visited, naming them after rivers of France — the Seine, the Loire — and then sailing farther north, they entered Port Royal Harbor, "finding the same one of the fayrest and greatest Havens of the worlde," says the quaint old translation of Thomas Hackit. Here they left behind a colony of thirty men, under Albert de la Pierria, to complete a fort called Charlesfort. It was the only Christian colony north of Mexico, and the site of the fort, though still disputed, was undoubtedly not far from Beaufort, South Carolina. The lonely colonists spent a winter of absolute poverty and wretchedness. They were fed by the Indians, and wronged them in return. They built for themselves vessels in which they sailed for France, reaching it after sufferings too great to tell.

Still another French Protestant colony followed in 1564, led by René de Laudonnière. He too sought the "River of May;" he too was cordially received by the Indians; and he built above what is now called St. John's Bluff, on the river of that name, a stronghold called Fort Caroline. "The place is so pleasant," wrote he, "that those which are melancholike would be enforced to change their humor." The adventures of this colony are told in the narrative of the artist Le Moyne — lately reproduced, with heliotypes of all his quaint illustrations, by J. R. Osgood & Co., Boston. These designs — some of which I am permitted by the publishers to copy — are so graphic that we seem in the midst of the scenes described.

INDIAN DWELLING AND CANOE.

They set before us the very costumes of the Frenchmen, and the absence of costume among the Indians. We see the domestic habits, the religious sacrifices, the warlike contests, the Indian faces alone being conventionalized, and made far too European for strict fidelity. We see also the animals that excited the artist's wonder, and especially the alligator, which is rendered with wonderful accuracy, though exaggerated in size. We see here also the column which had been erected by Ribaut on his previous voyage, and how the Indians had decked it, after worshipping there as at an altar.

.The career of the colony was a tragedy. Fort Caroline was built; the colonists mutinied, and sought to become buccaneers, "calling us cowards and greenhorns," says Le Moyne, "for not joining in the piracy." Failing miserably in this, and wearing out the patience of their generous Indian friends, they almost perished of famine. The very fact that they were a Protestant colony brought with it a certain disadvantage, so long as the colonists were French. Protestantism in England reached the lower classes, but never in France. The Hugue-

INDIANS DECORATING RIBAUT'S PILLAR.

nots belonged, as a rule, to the middle and higher classes, and the peasants, so essential to the foundation of a colony, would neither emigrate nor change their religion. There were plenty of adventurers, but no agriculturists. The English Hawkins visited and relieved them. Ribaut came from France and again gave them aid, and their lives were prolonged only to meet cruel destruction from the energy and perfidy of a Spaniard, Don Pedro de Menendez. He came with a great squadron of thirty-four vessels—his flag-ship being nearly a thousand tons burden—to conquer and settle the vast continent, then known as Florida. Parkman has admirably told the story of Menendez's victory; suffice it to say that he overcame the little colony, and then, after taking an oath upon the Bible, adding the sign of the cross, and giving a pledge, written and sealed, to spare their lives, he proceeded to massacre every man in cold blood, sparing only, as Le Moyne tells us, a drummer, a fifer, and a fiddler. It is the French tradition that he hanged his prisoners on trees, with this inscription: "I do this not as to Frenchmen, but as to Lutherans." This was the same Menendez who in that same year (1565) had founded the Spanish colony of St. Augustine, employing for this purpose the negro slaves he had brought from Africa—the first introduction, probably, of slave labor upon the soil now included in the United States. Menendez was the true type of the Spanish conqueror of that day—a race of whom scarcely one in a thousand, as poor Le Moyne declares, was capable of a sensation of pity.

Menendez thanked God with tears for his victory over the little garrison. But his act aroused a terrible demand for vengeance in France, and this eager desire was satisfied by a Frenchman—this time by one who was probably not a Huguenot, but a Catholic. Dominique de Gourgues had been chained to the oar as a galley-slave when a prisoner to the Spaniards, and finding his king unable or unwilling to avenge the insult given to his nation in America, De Gourgues sold his patrimony that he might organize an expedition of his own. It is enough to say that he absolutely annihilated, in 1568, the colony that Menendez had left behind him in Florida, and hanged the Spaniards to the same trees where they had hanged the French, nailing above them this inscription:

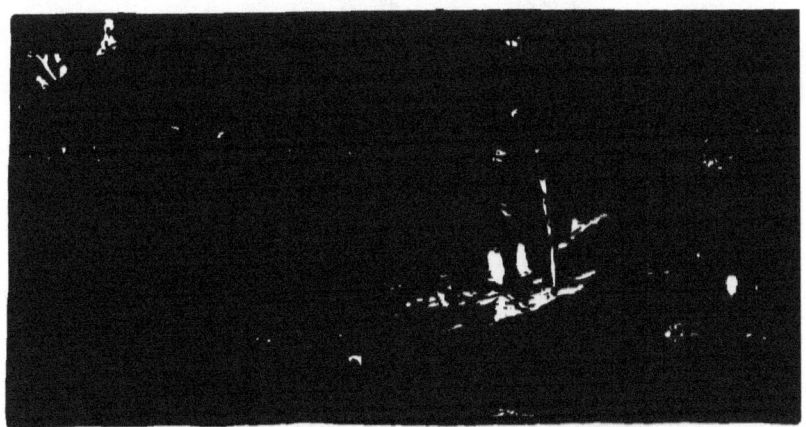

DOMINIQUE DE GOURGUES AVENGING THE MURDER OF THE HUGUENOT COLONY.

"I do this not as to Spaniards or Moors (*Marannes*), but as to traitors, robbers, and murderers."

All these southern and Protestant colonies failed at last. It was farther north, in the lands of the most zealous of Roman Catholics, and in the regions explored long since by Cartier, that the brilliant career of French colonization in America was to have its course. Yet for many years the French voyages to the north-eastern coasts of America were for fishing or trade, not religion: the rover went before the priest. The Cabots are said by Peter Martyr to have found in use on the Banks of Newfoundland the word *Baccalaos* as applied to cod-fish; and as this is a Basque word, the fact has led some writers to believe that the Basque fishermen had already reached there, though this argument is not now generally admitted. Cape Breton, which is supposed to be the oldest French name on the continent of North America, belongs to a region described on a Portuguese map of 1520 as "discovered by the Bretons." There were French fishing vessels off Newfoundland in 1517, and in 1578 there were as many as

THE FRENCH VOYAGEURS.

one hundred and fifty of these, all other nations furnishing but two hundred. Out of these voyages had grown temporary settlements, and the fur trade sprang up by degrees at Anticosti, at Sable Island, and especially at Tadoussac. It became rapidly popular, so that when two nephews of Cartier obtained a monopoly of it for twelve years, the news produced an uproar, and the patent was revoked. Through this trade Frenchmen learned the charm of the wilderness, and these charms attracted then, as always, a very questionable class of men. Cartier, in 1541, was authorized to ransack the prisons for malefactors. De la Roche, in 1598, brought a crew of convicts. De Monts, in 1604, was authorized to impress idlers and vagabonds for his colony. To keep them in order he brought both Catholic priests and Huguenot ministers, who disputed heartily on the way. "I have seen our curé and the minister," said Champlain, in Parkman's translation,

"HE BROUGHT BOTH CATHOLIC PRIESTS AND HUGUENOT MINISTERS, WHO DISPUTED HEARTILY ON THE WAY."

"fall to with their fists on questions of faith. I cannot say which had the more pluck, or which hit the harder, but I know that the minister sometimes complained to the Sieur de Monts that he had been beaten."

The Jesuits reached New France in 1611, and from that moment the religious phase of the emigration began. But their style of missionary effort was very unlike that severe type of religion which had made the very name of Christian hated in the days when Christian meant Spaniard, and when the poor Florida Indians had exclaimed, in despair, "The devil is the best thing in the world: we adore him." The two bodies of invaders held the same faith, acknowledged the same spiritual chief; but here the resemblance ended. From the beginning the Spaniards came as cruel and merciless masters; the Frenchmen, with few exceptions, as kindly and genial companions. The Spanish invaders were more liberal in the use of Scripture than any Puritan, but they were also much more formidable in the application of it. They maintained unequivocally that the earth belonged to the elect, and that they were the elect. The famous "Requisition," which was to be read by the Spanish commanders on entering each province for conquest, gave the full Bible narrative of the origin of the human race, announced the lordship of St. Peter, the gift of the New World to Spain by his successor the Pope; and deduced from all this the right to compel the natives to adopt the true religion. If they refused, they might rightfully be enslaved or killed. The learned Dr. Pedro Santander, addressing the king in 1557 in regard to De Soto's expedition, wrote thus:

> "This is the land promised by the Eternal Father to the faithful, since we are commanded by God in the Holy Scriptures to take it from them, being idolaters, and by reason of their idolatry and sin to put them all to the knife, leaving no living thing save maidens and children, their cities robbed and sacked, their walls and houses levelled to the earth."

In another part of the same address the author describes Florida as "now in possession of the Demon," and the natives as "lost sheep which have been snatched away by the dragon, the Demon." There is no doubt that a genuine superstition entered into the gloomy fanaticism of the Spaniards. When Columbus brought back from one of his voyages some native chiefs whose garments and ornaments were embroidered with cats and owls, the curate Bernaldez announced without hesitation that these grotesque forms represented the deities whom these people worshipped. It is astonishing how much easier it is to justify one's self in taking away a man's property or his life when one is thoroughly convinced that he worships the devil. At any rate, the Spaniards acted upon this principle. Twelve years after the first discovery of Hispaniola, as Columbus himself writes, six-sevenths of the natives were dead through ill-treatment.

But the French pioneers were perfectly indifferent to these superstitions; embroidered cat or Scriptural malediction troubled them very little. They came for trade, for exploration, for peaceful adventure, and also for religion; but almost from the beginning they adapted themselves to the Indians, urged on them their religion only in a winning way; and as to their ways of living, were willing to be more Indian than the Indians themselves. The instances of the contrary were to be found, not among the Roman Catholic French, but among the Huguenots in Florida.

The spirit which was exceptional in the benevolent Spanish monk Las Casas was common among French priests. The more profoundly they felt that the Indians were by nature children of Satan, the more they gave soul and body for their conversion. Père Le Caron, travelling with the Hurons, writes frankly about his infinite miseries, and adds: "But I must needs tell you what abundant consolation I found under all my troubles, for, alas! when one sees so many infidels needing nothing but a drop of water to make them children of God, he feels an inexpressible ardor to labor for their conversion, and sacrifice to it his repose and his life." At times, no doubt, the Frenchmen would help one Indian tribe against another, and this especially against the Iroquois; but in general the French went as friendly associates, the Spaniards as brutal task-masters.

The first French colonists were rarely such in the English or even the Spanish sense. They were priests or soldiers or traders—the latter at first predominating. They did not offer to buy the lands of the Indians, as the English colonists afterwards did, for an agricultural colony was not their aim. They wished to wander through the woods with the Indians, to join in their hunting and their wars, and, above all, to obtain their furs. For this they were ready to live as the Indians lived, in all their discomforts; they addressed them as "brothers" or as "children;" they married Indian wives with full church ceremonies. No such freedom of intercourse marked the life of any English settlers. The Frenchmen apparently liked to have the Indians with them; the savages were always coming and going, in full glory, about the French settlements; they feasted and slept beside the French; they were greeted with military salutes. The stately and brilliant Comte de Frontenac, the favorite officer of Turenne, and the intimate friend of La Grande Mademoiselle, did not disdain, when Governor-general of Canada, to lead in person the war-dance of his Indians, singing and waving the hatchet, while a wigwam full of braves, stripped and painted for war, went dancing and howling after him, shouting like men possessed, as the French narratives say. He himself admits that he did it deliberately, in order to adopt their ways. (*Je leur mis moy-mesme la hache à la main . . . pour m'accommoder à leurs façons de faire.*) Perhaps no single act ever done by a Frenchman explains so well how they won the hearts of the Indians.

The pageantry of the Roman Catholic Church had, moreover, its charm for native converts; the French officers taught them how to fight; the French priests taught them how to die. These heroic missionaries could bear torture like Indians, and could forgive their tormentors as Indians could not. This combination of gentleness with courage was something wholly new to the Indian philosophy of life. Père Brebeuf wrote to Rome from Canada: "That which above all things is demanded of laborers in this vineyard is an unfailing sweetness and a patience thoroughly tested." And when he died by torture in 1649 he so conducted himself that the Indians drank his blood, and the chief devoured his heart, in the hope that they might share his heroism.

But while the missionaries were thus gentle and patient with their converts, their modes of appeal included the whole range of spiritual terrors. Père Le Jeune wrote home earnestly for pictures of devils tormenting the soul with fire, serpents, and red-hot pincers; Père Garnier, in a manuscript letter copied by Mr. Parkman, asks for pictures of demons and dragons, and suggests that a single representation of a happy or beautiful soul will be enough. "The pictures must not be in profile, but in full face, looking squarely and with open eyes at the beholder, and all in bright colors, without flowers or animals, which only distract." But, after all, so essentially different was the French temperament from the Spanish that the worst French terrors seemed more kindly and enjoyable than the most cheerful form of Spanish devotion. The Spaniards offered only the threats of future torment, and the certainty of labor and suffering here. But the French won the Indians by precisely the allurements that to this day draw strangers from all the world to Paris—a joyous out-door life and an unequalled cookery. "I remember," says Lescarbot, describing his winter in Canada, "that on the 14th of January (1607), of a Sunday afternoon, we amused ourselves with singing and music on the river Équille, and that in the same month we went to see the wheat-fields two leagues from the fort, and dined merrily in the sunshine." At these feasts there was hardly a distinction between the courtly foreigner and the naked Indian, and even the coarse aboriginal palate felt that here was some one who would teach a new felicity. Mr. Parkman tells us of a convert who asked, when at the point of death, whether he might expect any pastry in heaven like that with which the French had regaled him.

In return for these blandishments it was not very hard for the Indians to accept the picturesque and accommodating faith of their guests. This was not at first done very reverently, to be sure. Sometimes when the early missionaries asked their converts for the proper words to translate the sacred phrases of the catechism, their mischievous proselytes would give them very improper words instead, and then would shout with delight whenever the priests began their lessons. Dr. George E. Ellis, in his valuable book "The Red Man and the White Man," points out that no such trick was ever attempted, so far as we know, beneath the graver authority of the apostle Eliot, when his version of the Scriptures was in progress. In some cases the native criticisms took the form of more serious remonstrance. Membertou, one of the most influential of the early Indian converts, said frankly that he did not like the petition for daily bread in the Lord's Prayer, and thought that some distinct allusion to moose meat and fish would be far better.

To these roving and companionable Frenchmen, or, rather, to the native canoe-men, who were often their half-breed posterity, was given at a later period the name *voyageurs* — a name still used for the same class in Canada, though it describes a race now vanishing. I have ventured to anticipate its date a little, and apply it to the French rovers of this early period, because it is one of those words which come spontaneously into use, tell their own story, and save much description. The character that afterwards culminated in the class called *voyageurs* was the character which lay behind all the early French enterprises. It implied those roving qualities which led the French to be pioneers in the fisheries and the fur trade; and which, even after the arrival of the Jesuit missionaries, still prevailed under the blessing of the Church. The Spaniards were gloomy despots; the Dutch and Swedes were traders; the English, at least in New England, were religious enthusiasts; the French were *voyageurs*, and even under the narrative of the most heroic and saintly priest we see something of the same spirit. The best early type of the *voyageur* temperament combined with the courage of the Church militant is to be found in Samuel de Champlain.

After all, there is no earthly immortality more secure than to have stamped one's name on the map; and that of Champlain will be forever associated with the beautiful lake which he first described, and to which the French missionaries vainly attempted to attach another name. Champlain was a Frenchman of good family, who had served in the army, and had, indeed, been from his childhood familiar with scenes of war, because he had dwelt near the famous city of Rochelle, the very hot-bed of the civil strife between Catholics and Huguenots. Much curiosity existing in France in regard to the great successes of Spain in America, he obtained naval em-

SAMUEL DE CHAMPLAIN.

ployment in the Spanish service, and visited, as commander of a ship, the Spanish-American colonies. This was in 1599, and he wrote a report on the condition of all these regions— a report probably fuller than anything else existing at that time, inasmuch as the Spaniards systematically concealed the details of their colonial wealth. Little did they know that they had in the humble French captain of the *Saint-Julian* an untiring observer, who would reveal to the acute mind of Henry the Fourth of France many of the secrets of Spanish domination; and would also disgust the French mind with pictures of the fanaticism of their rivals. In his report he denounced the cruelty of the Spaniards, described the way in which they converted Indians by the Inquisition, and made drawings of the burnings of heretics by priests. His observations on all commercial matters were of the greatest value, and he was the first, or one of the first, to suggest a ship-canal across the isthmus of Panama. Full of these vivid impressions of Spanish empire, he turned his attention towards the northern part of the continent, in regions unsettled by the Spaniards, visiting them first in 1603, under Pont-Gravé, and then in seven successive voyages. His narratives are minute, careful, and graphic; he explored river after river with the Indians, eating and sleeping with them, and recording laboriously their minutest habits. It is to his descriptions, beyond any others, that we must look for faithful pictures of the Indian absolutely unaffected by contact with white men; and his voyages, which have lately been translated by Dr. C. P. Otis, and published by the Prince Society, with annotations by Mr. E. F. Slafter, have a value almost unique.

Champlain himself may be best described as a devout and high-minded *voyageur*. He was a good Catholic, and on some of his exploring expeditions he planted at short intervals crosses of white cedar in token of his faith; but we see the born rover through the proselyting Christian. Look, for instance, at the spirit in which he dedicates his voyage of 1604 to the Queen Regent:

"MADAME,—Of all the most useful and excellent arts, that of navigation has always seemed to me to occupy the first place. For the more hazardous it is and the more numerous the perils and losses by which it is attended, so much the more is it esteemed and exalted above all others, being wholly unsuited to the timid and irresolute. By this art we obtain knowledge of different countries, regions, and realms. By it we attract and bring to our own land all kinds of riches, by it the idolatry of paganism is overthrown and Christianity proclaimed throughout all the regions of the earth. This is the art which from my early age has won my love, and induced me to expose myself all my life to the impetuous waves of the ocean, and led me to explore the coasts of a part of America, especially of New France, where I have always desired to see the lily flourish, and also the only religion, catholic, apostolic, and Roman."

Here we have the French lilies and the holy Catholic religion at the end, but the impulse of the *voyageur* through all the rest. We see here the born wanderer, as full of eagerness as Tennyson's Ulysses,

"Always roaming with a hungry heart."

And when we compare this frank and sailor-like address with the devout diplomacy, already quoted, of the Spanish doctor, we see in how absolutely different a spirit the men of these two nations approached the American Indians.

Champlain was an ardent lover of out-door life, and an intelligent field naturalist, and the reader finds described or mentioned in his narratives many objects now familiar, but then strange. He fully describes, for instance, the gar-pike of Western lakes, he mentions the moose under the Algonquin name "orignac," the seal under the name of "sea-lion," the musk-rat, and the horseshoe-crab. He describes almost every point and harbor on the north-east coast, giving the names by which many of them are since known; for instance, Mount Desert, which he calls *Isle des Monts Déserts*, meaning simply Desert

Mountains, so that the accent need not be laid, as is now usual, on the second syllable. We know from him that while yet unvisited by white men, the Indians of the Lake Superior region not only mined for copper, but melted it into sheets, and hammered it into shape, making bracelets and arrow-heads. Cartier, in 1535, had mentioned the same thing, but not so fully. And all Champlain's descriptions, whether of places or people,

CHAMPLAIN'S FORTIFIED RESIDENCE AT QUEBEC.

have the value that comes of method and minuteness. When he ends a chapter with "This is precisely what I have seen of this northern shore," or, "This is what I have learned from those savages," we know definitely where his knowledge begins and ends, and whence he got his information.

It is fortunate for the picturesqueness of his narrative that he fearlessly ventures into the regions of the supernatural, but always upon very definite and decided testimony. It would be a pity, for instance, to spare the Gougou from his pages. The Gougou was a terrible monster reported by the savages to reside on an island near the Bay of Chaleur. It was in the form of a woman, but very frightful, and so large that the masts of a tall vessel would not reach the waist. The Gougou possessed pockets, into which he — or she — used to put the Indians when caught; and those who had escaped said that a single pocket would hold a ship. From this receptacle the victims were only taken out to be eaten. Several savages assured Champlain that they had seen the creature; many had heard the horrible noises he made; and one French adventurer had sailed so near his dwelling-place as to hear a strange hissing from that quarter, upon which all his Indian companions hid themselves. "What makes me believe what they say," says Champlain, "is the fact that all the savages in general fear it, and tell such strange things about it that if I were to record all they say it would be regarded as a myth; but I hold that this is the dwelling-place of some devil that torments them in the above-mentioned manner. This is what I have learned about the Gougou."

Champlain has left a minute description, illustrated by his own pencil, of his successive fortified residences—first at what is now Douchet Island, named originally the Island of the Holy Cross, and afterwards at Port Royal and Quebec. Traces of the first-named encampment have been found in some cannon-balls, one of which is now in possession of the New England Historic-Genealogical Society. His journals vividly describe his winter discomforts in America, and the French devices that made them endurable. He also gives, as has been said, minute descriptions of the Indians, their homes and their hunting, their feasting and fighting, their courage and superstitions. His relations to them were, like those of other Frenchmen, for the most part kindly and generous. His most formidable act of kindness, if such it may be called, was when

"HE RESTED HIS MUSKET."

he first revealed to them the terrible power of fire-arms. He it was, of all men, who began for them that series of lessons in the military art by which the Frenchmen doubled the terrors of Indian warfare. Champlain has portrayed vividly for us with pen and pencil the early stages of that alliance which in later years made the phrase "French and Indian" the symbol of all that was most to be dreaded in the way of conflict. He describes picturesquely, for instance, an occasion when he and his Algonquin allies marched together against the Iroquois; and his Indians told him if he could only kill three particular chiefs for them they should win the day. Reaching a promontory which Mr. Slafter believes to have been Ticonderoga, they saw the Iroquois approaching, with the three chiefs in front, wearing plumes. Champlain then told his own allies that he was very sorry they could not understand his language better, for he could teach them such order and method in attacking their enemies that they would be sure of victory; but meanwhile he would do what he could. Then they called upon him with loud cries to stand forward; and so, putting him twenty paces in front, they advanced. Halting within thirty paces of the enemy, he rested his

musket against his cheek and aimed at one of the chiefs.
The musket—a short weapon, then called an arquebus—was
loaded with four balls. Two chiefs fell dead, and another man
was mortally wounded. The effect upon the Iroquois must
have been like that of fire from heaven. These chiefs were
dressed in armor made of cotton fibre, and arrow-proof, yet
they died in an instant! The courage of the whole band gave
way, and when another Frenchman fired a shot from the
woods, they all turned and fled precipitately, abandoning camp
and provisions—a whole tribe, and that one of the bravest,
routed by two shots from French muskets. This was in July,
1609.

On his voyage of the following year he also taught the
same Indians how to attack a fortified place. Until that time
their warlike training had taught them only how to track a
single enemy or to elude him; or at most, gathered in solid
masses, to pour in showers of arrows furnished with those
sharp stone heads so familiar in our collections. We know
from descriptions elsewhere given by Champlain that the chief
strategy of the Indians lay in arranging and combining these
masses of bowmen. This they planned in advance by means
of bundles of sticks a foot long, each stick standing for a soldier, with larger sticks for chiefs. Going to some piece of
level ground five or six feet square, the head chief stuck these
sticks in the ground according to his own judgment. Then
he called his companions, and they studied the arrangements.
It was a plan of the battle—a sort of Indian, *Kriegspiel*, like
the German military game that has the same object. The
warriors studied the sticks under the eye of the chief, and
comprehended the position each should occupy. Then they
rehearsed it in successive drills. We are thus able to understand—what would otherwise be difficult to explain—the compact and orderly array which Champlain's pictures represent.

It was with a band of warriors thus trained that Champlain

set forth from Quebec, in June, 1610, to search for a camp of Iroquois. The Indian guides went first, armed, painted, naked, light-footed, and five Frenchmen marched after them, arrayed in heavy corselets for defence, and bearing guns and ammunition. It was an alliance of hare and tortoise, but in this case the hare kept in front. Champlain describes their discom-

ATTACK ON AN IROQUOIS FORT.

forts as they tramped in their heavy accoutrements through pathless swamps, with water reaching to their knees, far behind their impatient leaders, whose track they found it hard to trace. Suddenly they came upon the very scene where the fight had begun, and when the savages perceived them, "they began to shout so that one could not have heard it thunder." In the midst of this tumult Champlain and his four companions approached the Iroquois fortress — built solidly of large trees arranged in a circle—and coolly began to fire their muskets through the logs at the naked savages within. He thus describes the scene, which is also vividly depicted in one of his illustrations, here given:

"You could see the arrows fly on all sides as thick as hail. The Iroquois were astonished at the noise of our muskets, and especially that the balls penetrated better than their arrows. They were so frightened at the effect produced that, seeing several of their companions fall wounded and dead, they threw themselves on the ground whenever they heard a discharge, supposing that the shots were sure. We scarcely ever missed firing two or three balls at one shot, resting our muskets most of the time on the side of their barricade. But seeing that our ammunition began to fail, I said to all the savages that it was necessary to break down their barricades and capture them by storm, and that in order to accomplish this they must take their shields, cover themselves with them, and thus approach so near as to be able to fasten stout ropes to the posts that supported the barricades, and pull them down by main strength, in that way making an opening large enough to permit them to enter the fort. I told them that we would meanwhile, by our musketry fire, keep off the enemy as they endeavored to prevent them from accomplishing this; also that a number of them should get behind some large trees which were near the barricade, in order to throw them down upon the enemy, and that others should protect them with their shields, in order to keep the enemy from injuring them. All this they did very promptly."

Thus were the military lessons begun—not lessons in the use of fire-arms alone, but in strategy and offensive tactics, to which the same class of instructors were destined later to add an improved mode of fortification. So completely did Champlain and his four Frenchmen find themselves the masters of the situation, that when some young fellows, countrymen of their own, and still better types of the *voyageur* than they themselves were, came eagerly up the river in some trading barks to see what was going on, Champlain at once ordered the savages who were breaking down the fortress to stop, "so that the new-comers should have their share in the sport." He then gave the guns to the young French traders, and let them amuse themselves by shooting down a few defenceless Iroquois before the walls fell.

At last the fort yielded. "This, then, is the victory obtained by God's grace," as Champlain proudly says. Out of a hundred defenders, only fifteen were found alive. All these were put to death by tortures except one, whom Champlain manfully claimed for his share, and saved; and he was perhaps the first to describe fully those frightful cruelties and that astonishing fortitude which have since been the theme of so much song and story, and to point out, moreover, that in these refinements of barbarity the women excceded the men. Later they were joined on the war-path by a large force of friendly Indians, "who had never before seen Christians, for whom they conceived a great admiration." This admiration was not destined, as in the case of the Spaniards and English, to undergo a stern reaction, but it lasted till the end of the French power on the American continent, and did a great deal to postpone that end. If the control of the New World could have been secured solely through the friendship and confidence of its native tribes, North America would have been wholly French and Roman Catholic to-day.

VI.

"*AN ENGLISH NATION.*"

SIR WALTER RALEIGH, just on the eve of his fall from greatness, and after the failure of nine successive expeditions to America, wrote these words: "I shall yet live to see it an English nation." He was mistaken; he did not live to see it, although his fame still lives, and what he predicted has in one sense come to pass. The vast difference that might exist between a merely English nation and an English-speaking nation had never dawned upon his mind. All that "History of the World" which he meditated in the Tower of London contained no panorama of events so wonderful as that which time has unrolled in the very scene of his labors.

We owe to Raleigh not merely the strongest and most persistent impulse towards the colonization of America, but also the most romantic and ideal aspects of that early movement. He it is who has best described for us the charm exercised by this virgin soil over the minds of cultivated men. Had he not sought to win it for a virgin queen, it would still have been "Virginia" to him. With what insatiable delight he describes the aspects of nature in this New World!

"I never saw a more beawtifull countrey, nor more liuely prospectes, hils so raised heere and there ouer the vallies, the riuer winding into diuers braunches, the plaines adioyning without bush or stubble, all faire greene grasse, the ground of hard sand easy to march on, eyther for horse or foote, the deare crossing in euery path, the birdes towardes the euening singing on euery tree, with a thousand seuerall tunes, cranes and herons of white, crimson, and carnation pearching on the riuers side, the ayre fresh with a gentle easterlie wind, and euery stone that we stooped to take vp promised eyther golde or siluer by his complexion."

Raleigh represents the imaginative and glowing side of American exploration—an aspect which, down to the days of John Smith, remained vividly prominent, and which had not wholly disappeared even under the graver treatment of the Puritans.

The very adventures of some of the early colonies seem to retain us in the atmosphere of those vanishing islands and enchanted cities of which the early English seamen dreamed. Raleigh sent his first colony to Virginia in 1585, under Ralph Lane; in 1586 he sent a ship with provisions to their aid, "who, after some time spent in seeking our colony up and down, and not finding them, returned with all the aforesaid provision unto England," the colonists having really departed "out of that paradise of the world," as Hakluyt says—in vessels furnished by Sir Francis Drake. Then followed Sir Richard Grenville with three vessels; but he could find neither relief-ship nor colony, and after some time spent in the same game of hide-and-seek, he landed fifteen men in the island of Roanoke, with two years' provisions, to take possession of the country. Then, in 1587, went three ships containing a colony of one hundred and fifty, under John White, with a chartered and organized corps of twelve assistants, under the sonorous name of "Governor and Assistants of the City of Raleigh in Virginia." They looked for Grenville's fifteen men, but found them not, and found only deer grazing on the melons that had grown within the roofless houses of Lane's colony. In spite of these dark omens, the new settlement was formed, and on the 18th of August, 1587—as we read in Captain John Smith's "Generall Historie of Virginia, New England, and the

Summer Isles"—"Ellinor, the Governour's daughter, and wife to Ananias Dare, was delivered of a daughter, in Roanoak, which, being the first Christian there borne, was called Virginia." Here at least was something permanent, definite, established — a birth and a christening, the beginning of "an English nation," transferred to American soil.

Alas! in all this pathetic series of dissolving hopes and lost colonies, the career of the little Virginia is the most touching. Governor White, going back to England for supplies soon after the birth of his grandchild, left in the colony eighty-nine men, seventeen women, and eleven children. He was detained three years, and on his return, in August, 1590, he found no trace of the colony except three letters "curiously carved" upon a tree—the letters CRO—and elsewhere, upon another tree, the word "CROATOAN." It had been agreed beforehand that should the colony be removed, the name of their destination should be carved somewhere conspicuously, and that if they were in distress a cross should be carved above. These trees bore no cross; but the condition of the buildings and buried chests of the colony indicated the work of savages. "Though it much grieved me," writes the anxious and wandering father in his narrative, "yet it did much comfort me that I did know they were at Croatoan." Before the ships could seek the island of Croatoan they were driven out to sea; but apparently those in charge of the expedition had resolved not to seek it, Governor White being but a passenger, and they having already anchored near that island and seen no signals of distress. Twenty years after, Powhatan confessed to Captain John Smith that he had been at the murder of the colonists. Strachey, secretary of the Jamestown settlement, found a report among the Indians of a race who dwelt in stone houses, which they had been taught to build by those English who had escaped the slaughter of Roanoke—these being farther specified as "fower men, two boyes, and one yonge mayde," whom a certain chief had preserved as his "slaves. Furthermore, the first Virginia settlers found at an Indian village a boy of ten, with yellow hair and whitish skin, who may have been a descendant of these ill-fated survivors. Thus vanishes from history the last of the lost colonies and every trace of Virginia Dare.

The first colonists farther north met with equal failure but less of tragedy. No children were born to them, no Christian maiden ever drifted away in the unfathomable ocean of Indian mystery; they consisted of men only, and this helped to explain their forlorn career. Bartholomew Gosnold crossed the Atlantic in 1602, following the route of Ribaut, who had wished to establish what are now called "ocean lanes"—at least so far as to keep the French vessels away from the Spaniards by following a more northern track. Gosnold landed at Cape Ann, then crossed Massachusetts Bay to Provincetown, and built a shelter on the Island of Cuttyhunk (called by him Elizabeth Island), in Buzzard's Bay. His house was fortified with palisades, thatched with sedge, and furnished with a cellar, which has been identified in recent times. He saw deer on the island, but no inhabitants; and the soil was "overgrown with wood and rubbish"—the latter including sassafras, young cherry-trees, and grape-vines. Here he wintered, but if he ever meant to found a colony—which is now doubted —it failed for want of supplies, and his vessel, the *Concord*, returned with all on board, his eight seamen and twenty planters, to England. They arrived there, as Gosnold wrote to his father, without "one cake of bread, nor any drink but a little vinegar left." But he had a cargo of sassafras root which was worth more than vinegar or bread, though it yielded little profit to Gosnold, since it was confiscated by Raleigh as being sole patentee of the region visited. This fragrant shrub, then greatly prized as a medicine, drew to America another expedition, following after Gosnold's, and headed by Martin Pring.

He sailed the next year (1603) with two vessels and forty-four men, not aiming at colonization, but at trade. He anchored either at Plymouth or Edgartown, built a palisaded fort to protect his sassafras-hunters, but found the Indians very inconvenient neighbors, and returned home. Waymouth came two years later, and sailed sixty miles up the Kennebec or Penobscot — it is not yet settled which —, and pronounced it "the most rich, beautiful, large, and secure harboring river that the world affordeth." But he did not stay long, and except for his enthusiasm over the country, and the fact that he carried home five Indians, his trip counted for no more than Pring's. Meanwhile De Monts and Champlain were busy in exploring on the part of the French; and Sir Ferdinando Gorges was planning one more fruitless colony for the English.

Gorges was probably a kinsman of Raleigh; he knew Waymouth, and took charge for three years of some of his Indian captives. With Sir John Popham he secured the incorporation of two colonies — to be called the First and the Second, and to be under charge of the Council of Virginia, appointed by the crown. The First, or London Colony, was to be planted in "South Virginia," from north latitude 34° to 38°, and the Second, or Plymouth Colony, was to be planted in "North Virginia," between 41° and 45° north latitude. Neither colony was to extend more than fifty miles inland, and there was to be an interval of a hundred miles between their nearest settlements. That gap of a hundred miles afterwards caused a great deal of trouble.

Three ships with a hundred settlers went from Plymouth, England, in 1607, reaching the mouth of the Sagadahoc, or Kennebec, August 8th. They held religious services according to the Church of England, read their patent publicly, and proceeded to dig wells, build houses, and erect a fort. Misfortune pursued them. Nearly half their number went back with the vessels. The winter was unusually severe. Their storehouse was burned; their president, George Popham, died; their patron in England, Sir John Popham, died also; their

"admiral," Raleigh Gilbert, was recalled to England by the death of his brother. In the spring all returned, and another colony was added to the list of unsuccessful attempts. It is useless to speculate on what might have been the difference in the destiny of New England had it succeeded; it failed, and the world never cares very much for failures. The contemporary verdict was that "the country was branded by the return of that plantation as being over-cold, and, in respect of that, not habitable for Englishmen." But the fortunate fact that two colonies were sent out together made the year 1607 the beginning of successful colonization in America, after all. The enterprise succeeded, not in New England, then called North Virginia, but in South Virginia, part of which territory still retains the name of the Virgin Queen. It succeeded not under the high-sounding name of Sir Ferdinando Gorges, but under the more plebeian auspices of John Smith.

John Smith was the last of the romantic school of explorers. It is impossible to tell who wrote all his numerous books, or where to draw the line in regard to his innumerable adventures. We shall never know the whole truth about Pocahontas or Powhatan. No matter; he was the ideal sailor, laboring to be accurate in all that relates to coasts and soundings, absolutely credulous as to all the wilder aspects of enterprise in a new world. He maintained the traditions of wonder; he would not have been surprised at Job Hartop's merman, or Ponce de Leon's old men made young, or Raleigh's headless Indians, or Champlain's Gougou. The flavor of all his narratives is that of insatiable and joyous adventure, not yet shadowed by that awful romance of supernatural terror which came in with the Puritans.

Yet his first service was in his accuracy of description. It is a singular fact pointed out by Kohl, that while the sixteenth century placed upon our maps with much truth the coasts of Newfoundland, Labrador, and Canada, the coasts of New England and New York were unknown till the beginning of the seventeenth. When Hudson sailed south of Cape Cod and entered the harbor of New York, he was justified in saying that he entered "an unknown sea." If the shore north of

POWHATAN Held this state & fashion when Capt. Smith was delivered to him prisoner 1607

Cape Cod was not an unknown region, it was due largely to Smith. While his companions were plundering or kidnapping negroes, at the time he first visited those shores, in 1614, he was drawing "a map from point to point, isle to isle, and harbor to harbor, with the soundings, sands, rocks, and landmarks." He first called the region New England, and first containing the orders from the King. This box designated as councillors the three sea-captains, with Edward Maria Wingfield (president), John Smith, John Martin, and John Kendall. Smith, however, because of some suspicion of mutinous bearing on the voyage, was excluded from office until June 10th.

It is possible that something of personal feeling may have entered into Smith's low opinion of these first colonists. He says of them, in his "Generall Historie:"

> "Being for most part of such tender educations, and small experience in Martiall accidents, because they found not English Cities, nor such fair houses, downe pillowes, tavernes, and ale-houses in euery breathing place, neither such plentie of gold and silver and dissolute libertie as they expected, had little or no care of anything but to pamper their bellies, to fly away with our Pinnaces, or procure their meanes to returne for *England.* For the Country was to them a misery, a ruine, a death, a hell, and their reports here and their actions there according."

They planted a cross at Fort Henry, naming it for the Prince of Wales, and they named the opposite cape for his brother, the Duke of York, afterwards Charles I. The next day they named another spot Point Comfort. Ascending the Powhatan River, called by them the James, they landed at a peninsula about fifty miles from the mouth, and resolved to build their town there. They went to work, sending Smith and others farther up the river to explore, and repelling the first Indian attack during their absence. In June Newport sailed for England, leaving three months' provisions for the colonists. Again the experiment was to be tried; again Englishmen found themselves alone in the New World. Captain John Smith, always graphic, has left a vivid picture of the discomforts of that early time:

> "When I first went to *Virginia*, I well remember, wee did hang an awning (which is an old saile) to three or foure trees to shadow us from the Sunne, our walls were rales of wood, our seats unhewed trees, till we cut plankes, our Pulpit a bar of wood nailed to two neighboring trees, in foule weather we shifted into an old rotten tent, for we had few better, and this came by the way of adventure for new; this was our Church, till wee built a homely thing like

a barne, set upon Cratchets, covered with rafts, sedge, and earth, so was also the walls: the best of our houses of the like curiosity, but the most part farre much worse workmanship, that could neither well defend wind nor raine, yet wee had daily Common Prayer morning and evening, every Sunday two Sermons, and every three moneths the holy Communion, till our Minister died, but our Prayers daily, with an Homily on Sundaies we continued two or three yeares after till more Preachers came, and surely God did most mercifully heare us, till the continuall inundations of mistaking directions, factions, and numbers of unprovided Libertines neere consumed us all, as the Israelites in the wildernesse."

The place was unhealthy; they found no gold; the savages were hostile; by September one-half of their own number had died, including Gosnold, and their provisions were almost exhausted. The council was reduced to three—Ratcliffe, Smith, and Martin. Later still their settlement was burned, and their food reduced to meal and water; the intrepid leadership of Smith alone saved them; and for years the colony struggled, as did the Plymouth colony a dozen years later, for mere existence. Its materials from the beginning were strangely put together—one mason, one blacksmith, four carpenters, fifty-two gentlemen, and a barber! The "first supply" in 1608 brought one hundred and twenty more, but not in much better combination—thirty-three gentle-

MAP OF JAMESTOWN SETTLEMENT, FROM CAPTAIN JOHN SMITH'S "HISTORIE OF VIRGINIA."

men, twenty-one laborers, six tailors, with apothecaries, perfumers, and goldsmiths, but still only one mechanic of the right sort. The "second supply," in the same year, brought seventy persons, including "eight Dutchmen and Poles," and, best of all, two women — Mistress Forrest and Anne Burras her maid — joined the company; and soon after, the maid was married to John Laydon, "which was the first marriage," Smith triumphantly says, "we had in Virginia." Smith had by this time become President of the Council, and was at last its only member. They had received supplies from England, but the continuance of these was very uncertain. Newport on his return trip had foolishly pledged himself not to return without a lump of gold, the discovery of a passage to the North Sea, some of the settlers of the lost colony, or a freight worth £2000. Unless this pledge was fulfilled, the colony was to be abandoned to its own resources; and fulfilled it never was.

Early in October, 1609, Smith sailed for England, leaving nearly five hundred settlers, with horses, cattle, cannon, fishing nets, and provisions. He never returned, though he made a successful voyage to New England. He apparently went away under a cloud, but with him went the fortunes of the colony. There followed a period known as "the starving time," which ended in the abandonment of the settlement, with its fifty or sixty houses and its defence of palisades. The colonists were met as they descended the river, in April, 1610, by Lord Delaware (or De la Warr) as he ascended with another party of settlers; and thenceforward the Virginia settlement was secure. Yet it did not grow strong; it was languishing in 1618, and it had an accession of doubtful benefit in 1619, when we read in Smith's "Generall Historie," as the statement of John Rolfe, "About the last of August came in a Dutch man-of-warre, and sold us twenty Negars." In 1621 came a more desirable accession, through the shipment by the company of "respectable young women" for wives of those colonists who

ARRIVAL OF THE YOUNG WOMEN AT JAMESTOWN.

would pay the cost of transportation—at first one hundred and twenty pounds of tobacco, afterwards one hundred and fifty. In July, 1620, the colony was four thousand strong, and shipped to England forty thousand pounds of tobacco. This was raised with the aid of many bound apprentices—boys and girls picked up in the streets of London and sent out—and of many "disorderly persons" sent by order of the King. But in the year 1624 only 1275 colonists were left in Virginia.

The colony would have been more prosperous, Captain John Smith thought, without the tobacco. "Out of the relicks of our miseries," he says, "time and experience had brought that country to a great happinesse, had they not so much doted on their tobacco, on whose firmest foundations there is small stability, there being so many good commodities beside." But their chief trouble, as he wrote from London in 1631 — the last year of his life — was always in the uncertain sway of the Virginia Company in London: "Their purses and lives were subject to some few here in London, who were never there, that consumed all in Arguments, Projects, Conclusions, altering everything yearely, as they altered opinions, till they had consumed more than £200,000 and neere 8000 men's lives."

Another voyager, also English, but in Dutch employ, following Smith across the ocean, rivalled his fame. It was a wondrous period, certainly, when a continent lay unexplored before civilized men, and a daring navigator could at a single voyage add to the map a whole mighty river, whereas now it sometimes takes many lives to establish a few additional facts as to the minor sources of some well-known stream. The name of Henry Hudson is as indelibly associated with the river he discovered as is the Rhine with the feudal castles that make its summits picturesque. The difference is that after the last stone of the last ruin has crumbled, the name of the great navigator will be as permanent as now. While Hudson was exploring what he called "The Great North River of New Netherlands," Champlain was within a few miles of him, on the lake that was to bear his name. Both he and Hudson were fortunate enough to have names sufficiently characteristic to keep their places on the map, while "Smith's Isles" soon yielded to the yet vaguer appellation of the "Isles of Shoals."

It has been well pointed out in the most recent sketch of the Dutch in America — that of Mr. Fernow, in the "Narrative and Critical History of America," edited by Justin Winsor — that the early Dutch explorations did not proceed from the love of discovery or of gold-seeking, but were an incident of European wars. Carlyle says that the Dutch might have kept on making butter and cheese forever had not the Spaniards hurried them into a war in order to make them believe in St. Ignatius. The Spaniards, he says, "never made them believe in him, but succeeded in breaking their own vertebral column, and raising the Dutch into a great nation." The Dutch West India Company was, according to Mr. Fernow, a political movement, planned in 1606, and revived in 1618—a scheme to destroy the results of Spanish conquest in America, under cover of finding a passage to Cathay.

Henry Hudson sailed in the employ of this company, in the vessel *Half-Moon*, April 4, 1609. He undertook the search for a north-west passage — to which there was an opening north of Virginia, as his friend, Captain John Smith, had assured him. Sailing up the river which now bears his name, he found no passage, but brought back reports of fur-bearing animals, which revived the Dutch Company, and secured for it a charter, granted in 1621. Before this Adrian Block had built a log fort on Manhattan Island, in 1614, and had called the settlement New Amsterdam; another fort was built near what is now Albany; another in what is now Gloucester, New Jersey; and in 1626 Peter Minuit bought the whole of Manhattan Island from the Indians. All these settlements were supposed to be within the hundred miles which were to separate the North and South Virginia settlements. The South Virginia colonists tried to drive out the Dutch in 1613, and Governor Bradford, in Plymouth, remonstrated in 1627 against the intruders, but they remained. The secret belief of the Dutch was that, after all, the English had secured only the two shells, while they had the oyster. For years the colony was rather like a commercial enterprise than like anything of larger expectations; but after a time, under the teaching of experience, a more liberal policy was practised, and settlers came from many sources—dissatisfied religionists from New England, escaped servants from Virginia, and rich and poor from Holland. In 1643 there were eighteen different nationalities represented in New Amsterdam.

The English had thus obtained a foothold in Virginia, and the Dutch had established themselves in New Netherlands, both being led by the love of discovery, or of trade, or of revenge against the Spaniards. All efforts had thus far failed to build a colony in New England. Captain Smith wrote that he was not so foolish as to suppose that anything but the prospect of great gain would induce people to settle in such a place. He was right; it was done with the prospect of great gain, but of a kind of which he had not dreamed. It is partly this new motive and partly the pivotal part it played in the colonization of America that has always given to the little colony of Plymouth an historic importance out of all proportion to its numbers, its wealth, or even its permanence of separate life.

The Pilgrims, as they have always been called, had separated for conscience' sake from the Church of England, had removed from England to Holland, and had dwelt there in that "common harbor of all heresies," as Bishop Hall called it, there increasing to the number of five hundred. The Dutch magistrates said, "These English have lived among us now these twelve years, and yet we have never had any suit or accusation against them." But it seemed likely that the wars between Spain and Holland would be renewed, making their place of refuge unsafe; and the children of the Pilgrims were growing up, whom their parents wished to hear speaking English rather than Dutch; and they desired also to do something "for the propagating and advancing of the Gospel of Christ in the remote parts of the world." So a hundred of their younger and stronger men and women were selected to go to America, and a portion of them sailed from Delft Haven in July, 1620; their pious minister, John Robinson, invoking a blessing upon their departure, and warning them, "The Lord hath more truth yet to seek out of His holy Word." Of their two ships, the *Mayflower* alone completed her voyage, and after touching at three English ports she still had a voyage of sixty-three days. The *Speedwell* put back in consequence of alarms needlessly spread by her captain, who had already repented of his promise to remain a year with the colony, and took this cowardly way to obtain relief from that pledge.

On the eastern coast of Massachusetts there is a cape which stretches far into the sea, "shaped like a sickle," as Captain John Smith said, but named less poetically "Cape Cod" by Gosnold, because of the multitudes of fish with which he had "pestered" his vessel there. If on the 9th of November (Old Style), in 1620, any stray Indian had been looking from the bluff where Highland Light now stands, he would have seen a lonely and weather-beaten vessel creeping slowly towards the land. It was the *Mayflower*, now more than two months at sea. She had met with such storms and had grown so leaky that it had been seriously proposed by the sailors, when half across the Atlantic, to return. But for the fact that some passenger had happened to bring a great iron screw with his baggage, it is doubtful if the little vessel could have made the passage. As it was, she was heavy and slow, and the passengers were full of joy when they saw Cape Cod. They very well knew what land it was, for the mates of the vessel had been there twice before, while one passenger had actually been as far as Virginia. But they did not mean to remain at Cape Cod, or indeed in New England at all. Ever since the failure of the Popham colony in Maine, twelve years before, New England had been thought to be a "cold, barren, mountainous, rocky desert," and had been abandoned as "uninhabitable by Englishmen." So the *Mayflower* did not at first anchor at Cape Cod, but tacked and sailed southward for half a day, meaning to reach the Hudson River. Then she got among dangerous shoals and currents, the wind moreover being contrary; and the captain, anxious for his vessel, and in a hurry to land his passengers, put about again and made Cape Cod Harbor.

"But here I cannot but stay and make a pause," says the old writer who first describes this voyage, "and stand half amazed at these poor people's condition; and so I think will the reader too, when he well considers the same. For having passed through many troubles, both before and upon the voyage, as aforesaid, they had now no friends to welcome them, nor inns to entertain and refresh them, no houses, much less towns, to repair unto." Before them lay an unknown wilderness. The nearest English settlement was five hundred miles away. They had expected to arrive in September, and it was November; they had expected to reach the Hudson River, and it was Cape Cod. "Summer being done," says the same writer—Bradford—"all things stand for them to look upon with a weather-beaten face; and the whole country being full of woods and thickets, represented a wild and savage hue. If they looked behind them there was the mighty ocean which they had passed, and was now a main bar and gulf to separate them from all the civil parts of the world." To be sure, they had still a ship; but the captain warned them daily that they must look out for a place to found their colony; that he could wait but little longer; that the provisions were diminishing every day, and he must and would keep enough for himself and crew to use on their return. Some of the crew were even less friendly in what they said, for some of these were heard to threaten that unless the place for their new colony were soon found, "they would turn them and their goods on shore and leave them."

Such was the position of the Pilgrims when the *Mayflower*

lay at anchor in Cape Cod Harbor. The first thing to be done was to select a place for their settlement. This, however, could not be done till the shallop, or sail-boat, was ready; and it would take several days, as they found. So they went to work on this, and meanwhile, for the sake of a mutual understanding among themselves, this agreement was drawn up and signed by all the men on board.

> "In the name of God, Amen. We, whose names are underwritten, the loyall subiects of our dread soveraigne lord, King James, by the grace of God, of Great Britaine, France, and Ireland King, Defender of the Faith, etc., having undertaken, for the glory of God and the advancement of the Christian faith, and honour of our King and country, a voyage to plant the first colony in the northerne parts of Virginia, doe, by these presents, solemnly and mutually, in the presence of God and one of another, covenant and combin ourselves together into a civill body politike, for our better ordering and preservation, and furtherance of the ends aforesaid; and by vertue hereof to enact, constitute, and frame such iust and equal lawes, ordinances, acts, constitutions, offices, from time to time, as shall be thought most meet and convenient for the generall good of the Colony; vnto which we promise all due submission and obedience. In witnesse whereof we haue hereunto subscribed our names. Cape Cod, 11 of November, in the year of the raigne of our soveraigne lord King Iames, of England, France, and Ireland 18, and of Scotland 54. Anno Domini 1620."

Here was the "social compact" in good earnest—a thing which philosophers have claimed to be implied in all human government, but which has rarely been put in a shape so unequivocal. Robinson's letter of advice to the company had recognized before they left Holland that they were "to become a body-politic," using among themselves civil government, and choosing their own rulers. As with most persons who write important documents, their work seemed less imposing to themselves than it has since appeared to others. They thought of discipline rather than of philosophy; they had secured a good working organization, and it was not till long after that the act was discovered to have been "the birth of popular constitutional liberty." Such as it was, it was signed by forty-one men, mostly heads of families. Against each name was placed the number represented by him, making a total of one hundred and one persons, though accurately revised estimates give one more.

This being signed, the people were eager to go on shore and examine the new country, even by venturing a little way. So a party landed for fuel, a portion of them being armed; they saw neither person nor house, but brought home a boat-load of juniper boughs, "which smelled very sweet and strong," and which became a frequent fuel with them. Then the women went ashore under guard the next Monday to do their washing, and we may well suppose that some of the twenty-eight children begged hard to go also, and offered much desultory aid in bringing water, while the men guarded and the women scrubbed. The more they knew of the land, the more they wished to know, and at last it was agreed that Captain Miles Standish and sixteen men, "with every man his musket, sword, and corselet," should be sent along the cape to explore. The muskets were matchlocks, and the corselet was a coat of mail, a heavy garment to be worn amid tangled woods and over weary sands.

The journal kept by this first party has been preserved. They found walnuts, strawberries, and vines, and came to some springs, where they sat down and drank their first New England water, as one of them says, "with as much delight as ever we drunk drink in all our lives." They saw no Indians, but found their houses and graves; they found also a basket holding three or four bushels of Indian corn of yellow, red, and blue, such as still grows in Cape Cod. This they took with them on their return, meaning to pay for it, which they afterwards did. Then they returned, and a few days after another party, twice as large, and including the captain of the *Mayflower*, set off in the shallop to make further explorations. All their adventures are preserved to us in the most graphic way by contemporary narratives. Then a third party of eighteen went out, including Carver, Standish, Bradford, and other leading men. They were attacked by Indians; they lost their rudder and their mast; they landed at last on Clark's Island, kept the Sabbath there, and on the 11th December, Old Style —commonly reckoned, but not quite accurately, as corresponding to the 22d of December, New Style—they made their first landing on Plymouth Rock. This place being approved, they returned to the *Mayflower*, and the vessel came into harbor five days later.

There they spent the winter—their first experience of a New England winter! They were ill housed, ill fed; part of them remained for several months on board the ship; one-half of them died during the first winter of scurvy and other diseases. At times, according to the diary of the heroic Bradford, there were but six or seven sound persons who could tend upon the sick and dying, "fetched them wood, made them fires, dressed them meat, made their beds, washed their loathsome clothes, clothed and unclothed them," two of these nurses being their spiritual and military leaders, Elder Brewster and Captain Miles Standish. The New Plymouth Colony never grew to be a strong one; its later history is merged in that of the Massachusetts Bay Colony, to which it led; but its success may be said to have been the turning-point in the existence of Raleigh's "English nation." The situation is thus briefly stated by the ablest historian who wrote in this continent before the Revolution, Governor Hutchinson:

"These were the founders of the colony of Plymouth. The settlement of this colony occasioned the settlement of Massachusetts Bay, which was the source of all the other colonies of New England. Virginia was in a dying state, and seemed to revive and flourish from the example of New England. I am not preserving from oblivion the names of heroes whose chief merit is the overthrow of cities, provinces, and empires, but the names of the founders of a flourishing town and colony, if not of the whole British empire in America."

In September, 1628, there came sailing into the harbor of

"AN ENGLISH NATION."

Naumkeag, afterwards called Salem, a ship bearing John Endicott, one of the six patentees of the "Dorchester Company," afterwards enlarged into the "Governor and Company of Mas-

JOHN ENDICOTT.

sachusetts Bay." Endicott had been appointed governor, and found on shore only a few settlers, Roger Conant and others, part of them strays from Plymouth, who were quite disposed to be impatient of his authority. There remains no record of his voyage, but an ample record of that of his successor in the emigration, Rev. Francis Higginson, who came as the spiritual leader — with his colleague Skelton — of the first large party of the Massachusetts Bay Colony. They came in summer (1629), and all their early impressions were in poetic contrast to the stern landing of the Pilgrims. Francis Higginson says, in his journal as preserved in Hutchinson's Collection:

> "By noon we were within three leagues of Cape Ann; and as we sailed along the coasts we saw every hill and dale and every island full of gay woods and high trees. The nearer we came to the shore the more flowers in abundance, sometimes scattered abroad, sometimes joined in sheets nine or ten yards long, which we supposed to be brought from the low meadows by the tide. Now what with fine woods and green trees by land, and these yellow flowers painting the sea, made us all desirous to see our new paradise of New England, whence we saw such forerunning signals of fertility afar off."

There came in this expedition five (or possibly six) ships, of which the *Mayflower* was one. They brought two hundred persons; whereas only some forty had arrived with Endicott; in the following year eight hundred came with Winthrop, who, being governor of the company itself, superseded all other authorities. It was the most powerful body of colonists that had yet reached America. Its members were by no means limited to Salem, nor did this long remain the centre of the colony. Charlestown was settled in 1629, and Dorchester, Roxbury, Boston, Medford, Watertown, and Cambridge in 1630.

The company itself was transplanted bodily from England. It was an organized government under a royal charter; the freemen were to meet four times a year and choose a governor, deputy-governor, and eighteen assistants, who were to meet once a month, and exercise all the functions of a State. As Mr. Lodge has tersely said, "It was the migration of a people, not the mere setting forth of colonists and adventurers." Considered as a colony, it was far larger and richer than that at Plymouth; it had chosen a more favorable situation, and it encountered less of hardship, though it had quite enough. Its leaders had not expected, in advance, to break with the Church of England, as had been done by the "Separatists" at Plymouth. "We will not say," said Francis Higginson, on looking back to the receding shores of England—

JOHN WINTHROP.

"we will not say, as the Separatists were wont to say at their leaving of England, 'Farewell, Babylon! farewell, Rome!' but we will say, 'Farewell, dear England! farewell, the Church of God in England, and all the Christian friends there.' . . . We go to practise the positive part of Church reformation, and to propagate the Gospel in America."

Yet, when once established on this soil, there was not

much difference in degree of independence between the two colonies. Indeed Endicott, when he sent back two turbulent Churchmen to England,—or when he defaced the cross, then deemed idolatrous, upon the English flag,—or when he suppressed Morton and his roisterers at Merry Mount,—went farther in the assertion of separate power than the milder authorities of Plymouth Colony ever went. Both colonies aimed at religious reformation. Neither colony professed religious toleration, though the Plymouth colony sometimes practised it. Rhode Island, on its establishment by Roger Williams, both professed and practised it; and though his banishment from Massachusetts was not on religious grounds alone, but partly from his contentious spirit in other ways, yet it resulted in good to the world, at last, through his high conceptions of religious liberty. In the New Hampshire settlements, which were formed as early as 1623, there was less of strictness in religion, and perhaps less of religion; nor was there ever any great rigidity of doctrine or practice in the few scattered villages of Maine. The two Connecticut colonies—Connecticut and New Haven—being framed at first by the direct emigration of whole religious societies, might have been supposed to carry some severity with them into their banishment; but they seemed to leave it behind, and were not sterner at the outset than the men of the other early settlements, even those of Virginia. What changes came over this type of manhood in the second generation, in the banishment of a colony and the asceticism of a life too restricted, we shall see. But these New England men were, at the outset, of as high a mould as ever settled a State. "God sifted a whole nation," said Stoughton, "that He might send choice grain over into this wilderness." Between the years 1629 and 1639, twenty thousand Puritans came to America; it was not a mere colonization, it was the transfer of a people.

Thus were four colonies established on the North Atlantic

coast before the year 1630, in the vast region once called Virginia. Three of them were English at the beginning—Virginia, New Plymouth, and Massachusetts Bay—and the other was destined to become such, changing its name from New Netherland to New York. These may be called the pioneer colonies; and if we extend our view to the year 1650, we take in three other colonies, Connecticut, Rhode Island, New Haven—which had gone forth from these—while two independent colonies, one English and one Swedish, had made separate settlements in Maryland and Delaware; thus making nine in all, of which seven were English.

The men of the Maryland settlement also called themselves, like those of Plymouth, "Pilgrims," but the name had not come to them by such arduous experience, and it has not attached itself to their descendants. The Roman Catholics and others who came to "Mary's Land" in the *Ark* and the *Dove*, in March, 1634, under Leonard Calvert, named their first settlement St. Mary's, in honor of Queen Henrietta Maria, and they called themselves "the Pilgrims of St. Mary's." The emigration was made up very differently from those which John Smith recorded in Virginia, for it consisted of but twenty "gentlemen" and three hundred laboring men. They came under a charter granted to George Calvert, Lord Baltimore, who had for many years been trying to establish a colony, which he called "Avalon," much farther north, and who had grown, in the words of a letter of the period, "weary of his intolerable plantation at Newfoundland, where he hath found between eight and nine months' winter, and upon the land nothing but rocks, lakes, or morasses like bogs, which one might thrust a pike down to the butt-head." But he died before the new charter was signed; and was succeeded by his son Cecil, the second Lord Baltimore, who fully adopted his father's plans, and amply defrayed the cost of the first expedition, this being £40,000.

There exists a graphic account of the voyage of the first Maryland settlers by Father White, their chaplain, in his re-

CECIL CALVERT, SECOND LORD BALTIMORE.

port to his religious superiors at Rome. He describes with delight his first ascent of the Potomac River, of which he says, "The Thames itself is a mere rivulet to it;" and when he reaches the St. Mary's River, where the colony was founded (March 27, 1634), he says, "The finger of God is in this, and He purposes some great benefit to this nation." He might well say that, for the career of the early Maryland colony was peaceful, tolerant, and honorable. It was the most nearly independent and self-governing of the early colonies, the King asking nothing of it but two Indian arrows each year, and one-fifth of its gold or silver. It was called "the land of the sanctuary;" all Christians were tolerated there, though it did not, like Rhode Island, expressly extend its toleration beyond Christianity. By degrees it passed under the charge of Puritans from Virginia, who proved themselves less liberal to Roman Catholics than the latter had been to them. But all working together laid the foundation of a new community, sharing in some respects the pursuits and destinies of Virginia, though more peaceful, and at times more prosperous.

The other independent colony came from Sweden — the only one ever planted by that nation. In the first years of Virginia emigration Lord Delaware, who was then governor, sailed up the river that took his name; but he left no settlement there. The Dutch afterwards tried to colonize it, but the Indians destroyed the colony. Then the great Protestant King of Sweden, Gustavus Adolphus, the "Lion of the North," resolved, at the suggestion of a Stockholm merchant, William Usselinx, to found a colony, which, unlike Virginia, should have no slaves, and which should be "the jewel of his kingdom." He died, and his little daughter Christina succeeded him; but the Prime-minister, Oxenstiern, carried out the original plan, sending fifty Swedes and Finlanders, in 1638, in two vessels commanded by Peter Minuit, who had previously been Governor of New Netherland. In spite of the loud protestations of the Dutch governor, Kieft, they established themselves on the river Delaware, and called their fort Christiana, in honor of the young queen. Four years after, a governor was sent out to them from Sweden, a lieutenant-colonel in the Swedish army, John Printz, described by one writer as a person "who weighed four hundred pounds, and drank three drinks at every meal." He built himself a house, let us hope on firm foundations, upon what is now called Province Island, at the mouth of the Schuylkill River. Meanwhile, the English from New Haven had settled within the bounds of the colony, and the Dutch had driven them away, and then trespassed themselves. Nevertheless there was a Swedish colony thus established in America, rivalling the Dutch of "New Netherland" in enterprise and industry, but destined to pass away and leave hardly a trace behind.

Such were the beginnings of European colonization along the Atlantic coast of North America. In the middle of the seventeenth century (1650) the condition of that coast was as follows. The New England colonies were of course English, and so were Virginia and Maryland; but the fertile region between these northern and southern colonies was claimed and occupied, as has been shown, by Holland and by Sweden. The French claimed the unsettled regions now known as the Carolinas and Georgia; the Spaniards held all beyond. Amid all these conflicting nationalities, what had become of Raleigh's dream? The seven English colonies, arranged in order of time, were as follows: Virginia, founded in 1607, and called to this day "the Old Dominion;" New Plymouth, founded in 1620, and still often called "the Old Colony;" Massachusetts Bay, 1628; Connecticut, 1633; Maryland, 1634; Rhode Island and Providence Plantations, 1636; New Haven, 1638. Four of these — the two Massachusetts and the two Connecticut colonies — had been leagued together since 1643 against the Indians and the Dutch; the others stood alone, each for itself. Among these scattered settlements, where was Raleigh's "English nation?" It existed in these germs.

VII.

THE HUNDRED YEARS' WAR.

EUROPEAN history makes much of the "Seven Years' War" and the "Thirty Years' War;" and when we think of a continuous national contest for even the least of those periods, there is something terrible in the picture. But the feeble English colonies in America, besides all the difficulties of pioneer life, had to sustain a warfare that lasted, with few intermissions, for about a hundred years. It was, moreover, a warfare against the most savage and stealthy enemies, gradually trained and re-enforced by the most formidable military skill of Europe. Without counting the early feuds, such as the Pequot War, there elapsed almost precisely a century from the accession of King Philip, in 1662, to the Peace of Paris, which nominally ended the last French and Indian War in 1763. During this whole period, with pacific intervals that sometimes lasted for years, the same essential contest went on; the real question being, for the greater part of the time, whether France or England should control the continent. The description of this prolonged war may therefore well precede any general account of the colonial or provincial life in America.

The early explorers of the Atlantic coast usually testify that they found the Indians a gentle, not a ferocious, people. They were as ready as could be expected to accept the friendship of the white race. In almost every case of quarrel the white men were the immediate aggressors, and where they were attacked without seeming cause—as when Smith's Virginian colony was assailed by the Indians in the first fortnight of its existence—there is good reason to think that the act of the Indians was in revenge for wrongs elsewhere. One of the first impulses of the early explorers was to kidnap natives for exhibition in Europe, in order to excite the curiosity of kings or the zeal of priests; and even where these captives were restored unharmed, the distrust could not be removed. Add to this the acts of plunder, lust, or violence, and there was plenty of provocation given from the very outset.

The disposition to cheat and defraud the Indians has been much exaggerated, at least as regards the English settlers. The early Spanish invaders made no pretence of buying one foot of land from the Indians, whereas the English often went through the form of purchase, and very commonly put in practice the reality. The Pilgrims, at the very beginning, took baskets of corn from an Indian grave to be used as seed, and paid for it afterwards. The year after the Massachusetts colony was founded, the court decreed: "It is ordered that Josias Plastowe shall (for stealing four baskets of corne from the Indians) returne them eight baskets againe, be fined five pounds, and hereafter called by the name of Josias, and not Mr., as formerly he used to be." As a mere matter of policy, it was the general disposition of the English settlers to obtain lands by honest sale; indeed, Governor Josiah Winslow, of Plymouth, declared, in reference to King Philip's War, that "before these present troubles broke out the English did not possess one foot of land in this colony but what was fairly obtained by honest purchase of the Indian proprietors." This policy was quite general. Captain West, in 1610, bought the site of what is now Richmond, Virginia, for some copper. The Dutch Governor Minuit bought the island of Manhattan, in 1626, for sixty gilders. Lord Baltimore's company purchased land for cloth, tools, and trinkets; the Swedes obtained the site of Christiana for a kettle; Roger Williams bought the island of Rhode Island for forty fathoms of white beads; and New Haven was sold to the whites, in 1638, for "twelve coats of English cloth, twelve alchemy spoons, twelve hoes, twelve hatchets, twelve porringers, twenty-four knives, and twenty-four cases of French knives and spoons." Many other such purchases will be found recorded by Dr. Ellis. And though the price paid might often seem ludicrously small, yet we must remember that a knife or a hatchet was really worth more to an Indian than many square miles of wild land; while even the beads were a substitute for wampum, or wompom, which was their circulating medium in dealing with each other and with the whites, and was worth, in 1660, five shillings a fathom.

So far as the mere bargaining went, the Indians were not individually the sufferers in the early days; but we must remember that behind all these transactions there often lay a theory which was as merciless as that quoted in a previous paper from the Spanish "Requisition," and which would, if logically carried out, have made all these bargainings quite superfluous. Increase Mather begins his history of King Philip's War with this phrase, "That the Heathen People amongst whom we live, and whose Land the Lord God of our Fathers hath given to us for a rightful Possession;" and it was this attitude of hostile superiority that gave the sting to all the relations of the two races. If a quarrel rose, it was apt to be the white man's fault; and after it had arisen, even the humaner Englishmen usually sided with their race, as when the peaceful Plymouth men went to war in defence of the Weymouth reprobates. This fact, and the vague feeling that an irresistible pressure was displacing them, caused most of the early Indian outbreaks. And when hostilities had once arisen, it was very rare for a white man of English birth to be found fighting against his own people, although it grew more and more common to find Indians on both sides.

As time went on, each party learned from the other. In the early explorations, as of Champlain and Smith, we see the Indians terrified by their first sight of fire-arms, but soon becoming skilled in the use of them. "The King, with fortie Bowmen to guard me," says Captain John Smith, in 1608, "entreated me to discharge my Pistoll, which they there presented to me, with a mark at sixscore to strike therewith; but to spoil the practise I broke the cocke, whereat they were much discontented." But writing more than twenty years later, in 1631, he says of the Virginia settlers, "The loving Salvages their kinde friends they trained up so well to shoot in a Peace [fowling-piece] to hunt and kill them fowle, they became more expert than our own countrymen." La Hontan, writing in 1703, says of the successors of those against whom Champlain had first used fire-arms, "The Strength of the Iroquese lies in engaging with Fire Arms in a Forrest, for they shoot very dexterously." They learned also to make more skilful fortifications, and to keep a regular watch at night, which in the time of the early explorers they had omitted. The same La Hontan says of the Iroquois, "They are as negligent in the night-time as they are vigilant in the day."

But it is equally true that the English colonists learned much in the way of forest warfare from the Indians. The French carried their imitation so far that they often disguised themselves to resemble their allies, with paint, feathers, and all; it was sometimes impossible to tell in an attacking party which warriors were French and which were Indians. Without often going so far as this, the English colonists still modified their tactics. At first they seemed almost irresistible because of their armor and weapons. In the very first year of the Plymouth settlement, when report was brought that their friend Massasoit had been attacked by the Narragansets, and a friendly Indian had been killed, the colony sent ten armed men, including Miles Standish, to the Indian town of Namasket (now Middleborough) to rescue or revenge their friend; and they succeeded in their enterprise, surrounding the chief's house, and frightening every one in a large Indian village by two discharges of their muskets.

But the heavy armor gradually proved a doubtful advantage against a stealthy and light-footed foe. In spite of the superior physical strength of the Englishman, he could not travel long distances through the woods or along the sands without lightening his weight. He learned also to fight from behind a tree, to follow a trail, to cover his body with hemlock boughs for disguise when scouting. Captain Church states in his own narrative that he learned from his Indian soldiers to march his men "thin and scattering" through the woods; that the English had previously, according to the Indians, "kept in a heap together, so that it was as easy to hit them as to hit a house." Even the advantage of fire-arms involved the risk of being without ammunition, so that the Rhode Island colony, by the code of laws adopted in 1647, required that every man between seventeen and seventy should have a bow with four arrows, and exercise with them; and that each father should furnish every son from seven to seventeen years old with a bow, two arrows, and shafts, and should bring them up to shooting. If this statute was violated a fine was imposed, which the father must pay for the son, the master for the servant, deducting it in the latter case from his wages.

Less satisfactory was the change by which the taking of scalps came to be a recognized part of colonial warfare. Hannah Dustin, who escaped from Indian captivity in 1698, took ten scalps with her own hand, and was paid for them. Captain Church, undertaking his expedition against the Eastern Indians, in 1705, after the Deerfield massacre, announced that he had not hitherto permitted the scalping of "Canada men," but should thenceforth allow it. In 1722, when the Massachusetts colony sent an expedition against the village of "praying Indians," founded by Father Rasle, they offered for each scalp a bounty of £15, afterwards increased to £100; and this inhumanity was so far carried out that the French priest himself was one of the victims. Jeremiah Bumstead, of Boston, made this entry in his almanac in the same year: "Aug. 22, 28 Indian scalps brought to Boston, one of which was Bombazen's [an Indian chief] and one fryer Raile's." Two years after, the celebrated but inappropriately named Captain Lovewell, the foremost Indian fighter of his region, came upon ten Indians asleep round a pond; he and his men killed and scalped them all, and entered Dover, New Hampshire, bearing the ten scalps stretched on hoops and elevated on poles. After receiving an ovation in Dover they went by water to Boston, and were paid a thousand pounds for their scalps. Yet Lovewell's party was always accompanied by a chaplain, and had prayers every morning and evening.

The most painful aspect of the whole practice lies in the fact that it was not confined to those actually engaged in fighting, but that the colonial authorities actually established a tariff of prices for scalps, including even non-combatants—so much for a man's, so much for a woman's, so much for a child's. Dr. Ellis has lately pointed out the striking circumstance that whereas William Penn had declared the person of an Indian to be "sacred," his grandson, in 1764, offered $134 for the scalp of an Indian man, $130 for that of a boy under ten, and $50 for that of a woman or girl. The habit doubtless began in the fury of retaliation, and was continued in order to conciliate Indian allies; and when bounties were offered to them, the white volunteers naturally claimed a share. But there is no doubt that Puritan theology helped the adoption of the practice. It was partly because the Indian was held to be something worse than a beast that he was treated with very little mercy. The truth is that he was viewed as a fiend, and there could not be much scruple about using inhumanities against a demon. Cotton Mather calls Satan "the old landlord" of the American wilderness, and says in his "Magnalia:" "These Parts were then covered with Nations of Barbarous Indians and Infidels, in whom the Prince of the Power of the Air did work as a Spirit; nor could it be expected that Nations of Wretches whose whole religion was the most Explicit sort of Devil-Worship should not be acted by the Devil to engage in some early and bloody Action for the Extinction of a Plantation so contrary to his Interests as that of New England was."

Before the French influence began to be felt there was very little union on the part of the Indians, and each colony adjusted its own relations with them. At the time of the frightful Indian massacre in the Virginia colony (March 22, 1622), when three hundred and forty-seven men, women, and children were murdered, the Plymouth colony was living in entire peace with its savage neighbors. "We have found the Indians," wrote Governor Winslow, "very faithful to their covenants of peace with us, very loving and willing to pleasure us. We go with them in some cases fifty miles into the country, and walk as safely and peaceably in the woods as in the highways of England." The treaty with Massasoit lasted for more than fifty years, and the first bloodshed between the Plymouth men and the Indians was incurred in the protection of the colony of Weymouth, which had brought trouble on itself in 1623. The Connecticut settlements had far more difficulty with the Indians than those in Massachusetts, but the severe punishment inflicted on the Pequots in 1637 quieted the savages for a long time. In that fight a village of seventy wigwams was destroyed by a force of ninety white men and several hundred friendly Indians; and Captain Underhill, the second in command, has left a quaint delineation of the attack.

There was a period resembling peace in the Eastern colonies for nearly forty years after the Pequot war, while in Virginia there were renewed massacres in 1644 and 1656. But the first organized Indian outbreak began with the conspiracy of King Philip in 1675, although the seeds had been sown before that chief succeeded to power in 1662. In that year Wamsutta, or Alexander, Philip's brother—both being sons of Massasoit—having fallen under some suspicion, was either compelled or persuaded by Major Josiah Winslow, afterwards the first native-born Governor of Plymouth, to visit that settlement. The Indian came with his whole train of warriors and women, including his Queen, the celebrated ".squaw sachem" Weetamo, and they stayed at Winslow's house. Here the chief fell ill. The day was very hot, and though Winslow offered his horse to the chief, it was refused, because there was none for his squaw or the other women. He was sent home because of illness, and died before he got half-way home. This is the story as told by Hubbard, but not altogether confirmed by other authorities. If true, it is interesting. as confirming the theory of that careful student, Mr. Lucien Carr, that the early position of women among the Indians was higher than has been generally believed. It is pretty certain, at any rate, that Alexander's widow, Weetamo, believed her husband to have been poisoned by the English, and she ultimately sided with Philip when the war broke out, and apparently led him and other Indians to the same view as to the poisoning. It is evident that from the time of Philip's accession to authority, whatever he may have claimed, his mind was turned more and more against the English.

It is now doubted whether the war known as King Philip's War was the result of such deliberate and organized action as was formerly supposed, but about the formidable strength of the outbreak there can be no question. It began in June, 1675; Philip was killed August 12, 1676, and the war was prolonged at the eastward for nearly two years after his death. Ten or twelve Puritan towns were utterly destroyed, many more damaged, and five or six hundred men were killed or missing. The war cost the colonists £100,000, and the Plymouth colony was left under a debt exceeding the whole valuation of its property — a debt ultimately paid, both principal and interest. On the other hand, the war tested and cemented the league founded in 1643 between four colonies — Massachusetts, Plymouth, New Haven, and Connecticut — against the Indians and Dutch, while this prepared the way more and more for the extensive combinations that came after. In this early war, as the Indians had no French allies, so the English had few Indian allies; and it was less complex than the later contests, and so far less formidable. But it was the first real experience on the part of the Eastern colonists of all the peculiar horrors of Indian warfare — the stealthy approach, the abused hospitality, the early morning assault, the maimed cattle, tortured prisoners, slain infants. All the terrors that now attach to a frontier attack of Apaches or Comanches belonged to the daily life of settlers in New England and Virginia for many years, with one vast difference, arising from the total absence in those early days of any personal violence or insult to women. By the general agreement of witnesses from all nations, including the women captives themselves, this crowning crime was then wholly absent. The once famous "white woman," Mary Jemison, who was taken prisoner by the Senecas at ten years old, in 1743 — who lived in that tribe all her life, survived two Indian husbands, and at last died at ninety — always testified that she had never received an insult from an Indian, and had never known of a captive's receiving any. She added that she had known few instances in the tribe of conjugal immorality, although she lived to see it demoralized and ruined by strong drink.

The English colonists seem never to have inflicted on the

Indians any cruelty resulting from sensual vices, but of barbarity of another kind there was plenty, for it was a cruel age. When the Narraganset fort was taken by the English, December 19, 1675, the wigwams within the fort were all set on fire, against the earnest entreaty of Captain Church; and it was thought that more than one-half the English loss—which amounted to several hundred—might have been saved had there been any shelter for their own wounded on that cold night. This, however, was a question of military necessity; but the true spirit of the age was seen in the punishments inflicted after the war was over. The heads of Philip's chief followers were cut off, though Captain Church, their captor, had promised to spare their lives; and Philip himself was beheaded and quartered by Church's order, since he was regarded, curiously enough, as a rebel against Charles the Second, and this was the State punishment for treason. Another avowed reason was, that "as he had caused many an Englishman's body to lye unburied," not one of his bones should be placed under ground. The head was set upon a pole in Plymouth, where it remained for more than twenty-four years. Yet when we remember that the heads of alleged traitors were exposed in London at Temple Bar for nearly a century longer—till 1772 at least—it is unjust to infer from this course any such fiendish cruelty as it would now imply. It is necessary to extend the same charity, however hard it may be, to the selling of Philip's wife and little son into slavery at the Bermudas; and here, as has been seen, the clergy were consulted and the Old Testament called into requisition.

While these events were passing in the Eastern settlements there were Indian outbreaks in Virginia, resulting in war among the white settlers themselves. The colony was, for various reasons, discontented; it was greatly oppressed, and a series of Indian murders brought the troubles to a climax. The policy pursued against the Indians was severe, and yet

DEATH OF KING PHILIP.

there was no proper protection afforded by the government; war was declared against them in 1676, and then the forces sent out were suddenly disbanded by the governor, Berkeley.

At last there was a popular rebellion, which included almost all the civil and military officers of the colony, and the rebellious party put Nathaniel Bacon, Jr., a recently arrived but very popular planter, at their head. He marched with five hundred men against the Indians, but was proclaimed a traitor by the governor, whom Bacon proclaimed a traitor in return. The war with the savages became by degrees quite secondary to the internal contests among the English, in the course of which Bacon took and burned Jamestown, beginning, it is said, with his own house; but he died soon after, the insurrection was suppressed, and the Indians were finally quieted by a treaty.

Into all the Indian wars after King Philip's death two nationalities besides the Indian and English entered in an important way. These were the Dutch and the French. It was the Dutch who, soon after 1614, first sold fire-arms to the Indians in defiance of their own laws, and by this means greatly increased the horrors of the Indian warfare. On the other hand, the Dutch did to the English colonists, though unintentionally, a service so great that the whole issue of the prolonged war may have turned upon it, because of the close friendship they established with the Five Nations, commonly called the Iroquois. These tribes, the Cayugas, Mohawks, Oneidas, Onondagas, and Senecas — afterwards joined by the Tuscaroras — held the key to the continent. Occupying the greater part of what is now the State of New York, they virtually ruled the country from the Atlantic to the Mississippi, and from the Great Lakes to the Savannah River. They were from the first treated with great consideration by the Dutch, and they remained, with brief intervals of war, their firm friends. One war, indeed, there was under the injudicious management of Governor Kieft, lasting from 1640 to 1643; and this came near involving the English colonies, while it caused the death of sixteen hundred Indians, first or last, seven hundred of these being massacred under the borrowed Puritan leader Captain Underhill. But this made no permanent interruption to the alliance between the Iroquois and the Dutch.

When the New Netherland yielded to the English, the same alliance was retained, and to this we probably owe the preservation of the colonies, their union against England, and the very existence of the present American nation. Yet the first English governor, Colden, has left on record the complaint of an Indian chief, who said that they very soon felt the difference between the two alliances. "When the Dutch held this country," he said, "we lay in their houses, but the English have always made us lie out-of-doors."

But if the Dutch were thus an important factor in the Indian wars, the French became almost the controlling influence on the other side. Except for the strip of English colonies along the sea-shore, the North American continent north of Mexico was French. This was not the result of accident or of the greater energy of that nation, but of a systematic policy, beginning with Champlain, and never abandoned by his successors. This plan was, as admirably stated by Parkman, "to influence Indian counsels, to hold the balance of power between adverse tribes, to envelop in the net-work of French power and diplomacy the remotest hordes of the wilderness." With this was combined a love of exploration, so great that it was hard to say which assisted the most in spreading their dominion—religion, the love of adventure, diplomatic skill, or military talent. These between them gave the interior of the continent to the French. One of the New York governors, wrote home that if the French were to hold all that they had discovered, England would not have a hundred miles from the sea anywhere.

France had early occupied Acadia, Canada, and the St. Lawrence on the north. Marquette rediscovered the Mississippi, and La Salle traced it, though Alvar Nuñez had crossed it, and De Soto had been buried beneath it. A Frenchman first crossed the Rocky Mountains; the French settled the Mississippi Valley in 1699, and Mobile in 1702. The great Western valleys are still full of French names, and for every one left, two or three have been blotted out. The English maps, down to the year 1763, give the name "New France" not to Canada only, but to the Ohio and Mississippi valleys. New France was vast; New England was a narrow strip along the shore. But there was a yet greater difference in the tenure by which the two nations held their nominal settlements. The French held theirs with the aid of a vast system of paid officials, priests, generals, and governors; the English colonists kept theirs for themselves, aided by a little chartered authority or deputed power. Moreover, the French retained theirs by a chain of forts and a net-work of trading posts; the English held theirs by sober agriculture. In the end the spade and axe proved mightier than the sword. What postponed the triumph was that the French, not the English, had won the hearts of the Indians.

This subject has been considered in a previous chapter, and need be only briefly mentioned here; but it should not be wholly passed by. To the Indian, the Frenchman was a daring swordsman, a gay cavalier, a dashing leader, and the most charming of companions; the Englishman was a plodding and sordid agriculturist. "The stoic of the woods" saw men infinitely his superiors in all knowledge and in the refinements of life, who yet cheerfully accepted his way of living, and took with apparent relish to his whole way of existence. Charlevoix sums it all up admirably: "The savages did not become French: the Frenchmen became savages." To the savage, at least, the alliance was inestimable. What saved the English colonies was the fact that it was not quite universal. It failed to reach the most advanced, the most powerful, and the most central race of savages—the tribes called Iroquois. It took the French a great many years to outgrow the attitude of hostility to these tribes which began with the attack of Champlain and a few Frenchmen on an Iroquois fort. Baron La Hontan, one of the few Frenchmen who were not also good Catholics, attributes this mainly to the influence of the priests. He says, in the preface to the English translation of his letters (1703): "Notwithstanding the veneration I have for the clergy, I impute to them all the mischief the Iroquese have done to the French colonies in the course of a war that would never have been undertaken if it had not been for the counsels of those pious churchmen." But whatever the cause, the fact was of vital importance, and proved to be, as has been already said, the turning-point of the whole controversy.

These being the general features of the French and Indian warfare, it remains only to consider briefly its successive stages. It took the form of a series of outbreaks, most of which were so far connected with public affairs in Europe that their very names often record the successive rulers under whose nominal authority they were waged. The first, known as "King William's War," and sometimes as "St. Castin's War," began in 1688, ten years after the close of King Philip's War, while France and England were still at peace. In April of the next year came the news that William of Orange had landed in England, and this change in the English dynasty was an important argument in the hands of the French, who insisted on regarding the colonists not as loyal Englishmen, but as rebels against their lawful king, James the Second. In reality the American collision had been in preparation for years. "About the year 1685," wrote the English visitor, Edward Randolph, "the French of Canada encroached upon the lands of the subjects of the crown of England, building forts upon the heads of their great rivers, and extending their bounds, disturbed the inhabitants." On the other hand, it must be remembered that England claimed the present territory of New

Brunswick and Nova Scotia, and the provincial charter of Massachusetts covered those regions. Thus each nationality seemed to the other to be trying to encroach, and each professed to be acting on the defensive. With this purpose the French directly encouraged Indian outbreaks. We now know, from the despatches of Denonville, the French Governor of Canada, that he claimed as his own merit the successes of the Indians; and Champigny wrote that he himself had supplied them with gunpowder, and that the Indians of the Christian villages near Quebec had taken the leading part.

Unluckily several of the provinces had just been brought together under the governorship of a man greatly disliked and distrusted, Sir Edmund Andros. In August this official, then newly placed in power, visited the Five Nations at Albany to secure their friendliness. During his absence there were rumors of Indian outbreaks at the East, and though he took steps to suppress them, yet nobody trusted him. The friendly Indians declared that "the Governor was a rogue, and had hired the Indians to kill the English," and that the Mohawks were to seize Boston in the spring. This rumor helped the revolt of the people against Andros; and after his overthrow the garrisons at the eastward were broken up, and the savage assaults recommenced. Cocheco, now Dover, New Hampshire, was destroyed; Pemaquid, a fort with seven or eight cannon, was regularly besieged by a hundred Christian Indians under their priest, Père Thury, who urged on the attack, but would not let the English be scalped or tortured. From the beginning the movements of the French and Indians were not impulsive outbreaks, as heretofore, but were directed by a trained soldier of fifty years' experience, the Count de Frontenac. There were no soldiers of experience among the colonists, and they fought like peasants against a regular army. Yet when, after a terrible Indian massacre at Schenectady, a Congress of delegates was held at New York, in May, 1690, they daringly planned an attack on the two strongholds, Quebec and Montreal. Winthrop of Connecticut was to take Montreal by a land expedition, and Sir William Phips, of Massachusetts — a rough sailor who had captured Port Royal — was sent by water with more than two thousand men against Quebec, an almost impregnable fortress manned by nearly three thousand. Both enterprises failed, and the Baron La Hontan wrote of Phips — in the English edition of his letters — that he could not have served the French better had he stood still with his hands in his pockets. The colonies were impoverished by these hopeless efforts, and the Puritans attributed their failure to "the frown of God." The Indians made fresh attacks at Pentucket (Haverhill) and elsewhere; but the Peace of Ryswick (September 20, 1697) stopped the war for a time, and provided that the American boundaries of France and England should remain the same.

A few more years brought new hostilities (May 4, 1702), when England declared war against France and Spain. This was called in Europe "The War of the Spanish Succession," but in America simply "Queen Anne's War." The Five Nations were now strictly neutral, so that New York was spared, and the force of the war fell on the New England settlements. The Eastern Indians promised equal neutrality, and one of their chiefs said, "The sun is not more distant from the earth than our thoughts from war." But they joined in the war just the same, and the Deerfield (Massachusetts) massacre, with the captivity of Rev. John Williams, roused the terror of all the colonists. Traces of that attack, in the form of tomahawk strokes upon doors, are still to be seen in Deerfield. The Governor of Massachusetts was distrusted; he tried in vain to take the small fort of Port Royal in Nova Scotia — "the hornets' nest," as it was called; but it was finally taken in 1710, and its name was changed to Annapolis Royal, afterwards Annapolis, in honor of the Queen.

The year after, a great expedition was sent from England

by St. John, afterwards Lord Bolingbroke, to effect the conquest of Canada. Fifteen ships of war, with five regiments of Marlborough's veterans, reached Boston in June, 1711. Provincial troops went from New York and New Jersey, as well as New England, and there were eight hundred Iroquois warriors. St. John wrote, " I believe you may depend upon our being, at this time, the masters of all North America." On the contrary, they did not become masters of an inch of ground; the expedition utterly failed, mainly through the incompetency of the commander, Admiral Sir Hovenden Walker; eight ships were wrecked, eight hundred and eighty-four men were drowned, and fleet and land-forces retreated. In April, 1713, the war nominally closed with the Peace of Utrecht, which gave to England Hudson Bay, Newfoundland, and Acadia—the last so poorly defined as to lead to much trouble at a later day.

But in Maine the Indian disturbances still went on. New forts were built by the colonists, and there were new attacks by the Abenaki tribe. Among these the most conspicuous figure was for a quarter of a century the Jesuit priest Père Rasle, who had collected a village of "praying Indians" at Norridgewock, and had trained a band of forty young men to assist, wearing cassock and surplice, in the services of the

FAC-SIMILE FROM MS. OF FATHER RASLE'S ABENAKI GLOSSARY.

Translation : "Having been for a year among the savages, I begin to arrange in order in the manner of a dictionary the words that I learn."

Church. There is in the Harvard College Library a MS. glossary of the Abenaki language in his handwriting. His whole career was one of picturesque self-devotion; but he belonged emphatically to the Church militant, and was in constant communication with the French Governor of Canada. His settlement was the head-quarters for all attacks upon the English colonists, and was finally broken up and annihilated by them on August 23, 1724. With him disappeared the Jesuit missions in New England, though there were scattering hostilities some time longer. On December 15, 1725, the Abenaki chiefs signed at Boston a treaty of peace, which is still preserved in the Massachusetts archives, and this compact was long maintained.

Nineteen years of comparative peace now followed,—by far the longest interval during the contest of a century. In 1744 came another war between England and France, known in Europe as "the War of the Austrian Succession," but in America as "King George's War," or as "Governor Shirley's War." Its chief event was that which was the great military surprise of that century, both at home and abroad—the capture of Louisburg in 1745. Hawthorne, in one of his early papers, has given a most graphic picture of the whole occurrence. A fleet sailed from Boston under Sir William Pepperrell, who led three thousand men to attack a stronghold which had been called the Gibraltar of America, and whose fortifications had cost five million dollars. The walls were twenty or thirty feet high, and forty feet thick; they were surrounded by a ditch eighty feet wide, and defended by two hundred and forty-three pieces of artillery, against which the assailants had eighteen cannon and three mortars. It seemed an enterprise as hopeless as that of Sir William Phips against Quebec, and yet it succeeded. To the amazement of all, the fortress surrendered after a siege of six weeks. The pious Puritans believed it a judgment of God upon the Roman Catholics, and held with delight a Protestant service in the chapel of the fort. When they returned they brought with them an iron cross from the chapel, and it now

SIR WILLIAM PEPPERRELL.
[From the painting in the Essex Institute.]

stands above the main entrance to the Harvard College library. But three years after (1748) the Peace of Aix-la-Chapelle provided for the mutual restoration of all conquests, and Louisburg was given back to the French.

Every step in this prolonged war taught the colonists the need of uniting. All the New England colonies had been represented at Louisburg by men, and New York, New Jersey, and Pennsylvania by money. New hostilities taking place in Nova Scotia and along the Ohio, what is called the "Old French War," or "French and Indian War," began, and at its very outset a convention of delegates met in Albany, coming from New England, New York, Pennsylvania, and Maryland. It was called by advice of the British ministry, and a committee of one from each colony was appointed to consider a plan of union. No successful plan followed, and a sarcastic Mohawk chief said to the colonists: "You desired us to open our minds and hearts to you. Look at the French; they are men; they are fortifying everywhere. But, we are ashamed to say it, you are like women, without any fortifications. It is but one step from Canada hither, and the French may easily come and turn you out-of-doors."

For the eight years following it seemed more than likely that the description would be fulfilled. The French kept resolutely at work, building forts and establishing garrisons, until they had a chain of sixty that reached from Quebec to New Orleans. Vainly did the Governor of Virginia send Washington, then a youth of twenty-one, to remonstrate with the French officers in 1753; he traversed the unbroken forests and crossed freezing rivers on rafts of ice; but to no result, except that it all contributed to the training of the future general. The English colonists achieved some easy successes —as in dispersing and removing the so-called " neutral French in Acadia"—a people whose neutrality, though guaranteed by treaty, did not prevent them from constantly recruiting the enemy's forces, and who were as inconvenient for neighbors as they are now picturesque in history. But when Braddock came with an army of English veterans to lead the colonial force he was ignominiously defeated, near Pittsburgh, Pennsylvania (July 9, 1755), and Washington and the provincial troops had to cover his retreat. All along the line of the colonies the Indian attacks only grew more terrible, the French telling the natives that the time had now come to drive the English from the soil. In Virginia, Washington wrote that the "supplicating tears of women and the moving petitions of the men melted him with deadly sorrow." Farther north, the French General Montcalm took fort after fort with apparent ease, and then the garrisons, as at Fort William Henry, were murdered by his Indians.

LOUIS JOSEPH MONTCALM.

"For God's sake," wrote the officer in command at Albany, to the Governor of Massachusetts, "exert yourself to save a province! New York itself may fall. Save a country! Prevent the downfall of the British government!" Dr. Jeremy Belknap, whom Bryant declares to have been the first person who made American history attractive, thus summed up the gloomy situation in the spring of 1757: "The great expense, the frequent disappointments, the loss of men, of forts, of stores, was very discouraging. The enemy's country was filled with prisoners and scalps, private plunder and public stores, and provisions which our people, as beasts of burden, had conveyed to them. These reflections were the dismal accompaniment of the winter."

What turned the scale was the energy of the new prime-minister, William Pitt. Under his inspiration the colonies raised men "like magic," we are told; the home government furnishing arms, equipments, and supplies; the colonies organizing, uniforming, and paying the troops, with a prospect of reimbursement. Events followed in quick succession. Abercrombie failed at Ticonderoga, but Bradstreet took Fort Frontenac; Prideaux took Niagara; Louisburg, Crown Point, and even Ticonderoga itself fell. Quebec was taken in 1759, Wolfe, the victor, and Montcalm, the defeated, dying alike almost in the hour when the battle was decided. Montreal soon followed; and in 1763 the Peace of Paris surrendered Canada to the English, with nearly all the French possessions east of the Mississippi. France had already given up to Spain all her claims west of the Mississippi, and her brilliant career as an American power was over. With her the Indian tribes were also quelled, except that the brief conspiracy of Pontiac came and went like the last flicker of an expiring candle; then the flame vanished, and the Hundred Years' War was at an end.

JAMES WOLFE.

VIII.

THE SECOND GENERATION OF ENGLISHMEN IN AMERICA.

WHEN a modern American makes a pilgrimage, as I have done, to the English village church at whose altars his ancestors once ministered, he brings away a feeling of renewed wonder at the depth of conviction which led the Puritan clergy to forsake their early homes. The exquisitely peaceful features of the English rural landscape—the old Norman church, half ruined, and in this particular case restored by aid of the American descendants of that high-minded emigrant; the old burial-ground that surrounds it, a haunt of such peace as to make death seem doubly restful; the ancestral oaks; the rooks that soar above them; the flocks of sheep drifting noiselessly among the ancient gravestones—all speak of such tranquillity as the eager American must cross the Atlantic to obtain. No Englishman feels these things as the American feels them; the antiquity, as Hawthorne says, is our novelty. But beyond all the charm of the associations this thought always recurs—what love of their convictions, what devotion to their own faith, must have been needed to drive the educated Puritan clergymen from such delicious retreats to encounter the ocean, the forest, and the Indians!

Yet there was in the early emigration to every American colony quite another admixture than that of learning and refinement; a sturdy yeoman element, led by the desire to better its condition and create a new religious world around it; and an adventurous element, wishing for new excitements. The popular opinion of that period did not leave these considerations out of sight, as may be seen by this London street ballad of 1640, describing the emigration:

> "Our company we feare not, there goes my Cosen Hanna,
> And Ruben doe perswade to goe his sister faire Susanna,
> W^th Abigall and Lidia, and Ruth noe doubt comes after,
> And Sara kinde will not stay behind my Cosen Constance dafter—
> Then for the truth's sake goe.
>
> "Nay Tom Tyler is p'pared, and ye Smith as black as a cole,
> And Ralph Cobbler too wth us will goe for he regards his soale,
> And the weaver honest Lyman, wth Prudence Jacobs daughter,
> And Agatha and Barrbarra professeth to come after—
> Then for the truth's sake goe."

There were also traces, in the emigration, of that love of wandering, of athletic sports and woodcraft, that still sends young men of English race to the far corners of the earth. In the Virginia colonization this element was large, but it also entered into the composition of the Northern colonies. The sister of Governor Winthrop wrote from England, in 1637, of her son, afterwards Sir George Downing, that the boy was anxious to go to New England; and she spoke of the hazard that he was in "by reson of both his father's and his owne strange inclination to the plantation sports." Upham accordingly describes this same youth in Harvard College, where he graduated in 1642, as shooting birds in the wild woods of Salem, and setting duck-decoys in the ponds. Life in the earlier days of the emigration was essentially a border life, a forest life, a frontier life — differing from such life in Australia or Colorado mainly in one wild dream which certainly added to its romance — the dream that Satan still ruled the forest, and that the Indians were his agents.

Whatever else may be said of the Puritan emigration, it

represented socially and intellectually much of what was best in the mother country. Men whose life in England would have been that of the higher class of gentry might have been seen in New England taking with their own hands from the barrel their last measure of corn, and perhaps interrupted by the sight of a vessel arriving in the harbor with supplies. These men, who ploughed their own fields and shot their own venison, were men who had paced the halls of Emanuel College at Cambridge, who quoted Seneca in their journals of travel, and who brought with them books of classic literature among their works of theology. The library bequeathed by the Rev. John Harvard to the infant college at Cambridge included Homer, Pliny, Sallust, Terence, Juvenal, and Horace. The library bought by the commissioners from the Rev. Mr. Welde, for the Rev. Mr. Eliot, had in it Plutarch's Morals and the plays of Aristophanes. In its early poverty the colony voted £400 to found Harvard College, and that institution had for its second president a man so learned, after the fashion of those days, that he had the Hebrew Bible read to the students in the morning, and the Greek Testament in the afternoon, commenting on both extemporaneously in Latin. The curriculum of the institution was undoubtedly devised rather with a view to making learned theologians than elegant men of letters — thus much may be conceded to Mr. Matthew Arnold—but this was quite as much the case, as Mr. Mullinger has shown, in the English Cambridge of the seventeenth century.

The year 1650 may be roughly taken as closing the first generation of the American colonists. Virginia had then been settled forty-three years, New York thirty-six, Plymouth thirty, Massachusetts Bay twenty-two, Maryland nineteen, Connecticut seventeen, Rhode Island fourteen, New Haven twelve, and Delaware twelve. A variety of industries had already been introduced, especially in the New England colonies. Boat-building had there begun, according to Colonel C. D. Wright, in 1624;

brick-making, tanning, and windmills were introduced in 1629; shoemaking and saw-mills in 1635; cloth mills in 1638; printing the year after; and iron foundries in 1644. In Virginia the colony had come near to extinction in 1624, and had revived under wholly new leadership. In New England, Brewster, Winthrop, Higginson, Skelton, Shepard, and Hooker had all died; Bradford, Endicott, Standish, Winslow, Eliot, and Roger Williams were still living, but past their prime. Church and State were already beginning to be possessed by a younger race, who had either been born in America or been brought as young children to its shores. In this coming race, also, the traditions of learning prevailed; the reading of Cotton Mather, for instance, was as marvellous as his powers of memory. When he entered Harvard College, at eleven, he had read Cicero, Terence, Ovid, Virgil, and the Greek Testament; wrote Latin with ease; was reading Homer, and had begun the Hebrew grammar. But the influences around these men were stern and even gloomy, though tempered by scholarship, by the sweet charities of home, and by some semblance of relaxation. We can hardly say that there was nothing but sternness when we find the Rev. Peter Thacher at Barnstable, Massachusetts—a man of high standing in the churches—mitigating the care of souls, in 1679, by the erection of a private nine-pin alley on his own premises. Still there was for a time a distinct deepening of shadow around the lives of the Puritans, whether in the Northern or Southern colonies, after they were left wholly to themselves upon the soil of the New World. The persecutions and the delusions belong generally to this later epoch. In the earlier colonial period there would have been no time for them, and hardly any inclination. In the later or provincial period society was undergoing a change, and wealth and aristocratic ways of living were being introduced. But it was in the intermediate time that religious rigor had its height.

Modern men habitually exaggerate the difference between

themselves and the Puritans. The points of difference are so great and so picturesque, we forget that the points of resemblance, after all, outweigh them. We seem more remote from

COTTON MATHER.

them than is really the case, because we dwell too much on secondary matters — a garment, a phrase, a form of service. Theologian and historian are alike overcome by this; as soon as they touch the Puritans all is sombre, there is no sunshine, no bird sings. Yet the birds filled the woods with their music then as now; children played; mothers talked pretty nonsense to their babies; Governor Winthrop wrote tender messages to his third wife in a way that could only have come of long and reiterated practice. We cannot associate a gloomy temperament with Miles Standish's doughty defiances, or with Francis Higginson's assertion that "a draught of New England air is better than a flagon of Old English ale." Their lives, like all lives, were tempered and moulded by much that was quite apart from theology—hard work in the woods, fights with the Indians, and less perilous field-sports. They were unlike modern men when they were at church, but not so unlike when they went on a bear-hunt.

In order to understand the course of Puritan life in America, we must bear in mind that the first-comers in the most strictly Puritan colonies were more and not less liberal than their immediate descendants. The Plymouth colony was more tolerant than the later colony of Massachusetts Bay, and the first church of the Massachusetts Bay colony was freer than those which followed it. The covenant drawn up for this Salem church in 1629 has seldom been surpassed in benignant comprehensiveness; it is thought that the following words constituted the whole of it: "We covenant with the Lord and one with another, and do bind ourselves, in the presence of God, to walk together in all His ways, according as He is pleased to reveal Himself to us in His blessed word of truth." This was drawn up, according to Mather, by the first minister of Salem; and even when this covenant was enlarged into a confession of faith by his son and successor, some years later, it nevertheless remained more liberal than many later covenants. The trouble was that the horizon for a time narrowed instead of widened. The isolation and privations of the colonial life produced their inevitable effect, and this tendency grew as the new generation developed.

But it must be noticed that even this early liberality never went so far as to lay down any high-sounding general principles of religious liberty, or to announce that as the corner-stone of the new enterprise. Here it is that great and constant injustice is done;—in attributing to these Puritans a principle of toleration which they never set up, and then reproaching them with being false to it. Even Mr. Francis Parkman, who seems to me to be, within his own domain, unquestionably the first of American historians, loses his habit of justice when he quits his Frenchmen and his Indians and deals with the Puritans. "At the outset," he says, in his "Pioneers of France," "New England was unfaithful to the principles of her existence. Seldom has religious toleration assumed a form more oppressive than among the Puritan exiles. New England Protestantism appealed to liberty; then closed the doors against her. On a stock of freedom she grafted a scion of despotism." Surely this is the old misstatement often made, often refuted. When were those colonists unfaithful to their own principle? When did they appeal to liberty? They appealed to truth. It would have been far better and nobler had they aimed at both, but in this imperfect world we have often to praise and venerate men for a single virtue. Anything but the largest toleration would have been inconsistency in Roger Williams, or perhaps—for this is less clearly established—in Lord Baltimore; but in order to show that the Puritans were false to religious liberty it must be shown that they had proclaimed it. On the contrary, what they sought to proclaim was religious truth. They lost the expansive influence of freedom, but they gained the propelling force of a high though gloomy faith. They lost the variety that exists in a liberal community where each man has his own opinion, but they gained the concentrated power of a homogeneous and well-ordered people.

There are but two of the early colonies of which the claim can be seriously made that they were founded on any principle of religious freedom. These two are Rhode Island and Maryland. It was said of the first by Roger Williams, its spiritual founder, that "a permission of the most paganish, Jewish, Turkish, or anti-Christian conscience" should be there granted "to all men of all nations and countries." Accordingly, the colony afforded such shelter on a very wide scale. It received Anne Hutchinson after she had set the State as well as Church in a turmoil at Boston, and had made popular elections turn on her opinions. It not only sheltered but gave birth to Jemima Wilkinson, prophetess of the "Cumberland Zealots," who might, under the stimulus of a less tolerant community, have expanded into a Joanna Southcote or a Mother Ann Lee. It protected Samuel Gorton, a man of the Savonarola temperament, of whom his last surviving disciple said, in 1771, "My master wrote in heaven, and none can understand his writings but those who live in heaven while on earth." It cost such an effort to assimilate these exciting ingredients that Roger Williams described Gorton, in 1640, as "bewitching and bemadding poor Providence," and the Grand Jury of Portsmouth, R. I., was compelled to indict him as a nuisance in the same year, on this count, among others, "that Samuel Gorton contumeliously reproached the magistrates, calling them Just-asses." Nevertheless, all these, and such as these, were at last disarmed and made harmless by the wise policy of Rhode Island, guided by Roger Williams, after he had outgrown the superfluous antagonisms of his youth, and had learned to be conciliatory in action as well as comprehensive in doctrine. Yet even he had so much to undergo in keeping the peace with all these heterogeneous materials that he recoiled at last from "such an infinite liberty of conscience," and declared that in the case of Quakers "a due and moderate restraint and punishment of these incivilities" was not only no persecution, but was "a duty and command of God."

Maryland has shared with Rhode Island the honor of having established religious freedom, and this claim is largely based upon the noble decree passed by its General Assembly in 1649:

"No person whatsoever in this province professing to believe in Jesus Christ shall from henceforth be any way troubled or molested for his or her religion, or in the free exercise thereof, or any way compelled to the belief or exercise of any other religion against his or her consent."

But it is never hard to evade a statute that seems to secure religious liberty, and this decree did not prevent the Maryland colony from afterwards enacting that if any person should deny the Holy Trinity he should first be bored through the tongue and fined or imprisoned; that for the second offence he should be branded as a blasphemer, the letter "B" being stamped on his forehead; and for the third offence should die. This was certainly a very limited toleration; and granting that it has a partial value, it remains an interesting question who secured it. Cardinal Manning and others have claimed this measure of toleration as due to the Roman Catholics, but Mr. E. D. Neill has conclusively shown that the Roman Catholic element was originally much smaller than was supposed, that the "two hundred Catholic gentlemen" usually claimed as founding the colony were really some twenty gentlemen and three hundred laboring men; that of the latter twelve died on shipboard, of whom only two confessed to the priests, thus giving a clew to the probable opinions of the rest; and that of the Assembly which passed the resolutions the majority were Protestants, and even Puritans. But granting to Maryland a place next to Rhode Island in religious freedom, she paid, like that other colony, what was then the penalty of freedom, and I must dwell a moment on this.

In those days religious liberty brought a heterogeneous and often reckless population; it usually involved the absence of a highly educated ministry; and this implied the want of a settled system of education, and of an elevated standard of public duty. These deficiencies left both in Rhode Island and in Maryland certain results which are apparent to this day. There is nothing more extraordinary in the Massachusetts and Connecticut colonies than the promptness with which they entered on the work of popular instruction. These little communities, just struggling for existence, marked out an educational system which had then hardly a parallel in the European world. In the Massachusetts Bay colony, Salem had a free school in 1640, Boston in 1642, or earlier, Cambridge about the same time, and the State, in 1647, marked out an elaborate system of common and grammar schools for every township—a system then without a precedent, so far as I know, in Europe. Thus ran the essential sentences of this noble document, held up to the admiration of all England by Lord Macaulay in Parliament:

... "Y^t learning may not be buried in ye grave of o^r fath^{rs} in ye church and comonwealth, the Lord assisting o^r endeavors—It is therefore ord^{r}ed, y^t ev^{r}y township in this iurisdiction, aft^r ye Lord heth increased y^m to ye number of 50 household^{rs}, shall then forthwth appoint one wthin their towne to teach all such children as shall resort to him to write and reade; ... and it is furth^r ordered, y^t where any towne shall increase to ye numb^r of 100 families or househould^s, they shall set up a grañer schoole, ye m^r thereof being able to instruct youth so farr as they may be fited for ye university."

The printing-press came with these schools, or before them, and was actively employed, and it is impossible not to recognize the contrast between such institutions and the spirit of that Governor of Virginia (Berkeley) who said, a quarter of a century later, "We have no free schools nor printing, and I hope shall not have these hundred years." In Maryland, convicts and indented servants were sometimes advertised for sale as teachers at an early day, and there was no public system until 1728. In Rhode Island, Newport had a public-school in 1640, but it apparently lasted but a year or two, nor was there a general system till the year 1800. These contrasts are mentioned for one sole purpose: to show that no single community unites all virtues, and that it was at that period very hard for religious liberality and a good school system to exist together.

There was a similar irregularity among the colonies in the

number of university-trained men. Professor F. B. Dexter has shown that no less than sixty such men joined the Massachusetts Bay colony within ten years of its origin, while after seventeen years of separate existence the Virginia colony held but two university men, Rev. Hant Wyatt and Dr. Pott; and Rhode Island had also but two in its early days, Roger Williams and the recluse William Blaxton. No one has more fully recognized the "heavy price paid" for this "great cup of liberty" in Rhode Island than her ablest scholar, Professor Diman, who employs precisely these phrases to describe it in his Bristol address; and who fearlessly points out how much that State lost, even while she gained something, by the absence of that rigorous sway and that lofty public standard which were associated with the stern rule of the Puritan clergy.

In all the early colonies, unless we except Rhode Island, the Puritan spirit made itself distinctly felt, and religious persecution widely prevailed. Even in Maryland, as has been shown, the laws imposed branding and boring through the tongue as a penalty for certain opinions. In Virginia those who refused to attend the Established Church must pay 200 pounds of tobacco for the first offence, 500 for the second, and incur banishment for the third. A fine of 5000 pounds of tobacco was placed upon unauthorized religious meetings. Quakers and Baptists were whipped or pilloried, and any ship-master conveying Nonconformists was fined. Even so late as 1741, after persecution had virtually ceased in New England, severe laws were passed against Presbyterians in Virginia; and the above-named laws of Maryland were re-enacted in 1723. At an earlier period, however, the New England laws, if not severer, were no doubt more rigorously executed. In some cases, to be sure, the so-called laws were a deliberate fabrication, as in the case of the Connecticut "Blue Laws," a code reprinted to this day in the newspapers, but which existed only in the active and malicious imagination of the Tory Dr. Peters.

The spirit of persecution was strongest in the New England colonies, and chiefly in Massachusetts, because of the greater intensity with which men there followed out their convictions. It was less manifest in the banishment of Roger Williams— which was, after all, not so much a religious as a political transaction—than in the Quaker persecutions which took place between 1656 and 1660. Whatever minor elements may have entered into the matter, these were undoubtedly persecutions based on religious grounds, and are therefore to be utterly condemned. Yet they were not quite so bad as a class of persecutions which had become familiar in Europe—forbidding heretics to leave the realm, and then tormenting them if they stayed. Not a Quaker ever suffered death except for voluntary action; that is, for choosing to stay, or to return after banishment. To demand that men should consent to be banished on pain of death seems to us an outrage; but it seemed quite otherwise, we must remember, to those who had already exiled themselves, in order to secure a spot where they could worship in their own way. Cotton Mather says, with some force:

> "It was also thought that the very Quakers themselves would say that if they had got into a Corner of the World, and with an immense Toyl and Charge made a Wilderness habitable, on purpose there to be undisturbed in the Exercises of their Worship, they would never bear to have New-Englanders come among them and interrupt their Publick Worship, endeavor to seduce their Children from it, yea, and repeat such Endeavors after mild Entreaties first, and then just Banishments, to oblige their departure."

We now see that this place they occupied was not a mere corner of the world, and that it was even then an essential part of the British dominions, and subject to British laws. We can therefore see that this was not the whole of the argument, and the Quakers might well maintain that they had a legal right to exercise their religion in America. The colonists seem to me to have strained much too far the power given them in their patent to "encounter, expulse, repel, and resist" all invaders when they applied it to these unwarlike visitors. Yet the Quakers were in a sense invaders, nevertheless; their latest and ablest defender, Mr. R. P. Hallowell, concedes as much when he entitles his history "The Quaker Invasion of Massachusetts;" and if an invasion it was, then Cotton Mather's *argumentum ad hominem* was quite to the point. Had the Quakers, like the Moravians, made settlements and cleared the forests for themselves, this argument would have been quite disarmed; and had those settlements been interfered with by the Puritans, the injustice would have been far more glaring; nor is it probable that the Puritans would have molested such colonies—unless they happened to be too near.

It must be remembered, too, that the Puritans did not view Quakers and other zealots as heretics merely, but as dangerous social outlaws. There was among the colonists a genuine and natural fear that if the tide of extravagant fanaticism once set in, it might culminate in such atrocities as had shocked all Europe while the Anabaptists, under John of Leyden, were in power at Münster. In the frenzied and naked exhibitions of Lydia Wardwell and Deborah Wilson they saw tendencies which might end in uprooting all the social order for which they were striving, and might lead at last to the revocation of their charter. I differ with the greatest unwillingness from my old friend Mr. John G. Whittier in his explanation of a part of these excesses. He thinks that these naked performances came from persons who were maddened by seeing the partial exposure of Quakers whipped through the streets. This view, though plausible, seems to me to overlook the highly wrought condition of mind among these enthusiasts, and the fact that they regarded everything as a symbol. When one of the very ablest of the Quakers, Robert Barclay, walked the streets of Aberdeen in sackcloth and ashes, he deemed it right to sacrifice all propriety for the sake of a symbolic act; and in just the same spirit we find the Quaker writers of that period de-

A QUAKER EXHORTER IN NEW ENGLAND.

fending these personal exposures, not by Mr. Whittier's reasons, but for symbolic ones. In Southey's "Commonplace-Book" there is a long extract, to precisely this effect, from the life of Thomas Story, an English Friend who had travelled in

America. He seems to have been a moderate man, and to have condemned some of the extravagances of the Ranters, but gravely argues that the Quakers might really have been commanded by God to exhibit their nakedness "as a sign."

Whatever provocation the Friends may have given, their persecution is the darkest blot upon the history of the time—darker than witchcraft, which was a disease of supernatural terror. And like the belief in witchcraft, the spirit of persecution could only be palliated by the general delusion of the age, by the cruelty of the English legislation against the Jesuits, which the Puritan Legislature closely followed as regarded Quakers; and in general by the attempt to unite Church and State, and to take the Old Testament for a literal modern statute-book. It must be remembered that our horror at this intolerance is also stimulated from time to time by certain extravagant fabrications which still appear as genuine in the newspapers; as that imaginary letter said to have been addressed by Cotton Mather to a Salem clergyman in 1682, and proposing that a colony of Quakers be arrested and sold as slaves. This absurd forgery appeared first in some Pennsylvania newspaper, accompanied by the assertion that this letter was in possession of the Massachusetts Historical Society. No such paper was ever known to that society; Cotton Mather was, at the time alleged, but nineteen years old, and the Quaker persecution had substantially ceased twenty years before. But when did such contradictions ever have any effect on the vitality of a lie?

The dark and intense convictions of Puritanism were seen at their highest in the witchcraft trials—events which took place in almost every colony at different times. The wonder is that they showed themselves so much less in America than in most European nations at the same period. To see this delusion in its most frightful form we must go beyond the Atlantic and far beyond the limits of English Puritanism. During its course 30,000 victims were put to death in Great Britain, 75,000 in France, 100,000 in Germany, besides those executed in Italy, Switzerland, and Sweden, many of them being burned. Compared with this vast estimate, which I take from that careful historian Mr. W. F. Poole, how trivial seem the few dozen cases to be found in our early colonies; and yet, as he justly remarks, these few have attracted more attention from the world than all the rest. Howell, the letter-writer, says, under date of February 22, 1647: "Within the compass of two years near upon 300 witches were arraigned, and the larger part of them executed, in Essex and Suffolk [England] only. Scotland swarms with them more and more, and persons of good quality are executed daily." In a single Swedish village threescore and ten witches were discovered, most of whom, including fifteen children, were executed, besides thirty children who were compelled to "run the gantlet" and be lashed on their hands once a week for a year. The eminent English judge Sir Matthew Hale, giving his charge at the trial for witchcraft of Rose Cullender and Anne Duny in 1668—a trial which had great weight with the American judges—said that he "made no doubt there were such Creatures as Witches, for the Scriptures affirmed it, and the Wisdom of all Nations had provided Laws against such Persons." The devout Bishop Hall wrote in England: "Satan's prevalency in this Age is most clear, in the marvellous numbers of Witches abiding in all places. Now hundreds are discovered in one Shire." It shows that there was, on the whole, a healthy influence exerted on Puritanism by American life when we consider that the witchcraft excitement was here so limited and so short-lived.

The first recorded case of execution for this offence in the colonies is mentioned in Winthrop's journal (March, 1646–47), as occurring at Hartford, Connecticut, where another occurred in 1648, there being also one in Boston that same year. Nine more took place in Boston and in Connecticut before the great outbreak at Salem. A curious one appears in the Maryland records of 1654 as having happened on the high seas upon a vessel bound to Baltimore, where a woman was hanged by the seamen upon this charge, the case being afterwards investigated by the Governor and Council. A woman was tried and acquitted in Pennsylvania in 1683; one was hanged in Maryland for this alleged crime by due sentence of court in 1685; and one or two cases occurred at New York. The excitement finally came to a head in 1692 at Salem, Massachusetts, where nineteen persons were hanged, and one "pressed to death" for refusing to plead — this being the regularly ordained punishment for such refusal. The excitement being thus relieved, a reaction followed. Brave old Samuel Sewall won for himself honor in all coming time by rising in his place in the congregation, and causing to be read an expression of regret for the part he had taken in the trials. The reaction did not at once reach the Southern colonies. Grace Sherwood was legally ducked for witchcraft in Virginia in 1705, and there was an indictment, followed by acquittal, in Maryland as late as 1712.

That the delusion reached this point was due to no hardened inhumanity of feeling; on the contrary, those who participated in it prayed to be delivered from any such emotion. "If a drop of innocent blood should be shed in the prosecution of the witchcrafts among us, how unhappy are we!" wrote Cotton

SAMUEL SEWALL.

[From the collections of the Massachusetts Historical Society.]

ARRESTING A WITCH.

Mather. Accordingly Mr. Poole has shown that this eminent clergyman, popularly identified beyond any one else with the witchcraft delusion, yet tried to have it met by united prayer rather than by the courts; would never attend any of the witchcraft trials; cautioned the magistrates against credulity, and kept secret to his dying day the names of many persons privately inculpated by the witnesses with whom he conversed. It was with anguish of spirit and the conscientious fidelity of the Anglo-Saxon temperament that these men entered upon the work. Happy would they have been could they have taken such supposed visitations lightly, as the Frenchmen on this continent have taken them. Champlain fully believed, as has been already stated, that there was a devil under the name of the Gougou inhabiting a certain island in the St. Lawrence; but he merely crossed himself, carolled a French song, and sailed by. Yet even in France, as has been seen, the delusion raged enormously; and to men of English descent, at any rate, it was no such light thing that Satan dwelt visibly in the midst of them. Was this to be the end of all their labors, their sacrifices? They had crossed the ocean, fought off the Indians, cleared the forest, built their quaint little houses in the clearing, extirpated all open vice, and lo! Satan was still there in concealment, like the fabled ghost which migrated with the family, being packed among the beds. There is no mistaking the intensity of their lament. See with what depth of emotion Cotton Mather utters it:

"'Tis a dark time, yea a black night indeed, now the Ty-dogs of the Pit are abroad among us, but *it is through the wrath of the Lord of Hosts!* . . . Blessed Lord! Are all the other Instruments of thy Vengeance too good for the chastisement of such Transgressors as we are? Must the very *Devils* be sent *out of their own plase* to be our troublers? . . . They are not swarthy Indians, but they are sooty Devils that are let loose upon us."

Thus wrote Cotton Mather, he who had sat at the bedside of the "bewitched" Margaret Rule and had distinctly smelled sulphur.

While the English of the second generation were thus passing through a phase of Puritanism more intense than any they brought with them, the colonies were steadily increasing in population, and were modifying in structure towards their later shape. Delaware had passed from Swedish under Dutch control, Governor Stuyvesant having taken possession of the colony in 1655 with small resistance. Then the whole Dutch territory, thus enlarged, was transferred to English dominion, quite against the will of the same headstrong governor, known as "Hardkoppig Piet." The Dutch had thriven, in spite of their patroons, and their slaves, and their semblance of aristocratic government; they had built forts in Connecticut, claimed Cape Cod for a boundary, and even stretched their demands as far as Maine. All their claims and possessions were at last surrendered without striking a blow. When the British fleet appeared off Long Island, the whole organized Dutch force included only some two hundred men fit for duty, scattered from Albany to Delaware; the inhabitants of New Amsterdam refused to take up arms, although Governor Stuyvesant would fain have had them, and he was so enraged that he tore to pieces the letter from Nicolls, the English commander, to avoid showing it. "The surrender," he said, "would be reproved in the fatherland." But the people utterly refused to stand by him, and he was thus compelled, sorely against his will, to surrender. The English entered into complete occupation; New Netherland became New York; all the Dutch local names were abolished, although destined to be restored during the later Dutch occupation, which again ceased in 1674. Yet the impress of that nationality remains to this day on the names, the architecture, and the customs of that region, and has indeed tinged those of the whole country; and the Dutch had securely founded what was from its early days the most cosmopolitan city of America.

Their fall left the English in absolute possession of a line of colonies that stretched from Maine southward. This now included some new settlements made during the period just described. Carolina, as it had been called a hundred years before by Jean Ribaut and his French Protestants, was granted,

PETER STUYVESANT TEARING THE LETTER DEMANDING THE SURRENDER OF NEW YORK.

in 1663, by King Charles the Second to eight proprietors, who brought with them a plan of government framed for them by the celebrated John Locke—probably the most absurd scheme of government ever proposed for a new colony by a philosopher, and fortunately set aside from the very beginning by the common-sense of the colonists. Being the most southern colony, Carolina was drawn into vexatious wars with the Spaniards, the French, and the Indians; but it was many years before it was divided by the King into two parts, and before Georgia was settled. Another grant by Charles the Second was more wisely planned, when in 1681 William Penn sent out some emigrants, guided by no philosopher except Penn himself, who came the following year. A great tract of country was granted to him as a sort of equivalent for a debt owed by the King to his father, Admiral Penn; the annual rent was to be two beaver-skins. Everything seemed to throw around the coming of William Penn the aspect of a lofty enterprise: his ship was named "*The Welcome;*" his new city was to be called "Brotherly Love," or "Philadelphia." His harmonious relations with the Indians have been the wonder of later times, though it must be remembered that he had to do with no such fierce tribes as had devastated the other colonies. Peace prevailed with sectarian zealots, and even towards those charged with witchcraft. Yet even Philadelphia did not escape the evil habits of the age, and established the whipping-post, the pillory, and the stocks—some of which Delaware, long a part of Pennsylvania, still retains. But there is no such scene of contentment in our pioneer history as that which the early annals of "Penn's Woods" (Pennsylvania) record.

Other great changes were meanwhile taking place. New Hampshire and New Jersey came to be recognized as colonies by themselves; the union of the New England colonies was dissolved; Plymouth was merged in Massachusetts, New Haven in Connecticut, Delaware temporarily in Pennsylvania. At the close of the period which I have called the second generation (1700) there were ten distinct English colonies along the coast —New Hampshire, Massachusetts, Rhode Island, Connecticut, New York, New Jersey, Pennsylvania, Maryland, Virginia, Carolina.

It is a matter of profound interest to observe that whatever may be the variations among these early settlements, we find everywhere the distinct traces of the old English village communities, which again are traced by Freeman and others to a Swiss or German origin. The founders of the first New England towns did not simply settle themselves upon the principle of "squatter sovereignty," each for himself; but they founded municipal organizations, based on a common control of the land. So systematically was this carried out that in an old town like Cambridge, Massachusetts, for instance, it would be easy at this day, were all the early tax lists missing, to determine the comparative worldly condition of the different settlers simply by comparing the proportion which each had to maintain of the great "pallysadoe," or paling, which surrounded the little settlement. These amounts varied from seventy rods, in case of the richest, to two rods, in case of the poorest; and so well was the work done that the traces of the "fosse" about the paling still remain in the willow-trees on the play-ground of the Harvard students. These early settlers simply reproduced, with a few necessary modifications, those local institutions which had come to them from remote ancestors. The town paling, the town meeting, the town common, the town pound, the fence-viewers, the field-drivers, the militia muster, even the tipstaves of the constables, are "survivals" of institutions older than the Norman conquest of England. Even the most matter-of-fact transactions of their daily life, as the transfer of land by giving a piece of turf, an instance of which occurred at Salem, Massachusetts, in 1696, sometimes carry us back to usages absolutely mediæval—in this case to the transfer "by turf and twig" so familiar to historians, although it is unsafe to press these analogies too far, since the aboriginal tribes sometimes practised the same usage. All that the New England settlers added to their traditional institutions —and it was a great addition—was the system of common schools. Beyond New England the analogies with inherited custom are less clear and unmistakable; but it is now maintained that the Southern "parish" and "county," the South Carolina "court-greens" and "common pastures," as well as the Maryland "manors" and "court-leets," all represent, under different combinations, the same inherited principle of communal sovereignty.

The period which I have assigned to the second generation in America may be considered to have lasted from 1650 to 1700. Even during this period there took place collisions of purpose and interest between the home government and the colonies. The contest for the charters, for instance, and the short-lived power of Sir Edmund Andros, occurred within the time which has here been treated, but they were the forerunners of a later contest, and will be included in another chapter. It will then be necessary to describe the gradual transformation which made colonies into provinces, and out of a varied emigration developed a homogeneous people; which taught the English ministry to distrust the Americans, while it unconsciously weaned the Americans from England; so that the tie which at first had expressed only affection, became at last a hated yoke, soon to be thrown aside forever.

IX.

THE BRITISH YOKE.

HOW deep and tender was the love with which the first American colonists looked back to their early home! Many proofs of this might be cited from their writings, but I know of none quite so eloquent as that burst of impassioned feeling in a sermon by William Hooke—cousin and afterwards chaplain of Oliver Cromwell—who came to America about 1636, and preached this discourse at Taunton, July 3, 1640, under the title, " New England's Teares for Old England's Feares." This whole production is marked by a learning and eloquence that remind us of one who may have been Hooke's fellow-student at Oxford, Jeremy Taylor; indeed it contains a description of a battle which, if Taylor had written it, would have been quoted in every history of English literature until this day. And in this sermon the clergyman thus speaks of the mother-country:

"There is no Land that claimes our name but *England;* wee are distinguished from all the Nations in the World by the name of *English.* There is no Potentate breathing that wee call our dread Sovereigne but King *Charles,* nor Lawes of any Land have civilized us but England's; there is no Nation that calls us Countrey-men but the *English.* Brethren! Did wee not there draw in our first breath? Did not the Sunne first shine there upon our heads? Did not that Land first beare us, even that pleasant Island, but for sinne, I would say, that Garden of the Lord, that Paradise?"

What changed all this deep tenderness into the spirit that found the British yoke detestable, and at length cast it off?

There have been many other great changes in America since that day. The American fields have been altered by the steady advance of imported weeds and flowers; the buttercup, the dandelion, and the ox-eyed daisy displacing the anemone and violet. The American physique is changed to a slenderer and more finely organized type; the American temperament has grown more sensitive, more pliant, more adaptive; the American voice has been shifted to a higher key, perhaps yielding greater music when fitly trained. Of all these changes we see the result, but cannot trace the steps; and it is almost as difficult to trace the successive impulses by which the love of everything that was English was transformed into a hatred of the British yoke.

Yet its beginnings may be observed in much that the colonists did, and in some things which they omitted. Within ten years after Hooke's loving reference to King Charles there was something ominous in the cool self-control with which the people of Massachusetts refrained from either approving or disapproving his execution. It was equally ominous when they abstained from recognizing the accession of Richard Cromwell, and when they let fifteen months pass before sending a congratulatory address to Charles the Second. It was the beginning of a policy of indifference more significant than any policy of resistance. When in 1660, under that monarch, the Act of Navigation was passed, prescribing that no merchandise should be imported into the plantations but in English vessels navigated by Englishmen, the New England colonies simply ignored it. During sixteen years the Massachusetts governor, annually elected by the people, never once took the oath which the Navigation Act required of him; and when the courageous Leverett was called to account for this he answered, "The King can in reason do no less than let us enjoy our liberties and trade, for we have made this large plantation of our own charge, without any contribution from the crown." Four years after the Act of Navigation, in 1664, the English fleet brought royal commissioners to Boston, with instructions aiming at further aggression; and there was great dignity in the response of the General Court, made through Governor Endicott, October 30, 1664: "The all-knowing God he knowes our greatest ambition is to liue a poore and quiet life in a corner of the world, without offence to God or man. Wee came not into this wilderness to seeke great things to ourselves, and if any come after vs to seeke them heere, they will be disappointed." They then declare that to yield to the demands of the commissioners would be simply to destroy their own liberties, expressly guaranteed to them by their King, and dearer than their lives.

The commissioners visited other colonies and then returned to Boston, where they announced that they should hold a court at the house of Captain Thomas Breedon on Hanover Street, at 9 A.M., May 24, 1665. It happened that a brother officer of Captain Breedon, one Colonel Cartwright, who had come over with the commissioners, was then lying ill with the gout at this same house. At eight in the morning a messenger of the General Court appeared beneath the window, blew an alarum on the trumpet, and proclaimed that the General Court protested against any such meeting. He then departed to make similar proclamation in other parts of the town; and when the royal commissioners came together they found nobody with whom to confer but the gouty and irate Colonel Cartwright, enraged at the disturbance of his morning slumbers. So perished all hope of coercing the Massachusetts colony at that time.

Thus early did the British yoke begin to make itself felt as a grievance. The Massachusetts men discreetly allayed the effect of their protest by sending his Majesty a ship-load of masts, the freight on which cost the colony £1600. For ten years the quarrel subsided: England had trouble enough with her neighbors without meddling with the colonies. Then the contest revived, and while the colonies were in the death-struggle of Philip's war, Edward Randolph came as commissioner with a king's letter in 1675. Two years later the Massachusetts colonists made for the first time the distinct assertion to the King, while pledging their loyalty, that "the laws of England were bounded within the four seas, and did not reach America," giving as a reason for this, "they [the colonists] not being represented in Parliament." Then followed the long contest for the charter, while Edward Randolph, like a sort of Mephistopheles, was constantly coming and going between America and England with fresh complaints and new orders, crossing the Atlantic eight times in nine years, and having always, by his own statement, "pressed the necessity of a general Governor as absolutely necessary for the honor and service of the crown." All this long series of contests has been minutely narrated by Mr. Charles Deane, with a thoroughness and clearness which would have won him a world-wide reputation had they only been brought to bear upon the history of some little European State. Again and again, in different forms, the attempt was made to take away the charters of the colonies; and the opposition was usually led, at least in New England, by the clergy. Increase Mather, in 1683–84, addressed a town-meeting in opposition to one such demand, and openly counselled that they should return Naboth's answer when Ahab asked for his vineyard, that they would not give up the inheritance of their fathers.

It must be remembered that all the early charters were defective in this, that they did not clearly define where the line was to be drawn between the rights of the local government and of the crown. We can see now that such definition would have been impossible; even the promise given to Lord Baltimore that Maryland should have absolute self-government did not avert all trouble. It is also to be remembered that there were great legal difficulties in annulling a charter, so long as the instrument itself had not been reclaimed by the power that issued it. We read with surprise of a royal scheme thwarted by so simple a process as the hiding of the Connecticut charter in a hollow tree by William Wadsworth; but an almost vital importance was attached in those days to the actual possession of the instrument. It was considered the most momentous of all the Lord Chancellor's duties—indeed, that from which he had his name (*cancellarius*)—to literally cancel and obliterate the King's letters-patent under the great seal. Hence, although the old charter of Massachusetts was vacated October 23, 1684, it has always been doubted by lawyers whether this was ever legally done, inasmuch as the old charter never was cancelled, and hangs intact in the office of the Massachusetts Secretary of State to this day. In 1686 came the new governor for the colonies—not the dreaded Colonel Kirke, who had been fully expected, but the less formidable Sir Edmund Andros.

The first foretaste of the provincial life, as distinct from the merely colonial, was in the short-lived career of this ruler. He came, a brilliant courtier, among the plain Americans; his servants wore gay liveries; Lady Andros had the first coach seen in Boston. He was at different times Governor of New York, President of New England, and Governor of Virginia. Everywhere he was received with aversion, but everywhere this was tempered by the feeling that it might have been worse, for it might have been Kirke. Yet there was exceeding frankness in the way the colonists met their would-be tyrant. When he visited Hartford, Connecticut, for instance, he met Dr. Hooker one morning, and said, "I suppose all the good people of Connecticut are fasting and praying on my account." The doctor replied, "Yes; we read, 'This kind goeth not out but by fasting and prayer.'" And it required not merely these methods, but something more, to eject Sir Edmund at last from the colonies.

The three years' sway of Sir Edmund Andros accustomed the minds of the American colonists to a new relation between themselves and England. Even where the old relation was not changed in form it was changed in feeling. The colonies which had seemed most secure in their self-government were liable at any moment to become mere royal provinces. Indeed, they

GOVERNOR ANDROS AND THE BOSTON PEOPLE.

were officially informed that his Majesty had decided to unite under one government "all the English territories in America, from Delaware Bay to Nova Scotia," though this was not really attempted. Yet charters were taken away almost at random, colonies were divided or united without the consent of their inhabitants, and the violation of the right of local government was everywhere felt. But in various ways, directly or indirectly, the purposes of Andros were thwarted. When the English revolution of 1688 came, his power fell without a blow, and he found himself in the hands of the rebellious men of Boston. The day had passed by when English events could be merely ignored, and so every colony proclaimed with joy the accession of William and Mary. Such men as Jacob Leisler, in New York, Robert Treat, in Connecticut, and the venerable Simon Bradstreet—then eighty-seven years old—in Massachusetts, were at once recognized as the leaders of the people. There was some temporary disorder, joined with high hope, but the colonies never really regained what they had lost, and henceforth held, more or less distinctly, the character of provinces, until they took their destiny, long after, into their own hands. It needed almost a century to prepare them for that event, not only by their increasing sense of grievance, but by learning to stretch out their hands to one another.

With the fall of the colonial charters fell the New England confederacy that had existed from 1643. There were other plans of union: William Penn formed a very elaborate one in 1698; others labored afterwards in pamphlets to modify his plan or to suggest their own. On nine different occasions, between 1684 and 1751, three or more colonies met in council, represented by their governors or by their commissioners, to consult on internal affairs, usually with reference to the Indians; but they apparently never had a thought of disloyalty, and certainly never proclaimed independence; nor did their meetings for a long time suggest any alarm in the minds of the British ministry. The new jealousies that arose related rather to commercial restrictions than to the form of government.

It is necessary to remember that even in colonial days, while it was of the greatest importance that the British law-makers should know all about the colonies, there was on their part even

THE BRITISH YOKE.

a denser ignorance as to American affairs than that which now impresses the travelling American in England. When he is asked if he came from America by land, it is only a matter for amusement; but when, as James Otis tells us—writing in 1764—it was not uncommon for official papers to come from an English Secretary of State addressed to "the Governor of the island of New England," it was a more serious matter. Under such circumstances the home government was liable at any minute to be swept away from all just policy by some angry tale told by Randolph or Andros. The prevalent British feeling towards the colonies was one of indifference, broken only by outbursts of anger, and spasms of commercial selfishness.

JAMES OTIS.
[From a painting by I. Blackburn, 1755.]

The event which startled the British ministry from this indifference was the taking of Louisburg in 1745, as described in a previous chapter. This success may have been, as has been asserted, only a lucky accident; no matter, it startled not only America, but Europe. That a fortress deemed impregnable by French engineers, and amply garrisoned by French soldiers, should have been captured by a mob of farmers and fishermen—this gave subject for reflection. "Every one knows the importance of Louisburg," wrote James Otis, proudly, "in the consuitations of Aix-la-Chapelle." Voltaire, in writing the history of Louis the Fifteenth, heads the chapter of the calamities of France with this event. He declares that the mere undertaking of such an enterprise showed of what a community was capable when it united the spirit of trade and of war. The siege of Louisburg, he says, was not due to the cabinet at London, but solely to the daring of the New England traders ("*ce fut le fruit de la hardiesse des marchands de la Nouvelle Angleterre*"). But while the feeling inspired on the European continent was one of respect, that created in England was mingled with dread. Was, then, the child learning to do without the parent? And certainly the effect on the minds of the Americans looked like anything but the development of humility. Already the colonies, from Massachusetts to Virginia, were eagerly planning the conquest of Canada, they to furnish the whole land-force, and Great Britain the fleet—a project which failed through the fears of the British ministry. The Duke of Bedford, then at the head of the naval service, frankly objected to it because of " the independence it might create in these provinces, when they shall see within themselves so great an army possessed by so great a country by right of conquest." And the Swedish traveller, Peter Kalm, writing three years later from New York, put the whole matter yet more clearly, thus: " There is reason for doubting whether the King, if he had the power, would wish to drive the French from their possessions in Canada. . . . The English government has therefore reason to regard the French in North America as the chief power that urges their colonies to submission." Any such impressions were naturally confirmed when, in 1748, the indignant American colonists saw Louisburg go back to the French under the treaty of Aix-la-Chapelle.

The trouble was that the British government wished the colonies to unite sufficiently to check the French designs, but not enough to assert their own power. Thus the ministry positively encouraged the convention of delegates from the New England colonies and from New York, Pennsylvania, and Maryland, which met at Albany on June 19, 1754. It was in this convention that Franklin began a course of national influence which was long continued, and brought forward his famous representation of the snake dismembered, with the motto "Unite or Die." He showed also his great organizing power by carrying through the convention a plan for a council of forty-eight members distributed among the different colonies, and having for its head a royal presiding officer with veto power. All the delegates, except those from Connecticut, sustained the plan; it was only when it went to the several colonies and the British ministry that it failed. Its ill-success in these two directions came from diametrically opposite reasons; the colonies thought that it gave them too little power, and the King's Council found in it just the reverse fault. It failed, but its failure left on the public mind an increased sense of divergence between England and America. Merely to have conceived such a plan was a great step towards the American Union that came afterwards; but still there was no conscious shrinking from the British yoke.

The ten colonies which had a separate existence in 1700 had half a century later grown to thirteen. Delaware, after having been merged in Pennsylvania, was again separated from it in 1703; North and South Carolina were permanently divided in 1729; Georgia was settled in 1733. No colony had a nobler foundation; it was planned by its founder—a British general and a member of Parliament—expressly as a refuge for poor debtors and other unfortunates; the colony was named Georgia in honor of the King, but it was given to the proprietors "in trust for the poor," and its seal had a family of silkworms, with the motto "Not for yourselves" (*Sic vos non vobis*). Oglethorpe always kept friendship with the Indians; he refused to admit either slavery or ardent spirits into the colony. But his successors did not adhere to his principles, and the colony was small and weak up to the time of the coming separation from England. Yet the growth of the colonies as a whole was strong and steady. Bancroft estimates their numbers in 1754 at 1,185,000 whites and 260,500 colored, making

GENERAL OGLETHORPE, FOUNDER OF GEORGIA.

in all nearly a million and a half. Counting the whites only, Massachusetts took the lead in population; counting both races, Virginia. "Some few towns excepted," wrote Dickinson soon after, "we are all tillers of the earth, from Nova Scotia to West Florida. We are a people of cultivators, scattered over an immense territory, communicating with each other by means of good roads and navigable rivers, united by the silken bands of mild government, all respecting the laws without dreading their power, because they are equitable."

But if the colonies had all been composed of peaceful agriculturists, the British yoke would have been easy. It was on the commercial settlements that the exactions of the home government bore most severely, and hence it was that the Eastern colonies, which had suffered most in the Indian wars, were again to endure most oppression. An English political economist of 1690, in a tract included in the "Harleian Miscellany," pointed out that there were two classes of colonies in America; that England need have no jealousy of those which raised only sugar and tobacco, and thus gave her a market; but she must keep anxious watch on those which competed with England in fishing and trade, and "threatened in time a total independence therefrom." "When America shall be so well peopled, civilized, and divided into kingdoms," wrote Sir Thomas Browne about the same time, "they are like to have so little regard of their originals as to acknowledge no subjection unto them." All the long series of arbitrary measures which followed were but the effort of the British government to avert this danger. The conquest of Canada, by making the colonies more important, only disposed the ministry to enforce obnoxious laws that had hitherto been dead letters.

Such laws were the "Navigation Act," and the "Sugar Act," and what were known generally as the "Acts of Trade," all aimed at the merchants of New England and New York. Out of this grew the "Writs of Assistance," which gave authority to search any house for merchandise liable to duty, and which were resisted in a celebrated argument by James Otis in 1761. Then came the "Declaratory Resolves" of 1764, which were the precursors of the "Stamp Act." The discussion occasioned by these measures was more important than any other immediate effect they produced; they afforded an academy of political education for the people. Those who had called themselves Whigs gradually took the name of Patriots, and from Patriots they became "Sons of Liberty." Every successive measure struck at once the double chord of patriotism and pocket, so that "Liberty and property" became the common cry. The colonists took the position, which is found everywhere in Otis's "Rights of the Colonies," that their claims were not dependent on the validity of their charters, but that their rights as British subjects were quite sufficient to protect them.

From this time forth the antagonism increased, and it so roused and united the people that the student wonders how it happened that the actual outbreak was delayed so long. It is quite remarkable, in view of the recognized differences among the colonies, that there should have been such unanimity in tone. There was hardly anything to choose, in point of weight and dignity, between the protests drawn up by Oxenbridge Thacher in Massachusetts, by Stephen Hopkins in Rhode Island, by the brothers Livingston in New York, and by Lee and Wythe in Virginia. The Southern colonies, which suffered least from the exactions of the home government, made common cause with those which suffered most. All the colonies claimed, in the words of the Virginia Assembly, "their ancient and indestructible right of being governed by such laws respecting their

LORD CHATHAM.
[After the picture by R. Brompton.]

internal polity and taxation as were derived from their own consent, with the approbation of their sovereign or his substitute."

The blow fell in 1765, with the Stamp Act—an act which would not have been unjust or unreasonable in England, and was only held so in America because it involved the principle of taxing where there was no representation. For a moment the colonies seemed stunned; then the bold protest of Patrick Henry in Virginia was taken up by James Otis in Massachusetts. He it was who proposed an "American Congress" in 1765, and though only nine out of the thirteen colonies sent delegates, this brought them nearer than ever before. It drew up its "Declaration of Rights." Then followed, in colony after colony, mobs and burnings in effigy; nobody dared to act as stamp officer. When the news reached England, the Earl of Chatham said: "The gentleman tells us that America is obstinate, America is almost in open rebellion. I rejoice that America has resisted." Then came the riot between people and soldiers, called the "Boston Massacre," in 1770, and the capture by the people of the armed British schooner *Gaspee*, off Rhode Island, in 1772. In 1773 the tea was thrown into the harbor at Boston; at Annapolis it was burned; at Charleston it was stored and left to spoil; at New York and Philadelphia it was returned. The next year came the Boston Port Bill, received with public mourning in the other colonies, and with grim endurance by the Bostonians. A thriving commercial city suddenly found itself unable to receive any vessel whose cargo had not been first landed at a port then thirty miles away by road —Marblehead—or to discharge any except through a customhouse at Plymouth, then forty miles by road in the other direction. All the industries of the place were stopped, and the price of fuel and provisions rose one-third; for every stick of wood and every barrel of molasses had to be landed first on the wharf at Marblehead, and then laboriously reshipped to Boston, or be sent on the long road by land. But as tyranny usually reacts upon itself, the voluntary contributions which came from all parts of the colonies to the suffering city did more to cement a common feeling than years of prosperity could have done.

In this chafed and oppressed position the people of Boston

THE "BOSTON MASSACRE."

awaited events, and the country looked on. Meanwhile the first Continental Congress had met at Philadelphia, September 5, 1774, with a sole view to procuring a redress of grievances, the people of every colony pledging themselves in one form or another to abide by the decision of this body. In July of that year, long before the thought of separation took shape even in the minds of the leaders, Ezra Stiles wrote this prophecy: "If oppression proceeds, despotism may originate an American Magna Charta and Bill of Rights, supported by such intrepid and persevering importunity as even sovereignty may hereafter judge it not wise to withstand. There will be a Runnymede in America." Such was the change from 1640 to 1774; the mother-country which to Hooke signified paradise, to Stiles signified oppression; the one clergyman wrote to deprecate war in England, the other almost invoked it in America.

The Congress met, every colony but little Georgia being soon represented. Its meeting signified that the colonies were at last united. In Patrick Henry's great opening speech he

BURNING OF THE "GASPEE."

said: "British oppression has effaced the boundaries of the several colonies; the distinctions between Virginians, Pennsylva-

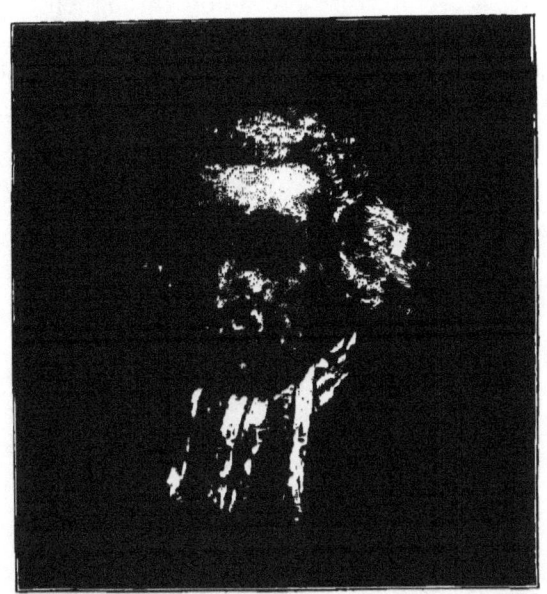

REV. EZRA STILES, D.D., LL.D., PRESIDENT OF YALE COLLEGE, 1777–1795.
[From the painting in the Trumbull Gallery, New Haven.]

nians, New-Yorkers, and New-Englanders are no more. I am not a Virginian, but an American."

There is, I think, an undue tendency in these days to exaggerate the differences between the colonies; and in bringing them to the eve of a great struggle it is needful to consider how far they were different, and how far they were one. In fact, the points of resemblance among the different colonies far exceeded the points of difference. They were mainly of the same English race; they were mainly Puritans in religion; they bore with them the local institutions and traditions; all held slaves, though in varying proportions. On the other hand, they were subject to certain variations of climate, pursuits, and local institutions; but, after all, these were secondary; the resemblances were more important.

The style of architecture prevailing throughout the colonies in the early part of the eighteenth century gives proof enough that the mode of living among the higher classes at that period must everywhere have been much the same. The same great square edifices, the same stacks of chimneys, the same tiles, the same mahogany stairways, and the same carving are still to be

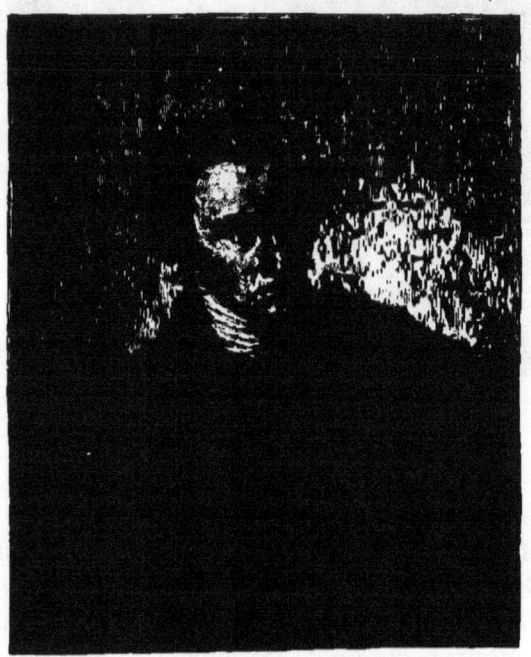

PATRICK HENRY.
[From the painting by Sully.]

seen in the old dwellings of Portsmouth, Newburyport, Salem, Boston, Newport, Philadelphia, Annapolis, and Norfolk. When Washington came from Mount Vernon to Cambridge as commander of the American army, he occupied as head-quarters a house resembling in many respects his own; and this was one of a line of similar houses, afterwards known as "Tory Row," and extending from Harvard College to Mount Auburn. These were but the types of the whole series of colonial or rather provincial houses, North and South. Sometimes they were built of wood, the oaken frames being brought from England, sometimes of bricks brought from Scotland, sometimes of stone. The chief difference between the Northern and Southern houses was that the chambers, being less important in a warm country, were less ample and comfortable in the Southern houses, and the windows were smaller, while for the same reason there was much more lavishness in the way of piazzas. Every one accustomed to the old Northern houses is surprised at the inadequate chambers of Mount Vernon, and it appears from the diary of Mr. Frost, a New England traveller in 1797, that he was then so struck with the smallness of the windows as to have made a note of it. The stairway at Arlington is singularly disproportioned to the external dignity of the house, and there is a tradition that at the funeral of Jefferson the stairway of his house at Monticello proved too narrow for the coffin, so that it had to be lowered from the window. All this was the result of the out-door climate, and apart from these trivial variations the life North and South was much the same—stately and ceremonious in the higher classes, with social distinctions much more thoroughly marked than we are now accustomed to remember.

We know by the private memoirs of the provincial period—for instance, from the charming recollections of Mrs. Quincy—that the costumes and manners of the upper classes were everywhere modelled on the English style of the period. Even after the war of independence, when the wealthier inhabitants of Boston had largely gone into exile at Halifax, the churches were still filled on important occasions with gentlemen wearing wigs, cocked hats, and scarlet cloaks; and before the Revolution the display must have been far greater. In Maryland, at a somewhat earlier period, we find an advertisement in the *Maryland Gazette* of a servant who offers himself "to wait on table, curry horses, clean knives, boots and shoes, lay a table, shave, and dress wigs, carry a lantern, and talk French; is as honest as the times will admit, and as sober as can be." From this standard of a servant's accomplishments we can easily infer the mode of life among the masters.

A striking illustration of these social demarcations is to be found in the general catalogues, now called "triennial," or "quinquennial," of our older colleges. Down to the year 1768 at Yale, and 1773 at Harvard, the students of each class will be found arranged in an order which is not alphabetical, as at the present day, but seems arbitrary. Not at all; they were arranged according to the social positions of their parents; and we know from the recollections of the venerable Paine Wingate that the first thing done by the college authorities on the admission of a new class was to ascertain by careful inquiry these facts. According to the result of the inquiry the young students were "placed" in the dining-hall and the recitation-room, and upon this was also based the choice of college rooms. Had they always retained this relative standing it would have been less galling, but while the most distinguished student could not rise in the list, the reprobates could fall; and the best scholar in the class might find himself not merely in a low position through his parentage, but flanked on each side by scions of more famed families who had been degraded by their own folly or vice. There could not be a more conclusive proof that American provincial society, even in the Eastern colonies, was founded, before the final separation from England, on an essentially aristocratic basis.

In the same connection it must be remembered that in the eighteenth century slavery gave the tone of manners through all the colonies. No matter how small the proportion of slaves, experience shows that it affected the whole habit of society.

AN OUT-OF-DOOR TEA-PARTY IN COLONIAL NEW ENGLAND.

In Massachusetts, in 1775, there was probably a population of some 350,000, of whom but 5000 were slaves. It was enough; the effect followed. It was in Cambridge, Massachusetts, not in Virginia, that Longfellow found his tradition of the lady who was buried by her own order with slave attendants:

> "At her feet and at her head
> Lies a slave to attend the dead;
> But their dust is as white as hers."

It is curious to compare the command of this dying woman of the Vassall race—whether it was an act of arrogance or of humility—with the self-humiliation of a Virginia dame of the same period, who directed the burial of her body beneath that portion of the church occupied by the poor, since she had despised them in life, and wished them to trample upon her when dead. Let us consider, by way of further illustration, the way of living on the Narraganset shore of Rhode Island, and see how closely it resembled that of Virginia.

The late venerable Isaac Peace Hazard, of Newport, Rhode Island, told me that his great-grandfather, Robert Hazard, of Narraganset, used in later life, when he had given away many of his farms to his children, to congratulate himself on the small limits to which he had reduced his household, having only seventy in parlor and kitchen. He occupied at one time nearly twelve thousand acres of land, and kept some four thousand sheep, from whose fleece his large household was almost wholly clothed. He had in his dairy twelve negro women, all slaves, and each having a young girl to assist her; each dairy-maid had the care of twelve cows, and they were expected to make from one to two dozen cheeses every day. This was the agricultural and domestic side; the social life consisted of one long series of gay entertainments, visiting from house to house, fox-hunting and horse-racing with the then famous breed of Narraganset pacers. Mr. Isaac Hazard had known old men who in their youth had gone to Virginia to ride their own horses at races, and kept open house for the Virginia riders in return. To illustrate how thoroughly the habits of slavery were infused into the daily life, he told me that another of these Narraganset magnates, his great-uncle, Rowland Robinson, said, impulsively, one day, "I have not servants enough; go fetch me some from Guinea." Upon this the master of a small packet of twenty tons, belonging to Mr. Robinson, fitted her out at once, set sail for Guinea, and brought home eighteen slaves, one of whom was a king's son. His employer burst into tears on their arrival, his order not having been seriously given. But all this was not in Maryland or Virginia; it was in Rhode Island, and on a part of Rhode Island so much a place of resort for the leading Boston families that a portion of it is called Boston Neck to this day.

These descriptions could be paralleled, though not fully, in all the Northern colonies. The description of the Schuyler family, and of their way of living at Albany, as given by Mrs. Grant of Laggan, about 1750, is quite on a par with these early scenes at Narraganset. In Connecticut it is recorded of John Peters, father of the early and malicious historian of that name, that he "aped the style of a British nobleman, built his house in a forest, kept his coach, and looked with some degree of scorn upon republicans." The stone house of the Lee family at Marblehead cost £10,000; the house of Godfrey Malbone at Newport cost £20,000; the Wentworth house at Portsmouth had fifty-two rooms. Through all the colonies these evidences of a stately way of living were to be found.

These facts are unquestionable, and would not so fully have passed out of sight but for another fact never yet fully explained. When the war of independence came it made no social change in the Southern provinces, but it made a social revolution in the Northern provinces. For some reason, perhaps only for the greater nearness to Nova Scotia, the gentry of New England took the loyal side and fled, while the gentry of Virginia fell in with the new movement, becoming its leaders. From my window, as I write, I have glimpses of some of the large houses of "Tory Row," in Cambridge, where, according to the contemporary description of the Baroness Riedesel, seven kindred families lived in the greatest luxury until the Revolution, all probably slave-holders, like the Vassalls, and some of them owning plantations in Jamaica. All fled, most of their estates were confiscated, and the war transferred the leadership of the New England colonies, as Professor Sumner has lately well shown in his "Life of Jackson," to a new race of young lawyers. Hence all the ante-Revolutionary life disappeared, and was soon forgotten; slavery disappeared also, while the self-same social order still subsisted in Virginia, though constantly decaying, until a more recent war brought that also to an end.

There was thus less of social difference among the colonies than is often assumed, but the difference in municipal institutions was considerable. Every colony, so far as it was left free to do it, recognized the principle of popular government, limiting the suffrage by age, sex, race, or property, but recognizing the control of a majority of qualified electors as binding. As a rule, this gave a political status to the laboring class in the Northern colonies, but not in those where slavery prevailed and the laboring class was of a different race. We naturally do not obtain from the books of the period so clear a picture of the lower order of inhabitants as of the higher; perhaps the liveliest is to be found in the description of General Riedesel, where he represents the yeomen of New England as being thickset, tolerably tall, wearing blue frocks girt by a strap, and having their heads surmounted by yellow wigs, "with the honorable visage of a magistrate beneath;" as being, moreover, rarely able to write; inquisitive, curious, and zealous to madness for liberty. These were the people—as seen, be it remembered, through the vexed eyes of a defeated prisoner —who made up the citizenship of the Northern colonies.

It is certain that the general model for the Colonial governments, and even for our present State governments, dates back to the organization of the Virginia House of Burgesses, in 1619; and all the colonies followed the same principle, with some important modifications. But when it came to the government of small local communities there was a great variation. The present system of New England town government had its beginning, according to Professor Joel Parker, in the action of the inhabitants of Charlestown, Massachusetts, when they adopted, on February 10, 1634–35, an order, which still stands on the record-book, "for the governm't of the Towne by Selectmen," thus giving to eleven persons, "wth the advice of Pastor and teacher desired in any case of conscience," the authority to manage their local affairs for one year. Since Professor Parker wrote, however, the researches of the Boston Record Commission have brought to light a similar grant of power by the planters of Dorchester (Oct. 8, 1633), authorizing twelve men, "selected of the company" to have charge of its affairs. This form of self-government, which could be perfectly combined with the existence of slavery on a small scale, was inconsistent with a system of great plantations, like those in the Southern colonies; and it was this fact more than anything else which developed such difference in character as really existed. The other fact that labor was held in more respect in the Northern colonies than in the Southern had doubtless something to do with it; but, after all, there was then less philosophizing on that subject than now, and the main influence was the town meeting. When John Adams was called upon by Major Langbourne to explain the difference of character between Virginia and New England, Mr. Adams offered to give him a receipt for creating a New England in Virginia. It consisted of four points, "town meetings, training-days, town schools, and ministers." Each colony really based its local institutions, in some form, on English traditions; but the system of town government, as it prevailed in the Eastern colonies, has struck deepest root, and has largely influenced the new civilization of the West. Thus, with varied preparation, but with a common need and an increasing unity, the several colonies approached the 19th of April, 1775, when the shot was fired that was "heard round the world."

X.

THE DAWNING OF INDEPENDENCE.

WHEN France, in 1763, surrendered Canada to England, it suddenly opened men's eyes to a very astonishing fact. They discovered that British America had at once become a country so large as to make England seem ridiculously small. Even the cool-headed Dr. Franklin, writing that same year to Mary Stevenson in London, spoke of England as "that petty island which, compared to America, is but a stepping-stone in a brook, scarce enough of it above water to keep one's shoes dry." The far-seeing French statesmen of the period looked at the matter in the same way. Choiseul, the Prime-minister who ceded Canada, claimed afterwards that he had done it in order to destroy the British nation by creating for it a rival. This assertion was not made till ten years later, and may very likely have been an after-thought, but it was destined to be confirmed by the facts.

We have now to deal with the outbreak of a contest which was, according to the greatest of the English statesmen of the period, "a most accursed, wicked, barbarous, cruel, unnatural, unjust, and diabolical war." No American writer ever employed to describe it a combination of adjectives so vigorous as those here brought together by the elder Pitt, afterwards Lord Chatham. The rights for which Americans fought seemed to them to be the common rights of Englishmen, and many Englishmen thought the same. On the other hand, we are now able to do justice to the position of those American loyalists who honestly believed that the attempt at independence was a mad one, and who sacrificed all they had rather than rebel against their King. "The annals of the world," wrote Massachusettensis, the ablest Tory pamphleteer in America, "have not been deformed with a single instance of so unnatural, so causeless, so wanton, so wicked a rebellion." When we compare this string of epithets employed upon the one side with those of Pitt upon the other, we see that the war at the outset was not so much a contest of nations as of political principles. Some of the ablest men in England defended the American cause; some of the ablest in the colonies took the loyal side.

Boston in the winter of 1774-75 was a town of some 17,000 inhabitants, garrisoned by some 3000 British troops. It was the only place in the Massachusetts colony where the royal governor exercised any real authority, and where the laws of Parliament had any force. The result was that its life was paralyzed, its people gloomy, and its commerce dead. The other colonies were still hoping to obtain their rights by policy or by legislation, by refusing to import or to consume, and they watched with constant solicitude for some riotous demonstration in Boston. On the other hand, the popular leaders in that town were taking the greatest pains that there should be no outbreak. There was risk of one whenever soldiers were sent on any expedition into the country. One might have taken place at Marshfield in January, one almost happened at Salem in February, yet still it was postponed. No publicity was given to the patriotic military organizations in Boston; as little as possible was said about the arms and stores that were gathered in the country. Not a life had been lost in any popular excitement since the Boston Massacre in 1770. The responsibility of the first shot, the people were determined, must rest upon the royal troops. So far was this carried that it was honestly attributed by the British soldiers to cowardice alone. An officer, quoted by

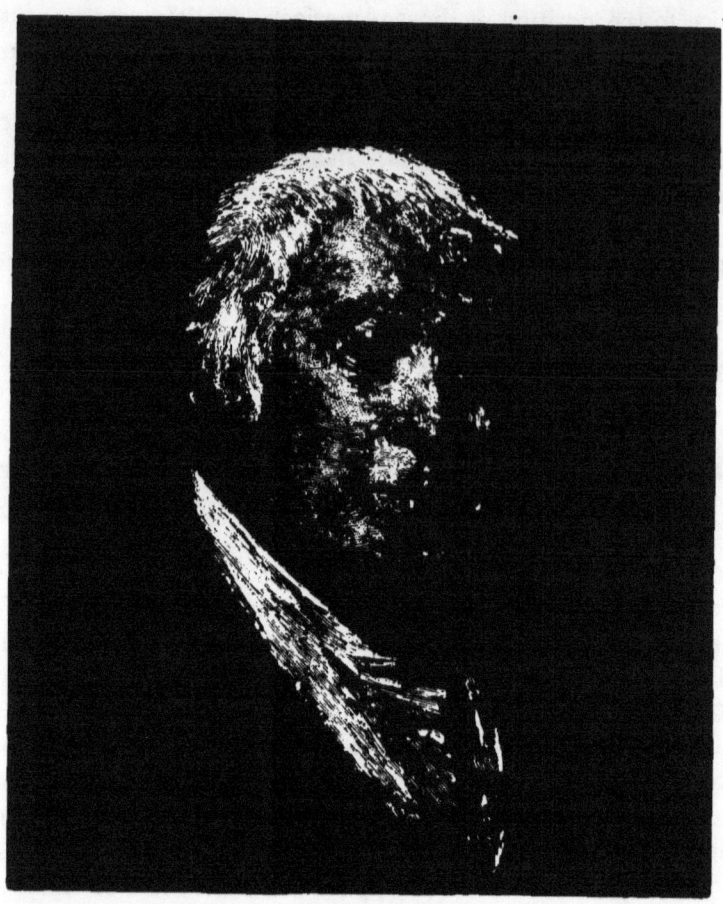

PAUL REVERE.

Frothingham, wrote home in November, 1774: "As to what you hear of their taking arms to resist the force of England, it is mere bullying, and will go no farther than words; whenever it comes to blows, he that can run the fastest will think himself best off; believe me, any two regiments here ought to be decimated if they did not beat in the field the whole force of the Massachusetts province; for though they are numerous, they are but a mere mob, without order or discipline, and very awkward at handling their arms."

But whatever may have been the hope of carrying their point without fighting, the provincial authorities were steadily collecting provisions, arms, and ammunition. Unhappily these essentials were hard to obtain. On April 19, 1775, the committees of safety could only count up twelve field-pieces in Massachusetts; and there had been collected in that colony 21,549 fire-arms, 17,441 pounds of powder, 22,191 pounds of ball, 144,699 flints, 10,108 bayonets, 11,979 pouches, 15,000 canteens. There were also 17,000 pounds of salt fish, 35,000 pounds of rice, with large quantities of beef and pork. Viewed as an evidence of the forethought of the colonists, these statistics are remarkable; but there was something heroic and indeed almost pathetic in the project of going to war with the British government on the strength of twelve field-pieces and seventeen thousand pounds of salt fish.

Yet when, on the night of the 18th of April, 1775, Paul Revere rode beneath the bright moonlight through Lexington to Concord, with Dawes and Prescott for comrades, he was carrying the signal for the independence of a nation. He had seen across the Charles River the two lights from the church-steeple in Boston which were to show that a British force was going out to seize the patriotic supplies at Concord; he had warned Hancock and Adams at Rev. Jonas Clark's parsonage in Lexington, and had rejected Sergeant Monroe's caution against unnecessary noise, with the rejoinder, "You'll have noise enough here before long—the regulars are coming out." As he galloped on his way the regulars were advancing with steady step behind him, soon warned of their own danger by alarm-bells and signal-guns. When Revere was captured by some British officers who happened to be near Concord, Colonel Smith, the commander of the expedition, had already halted, ordered Pitcairn forward, and sent back prudently for reinforcements. It was a night of terror to all the neighboring Middlesex towns, for no one knew what excesses the angry British troops might commit on their return march. The best picture we have of this alarm is in the narrative of a Cambridge woman, Mrs. Hannah Winthrop, describing "the horrors of that midnight cry," as she calls it. The women of that town were roused by the beat of drums and ringing of bells; they hastily gathered their children together and fled to the outlying farmhouses; seventy or eighty of them were at Fresh Pond, within hearing of the guns at Menotomy, now Arlington. The next day their husbands bade them flee to Andover, whither the college property had been sent, and thither they went, alternately walking and riding, over fields where the bodies of the slain lay unburied.

Before 5 A.M. on April 19, 1775, the British troops had reached Lexington Green, where thirty-eight men, under Captain Parker, stood up before six hundred or eight hundred to be shot at, their captain saying, " Don't fire unless you are fired on; but if they want a war, let it begin here." It began there; they were fired upon; they fired rather ineffectually in return, while seven were killed and nine wounded. The rest, after retreating, reformed and pursued the British towards Concord, capturing seven stragglers—the first prisoners taken in the war. Then followed the fight at Concord, where four hundred and fifty Americans, instead of thirty-eight, were rallied to meet the British. The fighting took place between two detachments at the North Bridge, where

> "once the embattled farmers stood,
> And fired the shot heard round the world."

There the American captain, Isaac Davis, was killed at the first shot—he who had said, when his company was placed at the head of the little column, " I haven't a man that is afraid to go."

LEXINGTON GREEN.—"IF THEY WANT A WAR, LET IT BEGIN HERE."

He fell, and Major Buttrick gave the order, "Fire! for God's sake, fire!" in return. The British detachment retreated in disorder, but their main body was too strong to be attacked, so they disabled a few cannon, destroyed some barrels of flour, cut down the liberty-pole, set fire to the court-house, and then began their return march. It ended in a flight; they were exposed to a constant guerilla fire; minute-men flocked behind every tree and house; and only the foresight of Colonel Smith in sending for reinforcements had averted a surrender. At 2 P.M., near Lexington, Percy with his troops met the returning fugitives, and formed a hollow square, into which they ran and threw themselves on the ground exhausted. Then Percy in turn fell back. Militia still came pouring in from Dorchester, Milton, Dedham, as well as the nearer towns. A company from Danvers marched sixteen miles in four hours. The Americans lost ninety-three in killed, wounded, and missing that day; the British, two hundred and seventy-three. But the important result was that every American colony now recognized that war had begun.

DR. JOSEPH WARREN.

How men's minds were affected may best be seen by a glimpse at a day in the life of one leading patriot. Early on the morning of the 19th of April, 1775, a messenger came hastily to the door of Dr. Joseph Warren, physician, in Boston, and chairman of the Boston Committee of Safety, with the news that there had been fighting at Lexington and Concord. Dr. Warren, doing first the duty that came nearest, summoned his pupil, Mr. Eustis, and directed him to take care of his patients for that day; then mounted his horse and rode to the Charlestown Ferry. As he entered the boat he remarked to an acquaintance: "Keep up a brave heart. They have begun it—that, either party can do; and we'll end it—that, only we can do." After landing in Charlestown he met a certain Dr. Welch, who says, in a manuscript statement: "Eight o'clock in the morning saw Dr. Joseph Warren just come out of Boston, horseback. I said, 'Well, they

GENERAL WILLIAM HEATH.

are gone out.' 'Yes,' he said, 'and we will be up with them before night.'" Apparently the two physicians jogged on together, tried to pass Lord Percy's column of reinforcements, but were stopped by bayonets. Then Dr. Welch went home, and Dr. Warren probably attended a meeting of the Committee of Safety, held "at the Black Horse in Menotomy," or West Cambridge. This committee had authority from the Provincial Congress to order out the militia, and General Heath, who was a member of the committee, rode to take command of the provincials, with Warren by his side, who was sufficiently exposed that day to have a musket-ball strike the pin out of the hair of his ear-lock. The two continued together till the British army had crossed Charlestown Neck on its retreat, and made a stand on Bunker Hill. There they were covered by the ships. The militia were ordered to pursue no further, and General Heath held the first council of war of the Revolution at the foot of Prospect Hill.

With the fervor of that day's experience upon him Warren wrote, on the day following, this circular to the town in behalf of the Committee of Safety. The original still exists in the Massachusetts archives, marked with much interlineation.

"GENTLEMEN,—The barbarous murders committed on our innocent brethren on Wednesday, the 19th instant, have made it absolutely necessary that we immediately raise an army to defend our wives and our children from the butchering hands of an inhuman soldiery, who, incensed at the obstacles they met with in their bloody progress, and enraged at being repulsed from the field of slaughter, will without the least doubt take the first opportunity in their power to ravage this devoted country with fire and sword. We conjure you, therefore, by all that is dear, by all that is sacred, that you give all assistance possible in forming an army. Our all is at stake. Death and devastation are the instant consequences of delay. Every moment is infinitely precious. An hour lost may deluge your country in blood, and entail perpetual slavery upon the few of your posterity who may survive the carnage. We beg and entreat, as you will answer to your country, to your own consciences, and, above all, as you will answer to God himself, that you will hasten and encourage by all possible means the enlistment of men to form the army, and send them forward to headquarters at Cambridge with that expedition which the vast importance and instant urgency of the affair demand."

It is always hard to interpret the precise condition of public feeling just before a war. It is plain that the Massachusetts committee expected something more than a contest of words when they made so many preparations. On the other hand, it is evident that hardly any one looked forward to any serious and prolonged strife. Dr. Warren wrote, soon after the 19th of April: "The people never seemed in earnest about the matter until after the engagement of the 19th ult., and I verily be-

FAC-SIMILE OF WARREN'S ADDRESS.

lieve that the night preceding the barbarous outrages committed by the soldiery at Lexington, Concord, etc., there were not fifty people in the whole colony that ever expected any blood would be shed in the contest between us and Great Britain."

Yet two days after the fight at Lexington the Massachusetts Committee of Safety resolved to enlist eight thousand men. Two days after that the news reached New York at noon. There was a popular outbreak; the royal troops were disarmed, the fort and magazines seized, and two transports for Boston unloaded. At five on Monday afternoon the tidings reached Philadelphia, when the bell in Independence Hall was rung, and the people gathered in numbers. When it got so far as Charleston, South Carolina, the people seized the arsenal, and the Provincial Congress proclaimed them "ready to sacrifice their lives and fortunes." In Savannah, Georgia, a mob took possession of the powder-magazine, and raised a liberty-pole. In Kentucky a party of hunters, hearing of the battle, gave their encampment the name of Lexington, which it still bears; and thus the news went on.

Meanwhile, on May 10th, the Continental Congress convened, and on the same day Ethan Allen took possession of the strong fortress of Ticonderoga. It was the first act of positive aggression by the patriotic party, for at both Lexington and Concord they were acting on the defensive. The expedition was planned in Connecticut and reinforced in Western Massachusetts, but the main reliance was to be placed on Ethan Allen and his "Green Mountain Boys," whose daring and energy were already well known. Benedict Arnold, who had been commissioned in Massachusetts for the same purpose, arrived only in time to join the expedition as a volunteer. On May 10, 1775, eighty-three men crossed the lake with Allen. When they had landed, he warned them that it was a dangerous enterprise, and called for volunteers. Every man volunteered. The rest took but a few moments. They entered with a war-whoop the open wicket-gate, pressing by the sentinel, and when the half-clad commander appeared and asked their authority, Allen answered with the words that have become historic, " In the name of the great Jehovah and the Continental Congress."

The Congress was only to meet that day, but it appeared already to be exercising a sort of antenatal authority; and a fortress which had cost eight million pounds sterling and many lives was placed in its hands by a mere stroke of boldness. Crown Point gave itself up with equal ease to Seth Warner, and another dramatic surprise was given to the new-born nation.

In the neighborhood of Boston the month of May was devoted to additional preparations, and to what are called, in the old stage directions of Shakespeare's plays, "alarums and excursions." At one time, when a sally from Boston was expected, the Committee of Safety ordered the officers of the ten nearest towns to assemble one-half the militia and all the minute-men, and march to Roxbury. While this was being done, General Thomas, with an ingenuity quite in the style of the above stage motto, marched his seven hundred men round and round a high hill, visible from Boston, to mislead the British. At another time, when men were more numerous, General Putnam marched all the troops in Cambridge, twenty-two hundred in number, to Charlestown Ferry, the column being spread over a mile and a half, and passing under the guns of the British without attack. At another time, "all of Weymouth, Braintree, and Hingham," according to Mrs. Adams, turned out to drive away a British detachment from Grape Island, where the Americans then landed, burned a quantity of hay, and brought away cattle. A larger skirmish took place at Noddle's Island, now East Boston, where the Americans destroyed a schooner, dismantled a sloop, and captured twelve swivels and four 4-pound cannon. Putnam commanded in this engagement, and the enthusiasm which it called out secured his unanimous election as major-general.

Meantime the Provincial troops were gathering for what the *Essex Gazette*, of June 8th, called, with rather premature admiration, "the grand American army"—an army whose returns for June 9th showed 7644 men. "Nothing could be in a more confused state," wrote Dr. Eliot, "than the army which first assembled at Cambridge. This undisciplined body of men were kept together by a few who deserved well of their country." President John Adams, writing long after (June 19, 1818), thus summed up the condition of these forces:

> "The army at Cambridge was not a national army, for there was no nation. It was not a United States army, for there were no United States. It was not an army of united colonies, for it could not be said in any sense that the colonies were united. The centre of their union, the Congress of Philadelphia, had not adopted nor acknowledged the army at Cambridge. It was not a New England army, for New England had not associated. New England had no legal legislature, nor any common executive authority, even upon the principles of original authority, or even of original power in the people. Massachusetts had her army, Connecticut her army, New Hampshire her army, and Rhode Island her army. These four armies met at Cambridge, and imprisoned the British army in Boston. But who was the sovereign of this united, or rather congregated, army, and who its commander-in-chief? It had none. Putnam, Poor, and Greene were as independent of Ward as Ward was of them."

This was the state of the forces outside, while the army inside was impatiently waiting for reinforcements, and chafing at the ignoble delay. On May 25th three British generals (Howe, Clinton, and Burgoyne) arrived with troops. The newspapers of the day say that when these officers were going into Boston harbor they met a packet coming out, when General Burgoyne asked the skipper of the packet what news there was. And being told that the town was surrounded by ten thousand country people, asked how many regulars there were in Boston; and being answered, "About five thousand," cried out, with astonishment, "What! and ten thousand peasants keep five thousand king's troops shut up! Well, let us get in, and we'll soon find elbow-room." After this conversation the nickname of "Elbow-room" was permanently fastened on General Burgoyne. He used to relate that after his reverses, while a prisoner of war, he was received with great courtesy by the people of Boston as he stepped from the Charlestown ferry-boat, but was a little annoyed when an old lady, perched on a shed above the crowd, cried out, in a shrill voice, "Make way! make way! The general's coming; give him elbow-room."

Two days before the battle of Bunker Hill, Mrs. Adams wrote to her husband, John Adams: "Gage's proclamation you will receive by this conveyance, and the records of time cannot produce a blacker page. Satan when driven from the realms of bliss exhibited not more malice. Surely the father of lies is superseded. Yet we think it the best proclamation he could have issued." This proclamation announced martial law, but offered pardon to those who would give in their allegiance to the government, "excepting only from the benefit of such pardon Samuel Adams and John Hancock, whose offences are of too flagitious a nature to admit of any other consideration than that of condign punishment." He afterwards remarked that the rebels added "insult to outrage" as, "with a preposterous parade of military arrangement, they affected to hold the army besieged."

Two things contributed to bring about the battle of Bunker Hill: the impatience of British troops under the "affectation" of a siege; on the other hand, the great increase of self-confidence among the provincials after Lexington and Concord. It was a military necessity, no doubt, for each side, to occupy the Charlestown heights; but there was also a growing disposition to bring matters to a crisis on the first favorable opportunity. Captain (afterwards Lord) Harris wrote home to England (June 12th): "I wish the Americans may be brought to a sense of their duty. One good drubbing, which I long to give them by way of retaliation, might have a good effect towards it." Dr. Warren, on the other hand, wrote (May 16th) that if General Gage would only make a sally from Boston, he would "gratify thousands who impatiently wait to avenge the blood of their murdered countrymen." With such dispositions on both sides, the collision could not be far off. Kinglake says that the reasons for a battle rarely seem conclusive except to a general who

THE DAWNING OF INDEPENDENCE. 255

has some positive taste for fighting. Had not something of this impulse existed on both sides in 1775, the American rebels would probably not have fortified Bunker Hill, or the English general might have besieged and starved them out without firing a shot.

SAMUEL ADAMS.

It is needless to add another to the innumerable descriptions of the battle of Bunker Hill. Every Englishman who comes to America feels renewed astonishment that a monument should have been built on the scene of a defeat. Every American school-boy understands that the monument celebrates a fact more important than most victories, namely, that the raw provincials faced the British army for two hours, they themselves being under so little organization that it is impossible to tell even at this day who was their commander; that they did this with only the protection of an unfinished earthwork and a rail fence, retreating only when their powder was out. Tried by the standards of regular warfare even at that day, a breastwork twice that of Bunker Hill would have been accounted but a moderate obstacle. When in the previous century the frightened citizens of Dorchester, England, had asked a military engineer whether their breastworks could resist Prince Rupert's soldiers, he answered, " I have seen them running up walls twenty feet high; these defences of yours may possibly keep them out half an hour." The flimsy defences of Bunker Hill kept back General Howe's soldiers for two hours, and until the untried provincials had fired their last shot. It was a fact worth a monument.

The best descriptions of the battle itself are to be found in the letters of provincial officers and soldiers preserved in the appendix to Richard Frothingham's "Siege of Boston." It is the descriptions of raw soldiers that are always most graphic; as they grow more familiar with war, their narratives grow tame. It is a sufficient proof of the impression made in England by the affair that the newspapers of that nation, instead of being exultant, were indignant or apologetic, and each had its own theory in regard to "the innumerable errors of that day," as the London *Chronicle* called them. Tried by this test of contemporary criticism, the Americans do not seem to have exaggerated the real importance of the event. " The ministerial troops gained the hill," wrote William Tudor to John Adams, "but were victorious losers. A few more such victories, and they are undone." By the official accounts these troops lost in killed and wounded 1054—about one in four of their number, including an unusually large proportion of officers—while the Americans lost but half as many, about 450, out of a total of from two to three thousand. But the numbers were nothing; the fact that the provincials had resisted regular troops was everything.

The "great American army" was still growing at Cambridge; it had been adopted by Congress, even before the battle, and George Washington, of Virginia, had been unanimously placed in command, by recommendation of the New England delegates. He assumed this authority beneath the historic elm-tree at Cambridge, July 3, 1775. On the 9th he held a council of war of the newly organized general officers. The whole force was still from New England, and consisted of 16,770 infantry and 585 artillerymen. These were organized in three divisions, each comprising two brigades, usually of six regiments each. They had a long series of posts to garrison, and they had nine rounds of ammunition per man. Worst of all, they were still, in the words of Washington, "a mixed multitude of people, under very little discipline." Their whole appearance under the new organization may be best seen from the contemporary description by the Rev. William Emerson, grandfather of our great poet and essayist:

"There is great overturning in the camp, as to order and regularity. New lords, new laws. The Generals Washington and Lee are upon the lines every day. New orders from his Excellency are read to the respective regiments every morning after prayers. The strictest government is taking place, and great distinction is made between officers and soldiers. Every one is made to know his place, and keep in it, or be tied up and receive thirty or forty lashes, according to his crime. Thousands are at work every day from four till eleven o'clock in the morning. It is surprising how much work has been done. The lines are extended almost from Cambridge to Mystic River, so that very soon it will be morally impossible for the enemy to get between the works, except in one place, which is supposed to be left purposely unfortified to entice the enemy out of their fortresses. Who would have thought, twelve months past, that all Cambridge and Charlestown would be covered over with American camps and cut up into forts and intrenchments, and all the lands, fields, orchards, laid common —horses and cattle feeding in the choicest mowing land, whole fields of corn eaten down to the ground, and large parks of well-regulated locusts cut down for firewood and other public uses! This, I must say, looks a little melancholy. My quarters are at the foot of the famous Prospect Hill, where such great preparations are made for the reception of the enemy. It is very diverting to walk among the camps. They are as different in their form as the owners are in their dress; and every tent is a portraiture of the temper and taste of the persons who encamp in it. Some are made of boards, and some of sail-cloth. Some partly of one, and some partly of the other. Again, others are made of stone and turf, brick or brush. Some are thrown up in a hurry; others curiously wrought with doors and windows, done with wreaths and withes, in the manner of a basket. Some are your proper tents and marquees, looking like the regular camp of the enemy. In these are the Rhode-Islanders, who are furnished with tent equipage and everything in the most exact English style. However, I think this great variety is rather a beauty than a blemish in the army."

All that was experienced on both sides at the beginning of the late American civil war, in respect to rawness of soldiery, inexperienced officers, short enlistments, local jealousies, was equally known in the early Continental army, and was less easily remedied. Even the four New England colonies that supplied the first troops were distrustful of one another and of Washington, and this not without some apparent reason. In a state of society which, as has been shown, was essentially aristocratic, they had suddenly lost their leaders. Nearly one-third of the community, including almost all those to whom social deference had been paid, had taken what they called the loyal, and others the Tory, side. Why should this imported Virginian be more trustworthy? Washington in turn hardly did justice to the material with which he had to deal. He found that in Massachusetts, unlike Virginia, the gentry were loyal to the King; those with whom he had to consult were mainly farmers and mechanics—a class such as hardly existed in Virginia, and which was then far rougher and less intelligent than the same class now is. They were obstinate, suspicious, jealous. They had lost their natural leaders, the rich men, the royal councillors, the judges, and had to take up with new and improvised guides—physicians like Warren—" Doctor-general" Warren, as the British officers called him,—or skilled mechanics like Paul Revere, or unemployed lawyers and business men like those whom Governor Shirley described as "that brace of Adamses." The few men of property and consequence who stood by them, as Hancock and Prescott, were the exceptions. There were few on the patriotic side of whom it could be said, as Hutchinson said of Oxenbridge Thacher, " He was not born a plebeian, but he was resolved to die one." Their line officers were men taken almost at random from among themselves, sometimes turning out admirably, sometimes shamefully. Washington cashiered a colonel and five captains for cowardice or dishonesty during the first summer. The Continental army as it first assembled in Cambridge was, as was said of another army on a later occasion, an aggregation of town-meetings, and, which is worse, of town-meetings from which all the accustomed leaders had suddenly been swept away. No historian has yet fully portrayed the extent to which this social revolution in New England embarrassed all the early period of the war, or shown how it made the early Continental troops chafe under Washington and Schuyler, and prefer in their secret souls to be led by General Putnam, whom they could call "Old Put," and who rode to battle in his shirt-sleeves.

And, on the other hand, we can now see that there was some foundation for these criticisms on Washington. With the highest principle and the firmest purpose, his views of military government were such as no American army in these days would endure for a month. His methods were simply despotic. He thought that the Massachusetts Provincial Legislature should impress men into the Revolutionary army, should provide them with food and clothes only, not with pay, and should do nothing for their families. He himself, having declined the offered $500 per month, served his country for his expenses only, and so, he thought, should they, overlooking the difference between those whose households depended only on themselves, and those who, like himself, had left slaves at work on their broad plantations. He thought that officers and men should be taken from different social classes, that officers should have power almost absolute, and that camp offences should be punished by the lash. These imperial methods produced a good effect, on the whole; probably it was best that the general should err on one side if the army erred on the other. But there is no doubt that much of the discontent, the desertion, the uncertain enlistments, of the next two years proceeded from the difficulty found by Washington in adapting himself to the actual condition of the people, especially the New England people. It is the highest proof of his superiority that he overcame not merely all other obstacles, but even his own mistakes.

Such as it was, the army remained in camp long enough to make everybody impatient. The delay was inevitable; it was easier to provide even discipline than powder; the troops kept going and coming because of short enlistments, and more than once the whole force was reduced to ten thousand men. With that patience which was one of Washington's strongest military qualities he withstood dissatisfaction within and criticism from without until the time had come to strike a heavier blow. Then, in a single night, he fortified Dorchester Heights, and this forced the evacuation of Boston. The British generals had to seek elbow-room elsewhere. They left Boston March 17, 1776, taking with them twelve hundred American loyalists, the bulk of what called itself "society" in New England. The navy went to Halifax, the army to New York, whither Washington soon took his Continental army also. Once there, he found new obstacles. From the very fact that they had not sent away their loyalists, there was less of unanimity among the New York people, nor had they been so well trained by the French and Indian wars. The New England army was now away from home; it was unused to marches or evolutions, but it had learned some confidence in itself and in its commander, though it did not always do credit to either. It was soon reinforced by troops from the Middle States, but a period of disaster fol-

SERGEANT JASPER AT THE BATTLE OF FORT MOULTRIE.

lowed, which severely tested the generalship of Washington. He no longer had, as in Massachusetts, all the loyalists shut up in the opposing camp; he found them scattered through the community. Long Island was one of their strongholds, and received the Continental army much less cordially than the British army was received at Staten Island. The Hudson River was debatable ground between opposing factions; Washington's own military family held incipient traitors. The outlook was not agreeable in any direction, at least in the Northern colonies, where the chief contest lay.

There was a disastrous advance into Canada, under Montgomery and Arnold, culminating in the defeat before Quebec December 30, 1775, and the retreat conducted the next spring by Thomas and Sullivan. It was clearly a military repulse, but it was a great comfort to John Adams, looking from the remoteness of Philadelphia, to attribute all to a quite subordinate cause. "Our misfortunes in Canada," he wrote to his wife, June 26, 1776, "are enough to melt a heart of stone. The small-pox is ten times more terrible than Britons, Canadians, and Indians together. This was the cause of our precipitate retreat from Quebec." Thus was disappointment slightly mitigated; but in the Carolinas, about the same time, it was the British who were disappointed, and the defence of Fort Moultrie especially gave comfort to all the patriotic party. It was a brilliant achievement, where the fate of Charleston and the Carolinas was determined by the defence of a fortress of palmetto logs, manned by less than five hundred men, under Moultrie, aided by Motte, Marion, and the since-renowned Sergeant Jasper. They had thirty-one cannon, but only a scanty supply of powder. Over them waved a flag of blue, with a crescent inscribed "Liberty." Against them was a squadron of British ships, some of them carrying fifty guns; and they defended themselves so successfully for ten hours that the British invasion was checked and then abandoned. This happened on June 28, 1776, just in time to counteract the discouragement that came from the fatal Canadian campaign.

The encouragement was needed. Just before the time when the Continental Congress had begun its preliminary work on the great Declaration, General Joseph Reed, the newly appointed adjutant-general, and one of Washington's most trusted associates, was writing thus from the field:

"With an army of force before, and a secret one behind, we stand on a point of land with six thousand old troops, if a year's service of about half can entitle them to this name, and about fifteen hundred raw levies of the province, many disaffected and more doubtful. Every man, from the general to the private, acquainted with our true situation, is exceedingly discouraged. Had I known the true posture of affairs, no consideration would have tempted me to take part in this scene; and this sentiment is universal."

XI.

THE GREAT DECLARATION.

IN the days of the Continental Congress the delegates used to travel to the capital, at the beginning of each session, from their several homes, usually on horseback; fording streams, sleeping at miserable country inns, sometimes weather-bound for days, sometimes making circuits to avoid threatened dangers, sometimes accomplishing forced marches to reach Philadelphia in time for some special vote. There lie before me the unpublished papers of one of the signers of the great Declaration, and these papers comprise the diaries of several such journeys. Their simple records rarely include bursts of patriotism or predictions of national glory, but they contain many plaintive chronicles of bad beds and worse food, mingled with pleasant glimpses of wayside chat, and now and then a bit of character-painting that recalls the jovial narratives of Fielding. Sometimes they give a passing rumor of "the glorious news of the surrendering of the Colonel of the Queen's Dragoons with his whole army," but more commonly they celebrate "milk toddy and bread and butter" after a wetting, or "the best dish of Bohea tea I have drank for a twelvemonth." When they arrived at Philadelphia, the delegates put up their horses, changed their riding gear for those garments which Trumbull has immortalized, and gathered to Independence Hall to greet their brother delegates, to interchange the gossip of the day, to repeat Dr. Franklin's last

TRUMBULL'S "SIGNING OF THE DECLARATION."

anecdote or Francis Hopkinson's last joke; then proceeding, when the business of the day was opened, to lay the foundation for a new nation.

"Before the 19th of April, 1775," said Jefferson, "I had never heard a whisper of a disposition to separate from the mother-country." Washington said: "When I first took command of the army (July 3, 1775), I abhorred the idea of independence; but I am now fully convinced that nothing else will save us." It is only by dwelling on such words as these that we can measure that vast educational process which brought the American people to the Declaration of Independence in 1776.

The Continental Congress, in the earlier months of that year, had for many days been steadily drifting on towards the distinct assertion of separate sovereignty, and had declared it irreconcilable with reason and a good conscience for the colonists to take the oaths required for the support of the government under the crown of Great Britain. But it was not till the 7th of June that Richard Henry Lee, of Virginia, rose and read these resolutions:

> "That these United Colonies are, and of right ought to be, free and independent States; that they are absolved from all allegiance to the British Crown, and that all political connection between them and the State of Great Britain is, and ought to be, totally dissolved.
>
> "That it is expedient forthwith to take the most effectual measures for forming foreign alliances.
>
> "That a plan of confederation be prepared and transmitted to the respective colonies for their consideration and approbation."

These resolutions were presented under direct instructions from the Virginia Assembly, the delegates from that colony selecting Mr. Lee as their spokesman. They were at once seconded, probably after previous understanding, by John Adams, of Massachusetts—Virginia and Massachusetts being then the leading colonies. It was a bold act, for it was still doubtful whether anything better than a degrading death would await these leaders if unsuccessful. Gage had written, only the year before, of the prisoners left in his hands at Bunker Hill, that "their lives were destined to the cord." Indeed the story runs that a similar threat was almost as frankly made to the son of Mr. Lee, then a school-boy in England. He was one day standing near one of his teachers, when some visitor asked the question: "What boy is that?" "He is the son of Richard Henry Lee, of America," the teacher replied. On this the visitor put his hand on the boy's head and said, "We shall yet see your father's head upon Tower Hill"—to which the boy answered, "You may have it when you can get it." This was the way in which the danger was regarded in England; and we know that Congress directed the secretary to omit from the journals the names of the mover and seconder of these resolutions. The record only says, "Certain resolutions respecting independence being moved and seconded, *Resolved*, That the consideration of them be deferred until to-morrow morning; and that the members be enjoined to attend punctually at ten o'clock, in order to take the same into their consideration."

On the next day the discussion came up promptly, and was continued through Saturday, June 8th, and on Monday, June 10th. The resolutions were opposed, even with bitterness, by Robert Livingston, of New York, by Dickinson and Wilson, of Pennsylvania, and by Rutledge, of South Carolina. The latter is reported to have said privately, "that it required the impudence of a New-Englander for them in their disjointed state to propose a treaty to a nation now at peace; that no reason could be assigned for pressing into this measure but the reason of every madman, a show of spirit." On the other hand, the impudence, if such it was, of John Adams, went so far as to defend the resolutions, as stating "objects of the most stupendous magnitude, in which the lives and liberties of millions yet unborn were intimately interested;" as belonging to "a revolution the most complete, unexpected, and remarkable of any in the history of nations." On Monday the resolutions were postponed, by a vote of seven colonies against five, until that day three weeks; and it was afterwards voted (June 11th), "in the mean while, that no time be lost, in case Congress agree thereto, that a committee be appointed to prepare a declaration to that effect." Of this committee Mr. Lee would doubtless have been the chairman, had he not been already on his way to Virginia, to attend the sick-bed of his wife. His associate, Thomas Jefferson, was named in his place, together with John Adams, of Massachusetts, Benjamin Franklin, of Pennsylvania, Roger Sherman, of Connecticut, and Robert R. Livingston, of New York.

This provided for the Declaration; and on the appointed day, July 1, 1776, Congress proceeded to the discussion of the momentous resolutions. Little remains to us of the debate, and the best glimpse of the opening situation is afforded to the modern reader through a letter written by Mr. Adams to Mercy Warren, the historian—a letter dated "Quincy, 1807," but not printed until within a few years, when it was inserted by Mr. Frothingham in the appendix to his invaluable "Rise of the Republic of the United States." The important passage is as follows:

"I remember very well what I did say; but I will previously state a fact as it lies in my memory, which may be somewhat explanatory of it. In the previous multiplied debates which we had upon the subject of independence, the delegates from New Jersey had voted against us; their constituents were informed of it and recalled them, and sent us a new set on purpose to vote for independence. Among these were Chief-justice Stockton and Dr. Witherspoon. In a morning when Congress met, we expected the question would be put and carried without any further debate; because we knew we had a majority, and thought that argument had been exhausted on both sides, as indeed it was, for nothing new was ever afterwards advanced on either side. But the Jersey delegates, appearing for the first time, desired that the question might be discussed. We observed to them that the question was so public, and had been so long discussed in pamphlets, newspapers, and at every fireside, that they could not be uninformed, and must have made up their minds. They said it was true they had not been inattentive to what had been passing abroad, but they had not heard the arguments in Congress, and did not incline to give their opinions until they should hear the sentiments of members there. Judge Stockton was most particularly importunate, till the members began to say, 'Let the gentlemen be gratified,' and the eyes of the assembly were turned upon me, and several of them said, 'Come, Mr. Adams; you have had the subject longer at heart than any of us, and you must recapitulate the arguments.' I was somewhat confused at this personal application to me, and would have been very glad to be excused; but as no other person rose, after some time I said, 'This is the first time in my life when I seriously wished for the genius and eloquence of the celebrated orators of Athens and Rome: called in this unexpected and unprepared manner to exhibit all the arguments in favor of a measure the most important, in my judgment, that had ever been discussed in civil or political society, I had no art or oratory to exhibit, and could produce nothing but simple reason and plain common-sense. I felt myself oppressed by the weight of the subject, and I believed if Demosthenes or Cicero had ever been called to deliberate on so great a question, neither would have relied on his own talents without a supplication to Minerva, and a sacrifice to Mercury or the God of Eloquence.' All this, to be sure, was but a flourish, and not, as I conceive, a very bright exordium; but I felt awkwardly. . . .

"I wish some one had remembered the speech, for it is almost the only one I ever made that I wish was literally preserved."

"John Adams," said Jefferson, long afterwards, to Mr. Webster and Mr. Ticknor, "was our Colossus on the floor. He was not graceful, nor elegant, nor remarkably fluent, but he came out occasionally with a power of thought and expression that moved us from our seats." It seems a pity that no adequate specimens remain to us of this straightforward eloquence; and yet it is cause for congratulation, on the whole, that the only speech fully written out after that debate was the leading argument for the negative. Long years have made us familiar with the considerations that led to national independence; the thing of interest is to know what was said against it; and this is just what we happen to know through the record of a single speech.

JOHN DICKINSON.

After any great measure has been carried through, men speedily forget the objections and the objectors, and in a hundred years can hardly believe that any serious opposition was ever made. How utterly has the name of John Dickinson passed into oblivion! and yet, up to the year 1776, he had doubtless contributed more than any one man, except Thomas Paine, to the political emancipation, so far as the press could effect it, of the American people. The "Farmer's Letters" had been reprinted in London with a preface by Dr. Franklin;

they had been translated into French, and they had been more widely read in America than any patriotic pamphlet, excepting only the "Common Sense" of Paine. Now their author is forgotten — except through the college he founded — because he shrunk at the last moment before the storm he had aroused. Who can deny the attribute of moral courage to the man who stood up in the Continental Congress to argue against independence? But John Adams reports that Dickinson's mother used to say to him: "Johnny, you will be hanged; your estate will be forfeited or confiscated; you will leave your excellent wife a widow," and so on; and Adams admits that if his wife and mother had held such language, it would have made him miserable at least. And it was under this restraining influence, so unlike the fearless counsels of Abby Adams, that Dickinson rose on that first of July, and spoke thus:

"I value the love of my country as I ought, but I value my country more; and I desire this illustrious assembly to witness the integrity, if not the policy, of my conduct. The first campaign will be decisive of the controversy. The Declaration will not strengthen us by one man, or by the least supply, while it may expose our soldiers to additional cruelties and outrages. Without some prelusory trials of our strength, we ought not to commit our country upon an alternative, where to recede would be infamy, and to persist might be destruction.

"No instance is recollected of a people without a battle fought, or an ally gained, abrogating forever their connection with a warlike commercial empire. It might unite the different parties in Great Britain against us, and it might create disunion among ourselves.

"With other powers it would rather injure than avail us. Foreign aid will not be obtained but by our actions in the field, which are the only evidences of our union and vigor that will be respected. In the war between the United Provinces and Spain, France and England assisted the provinces before they declared themselves independent; if it is the interest of any European kingdom to aid us, we shall be aided without such a declaration; if it is not, we shall not be aided with it. Before such an irrevocable step shall be taken, we ought to know the disposition of the great powers, and how far they will permit one or more of them to interfere. The erection of an independent empire on this continent is a phenomenon in the world; its effects will be immense, and may vibrate round the globe. How they may affect, or be supposed to affect, old establishments, is not ascertained. It is singularly disrespectful to France to make the Declaration before her sense is known, as we have sent an agent expressly to inquire whether such a Declaration would be acceptable to her, and we have reason to believe he is now arrived at the Court of Versailles. The measure ought to be delayed till the common interests shall in the best manner be consulted by common consent. Besides, the door to accommodation with Great Britain ought not to be shut, until we know what terms can be obtained from some competent power. Thus to break with her before we have compacted with another, is to make experiments on the lives and liberties of my countrymen, which I would sooner die than agree to make. At best, it is to throw us into the hands of some other power and to lie at mercy, for we shall have passed the river that is never to be repassed. We ought to retain the Declaration and remain masters of our own fame and fate."

These were the opinions of the "Pennsylvania Farmer," as condensed by Bancroft from Mr. Dickinson's own report, no words being employed but those of the orator. In the field some of the bravest men were filled with similar anxieties. The letter, already quoted, from the new adjutant-general, Joseph Reed, describing the military situation, was not laid before the Congress, indeed, but one from General Washington, giving essentially the same facts, was read at the opening of that day's session. In spite of this mournful beginning, and notwithstanding the arguments of Mr. Dickinson, the purpose of the majority in the legislative body was clear and strong; and the pressure from their constituencies was yet stronger. Nearly every colony had already taken separate action towards independence, and on that first day of July the Continental Congress adopted, in committee, the first resolution offered by the Virginia delegates. There were nine colonies in the affirmative, Pennsylvania and South Carolina voting in the negative, the latter unanimously, Delaware being divided, and New York not voting, the delegates from that colony favoring the measure, but having as yet no instructions.

When the resolutions came up for final action in convention the next day, the state of things had changed. Dickinson and Morris, of Pennsylvania, had absented themselves and left an affirmative majority in the delegation; Cæsar Rodney had returned from an absence and brought Delaware into line; and South Carolina, though still disproving the resolutions, joined in the vote for the sake of unanimity, as had been half promised by Edward Rutledge the day before. Thus twelve colonies united in the momentous action; and New York, though not voting, yet endorsed it through a State convention within a week. The best outburst of contemporary feeling over the great event is to be found in a letter by John Adams to his wife, dated July 3, 1776. He writes as follows:

"Yesterday the greatest question was decided which ever was debated in America, and a greater, perhaps, never was nor will be decided among men. . . . When I look back to 1761, . . . and recollect the series of political events, the chain of causes and effects, I am surprised at the suddenness as well as greatness of this revolution. Britain has been filled with folly, and America with wisdom. . . . It is the will of Heaven that the two countries should be sundered forever. It may be the will of Heaven that America shall suffer calamities still more wasting, and distresses yet more dreadful. . . . But I submit all my hopes and fears to an overruling Providence, in which, unfashionable as the faith may be, I firmly believe. . . .

"The second day of July, 1776, will be the most memorable epocha in the history of America. I am apt to believe that it will be celebrated by succeeding generations as the great anniversary festival. It ought to be commemorated as the day of deliverance, by solemn acts of devotion to God Almighty, . . . from one end of the continent to the other, from this time forward for evermore.

"You will think me transported with enthusiasm, but I am not. I am well aware of the toil and blood and treasure that it will cost us to maintain this declaration, and support and defend these States. Yet, through all the gloom, I can see the rays of ravishing light and glory; I can see that the end is worth all the means. And that posterity will triumph in that day's transaction, even though we should rue it, which I trust in God we shall not."

John Adams was mistaken in one prediction. It is the Fourth of July, not the Second, which has been accepted by Americans as "the most memorable epocha." This is one of the many illustrations of the fact that words as well as deeds are needful, since a great act may seem incomplete until it has been put into a fitting form of words. It was the vote of July 2d that changed the thirteen colonies into independent States; the Declaration of Independence only promulgated the fact and assigned its reasons. Had this great proclamation turned out to be a confused or ill-written document, it would never have eclipsed in fame the original Resolution, which certainly had no such weak side. But this danger was well averted, for the Declaration was to be drawn up by Jefferson, unsurpassed in his time for power of expression. He accordingly framed it; Franklin and Adams suggested a few verbal amendments;

HOUSE IN WHICH JEFFERSON WROTE THE DECLARATION, CORNER OF MARKET AND SEVENTH STREETS, PHILADELPHIA.

Sherman and Livingston had none to offer; and the document stood ready to be reported to the Congress.

Some of those who visit Philadelphia may feel an interest in knowing that the "title-deed of our liberties," as Webster called it, was written in "a new brick house out in the fields" —a house still standing, at the south-west corner of Market and Seventh streets, less than a quarter of a mile from Independence Square. Jefferson had there rented a parlor and bedroom, ready furnished, on the second floor, for thirty-five shillings a week; and he wrote the Declaration in this parlor, upon a little writing-desk, three inches high, which still exists. In that modest room we may fancy Franklin and Adams listening critically, Sherman and Livingston approvingly, to what was for them simply the report of a committee. Jefferson had written it, we are told, without the aid of a single book; he was merely putting into more systematic form a series of points long familiar; and Parton may be right in the opinion that the writer was not conscious of any very strenuous exercise of his faculties, or of any very eminent service done.

Nothing is so difficult as to transport ourselves to the actual mood of mind in which great historic acts were performed, or in which their actors habitually dwelt. Thus, on the seventh day of that July, John Adams wrote to his wife a description of the condition of our army, so thrilling and harrowing that it was, as he says, enough to fill one with horror. We fancy him spending that day in sackcloth and ashes; but there follows on the same page another letter, written to the same wife on the same day—a long letter devoted solely to a discourse on the varieties of English style, in which he urges upon her a careful reading of Rollin's "Belles-lettres" and the Epistles of Pliny the Younger. Yet any one who has ever taken part in difficult or dangerous actions can understand the immense relief derived from that half hour's relapse into "the still air of delightful studies." And it is probable that Jefferson and his companions, even while discussing the title-deed of our liberties, may have let their talk stray over a hundred collateral themes as remote from the immediate task as were Pliny and Rollin.

During three days—the second, third, and fourth of July—the Declaration was debated in the Congress. The most vivid historic glimpse of that debate is in Franklin's consolatory anecdote, told to Jefferson, touching John Thompson, the hatter.

The amendments adopted by Congress have always been accounted as improvements, because tending in the direction of conciseness and simplicity, though the loss of that stern condemnation of the slave-trade—"a piratical warfare against human

VIEW OF INDEPENDENCE HALL, THROUGH THE SQUARE.

nature itself"—has always been regretted. The amended document was finally adopted, like the Virginia resolution, by the vote of twelve colonies, New York still abstaining. If Thomas McKean's reminiscences at eighty can be trusted, it cost another effort to secure this strong vote, and Cæsar Rodney had again to be sent for to secure the Delaware delegation. McKean says, in a letter written in 1814 to John Adams, "I sent an express for Cæsar Rodney to Dover, in the county of Kent, in Delaware, at my private expense, whom I met at the Statehouse door on the 4th of July, in his boots; he resided eighty miles from the city, and just arrived as Congress met." Jefferson has, however, thrown much doubt over these octogenarian recollections by McKean, and thinks that he confounded the different votes together. There is little doubt that this hurried night-ride by Rodney was in preparation for the Second of July, not the Fourth, and that the vote on the Fourth went quietly through.

But the Declaration, being adopted, was next to be signed; and here again we come upon an equally great contradiction in testimony. This same Thomas McKean wrote in 1814 to ex-President Adams, speaking of the Declaration of Independence, "No man signed it on that day"—namely, July 4, 1776. Jefferson, on the other hand, writing some years later, thought that Mr. McKean's memory had deceived him, Jefferson himself asserting, from his early notes, that "the Declaration was reported by the Committee, agreed to by the House, and signed by every member present except Mr. Dickinson." But Jefferson, who was also an octogenarian, seems to have forgotten the subsequent signing of the Declaration on parchment, until it was recalled to his memory, as he states, a few years later. If there was a previous signing of a written document, the manuscript itself has long since disappeared, and the accepted historic opinion is that both these venerable witnesses were mistaken; that the original Declaration was signed only by the president and secretary, John Hancock and Charles Thomson, and that the general signing of the parchment copy took place on August 2d. It is probable, at least, that fifty-four of the fifty-six names were appended on that day, and that it was afterwards signed by Thornton, of New Hampshire, who was not then a member, and by McKean, who was then temporarily absent.

Jefferson used to relate, "with much merriment," says Parton, that the final signing of the Declaration was hastened by a very trivial circumstance. Near the hall was a large stable, whence the flies issued in legions. Gentlemen were in those days peculiarly sensitive to such discomforts by reason of silk

TABLE AND CHAIRS USED AT THE SIGNING OF THE DECLARATION.

stockings; and when this annoyance, superadded to the summer heat of Philadelphia, had become intolerable, they hastened to bring the business to a conclusion. This may equally well refer, however, to the original vote; flies are flies, whether in July or August.

American tradition has clung to the phrases assigned to the

different participants in this scene: John Hancock's commentary on his own bold handwriting, "There, John Bull may read my name without spectacles;" Franklin's, "We must hang together, or else, most assuredly, we shall all hang separately;" and the heavy Harrison's remark to the slender Elbridge Gerry, that in that event Gerry would be kicking in the air long after his own fate would be settled. These things may or may not have been said, but it gives a more human interest to the event when we know that they were even rumored. What we long to know is, that the great acts of history were done by men like ourselves, and not by dignified machines.

This is the story of the signing. Of the members who took part in that silent drama of 1776, some came to greatness in consequence, becoming presidents, vice-presidents, governors, chief-justices, or judges; others came, in equally direct consequence, to poverty, flight, or imprisonment. "Hunted like a fox by the enemy;" "a prisoner twenty-four hours without food," "not daring to remain two successive nights beneath one shelter"—these are the records we may find in the annals of the Revolution in regard to many a man who stood by John Hancock on that summer day to sign his name. It is a pleasure to think that not one of them ever disgraced, publicly or conspicuously, the name he had written. Of the rejoicings which, everywhere throughout the colonies, followed the signing, the tale has been often told. It has been told so often, if the truth must be confessed, that it is not now easy to distinguish the romance from the simple fact. The local antiquarians of Philadelphia bid us dismiss forever from the record the picturesque old bell-ringer and his eager boy, waiting breathlessly to announce to the assembled thousands the final vote of Congress on the Declaration. The tale is declared to be a pure fiction, of which there exists not even a local tradition. The sessions of Congress were then secret, and there was no expectant crowd outside. It was not till the fifth of

July that Congress sent out circulars announcing the Declaration; not till the sixth that it appeared in a Philadelphia newspaper; and not till the eighth that it was read by John Nixon in the yard of Independence Hall. It was read from an observatory there erected by the American Philosophical Society, seven years before, to observe the transit of Venus. The

TEARING DOWN THE KING'S ARMS FROM ABOVE THE DOOR IN THE CHAMBER OF THE SUPREME COURT ROOM IN INDEPENDENCE HALL, JULY 8, 1776.

king's arms over the door of the Supreme Court room in Independence Hall were torn down by a committee of the Volunteer force called "associators;" these trophies were burned in the evening, in the presence of a great crowd of citizens, and no doubt amid the joyful pealing of the old "Independence" bell. There is also a tradition that on the afternoon of that day, or possibly a day or two earlier, there was a joyful private

GARDEN-HOUSE, OWNED BY DR. ENOCH EDWARDS, WHERE JEFFERSON AND OTHERS CELEBRATED THE PASSAGE OF THE DECLARATION.

celebration of the great event, by Jefferson and others, at the garden-house of a country-seat in Frankford (near Philadelphia), then occupied by Dr. Enoch Edwards, a leading patriot of that time.

It is certain that a portion of the signers of the Declaration met two years after, for a cheery commemoration of their great achievement, in the Philadelphia City Tavern. The enjoyment of the occasion was enhanced by the recent deliverance of the city from the presence of General Howe, and by the contrast between this festival and that lately given by the

British officers to him, known in history as the "Meschianza." This chapter may well close with a passage from the manuscript diaries of William Ellery, now lying before me.

"On the glorious Fourth of July [1778], I celebrated in the City Tavern, with my brother delegates of Congress and a number of other gentlemen, amounting, in the whole, to about eighty, the anniversary of Independency. The entertainment was elegant and well conducted. There were four tables spread; two of them extended the whole length of the room, the other two crossed them at right angles. At the end of the room, opposite the upper table, was erected an Orchestra. At the head of the upper table, and at the President's right hand, stood a large baked pudding, in the centre of which was planted a staff, on which was displayed a crimson flag, in the midst of which was this emblematic device: An eye, denoting Providence; a label, on which was inscribed, 'An appeal to Heaven;' a man with a drawn sword in his hand, and in the other the Declaration of Independency, and at his feet a scroll inscribed, 'The declaratory acts.' As soon as the dinner began, the music, consisting of clarionets, hautboys, French horns, violins, and bass-viols, opened and continued, making proper pauses, until it was finished. Then the toasts, followed by a discharge of field-pieces, were drank, and so the afternoon ended. In the evening there was a cold collation and a brilliant exhibition of fireworks. The street was crowded with people during the exhibition. . . .

"What a strange vicissitude in human affairs! These, but a few years since colonies of Great Britain, are now free, sovereign, and independent States, and now celebrate the anniversary of their independence in the very city where, but a day or two before, General Howe exhibited his ridiculous *Champhaitre.*"

XII.

THE BIRTH OF A NATION.

"MY lords," said the Bishop of St. Asaph's, in the British House of Lords, "I look upon North America as the only great nursery of freedom left upon the face of the earth." It is the growth of freedom in this nursery which really interests us most in the Revolutionary period; all the details of battles are quite secondary. Indeed, in any general view of the history of a nation, the steps by which it gets into a war and finally gets out again are of more importance than all that lies between. No doubt every skirmish in a prolonged contest has its bearing on national character, but it were to consider too curiously to dwell on this, and most of the continuous incident of a war belongs simply to military history. If this is always the case, it is peculiarly true of the war of American Independence, which exhibited, as was said by the ardent young Frenchman, Lafayette, "the grandest of causes won by contests of sentinels and outposts."

The Declaration of Independence was publicly read throughout the colonies, and was communicated by Washington in a general order, July 9, 1776, with the following announcement: "The general hopes this important event will serve as an incentive to every officer and soldier to act with fidelity and courage, as knowing that now the peace and safety of his country depend (under God) solely on the success of our arms; and that he is now in the service of a State possessed of sufficient power to reward his merit and advance him to the highest honors of a free country." Thus early did this far-seeing Virginian give his allegiance to the new government as a nation,—terming it "a State," "a free country;" not an agglomeration of States only, or a temporary league of free countries. And he needed for his encouragement all the strength he could gain from this new-born loyalty.

It was a gloomy and arduous year, the year 1776. The first duty now assigned to Washington was that of sustaining himself on Long Island and guarding New York. Long Island was the scene of terrible disaster; the forces under Putnam were hemmed in and cut to pieces (August 27th), making Greenwood Cemetery a scene of death before it was a place of burial. In this fatal battle 8000 Americans, still raw and under a raw commander (Putnam), were opposed to 20,000 trained Hessian soldiers, supported by a powerful fleet. Washington decided to retreat from Long Island. With extraordinary promptness and energy he collected in a few hours, from a range of fourteen miles, a sufficient supply of boats—this being done in such secrecy that even his aides did not know it. For forty-eight hours he did not sleep, being nearly the whole time in the saddle. He sent 9000 men, with all their baggage and field artillery, across a rapid river nearly a mile wide, within hearing of the enemy's camp: "the best conducted retreat I ever read of," wrote General Greene. Then began desertions, by companies and almost by regiments. They continued during all his memorable retreat through the Jerseys, when his troops were barefooted and disheartened, and yet he contested every inch of ground. At the beginning of his march he heard of the loss of Fort Washington (November 16th) with 2600 men, their ordnance, ammunition, and stores. The day before he crossed the Delaware the British took possession of Newport, Rhode Island, signalling their arrival by burning the house of William Ellery, who had signed the great Declaration.

Yet amid all these accumulated disasters Washington wrote to Congress that he could see "without despondency even for a moment" what America called her "gloomy hours." He could breathe more freely at last when, on December 8th, he crossed the Delaware at Trenton with what the discouraged Reed had called "the wretched fragments of a broken army," now diminished to 3000 men. As his last boat crossed, the advanced guard of Howe's army reached the river, and looked eagerly for means of transportation. Washington had seized everything that could float upon the water within seventy miles.

On December 20, 1776, Washington told John Hancock, then President of the Congress, "Ten days more will put an end to the existence of our army." Yet at Christmas he surprised the Hessians at Trenton, recrossing the river and returning on his course with what was perhaps the most brilliant single stroke of war that he ever achieved. A few days later (January 3, 1777) he defeated Cornwallis at Princeton with almost equal ability; and all this he did with but 5000 men, one-half militia, the rest little more. During that year there had been in service 47,000 "Continentals" and 27,000 militia. Where were they all? These large figures had only been obtained through that system of short enlistments against which Washington had in vain protested—enlistments for three months, or even for one month. It is useless for this generation to exclaim against what may seem slowness or imbecility in the government of that day. Why, we ask, did they not foresee what the war would be? why did they not insist on longer enlistments? We have seen in our own time the uselessness of these questionings. Under popular institutions it is hard to convince a nation that a long war is before it; it is apt to be easily persuaded that peace will return in about sixty days; its strength is seen, if at all, in its reserved power and its final resources. The dawn of independence seemed overcast indeed when the campaign of 1776 closed, and Washington, with only three or four thousand men, went sadly into winter-quarters at Morristown.

In April, 1777, John Adams wrote proudly to his wife, " Two complete years we have maintained open war with Great Britain and her allies, and, after all our difficulties and misfortunes, are much abler to cope with them now than we were at the beginning." The year that followed was in many respects the turning-point of the Revolution. The British had formed a plan which, had it been carried out, might have resulted in a complete triumph for them. It was a project to take thorough possession of the whole line of the Hudson—Burgoyne coming down from the North, Howe going up from the South—thus absolutely cutting the colonies in two, separating New England from the rest, and conquering each by itself. Happily this was abandoned for a measure that had no valuable results, the possession of Philadelphia. It is true that in the effort to save that city, Washington sustained defeat at Brandywine (September 11, 1777), and only came near victory, without achieving it, at Germantown (October 4th). But the occupation of Philadelphia divided the British army—now nearly fifty thousand soldiers—while the American army, though it had shrunk to about half that number, remained more concentrated. Moreover, the luxurious winter in Philadelphia did the invading troops little good; while the terrible winter at Valley Forge was in one sense the saving of the Americans. There they came under the influence of trained foreign officers—Pulaski and Steuben, as well as the young Lafayette. Baron Steuben especially took the hungry soldiers and taught them what drill meant. Heretofore there had been a different drill for almost every regiment —a whole regiment numbering sometimes but thirty men—and many of these retained the practice learned in Indian warfare, of marching in single file.

Meanwhile at the North there occurred successes for the American army, which grew directly out of the abandonment of the British plan. Stark with New England troops defeated a detachment of Burgoyne's army near Bennington; and Gates took the whole of that army—five thousand men—prisoners at Saratoga, October 17, 1777. It seemed for the moment that this determined the fate of the war. That surrender is the only American battle included by Sir Edward Creasy in his "Fifteen Decisive Battles of the World," and yet for six years its decisiveness did not prove final and the war went on. Those who remember the sort of subdued and sullen hopefulness which prevailed, year in and year out, in the Northern States, during the late war for the Union, can probably conceive something of the mood in which the American people saw months and years go by during the Revolution without any very marked progress, and yet with an indestructible feeling that somehow the end must come. But the surrender of Burgoyne at least turned the scale in favor of the Americans, so far as the judgment of Europe was concerned. When the French minister, Vergennes, declared that "All efforts, however great, would be powerless to reduce a people so thoroughly determined to refuse submission," the alliance was a foregone conclusion. Dr. Franklin, with inexhaustible and wily good-nature, was always pressing upon the French ministry this same view, and the influence of Lafayette seconded it. Nations like to form alliances on the side that seems to be winning. Yet not even the French government wished to have the new nation too powerful; and Mr. John Jay has conclusively shown that Vergennes would have left the United States a very hampered and restricted nationality had not the vigor of Jay, well seconded by Adams, added, at a later period, an element of positive self-assertion beyond the good-nature of Franklin. Meanwhile, the first treaty with France—which was also the first treaty of the United States with any foreign government—was signed February 6, 1778, two months after the news of Burgoyne's surrender had reached Paris.

However high we rate the value of the French help, we must

remember that the alliance united England against the two nations. There were many who were by this time convinced that the work of conquest was hopeless. "The time may come," said the King to Lord North, in 1778, "when it will be wise to abandon all North America but Canada, Nova Scotia, and the Floridas; but then the generality of the nation must first see it in that light." If there is anything that is impressed upon the very school-books in connection with that period it is the obstinacy of King George III., and yet he had learned thus much. On the other hand, Lord Chatham, who had once said, "America has resisted; I rejoice, my lords," was now driven by the French alliance to take sides against America. He saw in the proposed independence only the degradation of the power of England before the French throne, and was carried from a sick-bed to speak against it in Parliament (April 7, 1778). "My lords," he said, "I rejoice that the grave has not closed upon me, that I am still alive to uplift my voice against the dismemberment of this ancient and most noble monarchy." As the Duke of Richmond essayed to answer, Chatham was seized with apoplexy, and was borne from the House to die. The young American government had gained a powerful alliance, but it had lost its best English friend. Richmond, Burke, and Fox supported its cause, but Chatham had roused the traditional pride of England against France, and Lord North was his successor. Then followed a period of which Washington wrote to George Mason (March 27, 1779) that he was for the first time despondent, and had beheld no day in which he thought the liberties of America so endangered. The war must still go on, and the French army and navy must cross the Atlantic for its prosecution. They were cordially welcomed by everybody except the German settlers of New York and Pennsylvania, who could not forget, as Mrs. Quincy's journal tells us, the excesses committed by the French troops in Germany.

The direct service done by the French alliance was of less

value than the moral support it brought. It occupied Newport, Rhode Island, in July, 1780, with nearly six thousand men in army and navy. The unpublished memorials of that time and place contain many delightful recollections of the charming manners of the French officers: of the Rochambeaux, father and son; of the Duc de Deux-Ponts, afterwards King of Bavaria; of the Prince de Broglie, guillotined in the Revolution; of the Swedish Count Fersen, "the Adonis of the camp," who afterwards acted as coachman for the French king and queen in their escape from Paris; of the Vicomte de Noailles and of Admiral de Ternay, the latter buried in Trinity Church yard in Newport. There are old houses in that city which still retain upon their window-panes the gallant inscriptions of those picturesque days, and there are old letters and manuscripts that portray their glories. One that lies before me describes the young noblemen driving into the country upon parties of pleasure, preceded by their running footmen—a survival of feudalism—tall youths in kid slippers and with leaping poles; another describes the reception of Washington by the whole French garrison, in March, 1781. It was a brilliant scene. The four French regiments were known as Bourbonnais, Soissonnais, Deux-Ponts, and Saintonge; they contained each a thousand men; and the cavalry troop, under De Lauzun, was almost as large. Some of these wore white uniforms, with yellow or violet or crimson lapels, and with black gaiters; others had a uniform of black and gold, with gaiters of snowy white. The officers displayed stars and badges; even the officers' servants were gay in gold and silver lace. Over them all and over the whole town floated the white flag of the Bourbons with the fleurs-delis. They were drawn up in open ranks along the avenue leading to the long wharf, which was just then losing its picturesque old name, Queen's Hithe. This gay army, whose fresh uniforms and appointments contrasted strangely with the worn and dilapidated aspect of the Continental troops, received Washington

THE FRENCH OFFICERS AT NEWPORT.

with the honors due to a marshal of France. In the evening a ball was given to the American generals; Washington opened the dance with the beautiful Miss Champlin: he chose for the figure the country-dance known as "A Successful Campaign," and, as he danced, the French officers took the instruments from the musicians, and themselves played the air and accompaniment.   Thus with characteristic graces began the French occupation of Newport, and it continued to be for them rather a holiday campaign, until the siege of Yorktown, Virginia, proved the qualities of their engineers and their soldiers.   After ten days of siege, the British army, overwhelmed and surrounded, had to surrender at last (October 19, 1781); and in the great painting which represents the scene, at the Versailles palace, General de Rochambeau is made the conspicuous figure, while Washington is quite secondary.

Meanwhile the successes of Paul Jones in sea-fighting gained still more the respect of Europe, and his victorious fight of three hours in the *Bonhomme Richard* against the *Serapis* (1779)—the two ships being lashed side by side—was the earliest naval victory gained under the present American flag, which this bold sea-captain was the first to unfurl.   Then the skilful campaigns of General Nathaniel Greene (1780) rescued the Carolinas from invasion; and the treason of Benedict Arnold, with his plan for surrendering to the British the "American Gibraltar"—West Point —created a public excitement only deepened by the melancholy death of Major André, who was hanged as a spy, Sept. 23, 1780. For nearly two years after the surrender of Cornwallis the British troops held the cities of New York, Charleston, and Savannah; and though they were powerless beyond those cities, yet it seemed to their garrisons, no doubt, that the war was not yet ended. Mrs. Josiah Quincy, visiting New York as a child, just before its evacuation by the British under Sir Guy Carleton, in 1783, says that she accompanied her mother, Mrs. Morton, to call on the wife of Chief-justice Smith, an eminent loyalist.   Their hostess brought in a little girl, and said, "This child has been born since the Rebellion." "Since the Revolution?" replied Mrs. Morton.   Mrs. Smith smiled, and said good-naturedly, "Well, well, Mrs. Morton, this is only a truce, not a peace; and we shall be back again in full possession in two years."   "This prophecy happily did not prove true," adds Mrs. Quincy, with exultant patriotism.

Independence was essentially secured by the preliminary articles signed in Paris on Jan. 20, 1783, although the final treaty was not signed till Sept. 3d. It was on April 18, 1783, that Washington issued his order for the cessation of hostilities, thus completing, as he said, the eighth year of the war. The army was disbanded Nov. 3d. The whole number of "Continentals,"

GENERAL SIR GUY CARLETON.

or regular troops, employed during the contest was 231,791. Of these Massachusetts had furnished 67,907, Connecticut 31,939, Virginia 26,678, Pennsylvania 25,678, and the other States smaller numbers, down to 2679 from Georgia. The expenditures of the war, as officially estimated in 1790, were nearly a hundred million dollars in specie ($92,485,693.15), and the debts, foreign expenditures, etc., swelled this to more than one hundred and thirty-five millions ($135,693,703). At the close, the army, which had been again and again on the verge of mutiny from neglect and privation, received pay for three months in six months' notes, which commanded in the market the price of two shillings for twenty shillings. The soldiers reached their homes, as Washington wrote to Congress, "without a settlement of their accounts, and without a farthing of money in their pockets."

Independence being thus achieved, what was to be done with it? Those who represented the nation in Congress, while generally agreed in patriotic feeling, were not agreed even on the fundamental principles of government. The Swiss Zubly, who represented Georgia, and who claimed to have been familiar with republican government ever since he was six years old, declared that it was "little better than a government of devils." John Adams heartily favored what he called republican government, but we know, from a letter of his to Samuel Adams (October 18, 1790), that he meant by it something very remote from our present meaning. Like many other men of modest origin, he had a strong love for social distinctions; he noted with satisfaction that there was already the semblance of an aristocracy in Boston; and he, moreover, held that the republican forms of Poland and Venice were worse, and the Dutch and Swiss republics but little better, than the old *régime* in France, whose abuses led to the Revolution. The republic of Milton, he thought, would imply "miseries," and the simple monarchical form would be better. He meant by republic, he said, simply a government in which "the people have collectively or by representation an essential share in the sovereignty"—such a share, for instance, as they have in England. This being the case, it is not strange that he should have regarded independence itself as but a temporary measure, a sort of protest, and should have looked forward without dismay to an ultimate reunion with England, under certain guarantees to be secured by treaty.

It is very fortunate that the institutions of America were not to depend on the speculations of any one man, even the wisest. Many persons think of the organization of the United States as being the work of a few leaders. Had this been the truth, the Continental government would have been organized first, and the State governments would have been built afterwards on its model. As a matter-of-fact, it was just the other way. While the great leaders were debating in Congress or negotiating in Europe, the question of government was settled by the reorganization of successive colonies into commonwealths, the work being done largely by men now forgotten. These men took the English tradition of local self-government, adapted it to the new situation, and adjusted it to a community in which kings and noblemen had already begun to fade into insignificance.

Even before independence was declared, some of the colonies—Massachusetts, New Hampshire, South Carolina, Virginia, and New Jersey—had begun to frame State governments on the basis of the old charter governments, but so hastily that their work needed in some cases to be revised. After the declaration, New York and Maryland followed soon, and then the rest. We find Jefferson writing to Franklin (August 13, 1777) that in Virginia "the people seem to have laid aside the monarchical and taken up the republican government with as much ease as would have attended their throwing off an old and putting on a new suit of clothes." All these commonwealths agreed, almost without consultation, on certain principles. All recognized the sovereignty of the people, or at least the masculine half of the people; all wished to separate Church and State; all distinguished, as did the unwritten constitution of England, between the executive, the judicial, and the legislative departments; all limited the executive department very carefully, as experience had taught them to do. Nowhere, except in Rhode Island and Pennsylvania, was there any recognition of the hereditary right to vote, this being in Rhode Island included in the royal charter under which that State governed itself, omitting only the part of royalty, till 1842. In short, all the scattered colonies shifted what had seemed the very basis of their structure, and yet found themselves, after all, in good condition. We have grown accustomed in these days to the readiness with which English-speaking men can settle down anywhere on the planet and presently organize free institutions; so that we hardly recognize what a wonder it seemed that thirteen colonies, even while engaged in a great war, should one by one quietly crystallize into shape.

The great difficulty was to unite these little commonwealths into a nation. It took one unsuccessful experiment to teach the way of success, and it is astonishing that it did not take a dozen. It was a strange period. The war had unsettled men's minds, as is done by all great wars. It had annihilated all loyalty to the king, but it had done much more than this. It had made the rich poor, and the poor rich; had filled the nation with almost irredeemable paper-money; had created a large class whose only hope was to evade payment of their debts. "Oh, Mr. Adams," said John Adams's horse-jockey client, "what great things have you and your colleagues done for us! We can never be grateful enough to you. There are no courts of justice now in this province, and I hope there never will be another."

The first experiment at national union was the Confederation. It was based essentially on a theory of Jefferson's. This theory was to make "the States one as to everything connected with foreign nations, and several as to everything purely domestic." For purposes of foreign commerce a Confederation must exist. To this all finally agreed, though with much reluctance. Indeed the original apostles of this theory did not much believe in any such commerce. Jefferson wrote from Paris (in 1785) that if he had his way "the States should practise neither commerce nor navigation," but should "stand with respect to Europe precisely on the footing of China." But he admitted that he could not have his way, and wrote to Monroe (December 11, 1785) from Paris: "On this side of the Atlantic we are viewed as objects of commerce only." Granting thus much, then, to be inevitable, how was little Rhode Island or Delaware to resist the aggressions of any European bully, or of those Algerine or Tripolitan pirates who then bullied even the bullies themselves? For this purpose, at least, there must be some joint action. How could the United States treat with any foreign government when, as Washington said (in 1785), they were "one nation to-day and thirteen to-morrow?" They must therefore unite sufficiently to make a treaty and enforce it, but no further. In other words, they undertook to build a house which should have an outside but no inside.

The Confederation was originally put in shape through a committee appointed by Congress, June 11, 1776, "to prepare and digest the form of a confederation to be entered into between these colonies." But the "articles" thus prepared were not accepted by Congress till November 15, 1777, and they had been much modified before they received the assent of the last of the States, on March 1, 1781. During all this time the affairs of the war were carried on loosely enough by Congress— still a single House—which had come to be familiarly known among the people as "King Cong." But this king had absolutely no power but in the impulsive support of the people. It was a thankless office to sit in Congress; the best men were more and more reluctant to serve there. To reach it, wherever it sat—Philadelphia, Baltimore, Lancaster, York, Princeton, or Annapolis—was to most of the members far more of a journey than to reach San Francisco or London from Philadelphia or Annapolis to-day. Inasmuch as all votes were taken by States —and every State had an equal vote, so long as there was one man to represent it—there was a strong temptation for delegates to absent themselves; and a single member from Delaware or Rhode Island could, if present, balance the whole representation from New York or Virginia. "It is enough to sicken one," wrote General Knox to Washington, in March, 1783, "to observe how light a matter many States make of their not being represented in Congress—a good proof of the badness of the present Constitution." Even on the great occasion when the resignation of Washington was to be received, there were present only twenty members, representing but seven of the colonies. "It is difficult," wrote M. Otto to the French government, "to assemble seven States, which form the number required to transact the least important business;" and he wrote again, a few months after, that the secret of the predominant influence of Massachusetts in the Congress was that she usually kept four or five able delegates there, while other States rarely had two. As we read the records we can only wonder that the organization did its work so well; and it is not at all strange that, as the same General Knox wrote to Washington, the favorite toasts in the army were, "Cement to the Union" and "A hoop to the barrel."

There were those who believed that nothing but the actual necessities of another war could really unite the colonies, and some patriots frankly wished for that calamity. M. Otto, writing home in December, 1785, to M. De Vergennes, declared that Mr. Jay was the most influential man in Congress, and that Mr. Jay had lately expressed in his hearing a wish that the Algerine pirates, then so formidable, would burn some of the maritime towns of the United States, in order to reunite the nation and call back the old feeling. "The majority of Congress perceive very clearly," he wrote, "that war would serve as a bond to the Confederation, but they cannot conceal the lack of means which they possess to carry it on with advantage."

This desperate remedy being out of the question, the "hoop to the barrel" must be put on by some more peaceful method.

Yet each way had its own perplexities. There were jealousies of long standing between North and South, between the colonies which were ready to abolish slavery and those which clung to it. Then the course of the Confederation had only increased the mutual distrust between the small and the large States. There were objections to a permanent president; some would have preferred, as a very few would still prefer, to have a system like that now prevailing in the Swiss Confederation, and to place at the head merely the chairman of a committee. Again, there existed a variety of opinions as to a Legislature of one or two Houses. It is said that when Jefferson returned from France he was breakfasting with Washington, and asked him why he agreed to a Senate.

"Why," said Washington, "did you just now pour that coffee into your saucer before drinking it?" "To cool it," said Jefferson; "my throat is not made of brass." "Even so," said Washington, "we pour our legislation into the Senatorial saucer to cool it."

Franklin, like Jefferson, approved only of the single chamber of deputies, and it has been thought that to his great influence in France, leading to the adoption of that method, were due some of the excesses of the French Revolution. The States of Pennsylvania and Georgia had, during the Confederation, but one legislative body; the Confederation itself had but one, and the great State of New York voted in the convention of 1787 against having more than one. Some of the most enlightened European reformers—Mazzini, Louis Blanc, Stuart Mill, even Goldwin Smith—have always believed the second House to be a source of weakness in American institutions, while the general feeling of Americans is overwhelmingly in its favor. Yet its mere existence is a type of that combination which is at the foundation of the national government. If Patrick Henry was right, if he had wholly ceased to be a Virginian in becoming an American, then there should be no separate representation of the States. If Jefferson was right —who considered the Union only a temporary device to carry the colonies through the war for Independence—then the States only should be represented, and they should weigh equally, whether small or large. But Elbridge Gerry included both

ELBRIDGE GERRY.

statements when he said: "We are neither the same nation nor different nations. We ought not, therefore, to pursue the one or the other of these ideas too closely." This statement is regarded by Von Holst, the acutest foreign critic of American institutions since De Tocqueville, as containing the whole secret of American history.

We are apt to suppose that the sentiment of union among the colonies, once formed, went steadily on increasing. Not at all; it went, like all other things, by action and reaction. It was before a shot was fired that Patrick Henry had thrilled the people's ears with his proud assertion of nationality. "The distinctions between Virginians, Pennsylvanians, New-Yorkers, and New-Englanders are no more. I am not a Virginian; I am an American." But as the war went on, the "people" of the United States came again to be loosely described as the "inhabitants" of the States. The separate commonwealths had the organization, the power, all but the army; and one of them, North Carolina, went so far as to plan a fleet. The Confederation was only, as it described itself, "a firm league of friendship;" the Continental government was once actually characterized in Massachusetts as a foreign power; it was the creation of war's necessities, while the States controlled the daily life. Washington had to complain that the States were too much engaged in their "local concerns," and he had to plead for the "great business of a nation." Fisher Ames wrote, "Instead of feeling as a nation, a State is our country." So far as the influence of foreign nations went, it tended only to disintegrate, not to unite. Even the one friendly government of Europe, the French, had no interest in promoting union; the cabinet at Versailles wrote to its minister in America (August 30, 1787) that it would not regret to see the Confederation broken up, and that it had recognized "no other object than to deprive Great Britain of that vast continent."

In short, the Confederation waned day by day; it had no power, for power had been carefully withheld from it; it had only influence, and, as Washington once said, "Influence is not government." Fisher Ames declared that "the corporation of a college or a missionary society were greater potentates than Congress. . . . The government of a great nation had barely revenue enough to buy stationery for its clerks, or to pay the salary of the door-keepers." It existed only to carry on the war as it best could, and when the war ended, the prestige of the Confederation was gone. There was left a people without a government, and this people was demoralized amid suc-

FISHER AMES.

cess, discontented in spite of its triumph. Washington thus despairingly summed up the situation: "From the high ground we stood upon, from the plain path which invited our footsteps, to be so fallen, so lost, is really mortifying; but virtue, I fear, has in some degree taken its departure from our land, and the want of a disposition to do justice is the source of our national embarrassments."

The downfall of the Confederation was greatly aided by the celebrated insurrection of Daniel Shays in Massachusetts—an occasion when armed mobs broke up the courts and interrupted all the orderly processes of law. This body numbered, according to the estimate of General Knox—who went to Springfield to provide for the defence of the arsenal against them—not less than twelve or fifteen thousand men, scattered through the New England States; and he estimated the whole force of their friends and supporters at two-sevenths of the population—not, as Von Holst says, one-half. The grounds of this insurrection were, as it seems to me, a shade more plausible, and hence more formidable, than the historians have recognized. As stated by Knox, these views were based expressly on the peculiar state of things at the close of a long and exhausting war, and amounted simply to the doctrine that, being narrowly rescued from shipwreck, the whole half-drowned company should share alike. As a result of the war, they urged, almost everybody was bankrupt. John Adams's horse-jockey client was really no worse off than the most sober and honest mechanic. Of the few who had any money, some were speculators and contractors, who had grown rich out of the government; others were Tories in disguise, who had saved their property from a just confiscation. All this property, having been saved from the British by the sacrifices of all, should in justice be shared among all. Yet they would not demand so much as that: let there be simply a remission of debts and a further issue of paper-money.

Audacious as this proposition now seems, it was not wholly inconsistent with some things that had gone before it. If Washington himself thought it fitting to celebrate the surrender of Cornwallis by a general release of prisoners from jail, why not now carry this rejoicing a little further, and have an equally

SHAYS'S MOB IN POSSESSION OF A COURT-HOUSE.

general release of those who were on their way to jail? Thus they reasoned, or might have reasoned, and all this helps us to understand a little better why it was that Jefferson did not share the general alarm at these doctrines, but, on the whole, rather approved of the outbreak. "Can history produce," he said, "an instance of rebellion so honorably conducted?" "God forbid we shall ever be without such a rebellion!" "A little rebellion now and then is a good thing." "An observation of this truth should render republican governors so mild as not to discourage them too much." Yet those who were on the spot saw in this rebellion not only the weakness of the general government, but that of the separate States as well. "Not only is State against State, and all against the Federal head," wrote General Knox to Washington, "but the States within themselves possess the name only, without having the essential concomitants of government.... On the very first impression of faction and licentiousness, the fine theoretic government of Massachusetts has given way."

Even before this insurrection, a convention, attended by five States only, had been held at Annapolis (September, 1786), with a view to some improved national organization. It called a general convention, which met at Philadelphia, having barely a quorum of States, on May 25, 1787. There the delegates sat amid constant interruptions and antagonisms, the majority of the New York delegation leaving once under protest, South Carolina protesting, Elbridge Gerry predicting failure, and Benjamin Franklin despairingly proposing to open the sessions thenceforward with prayer as the last remaining hope. Then the Constitution was adopted at last — only to come into new and more heated discussion in every State. We have in *The Federalist* Hamilton's great defence of it; but Patrick Henry himself turned his eloquence against it in Virginia, and Samuel Adams in Massachusetts. These were two very powerful opponents, who were well entitled to a voice; and in these two important States the Constitution was accepted by majorities so small that the change of a dozen votes would have caused defeat. In the New York Convention the vote stood 30 to 27; in

Rhode Island, 34 to 32; this being the last State to ratify, and the result being secured by a change of one vote under the instructions of a town-meeting in the little village of Middletown, too small, even at this day, to have a post-office. By a chance thus narrow was the United States born into a nation. The contest, as Washington wrote to Lee, was "not so much for glory as existence."

And as thus finally created the nation was neither English nor French, but American. It was in very essential features a new departure. It is common to say that the French Revolution brought with it French political theories in the United States. Edmund Burke wrote that the colonists were "not only devoted to liberty, but to liberty according to English ideas and on English principles," yet there is a prevalent impression that the influence of France converted this English feeling into a French habit of mind, and that the desire to legislate on the abstract rights of man came from that side of the English Channel. But Jefferson had never been in France, nor under any strong French influence, when he, as the Rev. Ezra Stiles said, "poured the soul of a continent into the monumental Act of Independence;" and Franklin had made but flying visits to Paris when he wrote in England, about 1770, those striking sentences, under the name of "Some Good Whig Principles," which form the best compendium of what is called Jeffersonian Democracy: "The *all* of one man is as dear to him as the *all* of another, and the poor man has an equal right, but more need, to have representatives in the legislature than the rich one." What are sometimes reproachfully called "transcendental politics"—political action, that is, based on an abstract theory—arose spontaneously in that age; the Constitution was based on them; and in urging them America probably influenced France more than France affected America. There is now a reaction against them, and perhaps it is as well that these oscillations of the pendulum should take place; but I am not one of those who believe that the people of the United States will ever outgrow the Declaration of Independence.

One of the most momentous acts of the Continental Congress had been to receive from the State of Virginia the gift of a vast unsettled territory north-west of the Ohio, and to apply to this wide realm the guarantee of freedom from slavery. This safeguard was but the fulfilment of a condition suggested by Timothy Pickering, when, in 1783, General Rufus Putnam and nearly three hundred army officers had proposed to form a new State in that very region of the Ohio. They sent in a memorial to Congress asking for a grant of land. Washington heartily endorsed the project, but nothing came of it. North Carolina soon after made a cession of land to the United States, and then revoked it; but the people on the ceded territory declared themselves for a time to be a separate State, under the name of Franklin. Virginia, through Thomas Jefferson, finally delivered a deed on March 1, 1784, by which she ceded to the United States all her territory north-west of the Ohio. The great gift was accepted, and a plan of government was adopted, into which Jefferson tried to introduce an antislavery ordinance, but he was defeated by a single vote. Again, in 1785, Rufus King, of Massachusetts, seconded by William Ellery, of Rhode Island, proposed to revive Jefferson's rejected clause, but again it failed, being smothered by a committee. It was not till July 13, 1787, that the statute passed by which slavery was forever prohibited in the territory of the North-west, this being moved by Nathan Dane as an amendment to an ordinance already adopted—which he himself had framed—and being passed by a vote of every State present in the Congress, eight in all. Under this statute the Ohio Company—organized in Boston the year before as the final outcome of Rufus Putnam's proposed colony of officers—bought from the government five or six millions of acres, and entered on the first great movement of emigration west of the Ohio. The report creating the colony provided for public-schools, for religious institutions, and for a university. The land was to be paid for in United States certificates of debt, and its price in specie was between eight and nine cents an acre. The settlers were almost wholly men who had served in the army, and were used to organization and discipline. The Indian title to the lands of the proposed settlement had been re-

THE INAUGURATION OF WASHINGTON.
[From the steel engraving by F. O'C. Darley in Irving's "Washington," by permission of G. P. Putnam's Sons.]

leased by treaty. It was hailed by all as a great step in the national existence, although it was really a far greater step than any one yet dreamed. "No colony in America," wrote Washington, "was ever settled under such favorable auspices as that which has just commenced at the Muskingum."

It had been provided that the new constitution should go

into effect when nine States had ratified it. That period having arrived, Congress fixed the first Wednesday in January, 1789, for the choice of Presidential electors, and the first Wednesday in March for the date when the new government should go into power. On March 4, 1789, the Continental Congress ceased to exist, but it was several weeks before either House of the new Congress was organized. On April 6th the organization of the two Houses was complete, the electoral votes were counted; and on April 21st John Adams took his seat as Vice-president in the chair of the Senate. On the 30th of April the streets around the old "Federal Hall" in New York City were so densely crowded that it seemed, in the vivid phrase of an eye-witness, "as if one might literally walk on the heads of the people." On the balcony of the hall was a table covered with crimson velvet, upon which lay a Bible on a crimson cushion. Out upon the balcony came, with his accustomed dignity, the man whose generalship, whose patience, whose self-denial, had achieved and then preserved the liberties of the nation; the man who, greater than Cæsar, had held a kingly crown within reach, and had refused it. Washington stood a moment amid the shouts of the people, then bowed, and took the oath, administered by Chancellor Livingston. At this moment a flag was raised upon the cupola of the hall; a discharge of artillery followed, and the assembled people again filled the air with their shouting. Thus simple was the ceremonial which announced that a nation was born.

XIII.

OUR COUNTRY'S CRADLE.

> "Peace, which in *our country's cradle*
> Draws the sweet infant breath of gentle sleep."
> SHAKESPEARE. *Richard II.*, i. 3.

THE year 1789 saw a new nation in its cradle in the city of New York. Liberty was born, but had yet to learn how to go alone. Political precedents were still to be established, social customs to be formed anew. New York City, the first seat of national government, had warmly welcomed Washington, though the State of New York had not voted for him; and now that he was in office, men and women waited with eager interest to see what kind of political and social life would surround him. The city then contained nearly thirty-three thousand people. It had long been more cosmopolitan than any other in the colonies, but it had also been longer occupied by the British, and had been more lately under the influence of loyal traditions and royal officials. This influence the languid sway of the "confederation" had hardly dispelled. What condition of things would the newly organized republic establish?

It was a period of much social display. Class distinctions still prevailed strongly, for the French Revolution had not yet followed the American Revolution to sweep them away. Employers were still called masters; gentlemen still wore velvets, damasks, knee-breeches, silk stockings, silver buckles, ruffled shirts, voluminous cravats, scarlet cloaks. The Revolution had made many poor, but it had enriched many, and money was lavishly spent. People gave great entertainments, kept tankards of punch on the table for morning visitors of both sexes, and returned in sedan-chairs from evening parties. Dr. Manasseh Cutler went to a dinner-party of forty-four gentlemen at the house of General Knox, just before his appointment as Secretary of War. All the guests were officers of the late Continental army, and every one, except Cutler himself, wore the badge of the Society of the Cincinnati. On another occasion he dined there with a French nobleman; the dinner was served "in high style, much in the French style." Mrs. Knox seemed to him to mimic "the military style," which he found "very disgusting in a female." This is his description of her head-dress: "Her hair in front is craped at least a foot high, much in the form of a churn bottom upward, and topped off with a wire skeleton in the same form, covered with black gauze, which hangs in streamers down her back. Her hair behind is in a large braid, and confined with a monstrous crooked comb."

Mrs. Knox's head-dress would have had no more importance than that of any other lady of the period, but that no other lady came so near to being the active head of American "society" at the outset of this government. General Knox and his wife were two people of enormous size—were, indeed, said to be the largest couple in New York—and they were as expansive in their hospitality as in their persons. The European visitors, who were abundant about that time, and especially the numerous Frenchmen who flocked to see the new republic—and who then, as now, gravitated naturally to that society where they were best amused—turned readily to Mrs. Knox's entertainments from those of Mrs. Washington. One traveller even complained of the new President that his bows were more distant and stiff than any he had seen in England. Of the other members of the cabinet, neither Hamilton, Jefferson, nor Randolph was in a position to receive company in the grand style, so that during the short period when New York was the seat of government, the house of the Knoxes in Broadway was emphatically the centre of social vivacity for the nation.

This was a matter of some importance when more political questions were settled at the dinner-table than in public debate, and when Washington himself would invite his subordinates to discuss affairs of State "over a bottle of wine." The social life of any community is always the foundation of its political life, and this was especially true when the United States began to exist, because there was a general suspicion in Europe that the new republic would be hopelessly plebeian. When we consider that even in 1845 an English lady of rank, trying to dissuade Dickens from visiting America, said, "Why do you not go down to Brighton, and visit the third and fourth rate people there?—that would be just the same," we know that she only expressed the current British feeling, which must have existed very much more strongly in 1789. What could be the social condition of that country whose highest official had never been in Europe, and did not speak French? Against this suspicion the six white horses of President Washington were a comparatively slight protest. Mere wealth can buy horses; indeed, they are among the first symptoms of wealth. To discerning observers the true mark of superiority was to be found in the grave dignity of the man. It is hard to see how he acquired that trait among the jovial fox-hunting squires in whose society he had been reared; perhaps his real training was in his long and silent expeditions in the woods. His manners and his bearing showed the marks of that forest life, and not of an artificial society; his gait, according to his enthusiastic admirer, William Sullivan, was that of a farmer or woodsman, not of a soldier; he reminded Josiah Quincy of the country gentlemen from Western Massachusetts, not accustomed to mix much in society, and not easy or graceful, though strictly polite. But the most genuine personal dignity he certainly had; his wife sustained him in it—at least until party bitterness began to prevail—and therefore the young French noblemen found his manners as unquestionably good as their own, though less pliant.

Nor were any of the members of his cabinet wanting in this respect. French society as well as French political principles had influenced Jefferson, and he showed by his flattering words to Madame De Brehan and other fine ladies that he had cultivated the arts of a courtier; Hamilton had refined manners, with the ready adaptation that came from his French blood and his West India birth; Randolph was called "the first gentleman of Virginia," though described by Sullivan as grave and heavy in aspect; while the cheerful Knox was a man of better early education than any of these, for he had been a bookseller, and his bookstore in Boston had been, it is recorded, "a great resort for the British officers and Tory ladies who were the *ton* at that period." Tried by the standard of the time, there was nothing to be ashamed of, but, indeed, quite the contrary, in the bearing of Washington's cabinet ministers. John Adams was Vice-president, and the Chief-justice was the high-minded John Jay. Both these men had agreeable and accomplished wives. Mrs. Adams was a woman of much social experience as well as talent and character. She describes Mrs. Jay as "showy but pleasing," and both these women appear to greatest advantage in their letters to their respective husbands. As to the households of the cabinet ministers, Jefferson was a widower; Mrs. Knox has already been characterized; and the French traveller Brissot described Mrs. Hamilton as "a charming woman, who joined to the graces all the candor and simplicity of the American wife." These made the leading official families at the seat of government.

The French Minister at that time was the Comte de Moustier, whose sister, Madame De Brehan, accompanied him to this country. Jefferson had assured her that her manners were a "model of perfection," while others found her "a little, singular, whimsical, hysterical old woman." His secretary of legation was M. Otto, part of whose keen and penetrating correspondence has lately been translated by Mr. Bancroft; he had married an American wife, one of the Livingston family. The English Consul-general, Sir John Temple, had also married an American, the daughter of Governor Bowdoin, of Massachusetts. These were the leading people "in society"—a society whose standard, after all, was not luxurious or extravagant. Oliver Wolcott wrote to his wife when he was invited to come to New York as Auditor of the Treasury: "The example of the President and his family will render parade and expense improper and disreputable." It is pleasant to add that after three months' stay at the seat of government, he wrote home to his mother, "Honesty is as much in fashion as in Connecticut."

Mrs. Washington's receptions were reproached as "introductory to the pageantry of courts," but it was very modest pageantry. Nothing could have been less festive or more harmless than the hospitality of the Presidential abode. An English manufacturer who was invited there to breakfast reports a meal of admirable simplicity—tea, coffee, sliced tongue, dry toast, and butter—"but no broiled fish, as is the general custom," he adds. At her evening receptions Mrs. Washington offered her guests tea and coffee with plum-cake; at nine she warned her visitors that the general kept early hours, and after this remark the guests had no choice but to do the same. At these entertainments of hers the President was but a guest—without his sword—and found it necessary also to retreat in good order at the word of command. His own receptions were for invited guests only, and took place every other week between three and four P.M. The President stood before the fireplace in full black velvet, with his hair powdered and gathered into a bag; he wore yellow gloves and silver buckles, with a steel-hilted sword in a white leather scabbard; he held in his hand a cocked hat with a feather. This is the description given by William Sullivan, in his "Familiar Letters on Public Characters."

If it was the object of Washington to make these occasions stiffer than the drawing-rooms of any crowned potentate, he succeeded. Names were announced, gentlemen were presented, the President bowed, but never shook hands; at a quarter past three the doors were closed, and the visitors formed a circle; the President made the circuit, addressing a few words to each; then they bowed and retired. It is hard to imagine that these mild entertainments could have been severely censured as extravagant or monarchical; one can better comprehend how the censure could be applied to the street equipage of the new President—the cream-colored carriage painted in medallions, and the liveries of white turned up with green. Yet these were, perhaps, more readily recognized as essential to the dignity of his station.

It was with the desire of promoting this dignity that the Senators of the new nation were anxious to give the President an official title. The plan was said to have originated with John Adams, who believed "splendor and majesty" to be important in a republic; and there was a joint committee of Congress to consider the matter. This committee reported against it, but the dissatisfied Senate still favored a title, as it well might, at a time when the Senators themselves were habitually called "Most Honorable." They proposed to call the Chief Magistrate "His Highness, the President of the United States of America, and Protector of their Liberties." The House objected; the country at large was divided. Chief-justice McKean proposed "His Serene Highness;" somebody else suggested "The President-general;" and Governor Sullivan thought that "His Patriotic Majesty" would not be inappropriate, since he represented the majesty of the people. Washington himself, it is said, favored "His High Mightiness," which was the phrase used by the Stadtholder of Holland. It was the common-sense of the nation that swept these extravagances aside; it was one

AT MRS. WASHINGTON'S RECEPTION.

of the many occasions in American history when the truth of Talleyrand's saying has been vindicated, that everybody knows more than anybody.

But when it became needful to go behind these externals, and to select a cabinet ministry for the actual work of government, the sane and quiet judgment of Washington made itself felt. At that period the cabinet consisted of but four persons, and it was the theory that it should not be made up of mere clerks and staff officers, but of the ablest and most conspicuous men in the nation. Washington being President, Adams and Jay having also been assigned to office, there naturally followed the two men who had contributed most in their different ways to the intellectual construction of the nation. Hamilton and Jefferson were brought together in the cabinet—the one as Secretary of the Treasury, the other as Secretary of State—not because they agreed, but because they differed. Tried by all immediate and temporary tests, it is impossible to deny to Hamilton the position of leading intellect during the constitutional period; and his clear and cogent ability contrasts strongly with the peculiar mental action, always fresh and penetrating, but often lawless and confused, of his great rival. Hamilton was more coherent, more truthful, more combative, more generous, and more limited. His power was as an organizer and advocate of measures, and this is a less secure passport to fame than lies in the announcement of great principles. The difference between Hamilton and Jefferson on questions of finance and States-rights was only the symbol of a deeper divergence. The contrast between them was not so much in acts as in theories; not in what they did, but in what they dreamed. Both had their visions, and held to them ardently, but the spirit of the nation was fortunately stronger than either; it made Hamilton support a republic against his will, and made Jefferson acquiesce, in spite of himself, in a tolerably strong central government.

There is not a trace of evidence that Hamilton, even when most denounced as a "monocrat" and a "monist," ever desired to bring about a monarchy in America. He no doubt believed the British constitution to be the most perfect model of government ever devised by man; but it is also true, as Jefferson himself admitted, that Hamilton saw the spirit of the American people to be wholly republican. This is just what Hamilton

ALEXANDER HAMILTON.
[From the portrait by Weimar, in the Governor's Room, New York City Hall.]

says of himself; all his action was based on the opinion "that the political principle of this country would endure nothing but republican government." Fisher Ames, his ablest ally, said the same as explicitly: "Monarchy is no path of liberty—offers no hopes. It could not stand; and would, if tried, lead to more agitation and revolution than anything else." What Hamilton and Ames believed—and very reasonably, so far as the mere teachings of experience went—was that a republic was an enormous risk to run; and they drew the very questionable conclusion that this risk must be diminished by making the republic as much like a monarchy as possible. For instance, if Hamilton could have had his way, only holders of real estate would have had the right to vote for President and Senators, and these would have held office for life, or at least during good behavior; the President would have appointed all the Governors of States, and they would have had a veto on all State legislation. All this he announced in the Constitutional Convention, with the greatest frankness, not hesitating to call even the British House of Lords "a most noble institution." Having thus indicated his ideal government, he accepted what he could get, and gave his great powers to carrying out a constitution about which he had serious misgivings. On the other hand, if Jefferson could have had his way, national organization would have been a shadow. "Were it left me to decide," he once wrote, "whether we should have a government without newspapers or a newspaper without a government, I should not hesitate a moment to prefer the latter." He accepted the constitution as a necessary evil, tempered by newspapers—then the very worst newspapers that ever flourished on American soil.

"Hamilton and I," wrote Jefferson, "were pitted against each other every day in the cabinet, like two fighting-cocks." The first passage between them was the only one in which Hamilton had clearly the advantage of his less practised antagonist, making Jefferson, indeed, the instrument of his own defeat. The transfer of the capital to the banks of the Potomac was secured by the first of many compromises between the Northern and Southern States, after a debate in which the formidable slavery question showed itself often, as it had shown itself at the very formation of the constitution. The removal of the capital was clearly the price paid by Hamilton for Jefferson's acquiescence in his first great financial measure. This measure was the national assumption of the State debts to an amount not to exceed twenty million dollars. It was met by vehement opposition, partly because it bore very unequally on the States, but mainly on the ground that the claims were in the hands of speculators, and were greatly depreciated. Yet it was an essential part of that great series of financial projects on which Hamilton's fame must rest, even more than on his papers in the *Federalist*—though these secured the adoption of the constitution. Three measures—the assumption of the State debts, the funding act, and the national bank—were what changed the bankruptcy of the new nation into solvency and credit. There may be question as to the good or bad precedents established by these enactments, but there can be no doubt as to their immediate success. Jefferson opposed them; it is certain that Jefferson never could have originated them or carried them through. The financial problem—the first, and in one sense the lowest problem to be met by the new government—was solved by Hamilton.

It seems curious to find in the correspondence of the public men of that day so little that relates to the appointment or removal of particular officials. One reason is that the officials were then so few. The whole number in civil office during Washington's administration were, in his own phrase, "a mere handful," and during his two Presidential terms he removed but eight, all for cause, this list not including Mr. Pinckney, the French Minister, who was recalled by desire of the government of that nation. The question of removal was almost wholly an abstract one, but, fortunately for us, the men of that period had a great taste for the abstract principles of government; and the consequence was that this particular question was debated as fully and ardently as if the number of officials had already been reckoned by tens of thousands. Many points in the prolonged controversy seem like the civil service discussions of to-day. The main debate took place in the House of Representatives, beginning June 16, 1789, and lasting four days; and it is fortunately preserved to us in full as a part of the appendix to "Elliott's Debates." It arose on the bill to establish the Department of Foreign Affairs, afterwards called the State Department. It was moved to strike out the words —as applied to the officer thus created—" to be removable from office by the President of the United States." The importance of the subject was amply recognized, Mr. Madison going so far as to say: " The decision that is at this time made will become the permanent exposition of the constitution; and on a permanent exposition of the constitution will depend the genius and character of the whole government." He and others took the ground that in no way could full executive responsibility be placed upon the President unless he had a corresponding power over his subordinates. All the familiar arguments in favor of a strong government were brought forward, and they were met by the obvious arguments against it. "This clause of the bill," said Mr. Page, of North Carolina, "contains in it the seeds of royal prerogative. Everything which has been said in favor of energy in the Executive may go to the destruction of freedom, and establish despotism. This very energy, so much talked of, has led many patriots to the Bastile, to the block, and to the halter."

Perhaps the ablest assailant of the power of removal was Elbridge Gerry, of Massachusetts — he through whom a new and permanent phrase was added to the American dialect in the word *gerrymander*. He claimed in this debate that unlimited removal from office belonged only to a king; that to a four years' President such power could only be made useful "by being the means of procuring him a re-election." If this step were taken, he said, the Presidency should be for life, or even hereditary. With some foresight of our later experience he added: "The officers, instead of being the machinery of the government, moving in regular order prescribed by the legislature, will be the mere puppets of the President, to be employed or thrown aside as useless lumber according to his fancy." His arguments did not prevail; the clause was retained by a vote of 34 to 20, and after some further modification the bill passed by a small majority in the House, and by the casting vote of the Vice-president in the Senate. The result of that vote has not been followed by quite the evils that Page and Gerry feared, but it has undoubtedly influenced, as Madison predicted, the genius and character of the whole government. It is to be remembered that no prophetic vision had yet revealed to any one the vast future population for which Congress was legislating, and Madison plainly thought himself making a very bold guess when he estimated that it might "in some years" double in number, and reach six millions.

On the 16th of July, 1790, Congress made up its mind to remove to the banks of the Potomac, but before the site was fixed upon, the seat of government was temporarily transferred (in November, 1790) to Philadelphia, then the largest town in the country, and claiming to be regarded as its metropolis. The French visitors criticised the city, found its rectangular formation tiresome, and the habits of its people sad; but Americans thought it gay and delightful. Brissot de Warville declared that the pretensions of the ladies were "too affected to be pleasing," and the Comte de Rochambeau said that the wives of merchants went to the extreme of French fashions. Mrs. John Adams, who had lived in Europe, complained of a want of etiquette, but found Philadelphia society eminently friendly and agreeable. Superior taste and a livelier wit were habitually claimed for the Philadelphia ladies. It was said by a vivacious maiden who went from that city to New York—Rebecca Franks, afterwards Lady Johnston—that the Philadelphia belles had "more cleverness in the turn of an eye than those of New York in their whole composition." In the latter city, she said,

MRS. BINGHAM.

there was no conversation without the aid of cards; in Philadelphia the chat never flagged. There were plenty of leading ladies. Mrs. Knox was still conspicuous, playing perpetual whist. Mrs. Bingham was the most charming of hostesses; and among women coming from other parts of the country, and celebrated for character or beauty, were Mrs. Theodore Sedgwick, of Massachusetts, and Mrs. Oliver Wolcott, of Litchfield,

Connecticut. It was of the latter that the story is told that the British Minister said to Senator Tracy, of Connecticut: "Your countrywoman would be admired at St. James's." "Sir," said the patriotic American, "she is admired even on Litchfield Hill."

There was in Philadelphia a theatre which was much attended, and which must have had a rather exceptional company for that period, inasmuch as Chief-justice Jay assured his wife that it was composed of "decent, moral people." In society, habits were not always quite moral, or conversation always quite decent. Gentlemen, according to John Adams, sat till eleven o'clock over their after-dinner wine, and drank healths in that elaborate way which still amazes the American visitor in England. Nay, young ladies, if we may accept Miss Rebecca Franks as authority, drank each other's health out of punch tankards in the morning. Gambling prevailed among both sexes. It was not uncommon to hear that a man or woman had lost three or four hundred dollars in an evening. An anonymous letter-writer, quoted in Mr. Griswold's "Republican Court," declares that some resident families could not have supported the cost of their entertainments and their losses at loo, but that they had the adroitness to make the temporary residents pay their expenses. At balls people danced country-dances, the partners being designated beforehand by the host, and being usually unchanged during the whole evening—though "this severity was sometimes mitigated," in the language of the Marquis de Chastellux—and the supper was served about midnight. Talleyrand, in later years, looking back on the Philadelphia of that period, found its luxury a theme for sarcasm in quality as well as quantity: *Leur luxe est affreux*, he said. Going beyond the strict circles of fashion, we find that some social peculiarities which we regard as recent seem to have existed in full force at the very foundation of the republic. The aversion of white Americans to domestic service, the social freedom given to young girls, the habit of eating hot bread — these form the constant theme of remark by the French visitors in the time of Washington. In some physiological matters American habits are now unquestionably modified for the better. Chastellux reports that at the best dinners of the period there was usually but one course besides the dessert; and Volney describes people as drinking very strong tea immediately after this meal, and clos-

MRS. THEODORE SEDGWICK.

ing the evening with a supper of salt meat. At other points, again, the national traits seem to have been bewilderingly transformed by the century that has since passed. The Chevalier de Beaujour describes Americans as usually having ruddy complexions, but without delicacy of feature or play of expression; whereas all these characteristics will be found by the testimony of later travellers to be now precisely reversed, the features having grown delicate, the expression vivacious, and the complexion pale.

The standard of women's education was still low, and in society they had to rely on native talent and the conversation of clever men; yet Mercy Warren's history had been accepted as a really able work, and Phillis Wheatley's poems had passed for a phenomenon. Mrs. Morton, of Massachusetts, also, under the name of "Philenia," had published a poem called "Beacon Hill," of which Robert Treat Paine, himself a man of ability, had written in this admiring strain:

> "Beacon shall live, the theme of future lays,
> Philenia bids; obsequious time obeys.
> Beacon shall live, embalmed in verse sublime,
> The new Parnassus of a nobler clime."

The original beacon has long since fallen; the hill to which it gave its name has been much cut down; and the fame of Philenia has been yet more sadly obliterated. Yet she and such as she undoubtedly contributed to the vague suspicions of monarchical design which began to array themselves against Washington. For did not these tuneful people write birthday odes to him; and were not birthday odes clearly monarchical?

Great men are sometimes influenced by minor considerations. It is probable that Washington's desire to retire from the Presidency after one term was largely due to the public criticisms on such innocent things as these melodious flatteries and Mrs. Washington's receptions. But he was still overwhelmingly popular, and his re-election in 1792 was unanimous; John Adams being again Vice-president, and the seat of government being still Philadelphia. It was thought at first by both Jefferson and Hamilton that the ceremony of a re-inaugration should be a wholly private one at the President's house, but it was finally decided by the cabinet that it should be public and in the Senate-chamber. Washington thus entered on a second term of office, which was destined to be far stormier than his first term. There were the Indian troubles to be settled, the whiskey insurrection in Pennsylvania to be curbed, and the balance of neutrality to be kept between France and England. The first two questions, though they seemed to belong to military matters alone, were yet complicated with politics, and the last was interwoven with the public affairs of all Europe. No President, except Abraham Lincoln, has ever yet had to deal with questions so difficult; and it is to be remembered that Lincoln had behind him the aid of national traditions already formed, while Washington dealt with a newly organized government, and had to create even the traditions.

The great scheme for filling the North-western Territory with settlers had seriously lagged. Great Britain still held her posts there; this encouraged the Indian tribes who had never been included in the treaty of peace. It was at this time that Kentucky earned the name of the "dark and bloody ground," more than fifteen hundred of her pioneer settlers having been killed or captured within a few years. General Mercer was sent against the Indians with a small body of men in 1790, and was defeated; General St. Clair was ordered out the following year, with a much larger force, and was beaten disastrously, losing nearly a thousand men and many cannon. Washington tried in vain to reach the Indians by treaty, and it took "Mad Anthony Wayne" and five thousand men to bring about peace at last. Near the site of what is now Cincinnati, Wayne made his winter camp in 1793; he built forts to strengthen his forward march, and in August, 1794, fought the battle of Maumee Rapids against Indians and Canadians, with the aid of eleven hundred Kentucky volunteers. In this battle he completely and finally routed the Miami Indians, with a loss of but one hundred men, and within sight of a British fort; and he forced the enemy to cease hostilities. On August 3, 1795, Wayne stood in presence of more than a thousand Indians at one of his forts, now Greenville, Ohio, and there made a treaty which put an end to the Indian wars. This, with the provisions of Jay's treaty with England, presently to be mentioned, flung open the Western country to the tide of settlers.

The French Revolution, passing from its period of promise into its epoch of terror, had divided American feeling as it had not before been sundered. This formidable French question had ceased to be a mere test of political sympathy; it was a matter of social feeling as well. England was the traditional enemy of the nation; France the traditional friend; yet France was causing horror to the world, while England stood for established order. Those who had tried to save the American experiment by keeping as near the English constitution as possible might well point to France as the example of the opposite method. Accordingly, the Federalists, who comprised the wealthier and more prominent class of the nation, renewed their fidelity to the English traditions. They called the Democrats *sans culottes*, and regarded them not merely as belonging to the less educated and less dignified class—which was true—but as socially polluted and degraded. When the President's wife found that her granddaughter, Nelly Custis, had been receiving a guest in her absence, she asked who it was; then noticing a stain where a head had rested against the straw-colored wall-paper, she exclaimed: "It was no Federalist: none but a filthy Democrat would mark the wall with his good-for-nothing head in that manner." Such remarks, when repeated from mouth to mouth, did not conduce to the amenities of life.

Yet the good lady had plenty of provocation. Much could be pardoned to a wife who had seen on printed handbills the coarse wood-cuts that represented Washington as placed upon the guillotine like the French king. Such a caricature, when injudiciously shown by Knox to the President at a cabinet meeting, drove him into "a transport of passion," according to the not always trustworthy record of Jefferson; how, then, could his wife be indifferent to it? There was really nothing serious to quarrel about in the home affairs of the country. The charge of monarchical tendencies amounted to nothing; the clearheaded Oliver Wolcott wrote that he could not find a man of sense who seriously believed it; and yet Washington was abused as if he carried a crown in his pocket. These attacks came most furiously from the poet Freneau in his *National Gazette*, established October 31, 1791; and Jefferson, in whose office Freneau was translating clerk, declared that this newspaper had saved the constitution, which was "galloping fast into monarchy;" that it had "checked the career of the Monocrats," and the like. Washington must have chafed all the more under these attacks because the editor, with persistent and painful courtesy, sent him four copies of every issue—a refinement of cruelty such as our milder times can hardly parallel.

All these troubles were exasperated by the arrival, on April 9, 1793, of the first envoy of the new French republic, M. Genet. He was received with a display of enthusiasm that might have turned any man's head, and his, apparently, needed no turning. His journey from Charleston, South Carolina, to Philadelphia was like the reception of Lafayette; all the triumphant rights of man were supposed to be embodied in him, and the airs he took upon himself seem now incredible. He undertook to fit out privateers in American ports, and to bring prizes into those ports for condemnation by French consuls; and when Washington checked this impertinence, he threatened to appeal from Washington to the people. The nation was instantly divided into two parties, and whatever extravagances the French sympathizers might commit, the Federalists doubled them in imagination. They sincerely believed that all sorts of horrors were transacted at the banquets given to Genet; that the guests in turn wore the red revolutionary cap—the *bonnet rouge*; that a roasted pig received the name of the slain King of France, and that the severed head was offered in turn to each guest, who exclaimed, theatrically, "Tyrant!" and struck it with his knife. These stories may have been chiefly false, but they produced as much effect as if they had been true. On the other hand, Genet behaved so foolishly and insolently that Jefferson had to abandon his cause. "If our citizens," he wrote, "have not already been shedding each other's blood, it is not owing to the moderation of Mr. Genet." Jefferson himself assented to Washington's proclamation of neutrality (April 22, 1793), though he rejoiced that it was not issued under that precise name. Indeed, throughout the excitement, Jefferson seems to have contributed only the needful influence to do justice to the French view of the question, and was less extravagant in that way than Hamilton on the other side.

But after all these extravagances, real or reputed, it was natural that every outbreak should be charged to the "democratic societies." Washington thought that they instigated the Whiskey Insurrection which arose in Pennsylvania in 1794 against the excise laws—an insurrection which denounced such laws as "the horror of all free States," and went so far as to threaten separation from the Union. It was Hamilton who had framed the law which caused the revolt, and Hamilton contributed the admirable suggestion by which it was quelled. His plan was to call out so large a force as instantly to overawe the insurrection and crush it without firing a shot. Washington accordingly summoned out 13,000 militia, and the work was done. Unfortunately it led to the reaction which usually follows a complete strategic success—people turn round and say that there never was any danger. The most skilful victories even in war are the bloodless ones, but it is apt to be bloodshed alone that wins laurels. It happened thus in this case. Jefferson declared the affair to have been merely a riot, and not nearly so bad as the excise law which created it; he held to the theory which he had announced during Shays's rebellion, that an occasional popular commotion was a good remedy for too much government.

Jay's treaty with England (November 19, 1794) was the turning-point of the personal popularity of Washington. From that time a large and increasing minority opposed the President with all the bitterness of the period; that is, furiously. The treaty secured the withdrawal of the British garrisons from the North-west, and it guaranteed payment from the British treasury for all illegal captures—a payment that amounted to ten millions of dollars. So far it might have been popular; but it provided also for the payment of all debts owed before the Revolution by Americans to British subjects, and this would have been enough to make it unpalatable. But it also had to encounter the rising sympathy for France, and this led to the most vehement opposition. The indignation against it broke out in mobs. Jay was burned or hanged in effigy in several cities; Adams was in one case hanged beside him, with a purse of English guineas in his hand; and the treaty itself was burned in Philadelphia by a mob of ten thousand people, before the windows of the British Minister. Hamilton, in speaking for it at a public meeting in New York, was assailed by a volley of stones. "Gentlemen," he said, "if you use such strong arguments, I must retire." But he only retired to write a series of papers in defence of the treaty, which was ratified by just the needful two-thirds vote, after a fortnight of discussion.

We think of those times as purer than the present; yet the perennial moaning over the decline of the republic had already begun in the first decade of its existence. Fauchet, the French minister who succeeded Genet, declared, truly or falsely, that Edmund Randolph, who was at first Attorney-general, but had now succeeded Jefferson as Secretary of State, had come to him and asked for a bribe to espouse the French side. "Thus," said the indignant Frenchman, "the consciences of the pretended patriots of America have already their prices. What will be the old age of this government if it is thus already decrepit!" And as to political violence, the habitual abuse of Washington went on increasing; the Democratic Republicans spoke of him habitually in their private meetings as "Montezuma;" they allowed him neither uprightness, nor pecuniary honesty, nor military ability, nor even personal courage. He himself wrote that every act of his administration was tortured, and the grossest misrepresentations made "in such exaggerated and indecent terms as could scarcely be applied to a Nero, to a notorious defaulter, or even to a common pickpocket."

His farewell address was made public in September, 1796, and he met Congress December 7th, for the last time. The electoral votes, as counted by the Senate in the following February (1797), showed John Adams, of Massachusetts, to have the highest number, and he was declared President-elect; while Jefferson, who had the next number, was pronounced to be the Vice-president-elect, according to a constitutional provision since altered. On his last day in office Washington wrote to Knox comparing himself to "the weary traveller who sees a resting-place, and is bending his body to lean thereon. To be suffered to do this in peace," he added, "is too much to be endured by some." Accordingly, on that very day a Philadelphia newspaper dismissed him with a final tirade, whose wild folly is worth remembering by all who think that political virulence is on the increase:

"'Lord now lettest thou Thy servant depart in peace, for mine eyes have seen Thy salvation!' This was the exclamation of a man who saw a flood of blessedness breaking in upon mankind. If ever there was a time that allowed this exclamation to be repeated, that time is the present. The man who is the source of all our country's misery is this day reduced to the rank of his fellow-citizens, and has no longer the power to multiply the woes of these United States. Now more than ever is the time to rejoice. Every heart which feels for the liberty and happiness of the people must now beat with rapture at the thought that this day the name of Washington ceases to give currency to injustice and to legalize corruption.... When we look back upon the eight years of Washington's administration, it strikes us with astonishment that one man could thus poison the principles of republicanism among our enlightened people, and carry his designs against the public liberty so far as to endanger its very existence. Yet such is the fact, and if this is apparent to all, this day should form a jubilee in the United States."

XIV.

THE EARLY AMERICAN PRESIDENTS.

AN acute foreign observer said well, in the days when John Adams was President, that there seemed to be in the United States many Englishmen, many Frenchmen, but very few Americans. The reason was that the French Revolution really drew a red-hot ploughshare through the history of America as well as through that of France. It not merely divided parties, but moulded them: gave them their demarcations, their watchwords, and their bitterness. The home issues were for a time subordinate, collateral; the real party lines were established on the other side of the Atlantic.

Up to the time when the Constitution was formed, it is curious to see that France was only the friend of the young nation, not its political counsellor. The proof of this is that, in the debates which formed the Constitution, France was hardly mentioned; the authorities, the illustrations, the analogies, were almost all English. Yet the leading statesmen of the period—Franklin, Jay, Adams, Jefferson—had been resident in Paris as diplomatists; and Hamilton was of French descent on the mother's side. France, however, gave them no model for imitation; the frame of government, where it was not English, was simply American. A few years more, and all was changed; in America, as in Europe, the French Revolution was the absorbing theme. The American newspapers of the day existed mainly to give information about foreign affairs; and they really gave more space to France than to their own country. They told something about the wrongs of the French people, though few besides Jefferson took them seriously to heart. They told a great deal about the horrors of the outbreak, and here men divided. American political parties are to-day still imbittered by the traditions of that great division.

COUNT FERSEN.

Those who had always distrusted the masses of the people inevitably began to distrust them more than ever. They read Burke's "Reflections on the French Revolution," they read Canning's editorials, and they attributed the French excesses to innate depravity, to atheism, to madness. Let the people have its own way, they argued, and it will always wish to cut off the heads of the better classes, or swing them up to the streetlantern. Those who thus reasoned were themselves the better classes, in the ordinary sense; they were the clergy, the lawyers, the planters, the merchants—the men who had, or thought they had, the largest stake in the country. The Frenchmen they had seen were the young men of rank and fortune who had helped America to fight through the Revolution — generous, high-souled, joyous young soldiers, of whom Lafayette was the conspicuous type. Of the same class were the Frenchmen who had visited America since the Revolution; who had been pleased with everything and had flattered everybody. The handsome Count Fersen, who had charmed all hearts at Newport, was the very man who had, in the disguise of a coachman, driven the French king and queen in their escape from Paris. Lauzun, the brilliant commander of French cavalry under Rochambeau, was also the picturesque hero who refused to have his hands tied on ascending the guillotine, but said gayly to the executioner, "We are both Frenchmen; we shall do our duty." Who could help sympathizing with these fine young fellows? But this revolutionist in the red cap, this Jacques with wooden shoes, these knitting women, these terrible *tricoteuses*, the Federalists had not seen; and doubtless the nearer they had seen them the less they would have liked them. Consequently, like Burke, they "pitied the plumage, but forgot the dying bird." To them everything French was now pernicious; the Reign of Terror was not much worse than was the career of those more moderate revolutionists who resisted that terror or fell beneath it. The opinions of this party were best represented by that celebrated periodical, the *Anti-Jacobin*, now chiefly remembered by Canning's best known poem, "The Needy Knife-Grinder." But the *Anti-Jacobin* lashed every grade of Frenchman and Frenchwoman with equal bitterness, if they took the side of the people; assailed Madame Roland and Madame De Staël as coarsely as it denounced Robespierre or Danton. The American Federalists held the same attitude.

To look below the surface of the French Revolution, to see in it the righting of a vast wrong, to find in that wrong some explanation of its very excesses, this view — now so generally accepted — was confined to a very few of the leaders: Jefferson, Samuel Adams, Albert Gallatin. Here, as is usual, the reformer found secret affinities with the demagogue. It is easier for the demagogue than for any one else to pose for a time as a reformer, and even to be mistaken for one; and on the other hand the reformer is always tempted to make excuses for the demagogue, since he himself has usually to wage war against the respectable classes. Some men were Federalists because they were high-minded, others because they were narrow-minded; while the more far-sighted, and also the less scrupulous, became Democrats—or, in the original name, Republicans. They used this last term not in the rather vague sense of current American politics, but in a much more definite manner. In calling themselves Republicans they sincerely believed that nobody else wished well to the republic. Thus the party lines which we should have expected to find drawn simply on American questions were in fact almost wholly controlled by European politics. The Federalists were in sympathy with England; the Democrats, or Republicans, with France; and this determined the history of the nation, its treaties and its parties, through a series of administrations.

The Federalist President-elect was John Adams—a man of great pith and vigor, whose letters and diaries are more racy than those of any man of that day, though his more elaborate writings are apt to be prolix and dull, like those of the others. He was a self-made man, as people say, and one who had a strong natural taste for rank and ceremony; even having, as John Randolph complained, "arms emblazoned on the 'scutcheon of the vice-regal carriage." The more he held to this aristocratic position, the more people remarked his original want of it; and there have lived within twenty years in Boston old ladies who still habitually spoke of him as "that cobbler's son." But he was a man, moreover, of extraordinary sense and courage, combined with an explosive temper, and a decided want of tact. He had at first the public sentiment of New England behind him, and a tolerably united party. Having been Vice-president under Washington, he seemed to be the natural successor; and the peculiar arrangement then prevailing, by which the Vice-president was not voted for as a distinct officer, but was simply

JOHN ADAMS.

[Engraved by G. Kruell, from the painting by Gilbert Stuart, owned by T. Jefferson Coolidge, Esq., Boston.]

the Presidential candidate who stood second on the list, led to many complications of political manœuvring, the result of which was that John Adams had 71 electoral votes, and became President, while Thomas Jefferson had 68 votes, and took the next place, greatly to his discontent. Adams and Jefferson were quite as inappropriately brought together in executive office as were Jefferson and Hamilton in the cabinet of Washington.

Abigail Adams, the President's wife, was undoubtedly the most conspicuous American woman of her day, whether by position or by character. When writing to her husband she often signed herself " Portia," in accordance with a stately and perhaps rather high-flown habit of the period; and she certainly showed qualities which would have done honor to either the Roman or Shakespearian heroine of that name. In her letters we see her thoroughly revealed. While the battle of Bunker Hill was in progress, she wrote that it was "dreadful but glorious;" and in the depression of the battle of Long Island she said, " If all America is to be ruined and undone by a pack of cowards and knaves, I wish to know it," and added, " Don't you know me better than to think me a coward?" When, first among American women, she represented her nation at the court of St. James, she met with equal pride the contemptuous demeanor of Queen Charlotte; and when her husband was chosen President, she wrote to him, " My feelings are not those of pride or ostentation upon the occasion; they are solemnized by a sense of the obligations, the important truths and numerous duties, connected with it." When finally, after four years, he failed of re-election, she wrote to her son: " The consequence to us is personally that we retire from public life. For myself and family I have few regrets. . . . If I did not rise with dignity, I can at least fall with ease." This was Abigail Adams. In person she was distinguished and noble rather than beautiful, yet it is satisfactory to know that when she was first presented at the British court she wore a white lutestring, trimmed with white crape, festooned with lilac ribbon and mock point-lace over a hoop of enormous extent, with a narrow train three yards long, looped up by a ribbon. She wore treble lace ruffles, a dress cap with long lace lappets, and two white plumes, these last doubtless soaring straight into the air above her head in the extraordinary style familiar to us in Gillray's caricatures of that period.

It was in those days no very agreeable task to be the wife of the President. Mrs. Adams has left on record a graphic sketch of the White House, where she presided for three months. The change in the seat of government had been decided upon for twelve years, yet the building was still a vast unfinished barrack, with few rooms plastered, no main stairway, not a bell within, not a fence without; it was distressingly cold in winter, while the Chief Magistrate of the United States could not obtain for love or money a man to cut wood for him in the forests which then surrounded Washington. From Washington to Baltimore extended an almost unbroken growth of timber, varied only by some small and windowless huts. There could as yet be in Washington no such varied companionship as had given attraction to the seat of government at New York and then at Philadelphia; yet at Georgetown there was a society which called itself eminently polite, and Mrs. Adams records that she returned fifteen calls in a single day.

Mr. Adams took his cabinet from his predecessor; it was not a strong one, and it was devoted to Hamilton, between whom and the new President there was soon a divergence, Hamilton being fond of power, and Adams having a laudable purpose to command his own ship. The figure of speech is appropriate, for he plunged into a sea of troubles, mainly created by the unreasonable demands of the French government. The French "Directory," enraged especially by Jay's treaty with England, got rid of one American minister by remonstrance, and drove out another with contempt. When Mr. Adams sent three special envoys, they were expected to undertake the most delicate negotiations with certain semi-official persons designated in their correspondence only by the letters X, Y, Z. The plan of this covert intercourse came through the private secretary of

ABIGAIL ADAMS.

M. de Talleyrand, then French Minister for Foreign Affairs; and the impudence of these three letters of the alphabet went so far as to propose a bribe of 1,200,000 francs (some $220,000) to be paid over to this minister. "You must pay money, a great deal of money," remarked Monsieur Y (*Il faut de l'argent, beaucoup de l'argent*). The secret of these names was kept, but the diplomatic correspondence was made public, and created much wrath in Europe as well as in America. Moreover, American vessels were constantly attacked by France, and yet Congress refused to arm its own ships. At last the insults passed beyond bearing, and it was at this time that "Millions for defence, not one cent for tribute," first became a proverbial phrase, having been originally used by Charles C. Pinckney, who, after having been expelled from France, was sent back again as one of the three envoys.

Then, with tardy decision, the Republicans yielded to the necessity of action, and the Federal party took the lead. War was not formally proclaimed, but treaties with France were declared to be no longer binding. An army was ordered to be created, with Washington as Lieutenant-general and Hamilton as second in command; and the President was authorized to appoint a Secretary of the Navy and to build twelve new ships-of-war. Before these were ready, naval hostilities had actually begun; and Commodore Truxton, in the U. S. frigate *Constellation*, captured a French frigate in West Indian waters (Feb. 9, 1799), and afterwards silenced another, which however escaped. Great was the excitement over these early naval successes of the young nation. Merchant-ships were authorized to arm themselves, and some three hundred acted upon this authority. It is to this period, and not as is commonly supposed to that of the Revolution, that Robert Treat Paine's song "Adams and Liberty" belongs. The result of it all was that France yielded. Talleyrand, the very minister who had dictated the insults, now disavowed them, and pledged his government to receive any minister the United States might send. The President, in the most eminently courageous act of his life, took the responsibility of again sending ambassadors; and did this without even consulting his cabinet, which would, as he well knew, oppose it.

They were at once received, and all danger of war with France was at an end.

This bold stroke separated the President permanently from at least half of his own party, since the Federalists did not wish for peace with France. His course would have given him a corresponding increase of favor from the other side, but for the great mistake the Federalists had made in passing certain laws, called the "Alien" law and the "Sedition" law; the first of these giving the President power to order any dangerous alien out of the country, and the second making it a penal offence to write anything false, scandalous, or malicious against the President or Congress. It was held, most justly, that this last law was directly opposed to the Constitution, which had been so amended as to guarantee freedom to the press. Looked at from this distance, it seems to have been one of those measures which inevitably destroy a party; and the Federalists certainly committed suicide when they passed it. It is clear that if it had stood, their own ablest newspapers four years after—Dennie's *Portfolio*, for instance—might have seen their proprietors imprisoned. These laws led to action almost equally extreme on the other side; the Republicans, powerless in Congress, fell back on their State Legislatures, and Kentucky and Virginia passed resolutions—drafted respectively by Jefferson and Madison—which went so near secession as to be quoted on that side at a later day. Kentucky distinctly resolved, in 1799, that any State might rightfully nullify any act of Congress which it regarded as unconstitutional.

Thus the bitterness grew worse and worse, till Adams dismissed from his cabinet the friends of Hamilton, calling them a "British faction." Hamilton, in turn, intrigued against Adams, and in 1800 the vote of South Carolina turned the scale in favor of the Republican electors. Jefferson and Burr, the two Republican nominees, had an equal number of votes—73; Adams having 65, Pinckney 64, and Jay 1. There was no choice, and the decision then went to the House of Representatives, which took six days to make its election, during which time the Constitution underwent such a party strain as has only once been equalled since that period. It ended in the election of Thomas Jefferson as President, and of Aaron Burr as Vice-president, and on March 4, 1801, they were sworn into office.

On the very day of his inauguration Jefferson took a step towards what he called simplicity, and what his opponents thought vulgarity. We know through an English traveller, John Davis, that, instead of driving with a coach-and-six to be inaugurated, the new President rode on horseback to the Capitol, without even a servant, tied his horse to the fence, and walked in. It was partly accidental—he was, at any rate, negotiating for a four-horse equipage in Virginia—but it was a characteristic accident. In the same way, thenceforward, instead of going with a state procession, at the opening of each Congress, to read his Message in person, as had hitherto been the custom, he sent it in writing. He would have no especial levees nor invited guests, but was accessible to any one at any hour. He was so unwilling to have his birthday celebrated that he concealed it as much as possible. These ways were criticised as those of a demagogue. The President was reproached with a desire to conciliate the mob, or, as it was then sometimes called—as, for instance, in Mrs. Adams's letters—the "mobility." His reason for sending a Message, according to that stout Federalist William Sullivan, was because a Speech could be answered, and a Message could not; although Sullivan asserts, in almost the next sentence, that Congress was utterly subservient to him, and it could therefore have made no difference. The discontinuance of formal levees is called by Sullivan "the abolition of all official dignity," and "descending to the lowest level."

Dennie's *Portfolio*, the best newspaper that had yet ap-

THOMAS JEFFERSON.

[Engraved by G. Kruell, from the painting by Gilbert Stuart, owned by T. Jefferson Coolidge, Esq., Boston.]

peared in the United States, contained, August 18, 1804, among eulogies of the poems of Burns, and burlesques upon the early lyrical effusions of Wordsworth, an imaginary diary, supposed to have been picked up near the White House in the previous February. In this the President was made to say: "Ordered my horse—never ride with a servant—looks proud—mob doesn't like it—must gull the boobies. Adams wouldn't bend so—would rather lose his place—knew nothing of the world." In another place he describes himself as meeting a countryman who took him for a Virginia overseer, and who talked politics. The countryman asked him to name one man of real character in the Democratic party. The President, after some stammering, suggested Jefferson, on which the countryman burst into a broad laugh, and asked him to enumerate his virtues—would he begin with his religion, chastity, courage, or honesty?—on which the President indignantly rode away. "Had he been as little as Sammy H. Smith," he adds, "I think I should have struck him." Ever since Jefferson's career as Governor of Virginia, the charge of personal cowardice had been unreasonably familiar.

The fictitious diary also contains some indecorous references to a certain "black Sally," a real or imaginary personage of that day whose companionship was thought discreditable to the President; also to the undoubted personal slovenliness of the Chief Magistrate—a point in which he showed an almost studied antagonism to the scrupulous proprieties of Washington. When Mr. Merry, the newly appointed British ambassador, went in official costume to be presented to the President at an hour previously appointed, he found himself, by his own narrative, "introduced to a man as the President of the United States, not merely in an undress, but actually standing in slippers down at the heels, and both pantaloons, coat, and underclothes indicative of utter slovenliness and indifference to appearance, and in a state of negligence actually studied." The minister went away with the very natural conviction that the whole scene was prepared and intended as an insult, not to himself, but to the sovereign whom he represented.

Mr. Merry's inference was probably quite unjust. A man may be habitually careless about his costume without meaning any harm by it; and the pre-eminent demagogue of the French Revolution, Robespierre, always appeared exquisitely dressed, and wore a fresh bouquet every day. Yet all these points of costume or propriety were then far weightier matters than we can now conceive. The habits of the last century in respect to decorum were just receding; men were—for better or worse—ceasing to occupy themselves about personal externals, and the customary suit of solemn black was only just coming into vogue. The old *régime* was dying, and its disappearance was as conspicuous in England as in France, in America as in England. This is easily illustrated.

If we were to read in some old collection of faded letters a woman's animated description of a country visit paid to one who seemed the counterpart of Addison's Sir Roger de Coverley, we should naturally assume that the date and address of the letter must be very far away in space and time. Suppose that the narrator should tell us of a fine country-house surrounded by lofty elms forming two avenues, the one leading to the high-road, the other to the village church. There are family portraits in the hall, a bookcase containing the first edition of the *Spectator*, and a buffet of old plate and rare china. The guest remains over Sunday, and her host, wearing wig and cocked hat and red cloak, escorts her down the avenue of elms through the rural church-yard to the village church. At every step they pass villagers who make profound obeisance, and at the conclusion of the service the whole congregation remains standing until this ancient gentleman and his friends have passed down the broad aisle. Who would not fancy this a scene from some English hamlet in the days of Queen Anne?

Yet it all took place in the present century, and in the quiet village of Harvard, Massachusetts, little more than thirty miles from Boston, and now only noted as the abode of a little Shaker community, and the scene of Howells's "Undiscovered Country." The narrator was the late Mrs. Josiah Quincy, and her host was Henry Bromfield, elder brother of the well-known benefactor of the Boston Athenæum. He was simply a "survival" of the old way of living. He spoke of State Street as King Street, and Summer Street as Seven-star Lane, and his dress and manners were like his phrases. Such survivals were still to be found, here and there all over the country, at the precise time when Jefferson became President, and shocked Mr. Merry with his morning slippers, and Mr. Sullivan by opening his doors to all the world.

For the rest, Jefferson's way of living in Washington exhibited a profuse and rather slovenly hospitality, which at last left him deeply in debt. He kept open house, had eleven servants (slaves) from his plantation, besides a French cook and steward and an Irish coachman. His long dining-room was crowded every day, according to one witness, who tested its hospitality for sixteen days in succession; it was essentially a bachelor establishment, he being then a widower, and we hear little of ladies among its visitors. There was no etiquette at these great dinners; they sat down at four and talked till midnight. The city of Washington was still a frontier settlement, in that phase of those outposts when they consist of many small cabins and one hotel at which everybody meets. The White House was the hotel; there was no "society" anywhere else, because no other dwelling had a drawing-room large enough to receive it. Pennsylvania Avenue was still an abyss of yellow mud, on which nobody could walk, and where carriages were bemired. Gouverneur Morris, of New York, described Washington as the best city in the world for a future residence. "We want nothing here," he said, "but houses, cellars, kitchens, well-informed men, amiable women, and other little trifles of this kind, to make our city perfect."

Besides new manners, the new President urged new measures; he would pay off the public debt, which was very well, though the main instrument by which it was to be paid was the Treasury system created by Hamilton. But to aid in doing this he would reduce the army and navy to their lowest point, which was not so well, although he covered this reduction in the case of the army by calling it — in a letter to Nathaniel Macon — "a chaste reformation." He pardoned those convicted under the Alien and Sedition laws, and he procured the removal of those officers appointed by President Adams at the last moment, and called "Midnight Judges," this being accomplished by a repeal of the law creating them. This repeal was an act which seemed to the Federalists unconstitutional, and its passage was their last great defeat. Under Jefferson's leadership the period of fourteen years of residence necessary for naturalization was reduced to five years. He sent Lewis and Clark to penetrate the vast regions west of the Mississippi, and encouraged Astor to found a settlement upon the Pacific coast. The Constitution was so amended as to provide for the Presidential election in its present form. The President's hostility could not touch the Bank of the United States, as established by Hamilton, for it was to exist by its charter till 1811; the excise law was early discontinued; the tariff question had not yet become serious, the tendency being, however, to an increase of duties. Slavery was occasionally discussed by pamphleteers. The officials of the civil service had not grown to be a vast army: instead of fifty thousand, there were then but five thousand, and of those Jefferson removed but thirty-nine. Yet even this mild degree of personal interference was severely criticised, for party bitterness had not abated. Violent squibs and handbills were still published; peaceful villages were divided against themselves. The late Miss Catharine Sedgwick, whose father

WASHINGTON IN 1800.

was Speaker of the House of Representatives, says that in a New England town, where she lived in childhood, the gentry who resided at one end were mainly Federalists, and the poorer citizens at the other end were Democrats. The travelling agent for the exchange of political knowledge was a certain aged horse, past service, and turned out to graze in the village street. He would be seen peacefully pacing one way in the morning, his sides plastered with Jeffersonian squibs, and he would return at night with these effaced by Federalist manifestoes.

Handbills and caricatures have alike disappeared; but one of the best memorials of the Jeffersonian side of the controversy is to be found in a very spicy correspondence carried on in 1807 between John Adams and Mercy Warren, and first published in the centennial volume of the Massachusetts Historical Society. Mercy Warren was a woman of rare ability and character, the sister of James Otis, the wife of General James Warren, and the author of a history of the American Revolution. John Adams, reading this book after his retirement from office, took offence at certain phrases, and corresponded with her at great length about them, showing in advancing years an undiminished keenness of mind and only an increase of touchy egotism. He makes it, for instance, a subject of sincere indignation when the lady in one case speaks of Franklin and Adams instead of Adams and Franklin. Mrs. Warren, on her side, shows to the greatest advantage, keeps her temper, and gives some keen home-thrusts. She makes it clear, in this correspondence, how strongly and indeed justly a portion of the most intelligent people of Mr. Adams's own State dreaded what she calls his "marked and uniform preference to monarchic usages;" she brings him to the admission that he hates "democratic" government, and likes better such republicanism as that of Holland—a nation which, as he himself says, "has no idea of any republic but an aristocracy"—and that he counts even England a republic, since a republic is merely "a government of more than one." She even quotes against him his own words, uttered in moments of excited impulse, recognizing monarchy as the probable destiny of the United States. But the most striking fact, after all, is that she, a refined and cultivated woman, accustomed to the best New England society of her time, is found dissenting wholly from the Federalist view of Jefferson. "I never knew," she bravely says, in answer to a sneer from Mr. Adams, "that 'my philosophical friend' Mr. Jefferson was afraid to do his duty in any instance. But this I know— he has dared to do many things for his country for which posterity will probably bless his memory; and I hope he will yet, by his wisdom, justice, moderation, and energy, long continue the blessings of peace in our country, and strengthen the republican system to which he has uniformly adhered." Such a tribute from a woman like Mercy Warren—a woman then nearly eighty years old, but still showing unimpaired those mental powers of which John Adams had before spoken in terms of

MERCY WARREN.

almost extravagant praise—is entitled to count for something against the bitterness of contemporary politicians.

There were now sixteen States, Vermont (1791), Kentucky

(1792), Tennessee (1796), having been added to the original thirteen. With these was soon associated Ohio (1802), and then no other was added until a vast acquisition of territory made it necessary. This was the province of Louisiana, which was obtained by Jefferson through one of those strokes of glaring inconsistency which his opponents called trick, and his admirers statesmanship. Monroe had been sent to France to buy the Floridas and the island of New Orleans, but he went beyond his instructions, and paid fifteen millions (April 30, 1803) for all the vast region then called Louisiana, comprising the island of New Orleans and all the continent west of the Mississippi River between the British possessions and what was then Mexico. The territory thus obtained was afterwards assumed to have extended to the Pacific Ocean, although this was a claim subject to much doubt. It was a most important acquisition, which more than doubled the original area of the United States, and saved it from being hemmed in between English Canada and French Florida. But here was a test of those rigid doctrines with which Jefferson was identified — of State rights and the strict construction of the Constitution. If the resolutions which he had drawn up for the State of Kentucky were true, then the purchase of Louisiana was wrong, for it was the exercise of a power not given by the Constitution, and it strengthened the nation enormously at the expense of the original States. Jefferson sustained it simply on the ground that the people needed it, and if they did so, a constitutional amendment would set all right. In other words, he violated what he himself had declared to be law, and suggested that a new law be passed to confirm his action. The new law—in the shape of an amendment to the Constitution—was in fact prepared, but never even offered, inasmuch as the popular voice ratified the purchase. Thus a precedent was created—that of the annexation of new territory —which was in accordance with Jefferson's immediate policy, but was fatal to his principles. The acquisition of Louisiana aided greatly in bringing about just that which he had opposed, the subordination of the States to the nation.

These things would have made enough of party bitterness, but what added to it was that parties still turned largely on European politics, and every fresh foreign newspaper added to the democratic flame. It was now France with which a treaty was to be made, and the debate ran almost as high as when Jay had negotiated with England, only that the arguments of the disputants were now reversed. But here, as in everything during Jefferson's earlier period, success awaited him. The French treaty was at length ratified; the Federalists were defeated all along the line. At the end of Jefferson's first term they were overwhelmingly beaten in the Presidential election, carrying only Connecticut and Delaware, with two electors in Maryland —14 electoral votes in all. Their unsuccessful candidates were Charles C. Pinckney and Rufus King; the successful ones were Thomas Jefferson, of Virginia, and George Clinton, of New York, both having 162 electoral votes, and Clinton taking the place of Aaron Burr, the most brilliant man of his time, who had now fallen from all public respect by his way of life, had made himself odious by shooting Hamilton in a duel, and was destined to come near conviction for treason through his project of setting up a separate government at the South-west. The new President and Vice-president were sworn into office March 4, 1805. They had behind them a strong majority in each House of Congress, and henceforth the Federalist party was only a minority, able and powerful, but destined to death.

Under the new administration the controlling effect of European strife was more and more felt in American affairs. Napoleon's "Decrees" and the British "Orders in Council" were equally disastrous to the commerce of the United States; and both nations claimed the right to take seamen out of United States vessels. "England," said Jefferson, "seems to have become a den of pirates, and France a den of thieves."

There was trouble with Spain also, backed by France, about the eastern boundaries of Louisiana. There was renewed demand for a navy, but the President would only consent to the building of certain little gun-boats, much laughed at then and ever since. They were to cost less than ten thousand dollars apiece, were to be kept on land under cover, and to be launched whenever they were needed, like the boats of our life-saving service; with these the fleets which had fought under Nelson were to be resisted. Yet a merely commercial retaliation was favored by Jefferson; and an act was passed to punish England by the prohibition of certain English goods. A treaty with that nation was made, but was rejected by the President, and all tended to increase the bitterness of feeling between the two nations. In June, 1807, the British frigate *Leopard* took four seamen by force from the United States frigate *Chesapeake*. "Never since the battle of Lexington," said Jefferson, "have I seen this country in such a state of exasperation as at present."

Then came that great political convulsion, the Embargo Act (December 22, 1807), prohibiting all commerce with all foreign countries, and thus instantly crushing all foreign trade which the two great European contestants had left. It kindled all the fires of hostility between the Federalists and Republicans—who had now fairly accepted the name of Democrats, a name borrowed from France, and fairly forced on them by their opponents. The act brought ruin to so many households that it might well be at least doubted whether it brought good to any. The very children of New England rose up against it, in the person of Bryant, who, when a boy of thirteen, wrote in opposition to it his first elaborate lay. It was believed by the Federalists to be aimed expressly at the Eastern States, yet John Quincy Adams, Senator from Massachusetts, supported it, and then resigned, his course being disapproved by his Legislature. He it was, however, who informed the President at last that the embargo could be endured no longer, and got it modified, in 1809, so as to apply only to England and France. Jefferson consented reluctantly even to this degree of pressure, but he wrote,

AARON BURR.

looking back upon the affair in 1816, "I felt the foundations of the government shaken under my feet by the New England township;" and he always urged thenceforward that the town system organized the voice of the people in a way with which no unwieldy county organization, such as prevailed at the South, could compete. Yet all but the commercial States sustained the embargo, and the Federalist party was left a broken and hopeless minority. Jefferson remained strong in popularity. His second term had secured a triumphant end to the long contest with Tripoli, whose insolent claims were checked by the successes of Decatur, and by a treaty (1805). An act had also been passed forever prohibiting the African slave-trade after January 1, 1808. Jefferson was urged to become for a third time a candidate for the Presidency, but wisely declined in favor of his friend Madison. In the election of 1808, James Madison, of Virginia, had 122 votes, C. C. Pinckney 47, and George Clinton 6, Mr. Madison being therefore elected; while on the vote for Vice-president George Clinton had a smaller majority. The third Chief Magistrate of the United States thus retired to private life after a career which has influenced American institutions to this day more profoundly than that of any other President.

Jefferson was a man full of thoughts and of studious purposes; trustful of the people, distrustful of the few; a generous friend, but a vehement and unscrupulous foe; not so much deliberately false as without a clear sense of truth; courageous for peace, but shrinking and vacillating in view of war; ignorant of his own limitations; as self-confident in financial and commercial matters, of which he knew little, as in respect to the principles of republican government, about which he showed more foresight than any man of his time. He may have underrated the dangers to which the nation might be exposed from ignorance and vice, but he never yielded, on the other hand, to the cowardice of culture; he never relaxed his faith in the permanence of popular government or in the high destiny of man.

Meanwhile John Adams, on his farm in Quincy, had been superintending his haymakers with something as near to peace of mind as a deposed President can be expected to attain. He was not a person of eminent humility, nor is it usually agreeable to a public man when his correspondence ceases to be counted by the thousand, and his letters shrink to two a week. His high-minded wife, more cordially accepting the situation, wrote with sincere satisfaction of skimming milk in her dairy at five o'clock in the morning. Each had perhaps something to say, when Jefferson was mentioned, about "Cæsar with a Senate at his heels," but it did not prevent the old friendship with Cæsar from reviving in later life. Jefferson had written to Washington long before, that even Adams's "apostasy to hereditary monarchy and nobility" had not alienated them; Adams saw in Jefferson, as time went on, the friend and even political adviser of his own son. Old antagonisms faded; old associations grew stronger; and the two aged men floated on, like two ships becalmed at nightfall, that drift together into port, and cast anchor side by side.

XV.

THE SECOND WAR FOR INDEPENDENCE.

JEFFERSON'S period of office lasted technically for eight years, but it is not wholly incorrect to estimate, as Mr. Parton suggests, that it endured for nearly a quarter of a century. Madison's and Monroe's administrations were but the continuation of it. The fourth and fifth Presidents had, indeed, so much in common that it was about an even chance which should take the Presidency first. Both had long been friends of Jefferson; both had something to do with reconciling him to the United States Constitution, which he had at first opposed. He himself would have rather preferred Monroe for his immediate successor, but the Legislature of Virginia pronounced in favor of Madison, who, like the two others, was a native of that then powerful State. It really made little difference which preceded. Josiah Quincy, in a famous speech, designated them simply as James I. and James II. The two were alike Jeffersonian; their administrations moved professedly in the line indicated by their predecessor, and the success of his policy must be tested in a degree by that of theirs. Both inherited something of his unpopularity with the Federalists, but Madison partially lived it down, and Monroe saw nearly the extinction of it. The Jeffersonian policy may, therefore, fairly be judged, not alone by its early storms, but by the calm which at last followed.

James Madison had been Secretary of State for eight years under Jefferson, and had not only borne his share earlier than this in public affairs, but had furnished a plan which formed the basis of the Constitution, and had afterwards aided Hamilton and Jay in writing *The Federalist* in support of it. For these reasons, and because he was the last survivor of those who signed the great act of national organization, he was called, before his death, "The Father of the Constitution." He was a man of clear head, modest manners, and peaceful disposition. His bitter political opponents admitted that he was honorable, well informed, and even, in his own way, patriotic; not mean or malignant. As to his appearance, he is described by one of these opponents, William Sullivan, as one who had "a calm expression, a penetrating blue eye, and who looked like a thinking man." In figure, he was small and rather stout; he was partially bald, wore powder in his hair, and dressed in black, without any of Jefferson's slovenliness. In speech he was slow and grave. Mrs. Madison was a pleasing woman, twenty years younger than himself, and they had no children.

Their arrival brought an immediate change in the manners of the President's house; they were both fond of society and ceremony, and though the new President claimed to be the most faithful of Jeffersonians, he found no difficulty in restoring the formal receptions which his predecessor had disused. These levees were held in what a British observer of that day called the "President's palace," a building which the same observer (Gleig) afterwards described as "small, incommodious, and plain," although its walls were the same with those of the present White House, only the interior having been burned by the British in the war soon to be described. Such as it was, it was thrown open at these levees, which every one was free to attend, while music played, and the costumes of foreign ambassadors gave, as now, some gayety to the scene. Mrs. Madison, according to a keen observer, Mrs. Quincy, wore on these occasions her carriage dress, the same in which she appeared on Sunday at the Capitol, where religious services were then held—"a purple velvet pelisse, and a hat trimmed with ermine. A very elegant costume," adds this feminine critic, "but not, I thought, appropriate to a lady receiving company at home." At another time Mr. and Mrs. Quincy dined at the President's house, "in the midst of the enemy's camp," they being the only Federalists among some five-and-twenty Democrats. The house, Mrs. Quincy tells us, was richly but incongruously furnished, "not of a piece, as we ladies say." On this occasion Mrs. Madison wore black velvet, with a very rich head-dress of *coquelicot* and gold, having on a necklace of the same color. At another time Mrs. Quincy went by invitation with her children, and was shown through the front rooms. Meeting the lady of the house, she apologized for the liberty, and Mrs. Madison said, gracefully, "It is as much your house as it is mine, ladies." The answer has a certain historic value; it shows that the spirit of Jefferson had already wrought a change in the direction of democratic feeling. Such a remark would hardly have been made by Mrs. Washington, or even by Mrs. Adams.

The tone of society in Washington had undoubtedly something of the coarser style which then prevailed in all countries. Men drank more heavily, wrangled more loudly, and there was a good deal of what afterwards came to be known as "plantation manners." The mutual bearing of Congressmen was that of courtesy, tempered by drunkenness and duelling; and it was true then, as always, that every duel caused ten new quarrels for each one that it decided. When Josiah Quincy, then the leader of the Federalists in Congress, made his famous speech against the invasion of Canada (January 5, 1813), and Henry Clay, then Speaker of the House, descended from the chair expressly to force him to the alternative of "a duel or disgrace"— as avowed by one of his friends to Mr. Quincy—it was not held to be anything but honorable action, and only the high moral courage of Mr. Quincy enabled him to avoid the alternative. On a later occasion, Mr. Grundy, of Tennessee, having to an-

JAMES MADISON.

[Engraved by G. Kruell, from the painting by Gilbert Stuart, owned by T. Jefferson Coolidge, Esq., Boston.]

swer another speech by Mr. Quincy, took pains to explain to him privately that though he must abuse him as a representative Federalist or else lose his election, he would endeavor to bestow the abuse like a gentleman. " Except Tim Pickering," said this frank Tennessean, " there is not a man in the United States so perfectly hated by the people of my district as yourself. By —— I must abuse you, or I shall never get re-elected. I will do it, however, genteelly. I will not do it as that —— fool Clay did it, strike so hard as to hurt myself. But abuse you I must." Seeing by this explanation what was the tone of Congressional manners when putting on gentility, we can form some conception of what they were on those more frequent occasions when they were altogether ungenteel.

But the amenities of Mrs. Madison and the gentilities of Mr. Grundy were alike interrupted by the excitements of war—" the war of 1812," habitually called " the late war " until there was one still later. For this contest, suddenly as it came at last, there were years of preparation. Long had the United States suffered the bitter experience of being placed between two contending nations, neither of which could be made into a friend, or easily reached as an enemy. Napoleon with his " Decrees," the British government with its " Orders in Council," had in turn preyed upon American commerce, and it was scarce reviving from the paralysis of Jefferson's embargo. At home, men were divided as to the remedy, and the old sympathies for France and for England re-appeared on each side. Unfortunately for the Federalists, while they were wholly right in many of their criticisms on the manner in which the war came about, they put themselves in the wrong as to its main feature. We can now see that in their just wrath against Napoleon they would have let the nation remain in a position of perpetual childhood and subordination before England. No doubt there were various points at issue in the impending contest, but the most important one, and the only one that remained in dispute all through the war, was that of the right of search and impressment—the English claiming the right to visit American vessels, and impress into the naval service any sailors who appeared to be British subjects. The one great object of the war of 1812 was to get rid of this insolent and degrading practice.

It must be understood that this was not a question of reclaiming deserters from the British navy, for the seamen in question had very rarely belonged to it. There existed in England at that time an outrage on civilization, now abandoned, called impressment, by which any sailor and many who were not sailors could be seized and compelled to serve in the navy. The horrors of the "press-gang," as exhibited in the sea-side towns of England, have formed the theme of many novels. It was bad enough at home, but when applied on board the vessels of a nation with which England was at peace, it became one of those outrages which only proceed from the strong to the weak, and are never reciprocated. Lord Collingwood said well, in one of his letters, that England would not submit to such an aggression for an hour. Merely to yield to visitation for such a purpose was a confession of national weakness; but the actual case was far worse than this. Owing to the similarity of language, it was always difficult to distinguish between English and American seamen; and the temptation was irresistible to the visiting officer, anxious for the enlargement of his own crew, to give England the benefit of the doubt. The result was that an English lieutenant, or even midshipman, once on board an American ship, was, in the words of the English writer Cobbett, "at once accuser, witness, judge, and captor," and we have also Cobbett's statement of the consequences. "Great numbers of Americans have been impressed," he adds, "and are now in our navy.... That many of these men have died on board our ships, that many have been worn out in the service, there is no doubt. Some obtain their release through the application of the American Consul, and of these the sufferings have been in many in-

stances very great. There have been instances where men have thus got free after having been flogged through the fleet for desertion." Between 1797 and 1801 more than two thousand applications for impressed seamen were made through the American Minister; and of these only one-twentieth were proved to be British subjects, though nearly one-half were retained for further proof. When the *Hornet* captured the British sloop *Peacock*, the victors found on board three American seamen who had been forced, by holding pistols at their heads, to fight against their own countrymen. Four American seamen on the British ship *Actæa* were ordered five dozen lashes, then four dozen, then two dozen, then kept in irons three months, for refusing to obey orders under similar circumstances. There was nothing new about the grievance; it had been the subject of indignant negotiation since 1789. In 1796 Timothy Pickering, Secretary of State, a representative Federalist, had denounced the practice of search and impressment as the sacrifice of the rights of an independent nation, and lamented "the long and fruitless attempts" to correct it. In 1806 the merchants of Boston had called upon the general government to "assert our rights and support the dignity of the United States;" and the merchants of Salem had offered to "pledge their lives and properties" in support of necessary measures of redemption. Yet it shows the height of party feeling that when, in 1812, Mr. Madison's government finally went to war for these very rights, the measure met with the bitterest opposition from the whole Federalist party, and from the commercial States generally. A good type of the Federalist opposition on this particular point is to be found in the pamphlets of John Lowell.

John Lowell was the son of the eminent Massachusetts judge of that name; he was a well-educated lawyer, who was president of the Massachusetts Agricultural Society, and wrote under the name of "A New England Farmer." In spite of the protests offered half a dozen years before by his own neighbors, he declared the whole outcry against impressment to be a device of Mr. Madison's party. The nation, he said, was "totally opposed to a war for the purpose of protecting British seamen against their own sovereign." The whole matter at issue, he asserted, was "the protection of renegadoes and deserters from the British navy." He argued unflinchingly for the English right of search, called it a "consecrated" right, maintained that the allegiance of British subjects was perpetual, and that no residence in a foreign country could absolve them. He held that every sailor born in Great Britain, whether naturalized in America or not, should be absolutely excluded from American ships; and that, until this was done, the right to search American vessels and take such sailors out was the only restraint on the abuse. He was a man of great ability and public spirit, and yet he held views which now seem to have renounced all national self-respect. While such a man, with a large party behind him, took this position, it must simply be said that the American republic had not yet asserted itself to be a nation. Soon after the Revolution, when some one spoke of that contest to Franklin as the war for independence, he said, "Say rather the war of the Revolution; the war for independence is yet to be fought." The war of 1812 was just the contest he described.

To this excitement directed against the war, the pulpit very largely contributed, the chief lever applied by the Federalist clergy being found in the atrocities of Napoleon. "The chieftain of Europe, drunk with blood, casts a look upon us; he raises his voice, more terrible than the midnight yell of savages at the doors of our forefathers." These melodramatic words are from a sermon, once famous, delivered by Rev. Daniel Parish, of Byfield, Massachusetts, on Fast Day, 1810. Elsewhere he says: "Would you establish those in the first offices of the land who will poison the hearts of your children with infidelity, who will harness them in the team of Hollanders and Germans and Swiss and Italians to draw the triumphal car of

Napoleon? Are you nursing your sons to be dragged into his armies?" The climax was reached when one pulpit orator wound up his appeal by asking his audience if they were ready to wear wooden shoes, in allusion to the *sabots* of the French peasants.

A curious aspect of the whole affair was the firm conviction of the Federalists that they themselves were utterly free from all partisan feeling, and that what they called the "Baleful Demon, Party," existed only on the other side. For the Democrats to form Jacobin societies was an outrage; but the "Washington Benevolent Societies" of the Federalists were claimed to be utterly non-political, though they marched with banners, held quarterly meetings, and were all expected to vote one way. At one of their gatherings, in 1789, there was a company of "School-boy Federalists" to the number of two hundred and fifty, uniformed in blue and white, and wearing Washington's Farewell Address in red morocco around their necks. It was a sight hardly to be paralleled in the most excited election of these days; yet the Federalists stoutly maintained that there was nothing partisan about it; the other side was partisan. They admired themselves for their width of view and their freedom from prejudice, and yet they sincerely believed that the mild and cautious Madison, who would not have declared war with England unless forced into it by others, was plotting to enslave his own nation for the benefit of France. The very names of their pamphlets show this. One of John Lowell's bears on the title-page "*Perpetual War* the policy of Mr. Madison ... the important and interesting subject of a *conscript militia*, and an immense standing army of guards and spies under the name of a *local volunteer corps*." The Federalist leaders took distinctly the ground that they should refuse to obey a conscription law to raise troops for the conquest of Canada; and when that very questionable measure failed by one vote in the Senate, the nation may have escaped a serious outbreak. Had the law passed and been enforced, William Sullivan ominously declares, "No doubt the citizens would have armed, and might have marched, but not, it is believed, to Canada." This was possibly overstated; but the crisis thus arising might have been a formidable matter.

It might, indeed, have been far more dangerous than the Hartford Convention of 1814, which was, after all, only a peaceable meeting of some two dozen honest men, with George Cabot at their head—men of whom very few had even a covert purpose of dissolving the Union, but who were driven to something very near desperation by the prostration of their commerce and the defencelessness of their coast. They found themselves between the terror of a conscription in New England and the outrage of an invasion of Canada. They found the President calling in his Message of November 4, 1812, for new and mysterious enactments against "corrupt and perfidious intercourse with the enemy, not amounting to treason," and they did not feel quite sure that this might not end in the guillotine or the lamp-post. They saw what were called "the horrors of Baltimore" in a mob where the blood of Revolutionary officers had been shed in that city under pretence of suppressing a newspaper. No one could tell whither these things were leading, and they could at least protest. The protest will always be remarkable from the skill with which it turned against Jefferson and Madison the dangerous States-rights doctrines of their own injurious Virginia and Kentucky resolutions. The Federalist and Democratic parties had completely shifted ground; and we can now see that the Hartford Convention really strengthened the traditions of the Union by showing that the implied threat of secession was a game at which two could play.

It must be remembered, too, in estimating the provocation which led to this famous convention, that during all this time the commercial States were most unreasonably treated. In the opinion of Judge Story, himself a moderate Republican and a member of Congress, "New England was expected, so far as the Republicans were concerned, to do everything and have nothing. They were to obey, but not to be trusted." Their commerce, which had furnished so largely the supplies for the nation, was viewed by a great many not merely with indifference, but with real dislike. Jefferson, whose views had more influence than those of any ten other men, still held to his narrow Virginia-planter opinion that a national business must somehow be an evil; and it was hard for those whose commerce his embargo had ruined to be patient while he rubbed his hands and assured them that they would be much better off without any ships. When the war of 1812 was declared, the merchants of Boston and Salem had—as it was estimated by Mr. Isaac P. Davis, quoted in the memoirs of Mrs. Quincy—twenty million dollars' worth of property on the sea and in British ports. The war sacrificed nearly all of it, and the losers were expected to be grateful. In a letter to the Legislature of New Hampshire, four years before (August, 1808), Jefferson had calmly recommended to the people of that region to retire from the seas and "to provide for themselves [ourselves] those comforts and conveniences of life for which it would be unwise ever to recur to other countries." Moreover, it was argued, the commercial States were almost exclusively the sufferers by the British intrusions upon American vessels; and if they did not think it a case for war, why should it be taken up by the States which were not hurt by it? Again, the commercial States had yielded to the general government the right of receiving customs duties and of national defence, on the express ground of receiving protection in return. Madison had pledged himself—as he was reminded in the once famous "Rockingham County [New Hampshire] address," penned by young Daniel Webster—to give the nation a navy; and it had resulted in Mr. Jefferson's hundred and fifty little gun-boats, and some twenty larger vessels. As for the army, it consisted at this time of about three thousand men all told. The ablest men in the President's cabinet—Gallatin and Pinkney—were originally opposed to the war. The only member of that body who had any personal knowledge of military matters was Colonel James Monroe, Secretary of State; and it was subsequently thought that he knew just enough to be in the way. Nevertheless, the war was declared, June 18, 1812—declared reluctantly, hesitatingly, but at last courageously. Five days after the declaration the British "Orders in Council," which had partly caused it, were revoked; but hostilities went on. In the same autumn Madison was re-elected President, receiving 128 electoral votes against 89 for De Witt Clinton; Elbridge Gerry, of Massachusetts, being chosen Vice-president. A sufficient popular verdict was thus given, and the war was continued.

In its early period much went wrong. British and Indians ravaged the North-western frontier; General Hull invaded Canada in vain, and finally surrendered Detroit (August 15, 1812). He was condemned by court-martial, and sentenced to be shot, but was pardoned because of his Revolutionary services; and much has since been written in his vindication, making it altogether probable that he was simply made the scapegoat of an inefficient administration. To the surprise of every one, it was upon the sea, not the land, that the United States proved eminently successful, and the victory of the *Constitution* over the *Guerrière* was the first of a long line of triumphs. The number of British war vessels captured during the three years of the war was 56, with 880 cannon; the number of American war vessels only 25, with 350 guns; and there were, besides these, thousands of merchant-vessels taken on both sides by privateers. But these mere statistics tell nothing of the excitement of those picturesque victories which so long thrilled the heart of every American school-boy with the conviction that this nation was the peer of the proudest upon the seas. Yet the worst predictions of the Federalists did not exaggerate the injury done by the war to American commerce; and the highest expectations of the other party did no more than justice to the national prestige gained by the successes of the American navy. It is fairly to be remembered to the credit of the Federalists, however, that but for their urgent appeals there would have been no navy, and that it was created only by setting aside Jefferson's pet theories of sea defence. The Federalists could justly urge, also, that the merchant-service was the only nursery of seamen, and that with its destruction the race of American sailors would die out—a prediction which the present day has seen almost fulfilled.

But, for the time being, the glory of the American navy was secure; and even the sea-fights hardly equalled the fame of Perry's victory on Lake Erie, immortalized by two phrases, Lawrence's "Don't give up the ship," which Perry bore upon his flag, and Perry's own brief despatch, "We have met the enemy, and they are ours." Side by side with this came Harrison's land victories over the Indians and English in the Northwest. Tecumseh, who held the rank of brigadier-general in the British army, had, with the aid of his brother, "the Prophet," united all the Indian tribes in a league. His power was broken by Harrison in the battle of Tippecanoe (November 7, 1811), and finally destroyed in that of the Thames, in Canada (October 5, 1813), where Tecumseh fell.

But the war, from the first, yielded few glories to either side by land. The Americans were still a nation of woodsmen and sharp-shooters, but they had lost the military habit, and they had against them the veterans of Wellington, and men who boasted —to Mrs. Peter, of Washington—that they had not slept under a roof for seven years. Even with such men, the raid on the city of Washington by General Ross was a bold thing—to march with four thousand men sixty miles into an enemy's country, burn its Capitol, and retreat. Had the Americans renewed the tactics of Concord and Lexington, and fought from behind trees and under cover of brick walls, the British commander's losses might have been frightful; but to risk a pitched battle was to leave themselves helpless if defeated. The utter rout of the Americans at Bladensburg left Washington to fall defenceless into the hands of the enemy. The accounts are still somewhat confused, but the British statement is that, before entering the city, General Ross sent in a flag of truce, meaning to levy a contribution, as from a conquered town; and the flag of truce being fired upon, the destruction of the town followed. Washington had then less than a thousand houses; the British troops set fire to the unfinished Capitol with the Library of Congress, to the Treasury Buildings, the Arsenal, and a few private dwellings. At the President's house —according to their own story, since doubted—they found dinner ready, devoured it, and then set the house on fire. Mr. Madison sent a messenger to his wife to bid her flee. She wrote to her sister, ere going, "Our kind friend Mr. Carroll has come to hasten my departure, and is in a very bad humor with me because I insist on waiting till the large picture of General Washington is secured, and it requires to be unscrewed from the wall." She finally secured it, put it into the hands of two gentlemen passing by, Mr. Jacob Barker and Mr. De Peyster, and went off in her carriage with her sister, Mrs. Cutts. The Federalist papers made plenty of fun of her retreat, and Mr. Lossing has preserved a fragment of one of their ballads in which she is made to say to the President, in the style of John Gilpin,

>"Sister Cutts and Cutts and I,
>And Cutts's children three,
>Shall in the coach, and you shall ride
>On horseback after we."

But, on the whole, the lady of the Presidential "palace" carried off more laurels from Washington than most American men.

The news of the burning of Washington was variously received in England: the British *Annual Register* called it "a return to the times of barbarism," and the London *Times* saw in it, on the contrary, the disappearance of the American republic, which it called by the withering name of an "association." "That ill-organized association is on the eve of dissolution, and the world is speedily to be delivered of the mischievous example of the existence of a government founded on democratic rebellion." But the burning had, on the contrary, just the opposite effect from this. After Washington had fallen, Baltimore seemed an easy prey; but there was a great rising of the people; the British army was beaten off—the affair turning largely on the gallant defence of Fort McHenry by Colonel George Armistead—and General Ross was killed. It was at this time that Key's lyric "The Star-spangled Banner" was written, the author being detained on board the cartel-ship *Minden* during the bombardment. Before this there had been various depredations and skirmishes along the coast of Maine, and a courageous repulse of the British at Stonington, Connecticut. Afterwards came the well-fought battle of Lundy's Lane, and the closing victory of New Orleans, fought after the treaty of peace had been actually signed, and unexpectedly leaving the final laurels of the war in the hands of the Americans.

After this battle an English officer visiting the field saw within a few hundred yards "nearly a thousand bodies, all arrayed in British uniforms," and heard from the American officer in command the statement that the American loss had consisted only of eight men killed and fourteen wounded. The loss of the English was nearly twenty-one hundred in killed and wounded, including two general officers. A triumph so overwhelming restored some feeling of military self-respect, sorely needed after the disasters at Washington. "There were," says the Federalist William Sullivan, "splendid processions, bonfires, and illuminations, as though the independence of the country had been a second time achieved." Such, indeed, was the feeling, and with some reason. Franklin's war for independence was at an end. The battle took place January 8, 1815, but the treaty of peace had been signed at Ghent on the day before Christmas. The terms agreed upon said not one word about impressment or the right of search, but the question had been practically settled by the naval successes of the United States;

FRANCIS SCOTT KEY AT SEVENTEEN.
[From a photograph owned by his daughter, Mrs. G. H. Pendleton.]

and so great were the rejoicings on the return of peace that even this singular omission seemed of secondary importance.

The verdict of posterity upon the war of 1812 may be said to be this: that there was ample ground for it, and that it completed the work of the Revolution; and yet that it was the immediate product of a few ambitious men, whose aims and principles were not really so high as were those of many who opposed the war. The outrageous impressment of American seamen touched a point of national pride, and justly; while the United States submitted to this it certainly could not be called an independent nation; and the abuse was in fact ended by the war, even though the treaty of peace was silent. On the other side, the dread entertained of Napoleon by the Federalists was perfectly legitimate; and this, too, time has justified. But this peril was really far less pressing than the other: the United States needed more to be liberated from the domineering attitude of England than from the remoter tyranny of Napoleon, and it was therefore necessary to reckon with England first. In point of fact, the Federalists did their duty in action; the commonwealth of Massachusetts furnished during those three years more soldiers than any other; and the New England States, which opposed the war, sent more men into the field than the Southern States, which brought on the contest. Unfortunately the world remembers words better than actions— *litera scripta manet*—and the few questionable phrases of the Hartford Convention are now more familiar in memory than the fourteen thousand men whom Massachusetts raised in 1814, or the two millions of dollars she paid for bounties.

The rest of Mr. Madison's administration was a career of peace. Louisiana had long since (April 30, 1812) become a State of the Union, and Indiana was also admitted (December 11, 1816). An act was passed, under the leadership of Mr. Lowndes, of South Carolina, providing for the payment, in instalments of ten millions of dollars annually, of the national debt of one hundred and twenty millions. Taxes were reduced, the tariff was slightly increased, and in April, 1816, a national bank was chartered for a term of twenty years. Here, as in some other matters, at least one of the parties proved to have changed ground, and the Democratic Republican newspapers began eagerly to reprint Hamilton's arguments for a bank—arguments which they had formerly denounced and derided. To the Federalists the passage of the bank act was a complete triumph, and while their own party disappeared, they could feel that some of its principles survived. A national bank was their policy, not that of Jefferson; and Jefferson and Madison had, moreover, lived to take up those theories of a strong national government which they had formerly called monarchical and despotic. The Federalists had indeed come equally near to embracing the extreme States-rights doctrines which their opponents had laid down; but the laws of physical perspective seem to be reversed in moral perspective, so that our own change of position seems to us insignificant, while an equal change on the other side looks conspicuous and important. Be this as it may, Mr. Madison's administration closed in peace, partly the peace of good-nature, partly of fatigue. The usual nominations were made for the Presidency by the Congressional caucuses, but when it came to the voting it was almost all one way. The only States choosing Federalist electors were Massachusetts, Connecticut, and Delaware. James Monroe—Josiah Quincy's "James the Second"—had 183 electoral votes, against 34 for Rufus King, so that four years more of yet milder Jeffersonianism were secured. The era of bitterness had passed, and the "era of good feeling" was at hand.

XVI.

THE ERA OF GOOD FEELING.

MANY Presidents of the United States have served their country by remaining at Washington, but probably James Monroe was the only one who ever accomplished great good by going on an excursion. Few battles in the Revolution were of so much benefit to the nation as the journey which, in 1817, the President decided to undertake. There were two especial reasons for this beneficent result: the tour reconciled the people to the administration, and it reconciled the administration to what seemed the really alarming growth of the people.

The fact that Monroe was not generally held to be a very great man enhanced the value of this expedition. He had been an unfortunate diplomatist, retrieving his failures by good-luck; as a soldier, he had blundered at Washington, and yet had retained enough of confidence to be talked of as probable commander of a Canadian invasion. All this was rather advantageous. It is sometimes a good thing when a ruler is not personally eminent enough to obscure his office. In such a case, what the man loses the office may gain. Wherever Washington went he was received as a father among grateful children; Adams had his admirers, Jefferson his adorers; Madison had carried through a war which, if not successful, was at least a drawn game. All these, had they undertaken what play-actors call "starring in the provinces," would have been received as stars, not as officials. Their applauses would have been given to the individual, not the President. But when Monroe travelled, it was simply the Chief Magistrate of the nation who met the eyes of men. He was not a star, but a member of the company, a stock actor, one of themselves. In the speeches with which he was everywhere received there was very little said about his personality; it was the head of the nation who was welcomed. Thus stripped of all individual prestige, the occasion appealed to every citizen. For the first time the people of the United States met their President as such, and felt that they were a nation.

It was at the end of sixteen years of strife—political strife more bitter than can easily be paralleled in these calmer days. The result of this contest may in some respects have been doubtful, but on one point at least it was clear. It had extinguished the colonial theory of government, and substituted the national. Hamilton and the Federalists, with all their high qualities, had still disbelieved in all that lay beyond the domain of experience. But experience, as Coleridge said, is like the stern-lights of a ship, illumining only the track already passed over. Jefferson, with all his faults, had steered for the open sea. Madison's war had impoverished the nation, but had saved its self-respect. Henceforward the American flag was that of an independent people—a people ready to submit to nothing, even from England, which England would not tolerate in return. And it so happened that all the immediate honor of this increased self-respect belonged, or seemed to belong, to the party in power. Jefferson was the most pacific of men, except Madison; both dreaded a standing army, and shrank with reluctance from a navy; yet the laurels of both arms of the service, such as they were, went to Madison and Jefferson. The Federalists, who had begged for a navy, and had threatened to raise an army on their own account, now got no credit for either. That party held, on the whole, the best educated, the most high-minded, the most solvent part of the nation, yet it had been wrecked by its own want of faith. When in the Electoral College Monroe had 183 votes, against 34 for Rufus King, it was plain that the contest was at an end, and that the nation was ready to be soothed. Monroe was precisely the sedative to be applied, and his journey was the process of application.

So much for the people; but there were also anxieties to be quieted among the nation's statesmen. Not only did the people need to learn confidence in their leaders, but the leaders in the people. It was not that republican government itself was on trial, but that its scale seemed so formidable. Nobody doubted that it was a thing available among a few mountain communities, like those of Switzerland. What even the Democratic statesmen of that day doubted—and they had plenty of reason for the fear—was the possibility of applying self-government to the length and breadth of a continent peopled by many millions of men. They were not dismayed by the principle, but by its application; not by the philosophy, but the geography. Washington himself, we know, was opposed to undertaking the ownership of the Mississippi River; and Monroe, when a member of the Virginia Convention, had argued against the adoption of the United States Constitution for geographical reasons. "Consider," he said, "the territory lying between the Atlantic Ocean and the Mississippi. Its extent far exceeds that of the German Empire. It is larger than any territory that ever was under any one free government. It is too extensive to be governed but by a despotic monarchy." This was the view of James Monroe in 1788, at a time when he could have little dreamed of ever becoming President. He was heard with respect, for he had been one of the Virginia committee-men who had transferred the North-western lands to the United States government, and he was one of the few who had personally visited them. Yet he had these fears, and the worst of the alarm was that it had some foundation. But for the unexpected alliances of railway and telegraph, does anybody believe that Maine,

Louisiana, and California would to-day form part of the same nation? In the mean time, while waiting for those mighty coadjutors, the journey of Mr. Monroe relieved anxiety in a very different manner, by revealing the immense strength to which the national feeling had already grown. At any rate, after this experience he expressed no more solicitude. In his message on internal improvements, written five years after his journey, he described the American system of government as one "capable of expansion over a vast territory."

Monroe himself was now fifty-nine years old, and formed in physical appearance a marked contrast to the small size and neat, compact figure of his predecessor. He was six feet high, broad-shouldered, and rather raw-boned, with grayish-blue eyes, whose frank and pleasing expression is often mentioned by the writers of the period, and sometimes cited in illustration of Jefferson's remark that Monroe was "a man whose soul might be turned inside out without discovering a blemish to the world." He was dignified and courteous, but also modest, and even shy, so that his prevailing air was that of commonplace strength and respectable mediocrity. After all the political excitements of the past dozen years, nothing could be more satisfactory than this. People saw in him a plain Virginia farmer addressing audiences still mainly agricultural. Ralph Waldo Emerson once said to me, when looking for the first time on John P. Hale, of New Hampshire, then at the height of a rather brief eminence: "What an average man he is! He looks just like five hundred other men. That must be the secret of his power." It was precisely thus with Monroe. He had in his cabinet men of talents far beyond his own—Adams, Calhoun, Crawford, Wirt; Jefferson and Madison yet lived, his friends and counsellors; Jackson, Clay, Webster, and Benton were just coming forward into public life; but none of all these gifted men could have re-assured the nation by their mere aspect, in travelling through it, as he did. Each of these men, if President, would have been

JAMES MONROE.
[From the painting by Gilbert Stuart, owned by T. Jefferson Coolidge, Esq., Boston

something more than the typical official. Monroe precisely filled the chair, and stood for the office, not for himself.

He left Washington June 2, 1817, accompanied only by his private secretary, Mr. Mason, and by General Joseph G. Swift, the Chief Engineer of the War Department. The ostensible object of his journey was to inspect the national defences. This explained his choice of a companion, and gave him at each point an aim beyond the reception of courtesies. With this nominal errand he travelled through Maryland to New York City, traversed Connecticut and Rhode Island, Massachusetts, New Hampshire, and Maine, then a district only. He went southward through Vermont, visited the fortifications at Plattsburg, travelled through the forests to the St. Lawrence, inspected Sackett's Harbor and Fort Niagara; went to Buffalo, and sailed through Lake Erie to Detroit. Thence he turned eastward again, returning through Ohio, Pennsylvania, and Maryland. He reached home September 17th, after an absence of more than three months.

During all this trip there occurred not one circumstance to mar the reception of the President, though there were plenty of hardships to test his endurance. Everywhere he was greeted with triumphal arches, groups of school-children, cavalcades of mounted citizens, and the roar of cannon. The Governor of Massachusetts, by order of the Legislature, provided him with a military escort from border to border; no other State apparently did this, though the Governor of New Hampshire apologized for not having official authority to follow the example. Everywhere there were addresses of welcome by eminent citizens. Everywhere the President made answer. Clad in the undress uniform of a Revolutionary officer—blue coat, light underclothes, and cocked hat—he stood before the people a portly and imposing figure, well representing the men who won American freedom in arms. His replies, many of which are duly reported, seem now laudably commonplace and reasonably brief; but they were held at the time to be "elegant and impressive."

We see a lingering trace of the more ceremonial period of Washington and Adams when the semi-official historian of Monroe's travels reports that in approaching Dartmouth, New Hampshire, "although the road was shrouded in clouds of dust, he *condescended* to leave his carriage and make his entry on horseback." The more eminent Federalist leaders, except Mr. H. G. Otis, took apparently no conspicuous part in the reception; but their place was supplied by others. Elder Goodrich of the Enfield (New Hampshire) Shakers, addressed him with " I, James Goodrich, welcome James Monroe to our habitations;" and the young ladies of the Windsor (Vermont) Female Academy closed their address by saying, "That success may crown all your exertions for the public good is the ardent wish of many a patriotic though youthful female bosom." Later, when traversing "the majestic forests" near Ogdensburg, New York, "his attention was suddenly attracted by an elegant collation, fitted up in a superior style by the officers of the army and the citizens of the country. He partook of it with a heart beating in unison with those of his patriotic countrymen by whom he was surrounded, and acknowledged this unexpected and romantic civility with an unaffected and dignified complaisance."

Philadelphia had at this time a population of 112,000 inhabitants; New York, of 115,000; Baltimore, of 55,000; Boston, of 40,000; Providence, of 10,000; Hartford, of 8000; Pittsburg, of 7000; Cincinnati, of 7000; St. Louis, of 3500; Chicago was but a fort. The Ohio River was described by those who narrated this journey as an obscure and remote stream that had "for nearly six thousand years rolled in silent majesty through the towering forests of the New World." "It would not be," says a writer of that period, "the madness of a deranged imagination to conclude that this stream in process of time will become as much celebrated as the Ganges of Asia, the Nile of

Africa, and the Danube of Europe. In giving this future importance to the Ohio, the Mississippi and the Missouri cannot be forgotten as exceeding it in length and in importance. These astonishing streams may hereafter, as civilization progresses in the present wilds of the American republic, become rivals to the Ohio." When we consider that the region thus vaguely indicated is now the centre of population for the nation, we learn what a little world it was, after all, which was embraced in the Presidential tour of James Monroe. Even of that small realm, however, he did not see the whole during these travels. We know from a letter of Crawford to Gallatin, quoted by Mr. Gilman, that a good deal of jealousy was felt in the Southern States at Monroe's "apparent acquiescence in the seeming man-worship" at the North; and Crawford thinks that while the President had gained in health by the trip, he had "lost as much as he had gained in popularity." The gain was, however, made where he most needed it, and another tour to Augusta, Nashville, and Louisville soon restored the balance.

The President being established at the seat of government, the fruits of his enlarged popularity were seen in the tranquillity and order of his administration. The most fortunate of officials, he was aided by the general longing for peace. He was yet more strengthened by the fact that he was at the same time governing through a Democratic organization and on Federalist principles. Nominally he held the legitimate succession to Jefferson, having followed, like Madison, through the intermediate position, that of Secretary of State, which was in those days what the position of Prince of Wales was and is in England. But when it came to political opinions, we can now see that all which Federalism had urged—a strong government, a navy, a national bank, a protective tariff, internal improvements, a liberal construction of the Constitution—all these had become also Democratic doctrines. Were it not for their traditional reverence for Jefferson's name, it would sometimes have been hard to tell Madison and Monroe from Federalists. In a free country, when a party disappears, it is usually because the other side has absorbed its principles. So it was here, and we never can understand the extinction of Federalism unless we bear this fact in mind. In the excitement of contest the combatants had already changed weapons, and Federalism had been killed, like Laertes in "Hamlet," by its own sword. For the time, as Crawford wrote, all were Federalists, all Republicans.

Henry Clay, who remains to us as a mere tradition of winning manners and ready eloquence, was almost unanimously elected and re-elected as Speaker of the House. But Clay was a Federalist without knowing it; he wished to strengthen the army, to increase the navy, to make the tariff protective, to recognize and support the South American republics. General Jackson too, the chief military hero of the period, developed the national impulse in a way that Jefferson would once have disapproved, by entering the territory of Spanish Florida (in 1818) to fight the Seminoles, and by putting to death as "outlaws and pirates" two British subjects, Arbuthnot and Ambrister, who led the Indians. Then the purchase of Florida for five millions was another bold step on the part of the central government, following a precedent which had seemed very questionable when Jefferson had annexed Louisiana. While buying this the nation yielded up all claim to what was afterwards Texas; and all these events built up more and more the national feeling—which was the bequest of Federalism—as distinct from the separate State feeling which was the original Democratic stock in trade.

It is the crowning proof of the pacified condition to which parties were coming that this peace survived what would have been, under other circumstances, a signal of war—the first and sudden appearance of the vexed question of slavery. It came upon the nation, as Jefferson said, "like a fire-ball in the night." It had slumbered since the adoption of the Constitution, and came up as an incident of the great emigration westward. For

HENRY CLAY.
(From a drawing by Davignon, owned by Louis R. Menger, Esq.)

a time, in admitting new States, it was very easy to regard the Ohio River as a sort of dividing line, and to alternately admit a new Free State above it and a new Slave State below it. In this way had successively come in Louisiana (1812), Indiana (1816), Mississippi (1817), Illinois (1818), Alabama (1819). But when the process reached Maine and Missouri the struggle began. Should slavery extend beyond the Ohio border into the great Louisiana purchase? Again was every aspect of the momentous question debated with ardor, Rufus King leading one side, John Randolph the other, each side invoking the traditions of the fathers, and claiming to secure the safety of the nation. "At our evening parties," says John Quincy Adams in his diary, "we hear of nothing but the Missouri question and Mr. King's speeches." The contest was ended by Mr. Clay's great effort of skill, known in history as the Missouri Compromise. The result was to admit both Maine (1820) and Missouri (1821), with a provision thenceforward excluding slavery north of the line of 36° 30', the southern boundary of Missouri. John Randolph called it "a dirty bargain," and christened those Northern men who had formed it "dough-faces"—a word which became thereafter a part of the political slang of the nation.

Monroe, in a private letter written about this time (Feb. 15, 1820), declared his belief that "the majority of States, of physical force, and eventually of votes in both Houses," would be ultimately "on the side of the non-slave-holding States." As a moderate Virginia slave-holder he recognized this as the probable condition of affairs. On the other hand, John Quincy Adams, strong in antislavery feeling, voted for the compromise, and afterwards expressed some misgivings about it. He held it to be all that could have been effected under the Constitution, and he shrank from risking the safety of the Union. "If the Union must be dissolved," he said, "the slavery question is precisely the question upon which it ought to break. *For the present, however, this contest is laid to sleep.*" And it slept for many years.

During two sessions of Congress the Missouri question troubled the newly found quiet of the nation, but it did not make so much as a ripple on the surface of the President's popularity. In 1820 the re-election of Monroe would have been absolutely unanimous had not one dissatisfied elector given his vote for John Quincy Adams, the tradition being that this man did not wish any other President to rival Washington in unanimity of choice. The Vice-president, Daniel D. Tompkins, was re-elected with less complete cordiality, there being fourteen votes against him in the Electoral College. Then followed the second administration of Monroe, to which was given, perhaps by the President himself, a name which has secured for the whole period a kind of peaceful eminence. It was probably fixed and made permanent by two lines in Halleck's once famous poem of "Alnwick Castle," evidently written during the poet's residence in England in 1822–23. Speaking of the change from the feudal to the commercial spirit, he says:

> " 'Tis what 'our President,' Monroe,
>   Has called 'the era of good feeling.'
> The Highlander, the bitterest foe
>   To modern laws, has felt their blow,
>   Consented to be taxed, and vote,
>   And put on pantaloons and coat,
>   And leave off cattle-stealing."

It would seem from this verse that Monroe himself was credited with the authorship of the phrase; but I have been unable to find it in his published speeches or messages, and it is possible that it may be of newspaper origin, and that Halleck, writing in England, may have fathered it on the President himself. This is the more likely because even so mild a flavor of facetiousness as this was foreign to the character of Monroe.

Under these soothing influences, at any rate, the nation, and especially its capital city, made some progress in the amenities and refinements of life. It was a period when the social etiquette of Washington City was going through some changes; the population was growing larger, the classes were less distinct, the social duties of high officials more onerous. The diary of John Quincy Adams records cabinet meetings devoted to such momentous questions as who should make the first call, and who should be included in the official visiting lists. Mrs. Monroe, without a cabinet council, made up her own mind to retrench some of those profuse civilities with which her predecessor had fatigued herself. Mrs. Madison, a large, portly, kindly dame, had retired from office equally regretted by the poor of Washington and by its high life; but she had gained this popularity at a severe cost. She had called on all conspicuous strangers; Mrs. Monroe intended to call on nobody. Mrs. Madison had been always ready for visitors when at home; her successor proposed not to receive them except at her regular levees. The ex-Presidentess had presided at her husband's dinner-parties, and had invited the wives of all the men who were to be guests; Mrs. Monroe stayed away from the dinner-parties, and so the wives were left at home. Add to this that her health was by no means strong, and it is plain that there was great ground for a spasm of unpopularity. She, however, outlived it, re-established her social relations, gave fortnightly receptions, and won much admiration, which she probably deserved. She was by birth a Miss Kortwright, of New York, a niece of General Knox, and when she accompanied her husband on his embassy to Paris she had there been known as "la belle Américaine." She was pronounced by observers in later life to be "a most regal-looking lady," and her manners were described as "very gracious." At her final levee in the White House "her dress was superb black velvet; neck and arms bare, and beautifully formed; her hair in puffs, and dressed high on the head, and ornamented with white ostrich plumes; around her neck an elegant pearl necklace." Her two fair daughters—her only children, Mrs. Hay and Mrs. Gouverneur—assisted at this reception.

Such was the hostess, but her drawing-rooms, by all contemporary accounts, afforded a curious social medley. The well-defined gentry of the Revolutionary period was disappearing, and the higher average of dress and manners had not begun to show itself—that higher average which has since been rapidly developed by the influence of railroads and newspapers, joined with much foreign travel and a great increase in wealth. It was a period when John Randolph was allowed to come to dinner-parties "in a rough, coarse, short hunting coat, with small-clothes and boots, and over his boots a pair of coarse coating leggings, tied with strings around his legs." At Presidential receptions, in the words of an eye-witness, "ambassadors and consuls, members of Congress and officers of the army and navy, greasy boots and silk stockings, Virginia buckskins and Yankee cowhides, all mingled in ill-assorted and fantastic groups."

Houses in Washington had become much larger than formerly, and a similar expansion had been seen in the scale of entertainments. It is not uncommon to find records of evening parties, at which five or six hundred persons were present, filling five or six rooms. When John Quincy Adams, then Secretary of State, gave a reception to the newly arrived hero, General Andrew Jackson, eight rooms were opened, and there were a thousand guests. It was regarded as the finest entertainment ever given in Washington, and showed, in the opinion of Senator Mills, of Massachusetts, "taste, elegance, and good-sense" on the part of Mrs. Adams. Elsewhere he pronounces her "a very pleasant and agreeable woman," but adds, "the Secretary has no talent to entertain a mixed company, either by conversation or manners." Other agreeable houses were that of Mr. Bagot, the British Minister, whose wife was a niece of the Duke of Wellington, and that of M. Hyde de Neuville, the French Minister, each house being opened for a weekly reception, whereas the receptions at the White House took place but once a fortnight. At these entertainments they had music, cards, and dancing—country-dances, cotillions, with an occasional Scotch reel. It was noticed with some surprise that even New England ladies would accept the hospitalities of Madame de

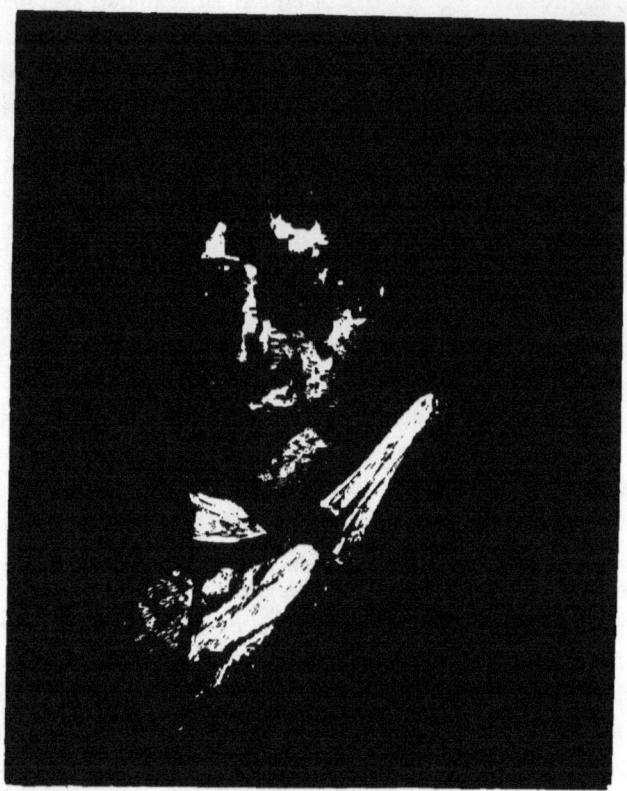

JOHN RANDOLPH.
[From an early portrait by Stuart, now at Williamsburgh, Va.]

Neuville on Saturday evenings, and would dance on what they had been educated to regard as holy time.

Among the most conspicuous of these ladies was Mrs. Jonathan Russell, of Boston, full of sense and information, but charged with some eccentricities of costume; the reigning belle seems to have been the wife of Commodore Hull; and one of the most conspicuous figures was Miss Randolph, of Virginia, daughter of the governor of that State, and granddaughter of ex-President Jefferson—a damsel who had plenty of brains, and could talk politics with anybody; but was no favorite with the ladies. Among the men, John Randolph was the most brilliant and interesting, and all the more so from his waywardness and insolence. In public life he preceded Calhoun in the opinions which have made the latter famous; and in private life he could, if he chose, be delightful. "He is now," Mr. Mills writes to his wife in 1822, "what he used to be in his best days—in good spirits, with fine manners and the most fascinating conversation. I would give more to have you see *him* than any man living on the earth." Add to these Messrs. Clay, Webster, Crawford, Van Buren, Rufus King, and many other men of marked ability, but of varied social aptitude, and we have the Washington of that day. By way of background there was the ever-present shadow of slavery; and there were occasional visits from Indian delegations, who gave war-dances before the White House in the full glory of nakedness and paint.

In considering this social development we must remember that under Monroe's administration American literature may be said to have had its birth. Until about his time prose and verse were mainly political; and the most liberal modern collection would hardly now borrow a single poem from the little volume called the "Columbian Oracle," in which were gathered, during the year 1794, the choicest effusions of Dwight and Humphreys, Barlow and Freneau. Fisher Ames, perhaps the most accomplished of the Federalists, and the only one who took the pains to make "American Literature" the theme of an essay, had declared, in 1808, that such a literary product would never exist until the course of democracy should be ended, and despotism should have taken its place. "Shall we match Joel Barlow against Homer or Hesiod?" he asked. "Can Thomas

Paine contend with Plato?... Liberty has never lasted long in a democracy, nor has it ever ended in anything better than despotism. With the change of our government, our manners and sentiments will change. As soon as our emperor has destroyed his rivals and established order in his army, he will desire to see splendor in his court, and to occupy his subjects with the cultivation of the sciences."

It was something when the matter of a national literature came to be treated, not thus despairingly, but jocosely. This progress found a voice, four years later, in Edward Everett, who, in his Cambridge poem on "American Poets" (1812), prophesied with a little more of hope. He portrayed, indeed, with some humor, the difficulties of the native bard, since he must deal with the Indian names, of which nobody then dreamed that they could ever be thought tuneful:

> "A different scene our native poet shames
> With barbarous titles and with savage names.
> When the warm bard his country's worth would tell,
> Lo Mas-sa-chu-setts' length his lines must swell.
> Would he the gallant tales of war rehearse,
> 'Tis graceful Bunker fills the polished verse.
> Sings he, dear land, those lakes and streams of thine,
> Some mild Memphremagog murmurs in his line,
> Some Ameriscoggin dashes by his way,
> Or smooth Connecticut softens in his lay.
> Would he one verse of easy movement frame,
> The map will meet him with a hopeless name;
> Nor can his pencil sketch one perfect act
> But vulgar history mocks him with a fact."

Still, he thought, something might be done by-and-by, even with materials so rough:

> "Oh yes! in future days our western lyres,
> Tuned to new themes, shall glow with purer fires,
> Clothed with the charms, to grace their later rhyme,
> Of every former age and foreign clime.
> Then Homer's arms shall ring in Bunker's shock,
> And Virgil's wanderer land on Plymouth rock;

> Then Dante's knights before Quebec shall fall,
> And Charles's trump on trainband chieftains call.
> Our mobs shall wear the wreaths of Tasso's Moors,
> And Barbary's coast shall yield to Baltimore's.
> Here our own bays some native Pope shall grace,
> And lovelier beauties fill Belinda's place."

It was all greatly applauded, no doubt, as in the best vein of the classic Everett; and it was in Monroe's time, five or ten years later, that the fulfilment actually began. He certainly could not be called an emperor, nor could his court be termed splendid; yet it was under this plain potentate that a national literature was born.

The English Sydney Smith wrote in 1818, one year after Monroe's accession to office: "There does not appear to be in America at this time one man of any considerable talents." But an acuter and severer literary critic, Lord Jeffrey, wrote, four years later (January 27, 1822): "The true hope of the world is with you in America—in your example now, and in fifty years more, I hope, your influence and actual power." It was midway between these two dates that the veteran publisher Mr. S. G. Goodrich, in his "Recollections," placed the birth-time of a national literature. "During this period," he says, "we began to have confidence in American genius, and to dream of literary ambition." The *North American Review* was established in 1815; Bryant's "Thanatopsis" appeared in 1817; Irving's "Sketch-Book" in 1818; Cooper's "Spy" in 1822. When Monroe went out of office, in 1825, Emerson was teaching school, Whittier was at work on his father's farm, Hawthorne and Longfellow were about to graduate from college; but American literature was born.

People still maintained—as a few yet hold—that these various authors succeeded in spite of the national atmosphere, not by means of it. It seems to me easy to show, on the contrary, that they all impressed themselves on the world chiefly by using the materials they found at home. Longfellow, at first steeped

RUFUS KING.
[From the painting by Gilbert Stuart, owned by A. Gracie King, Esq.]

in European influences, gained in strength from the time he touched his native soil; nor did he find any difficulty in weaving into melodious verse those Indian names which had appalled Mr. Everett. Irving, the most exotic of all these writers, really made his reputation by his use of what has been called "the Knickerbocker legend." He did not create the traditions of the Hudson; they created him. Mrs. Josiah Quincy, sailing up that river in 1786, when Irving was a child three years old, records that the captain of the sloop had a legend, either supernatural or traditional, for every scene, "and not a mountain reared its head unconnected with some marvellous story." The legends were all there ready for Irving, just as the New England legends were waiting for Whittier. Once let the man of genius be born, and his own soil was quite able to furnish the food that should rear him.

Apart from this social and literary progress, two especial points marked the administration of Monroe, both being matters whose importance turned out to be far greater than any one had suspected. The first was the introduction of a definite term of office for minor civil officers. When the First Congress asserted the right of the President to remove such officials at all, it was thought a dangerous power. In practice that power had been but little used, and scarcely ever for political purposes, when William H. Crawford, Secretary of the Treasury, was touched with Presidential ambition. Most of the minor officials being then in his department, he conceived the plan of pushing through a bill to make them removable every four years. It seemed harmless. The apparent object was to get rid of untrustworthy revenue officers. It was enacted with so little discussion that Benton's "Abridgment of Debates" does not mention its passage. It was signed by the President "unwarily," as John Quincy Adams tells us, on May 15, 1820; and instantly, as the same authority asserts, all the Treasury officials became "ardent Crawfordites." Jefferson and Madison utterly disapproved of the new system; so did Adams, so did Calhoun, so did Webster; but it has remained unchanged until this day, for good or for evil.

It so happens that this law has never until lately been identified with the period of Monroe; it was enacted so quietly that its birthday was forgotten. Not so with another measure, which was not indeed a law, but merely the laying down of a principle, ever since known as the "Monroe doctrine;" this being simply a demand of non-interference by foreign nations with the affairs of the two American continents. There has been a good deal of dispute as to the real authorship of this announcement, Charles Francis Adams claiming it for his father, and Charles Sumner for the English statesman Canning. Mr. Gilman, however, in his late memoir of President Monroe, has shown with exhaustive research that this doctrine had grown up gradually into a national tradition before Monroe's time, and that he merely formulated it, and made it a matter of distinct record. The whole statement is contained in a few detached passages of his message of December 2, 1823. In this he announces that "the American continents, by the free and independent condition which they have assumed and maintain, are not to be considered as subjects for colonization by European powers." Further on he points out that the people of the United States have kept aloof from European dissensions, and ask only in return that North and South America should be equally let alone. "We should consider any attempt on their part to extend their system to any portion of this hemisphere as dangerous to our peace and safety;" and while no objection is made to any existing colony or dependency of theirs, yet any further intrusion or interference would be regarded as "the manifestation of an unfriendly spirit towards the United States." This, in brief, is the "Monroe doctrine" as originally stated; and it will always remain a singular fact that this President—the least original or commanding of those who early held that office—should yet be the only one whose name is identified with what amounts to a wholly new axiom of international law.

Apart from this, Mr. Monroe's messages, which fill as many pages as those of any two of his predecessors, are conspicuously hard reading; and the only portions to which a student of the present day can turn with any fresh interest are those which measure the steady progress of the nation. "Twenty-five years ago," he could justly say—looking back upon his own first diplomatic achievement—"the river Mississippi was shut up, and our Western brethren had no outlet for their commerce. What has been the progress since that time? The river has not only become the property of the United States from its source to the ocean, with all its tributary streams (with the exception of the upper part of the Red River only), but Louisiana, with a fair and liberal boundary, on the western side, and the Floridas on the eastern, have been ceded to us. The United States now enjoy the complete and uninterrupted sovereignty over the whole territory from St. Croix to the Sabine." This was written March 4, 1821. Nevertheless, the President could not, even then, give his sanction to any national efforts for the improvement of this vast domain; and he vetoed, during the following year, the "Cumberland Road" bill, which would have led the way, he thought, to a wholly unconstitutional system of internal improvements. With this exception his administration came into no very marked antagonism to public sentiment, and even in dealing with this he went to no extremes, but expressed willingness that the national road should be repaired, not extended.

And while he looked upon the past progress of the nation with wonder, its destiny was to him a sealed book. Turning from all this record of past surprises, he could find no better plan for the future development of the post-office department, for instance, than to suggest that all the mails of the nation might profitably be carried thenceforward on horseback. As a crowning instance of how little a tolerably enlightened man may see into the future, it would be a pity not to quote the passage from this veto message of May 4, 1822:

"Unconnected with passengers and other objects, it cannot be doubted that the mail itself may be carried in every part of our Union, with nearly as much economy and greater despatch, on horseback, than in a stage; and in many parts with much greater. In every part of the Union in which stages can be preferred the roads are sufficiently good, provided those which serve for every other purpose will accommodate them. In every other part, where horses alone are used, if other people pass them on horseback, surely the mail-carrier can. For an object so simple and so easy in the execution it would doubtless excite surprise if it should be thought proper to appoint commissioners to lay off the country on a great scheme of improvement, with the power to shorten distances, reduce heights, level mountains, and pave surfaces."

Those who have traversed on horseback, even within twenty years, those miry Virginia roads and those treacherous fords with which President Monroe was so familiar, will best appreciate this project for the post-office accommodations of a continent—a plan "so simple and easy in the execution." Since then the country has indeed been laid off "in a great scheme of improvement," distances have been shortened, heights reduced, and surfaces paved, even as he suggested, but under circumstances which no President in 1822 could possibly have conjectured. Indeed, it was not till the following administration, that of John Quincy Adams, that the first large impulse of expansion was really given, and the great western march began.

XVII.

THE GREAT WESTERN MARCH.

THE four years' administration of John Quincy Adams is commonly spoken of as a very uninteresting period, but it was in one respect more important than the twenty years that went before it or the ten years that followed. For the first time the inhabitants of the United States began to learn in how very large a country they lived. From occupying a mere strip of land on the Atlantic they had spread already through New York and Ohio; but it was by detached emigrations, of which the nation was hardly conscious, by great single waves of population sweeping here and there. After 1825 this development became a self-conscious and deliberate thing, recognized and legislated for, though never systematically organized by the nation. When, between 1820 and 1830, Michigan Territory increased 260 per cent., Illinois 180 per cent., Arkansas Territory 142 per cent., and Indiana 133 per cent., it indicated not a mere impulse but a steady progress, not a wave but a tide. Now that we are accustomed to the vast statistics of to-day, it may not seem exciting to know that the population of the whole nation rose from nearly ten millions (9,633,822) in 1820 to nearly thirteen (12,866,020) in 1830; but this gain of one-third was at the time the most astounding demonstration of national progress. It enables us to understand the immense importance attached in John Quincy Adams's time to a phrase now commonplace and almost meaningless—" internal improvements." It is true that during his term of office more commercial treaties were negotiated than under all his predecessors; but this, after all, was a minor benefit. The foreign commerce of the United States is now itself, comparatively speaking, subordinate; it is our vast internal development that makes us a nation. It is as the great epoch of internal improvements that the four years from 1825 to 1829 will forever be momentous in the history of the United States.

In 1825 the nation was in the position of a young man who has become aware that he owns a vast estate, but finds it to be mostly unproductive, and hardly even marketable. Such a person sometimes hits upon an energetic agent, who convinces him that the essential thing is to build a few roads, bridge a few streams, and lay out some building lots. It was just in this capacity of courageous adviser that John Quincy Adams was quite ready to offer himself. On the day of his inauguration the greater part of Ohio was yet covered with forests, and Illinois was a wilderness. The vast size of the country was still a source rather of anxiety than of pride. Monroe had expressed the fear that no republican government could safely control a nation reaching so far as the Mississippi; and Livingston, after negotiating for the purchase of Louisiana, had comforted himself with the thought that a large part of it might probably be resold. At that time this enormous annexation was thought to endanger the very existence of the original thirteen States.

This was perhaps nowhere more frankly stated than by an able Fourth-of-July orator at Salem, Massachusetts, in 1813, Benjamin R. Nichols. He declares, in this address, that to admit to the Union new States formed out of new territory is "to set up a principle which, if submitted to, will make us more dependent than we were as colonies of Great Britain. If a majority of Congress have a right of making new States where they please, we shall probably soon hear of States formed for us in East and West Florida; and, should it come within the scope of the policy of our rulers, of others as far as the Pacific Ocean. If all this be right, the consequence is that the people of New England, in case of any disturbances in these newly created States, may, under pretence of suppressing insurrections, be forced to march, in obedience to the Constitution, to the remotest corners of the globe." In other words, that which now makes the crowning pride of an American citizen, that the States of the Union are spread from the Atlantic to the Pacific, was then held up by a patriotic Federalist as the very extreme of danger. The antidote to this deadly peril, the means of establishing some communication with these " remotest corners of the globe," had necessarily to be found, first of all, in internal improvements. At least, under these circumstances of alarm, a highway or two might be held a reasonable proposition; and the new President, in his inaugural address, approached the subject with something of the lingering stateliness of those days:

"The magnificence and splendor of their public works are among the imperishable glories of the ancient republics. The roads and aqueducts of Rome have been the admiration of all after-ages, and have survived thousands of years, after all her conquests have been swallowed up in despotism, or become the spoil of barbarians. Some diversity of opinion has prevailed with regard to the powers of Congress for legislation upon subjects of this nature. The most respectful deference is due to doubts originating in pure patriotism, and sustained by venerated authority. But nearly twenty years have passed since the construction of the first national road was commenced. The authority for its construction was then unquestioned. To how many thousands of our countrymen has it proved a benefit? To what single individual has it ever proved an injury?"

It has already been pointed out that when John Quincy Adams became President the nation had been governed for a quarter of a century by Democratic administrations, acting more and more on Federalist principles. The tradition of States-rights had steadily receded, and the reality of a strong and expanding nation had taken its place. The very men who had at first put into the most definite shape these States-rights opinions had, by their action, done most to overthrow

JOHN QUINCY ADAMS.

[From the painting by G. P. A. Healy, in the Corcoran Gallery, Washington.]

them, Jefferson above all. By the purchase of Louisiana he had, perhaps unconsciously, done more than any President before him to make national feeling permanent. Having, by a happy impulse, and in spite of all his own theories, enormously enlarged the joint territory, he had recognized the need of opening and developing the new possession; he had set the example of proposing national appropriations for roads, canals, and even education; and had given his sanction (March 24, 1806) to building a national road from Maryland to Ohio, first obtaining the consent of the States through which it was to pass. To continue this policy would, he admitted, require constitutional amendments, but in his closing message he favored such alterations. It was but a step from favoring constitutional amendments for this purpose to doing without them; Jefferson, Madison, Monroe had done the one, John Quincy Adams did the other.

Of course it took the nation by surprise. Nothing astonishes people more than to be taken at their word, and have their own theories energetically put in practice. Others had talked in a general way about internal improvements; under President Monroe there had even been created (April 30, 1824) a national board to plan them; but John Quincy Adams really meant to have them; and his very first message looked formidable to those who supposed that because he had broken with the Federalists he was therefore about to behave like an old-fashioned Democrat. In truth he was more new-fashioned than anybody. This is the way he committed himself in this first message:

"While foreign nations, less blessed with that freedom which is power than ourselves, are advancing with gigantic strides in the career of public improvement, were we to slumber in indolence, or fold up our arms and proclaim to the world that we are palsied by the will of our constituents, would it not be to cast away the bounties of Providence, and doom ourselves to perpetual inferiority? In the course of the year now drawing to its close, we have beheld, under the auspices and at the expense of one State of this Union, a new university unfolding its portals to the sons of science, and holding up the torch of human improvement to eyes that seek the light. We have seen, under the persevering and enlightened enterprise of another State, the waters of our western lakes mingle with those of the ocean. If undertakings like these have been accomplished in the compass of a few years by the authority of single members of our confederation, can we, the representative authorities of the whole Union, fall behind our fellow-servants in the exercise of the trust committed to us for the benefit of our common sovereign, by the accomplishment of works important to the whole, and to which neither the authority nor the resources of any one State can be adequate?"

Nor was this all. It is curious to see that the President's faithful ally, Mr. Rush, Secretary of the Treasury, went far beyond his chief in the tone of his recommendations, and drifted into what would now be promptly labelled as Communism. When we read as an extreme proposition in these days, in the middle of some mildly socialistic manifesto, the suggestion that there should be a national bureau "whereby new fields can be opened, old ones developed, and every labor can be properly directed and located," we fancy it a novelty. But see how utterly Mr. Rush surpassed these moderate proposals in one of his reports as Secretary of the Treasury. He said that it was the duty of government

"to augment the number and variety of occupations for its inhabitants; to hold out to every degree of labor and to every manifestation of skill its appropriate object and inducement; to organize the whole labor of a country; to entice into the widest ranges its mechanical and intellectual capacities, instead of suffering them to slumber; to call forth, wherever hidden, latent ingenuity, giving to effort activity, and to emulation ardor; to create employment for the greatest amount of numbers by adapting it to the diversified faculties, propensities, and situations of men, so that every particle of ability, every shade of genius, may come into requisition."

Let us now turn to the actual advances made under the guidance of Mr. Adams. Nothing in the history of the globe is so extraordinary in its topographical and moral results as the vast western march of the American people within a hundred years. Let us look, for instance, at some contemporary map of what constituted the northern part of the United States in 1798. The western boundary of visible settlement is the Genesee River of New York. The names on the Hudson are like the names of to-day; all beyond is strange. No railroad, no canal; only a turnpike running to the Genesee, and with no farther track to mark the way through the forest to "Buffaloe," on the far-off lake. Along this turnpike are settlements, "Schenectady," "Canajohary," "Schuyler or Utica," "Fort Stenwick or Rome," "Oneida Cassle," "Onondaga Cassle," "Geneva," and "Canandargue," where the road turns north to Lake Ontario. Forests cover all Western New York, all North-western Pennsylvania. Far off in Ohio is a detached region indicated as "the Connecticut Reserve, conceded to the families who had been ruined during the war of Independence"—whence our modern phrase "Western Reserve." The summary of the whole map is that the nation still consists of the region east of the Alleghanies, with a few outlying settlements, and nothing more.

Now pass over twenty years. In the map prefixed to William Darby's "Tour from New York to Detroit," in 1818—this Darby being the author of an emigrant's guide, and a member of the New York Historical Society—we find no State west of the Mississippi except Missouri, and scarcely any towns in Indiana or Illinois. Michigan Territory is designated, but across the whole western half of it is the inscription, "This part very imperfectly known." All beyond Lake Michigan and all west of the Mississippi is a nameless waste, except for a few names of rivers and of Indian villages. This marks the progress—and a very considerable progress—of twenty years. Writing from Buffalo (now spelled correctly), Darby says: "The beautiful and highly cultivated lands of the strait of Erie are now a specimen of what in forty years will be the landscape from Erie to Chicaga [sic]. It is a very gratifying anticipation to behold in fancy the epoch to come when this augmenting mass of the population will enjoy, in the interior of this vast continent, a choice collection of immense marts where the produce of the banks of innumerable rivers and lakes can be exchanged."

Already, it seems, travellers and map-makers had got from misspelling "Buffaloe" to misspelling "Chicaga." It was a great deal. The *Edinburgh Review* for that same year (June, 1818), in reviewing Birkbeck's once celebrated "Travels in America," said:

> "Where is this prodigious increase of numbers, this vast extension of dominion, to end? What bounds has nature set to the progress of this mighty nation? Let our jealousy burn as it may, let our intolerance of America be as unreasonably violent as we please, still it is plain that she is a power in spite of us, rapidly rising to supremacy; or, at least, that each year so mightily augments her strength as to overtake, by a most sensible distance, even the most formidable of her competitors."

This was written, it must be remembered, when the whole population of the United States was but little more than nine millions, or about the number now occupying New York and Pennsylvania.

What were the first channels for this great transfer of population? They were the great turnpike-road up the Mohawk Valley, in New York; and farther south, the "National Road," which ended at Wheeling, Virginia. Old men, now or recently living—as, for instance, Mr. Sewall Newhouse, the trapper and trap-maker of Oneida—can recall the long lines of broad-wheeled wagons, drawn by ten horses, forty of these teams sometimes coming in close succession; the stages, six of which were sometimes in sight at once; the casualties, the break-downs, the sloughs of despond, the passengers at work with fence-rails to pry out the vehicle from a mud-hole. These sights, now disappearing on the shores of the Pacific, were then familiar in the heart of what is now the East. This was the tide flowing westward; while eastward, on the other hand, there soon began a counter-current of flocks and herds sent from the new settlements to supply the older States. As early as 1824 Timothy Flint records meeting a drove of more than a thousand cattle and swine, rough and shaggy as wolves, guided towards the

Philadelphia market by a herdsman looking as untamed as themselves, and coming from Ohio—"a name which still sounded in our ears," Flint says, "like the land of savages."

The group so well known in our literature, the emigrant family, the way-side fire, the high-peaked wagon, the exhausted oxen—this picture recedes steadily in space as we come nearer to our own time. In 1788 it set off with the first settlers from Massachusetts to seek Ohio; in 1798 it was just leaving the Hudson to ascend the Mohawk River; in 1815 the hero of "Lawrie Todd" saw it at Rochester, New York; in 1819 Darby met it near Detroit, Michigan; in 1824 Flint saw it in Missouri; in 1831 Alexander depicted it in Tennessee; in 1843 Margaret Fuller Ossoli sketched it beyond Chicago, Illinois; in 1856 I myself saw it in Nebraska and Kansas; in 1864 Clarence King described it in his admirable sketch, "Way-side Pikes," in California; in 1882 Mrs. Leighton, in her graphic letters, pictures it at Puget Sound; beyond which, as it has reached the Pacific, it cannot advance. From this continent the emigrant group in its original form has almost vanished; the process of spreading emigration by steam is less picturesque but more rapid.

The newly published volumes of the United States Census for 1880 give, with an accuracy and fulness of detail such as were before unexampled, the panorama of this vast westward march. It is a matter of national pride to see how its ever-changing phases have been caught and photographed in these masterly volumes, in a way such as the countries of the older world have never equalled, though it would seem so much easier to depict their more fixed conditions. The Austrian newspapers complain that no one in that nation knows at this moment, for instance, the centre of Austrian population; while the successive centres for the United States are here exhibited on a chart with a precision as great, and an impressiveness to the imagination as vast, as when astronomers represent for us the successive positions of a planet. Like the shadow thrown by the hand of some great clock, this inevitable point advances year by year across the continent, sometimes four miles a year, sometimes eight miles, but always advancing. And with this striking summary the census report gives us a series of successive representations on colored charts, at ten-year intervals, of the gradual expansion and filling in of population over the whole territory of the United States. No romance is so fascinating as the thoughts suggested by these silent sheets, each line and tint representing the unspoken sacrifices and fatigues of thousands of nameless men and women. Let us consider for a moment these successive indications.

In the map for 1790 the whole population is on the eastern slope of the Appalachian range, except a slight spur of emigra-

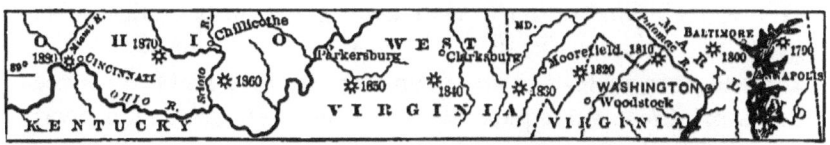

MAP SHOWING THE MOVEMENT OF THE CENTRE OF POPULATION WESTWARD ON THE THIRTY-NINTH PARALLEL.

tion reaching westward from Pennsylvania and Virginia, and a detached settlement in Kentucky. The average depth of the strip of civilization, measuring back from the Atlantic westward, is but three hundred and fifty-five miles. In 1800 there is some increase of population within the old lines, and a western movement along the Mohawk in New York State, while the Kentucky group of inhabitants has spread down into Tennessee. In 1810 all New York, Pennsylvania, and Kentucky are well sprinkled with population, which begins to invade southern Ohio also, while the territory of Orleans has a share; although Michigan, Indiana, Illinois, Missouri, the Mississippi territory—including Mississippi and Alabama—are still almost or quite untouched.

In 1820 Ohio, or two-thirds of it, shows signs of civilized occupation; and the settlements around Detroit, which so impressed Darby, have joined those in Ohio; Tennessee is well occupied, as is southern Indiana; while Illinois, Wisconsin, Alabama, have little rills of population adjoining the Indian tribes, which are not yet removed, and still retard Southern settlements. In 1830 —Adams's administration being now closed—Indiana is nearly covered with population, Illinois more than half; there is hardly any unsettled land in Ohio, while Michigan is beginning to be occupied. Population has spread up the Missouri to the north of Kansas River; and farther south, Louisiana, Alabama, and Arkansas begin to show for something. But even in 1830 the centre of population is in Moorefield, Virginia, and is not yet moving westward at the rate of more than five miles a year.

This year of 1830 lying beyond the term of John Quincy Adams's administration, I shall here follow the statistics of the great migration no farther. Turn now to his annual message, and see how, instead of the doubts or cautious hints of his predecessors, these State papers are filled with suggestions of those special improvements which an overflowing Treasury enabled him to secure. In his third annual message, for instance, he alludes to reports ready for Congress, and in some cases acted upon, in respect to the continuance of the national road from Cumberland eastward, and to Columbus and St. Louis westward; other reports as to a national road from Washington to Buffalo, and a post-road from Baltimore to Philadelphia; as to a canal from Lake Pontchartrain to the Mississippi; as to another to be cut across Florida; another to connect Mobile and Pensacola; another to unite the Coosa and Hiwassee rivers in Alabama. There are reports also on Cape Fear; on the Swash in Pamlico Sound; on La Plaisance Bay in Michigan; on the Kennebec and Saugatuck rivers; on the harbors of Edgartown, Hyannis, and Newburyport. What has been already done, he says, in these and similar directions, has cost three or four millions of dollars annually, but it has been done without creating a dollar of taxes or debt; nor has it diminished the payment of previous debts, which have indeed been reduced to the extent of sixteen millions of dollars in three years. But this was only a partial estimate. During the whole administration of John Quincy Adams, according to the *American Annual Register*, more than a million of dollars were devoted to the light-house system; half a million to public buildings; two millions to arsenals and armories; three millions to coast fortifications; three millions to the navy; and four millions to internal improvements and scientific surveys. Including smaller items, nearly fourteen millions were expended under him for permanent objects, besides five millions of dollars for pensions; a million and a half for the Indian tribes; thirty millions for the reduction of the public debt; and a surplus of five millions for his successor. Here was patriotic house-keeping indeed for the vast family of the nation, and yet this administration has very commonly been passed over as belonging to those times of peace that have proverbially but few historians.

Let us return to the actual progress of the great western march. The Ohio River being once reached, the main channel of emigration lay in the watercourses. Steamboats as yet were but beginning their invasion, amid the general dismay and cursing of the population of boatmen that had rapidly established itself along the shore of every river. The early water life of the Ohio and its kindred streams was the very romance of emigration; no monotonous agriculture, no toilsome wood-chopping, could keep back the adventurous boys who found delight in the endless novelty, the alternate energy and repose of a floating existence on those delightful waters. The variety of river craft corresponded to the varied tastes and habits of the boatmen. There was the great barge with lofty deck, requiring twenty-five men to work it up-stream; there was the long keel-boat, carrying from fifteen to thirty tons; there was the Kentucky "broad-horn," compared by the emigrants of that day to a New England pigsty set afloat, and sometimes built one hundred feet long, and carrying seventy tons; there was the "family boat," of like structure, and bearing a whole household, with cattle, hogs, horses, and sheep. Other boats were floating tin shops, blacksmiths' shops, whiskey shops, dry-goods shops. A few were propelled by horse-power. Of smaller vessels there were "covered sleds," "ferry flats," and "Alleghany skiffs;" "pirogues" made from two tree trunks, or "dug-outs" consisting of one. These boats would set out from Pittsburg for voyages of all lengths, sometimes extending over three thousand miles, and reaching points on the Missouri, Arkansas, and Red rivers. Boats came to St. Louis from Montreal with but few "portages" or "carries" on the way; and sometimes arrived from Mackinaw, when the streams were high and the morasses full, without being carried by hand at all.

The crews were carefully chosen; a "Kentuck," or Kentuckian, was considered the best man at a pole, and a "Kanuck," or French Canadian, at the oar or the "cordelle," the rope used to haul a boat up-stream. Their talk was of the dangers of the river; of "planters and sawyers," meaning tree trunks embedded more or less firmly in the river; of "riffles," meaning ripples; and of "shoots," or rapids (French, *chutes*). It was as necessary to have violins on board as to have whiskey, and all the traditions in song or picture of "the jolly boatmen" date back to that by-gone day. Between the two sides of the river there was already a jealousy. Ohio was called "the Yankee State;" and Flint tells us that it was a standing joke among the Ohio boatmen, when asked their cargo, to reply, "Pit-coal indigo, wooden nutmegs, straw baskets, and Yankee notions." The same authority describes this sort of questioning as being inexhaustible among the river people, and asserts that from one descending boat came this series of answers, all of which proved to be truthful: "Where are you from?" "Redstone." "What's your lading?" "Millstones." "What's your captain's name?" "Whetstone." "Where are you bound?" "To Limestone."

All this panorama of moving life was brought nearly to a close, during the younger Adams's administration, by the introduction of steamboats, though it was prolonged for a time upon the newly built canals. Steamboats were looked upon, as Flint tells us, with "detestation" by the inhabitants, though they soon learned to depend upon them, and to make social visits in them to friends a hundred miles away. In 1812 Fulton's first Western boat, the *Orleans*, went down the Ohio, and in 1816 the *Washington* proved itself able to stem the current in returning. But for a time canals spread more rapidly than steamboats. Gouverneur Morris had first suggested the Erie Canal in 1777, and Washington had indeed proposed a system of such water-ways in 1774. But the first actual work of this kind in the United States was that dug around Turner's Falls, in Massachusetts, soon after 1792. In 1803 De Witt Clinton again proposed the Erie Canal. It was begun in 1817, and opened July 4, 1825, being cut mainly through a wilderness. The effect produced on public opinion was absolutely startling. When men found that the time from Albany to Buffalo was reduced one-half, and that the freight on a ton of merchandise was cut down from $100 to $10, and ultimately to $3, similar enterprises sprang into being everywhere. The most conspicuous of these was the Chesapeake and Ohio Canal, from Georgetown to Pittsburg, which was surveyed and planned by the national board of internal improvements, created just before Mr. Adams's accession. On July 4, 1828, the first blow in the excavation was struck by the President. He had a habit of declining invitations to agricultural fairs and all public exhibitions, but was persuaded to make a speech and put the first spade in the ground for this great enterprise. The soil was for some reason so hard that it would scarcely give way, so the President took off his coat, and tried again and again, at last raising the sod, amid general applause. It was almost the only time during his arduous life when he paused to do a picturesque or symbolic act before the people.

Thus, by various means, the great wave swept westward. Massachusetts, Connecticut, and New Jersey filled up Ohio; North Carolina and Virginia populated Kentucky and Tennessee; Canada sent its emigrants into Illinois and Indiana, and all down the Mississippi. The new settlers, being once launched in the free career of the West, developed by degrees a new type of character. Everywhere there was a love of the frontier life, of distance, isolation, of "range," as the Kentuckians of that day called it. There was a charming side to it all. There was no more fascinating existence anywhere than that of the pioneer hunters in the yet unfelled forests, and the lasting popularity of Cooper's novels proves the permanent spell exercised by this life over the imagination. No time will ever diminish the picturesqueness of Daniel Boone's career in Kentucky, for instance, amid the exquisite beauty of the regions near Lexington, woods carpeted with turf like an English park, free from underbrush, with stately trees of every variety, and fresh, clear streams everywhere; or beside the salt springs of the Licking Valley, where Simon Kenton saw from twenty to thirty thousand buffaloes congregated at a time. What were the tame adventures of Robin Hood to the occasion when these two pioneer hunters, Boone and Kenton, approached the Licking Valley, each alone, from opposite points, each pausing to reconnoitre before leaving the shelter of the woods, and each recognizing the presence of another human being in the valley? Then began a long series of manœuvres on the part of each to discover who the other was, without self-betrayal; and such was their skill that it took forty-eight hours before either could make up his mind that the other was a white man and a friend, not an Indian and a foe.

But there was to all this picture a reverse side that was less charming. For those who were not content to spend their lives as woodsmen in Kentucky, and preferred to seek Ohio as agriculturists, how much of sacrifice there was! what weary years of cold, poverty, discomfort! This letter, quoted in Perkins's "Fifty Years of Ohio," as written in 1818 from Marietta, gives a glimpse through the door-way of a thousand cabins:

> "Marietta I find a poor, muddy hole; the mud here is more disgreeable than snow in Massachusetts. My advice to all my friends is not to come to this country. There is not one in a hundred but what is discontented; but they cannot get back, having spent all their property in getting here. It is the most broken country that I ever saw. Poor, lean pork at twelve cents; salt, four cents; poor, dry fish, twenty cents. The corn is miserable, and we cannot get it ground; we have to pound it. Those that have lanterns grate it. Rum, twenty-five cents a gill; sugar, thirty-seven cents a pound; and no molasses! This country has been the ruin of a great many poor people; it has undone a great many poor souls forever."

Meantime, at Washington, there had been a great increase in wealth and social refinement since the earlier days. Mr. Josiah Quincy, in his "Recollections of Washington Society in 1826," presents for us a polished and delightful community, compared to that which had preceded it. Himself a handsome young Bostonian, with the prestige of a name already noted, he found nothing but sunshine and roses in his path through the metropolis. Names now historic glitter through his pages; he went to balls under the escort of Mr. and Mrs. Daniel Webster; his first entertainment was at Mrs. William Wirt's, where he met Miss Henry, Patrick Henry's daughter, who played the piano and sang to the harp. The belles of the day smiled upon him: Miss Catherine van Rensselaer, of Albany, and Miss Cora Livingston, the same who in her old age, as Mrs. Barton, sold the great Shakespearian library to the city of Boston. The most conspicuous married belle of that day was known as Mrs. Florida White, so called because her husband represented that region, then new and strange. More eccentric than this *sobriquet* were the genuine names in the household of Mrs. Peter, granddaughter of Mrs. Washington, and the fiercest of Federalists, who had named her daughters America, Columbia, and Britannia—the last by way of defiance, it was said, to Jefferson. With these various charmers Mr. Quincy attended many a ball in Washington, these entertainments then keeping modest hours —from eight to eleven. He saw a sight not then considered so modest—the introduction, in 1826, of the first waltz, danced with enthusiasm by Baron Stackelburg, who whirled through it without removing his huge dragoon spurs, and was applauded at the end for the skill with which he avoided collisions that might have been rather murderous.

The young Bostonian also went to dinner-parties; sometimes at the White House, either formal state dinners of forty gentlemen and ladies, or private occasions, less elaborate, where he alone among witnesses found the President "amusing." He gives also an agreeable picture of the home and household manners of Daniel Webster, not yet fallen into those questionable private habits which the French M. Bacourt, sixteen years afterwards, too faithfully chronicled. Mr. Quincy also found the Vice-president, John C. Calhoun, a man most agreeable in his own house, while Miss Calhoun had an admirable gift for political discussion. The presence of these eminent men lent a charm even to the muddy streets and scattered houses of the Washington of that day. The two branches of government then met in small, ill-arranged halls, the House of Representatives having huge pillars to intercept sight and sound, with no gallery for visitors, but only a platform but little higher than the floor. In this body the great Federal party had left scarcely a remnant of itself, Mr. Elisha Potter, of Rhode Island, describing vividly to Mr. Quincy a caucus held when the faithful few had been reduced to eleven, and could only cheer themselves with the thought that the Christian apostles, after the desertion of Judas, could number no more. The Houses of Congress were still rather an arena of debating than for set speeches, as now; and they had their leaders, mostly now fallen into that oblivion which waits so surely on merely political fame. Daniel Webster, to be sure, was the great ornament of the Senate; but McDuffie, of South Carolina, and Storrs, of New York, members of the House, had then a national reputation for eloquence, though they now are but the shadows of names. To these must be added Archer, of Virginia, too generally designated as "Insatiate Archer," from his fatal long-windedness.

For the first time in many years the White House was kept in decent order again; all about it had for years—if we may trust Samuel Breck's testimony—worn the slipshod, careless look of a Virginia plantation. Fence-posts fell and lay broken on the ground for months, although they could have been repaired in half an hour; and the grass of the lawns, cut at long intervals, was piled in large stacks before the drawing-room windows. Fifty thousand dollars spent on the interior in Monroe's time had produced only a slovenly splendor, while the fourteen thousand appropriated to Adams produced neatness at least. Manners shared some of the improvement, in respect to order and decorum at least, though something of the profuse Virginia cordiality may have been absent. It was an intermediate period, when, far more than now, the European forms were being tried, and sometimes found wanting. In Philadelphia, where the social ambition was highest, Mr. William Bingham had entertainments that were held to be the most showy in America. He had, as in England, a row of liveried servants, who repeated in loud tone, from one to another, the name of every guest. A slight circumstance put an end to the practice. On the evening of a ball an eminent physician, Dr. Kuhn, drove to the door with his step-daughter, and was asked his name by the lackey. "The doctor and Miss Peggy," was the reply. "The doctor and Miss Peggy," was echoed by the man at the door, and hence by successive stages to the drawing-room. "The doctor and Miss Peggy" (Miss Markoe, afterwards Mrs. Benjamin Franklin Bache) became the joke of the town; and

JOHN C. CALHOUN.

[From the painting by De Block, owned by John C. Calhoun, Esq.]

the practice was soon after changed, carrying with it the humbler attempts at imitation in Washington. Samuel Breck, who tells the story, rejoices that among the other failures in aping foreign manners were "the repeated attempts of our young dandies to introduce the mustache on the upper lip." "And so," he adds, "with the broadcloth gaiters and other foreign costumes. They were neither useful nor ornamental, and would not take with us. So much the better."

The President himself, in the midst of all this, lived a life so simple that the word Spartan hardly describes it. He was now sixty years old. Rising at four or five, even in winter, he often built his own fire, and then worked upon his correspondence and his journal, while the main part of the day was given to public affairs, these being reluctantly interrupted to receive a stream of visitors. In the evening he worked again, sometimes going to bed at eight or nine even in summer. His recreations were few—bathing in the Potomac before sunrise, and taking a walk at the same hour, or a ride later in the day, or sometimes the theatre, such as it was. For social life he had little aptitude, though he went through the forms of it. This is well illustrated by one singular memorandum in his diary: "I went out this evening in search of conversation, an art of which I never had an adequate idea.... I never knew how to make, control, or change it. I am by nature a silent animal, and my dear mother's constant lesson in childhood that little children should be seen and not heard confirmed me in what I now think a bad habit."

It is to be observed that the influence of political wire-pulling first began to be seriously felt at this period. We commonly attribute its origin to Jackson, but it really began, as was explained in a previous chapter, with Crawford. As the end of Monroe's administration drew near, there were, it must be remembered, five candidates in the field for the succession—Crawford, Clay, Calhoun, Adams, and Jackson. Calhoun withdrew, was nominated for Vice-president, and was triumphantly elected; but for President there was no choice. Jackson had 99 electoral votes, Adams 84, Crawford 41, Clay 37. The choice was thrown into the House of Representatives, and took place February 9, 1825. Two distinguished men were tellers, Daniel Webster and John Randolph. They reported that Mr. Adams had 13 votes, General Jackson 7, Mr. Crawford 4; and that Mr. Adams was therefore elected. The explanation was that Mr. Clay's forces had been transferred to Mr. Adams, and when, after his inauguration, Mr. Clay was made Secretary of State, the cry of "unholy coalition" was overwhelming. It was, John Randolph said, "a combination hitherto unheard of, of the Puritan and the Blackleg—of Blifil and Black George"—these being two characters in Fielding's "Tom Jones." This led to a duel between Clay and Randolph, in which neither party fell. But the charge remained. Jackson and Calhoun believed it during their whole lives, though the publication of John Quincy Adams's "Diary" has made it clear that there was no real foundation for it.

The influence, since called "the machine," in politics was systematically brought to bear against Mr. Adams during all the latter part of his administration. Having the reluctance of a high-minded statesman to win support by using patronage for it, he unluckily had not that better quality which enables a warm-hearted man to secure loyal aid without raising a finger. The power that he thus refused to employ was simply used against him by his own subordinates. We know by the unerring evidence of his own diary that he saw clearly how his own rectitude was injuring him, yet never thought of swerving from his course. One by one the men dependent on him went over, beneath his eyes, to the camp of his rival; and yet so long as each man was a good officer he was left untouched. Mr. Adams says in his "Diary" (under date of May 13, 1825), when describing his own entrance on office: "Of the custom-house officers throughout the Union two-thirds were probably opposed to my election. They were all now in my power, and I had been urged very earnestly from various quarters to sweep away my opponents, and provide with their places for my friends." This was what he absolutely refused to do. In these days of civil service reform we go back with pleasure to his example; but the general verdict of the period was that this course may have been very heroic, but it was not war.

It must always be remembered, moreover, in our effort to understand the excitement of politics fifty years ago, that the Presidential candidates were then nominated by Congressional caucus. The effect was to concentrate in one spot the excitement and the intrigues that must now be distributed through the nation. The result was almost wholly evil. "It places the President," John Quincy Adams wrote just before his election, "in a state of subserviency to the members of the Legislature, which ... leads to a thousand corrupt cabals between the members of Congress and heads of departments. ... The only possible chance for a head of a department to attain the Presidency is by ingratiating himself with the members of Congress." The result was that these Congressmen practically selected the President. For political purposes, Washington was the focus of all that political agitation now distributed over various cities; it was New York, Cincinnati, Chicago, all in one. It was in a centre of politics like this, not in the present more metropolitan Washington, that John Quincy Adams stood impassive — the object of malice, of jealousy, of envy, of respect, and perhaps sometimes even of love.

He was that most unfortunate personage, an accidental President — one chosen not by a majority or even a plurality of popular or electoral votes, but only by the process reluctantly employed in case these votes yield no choice. The popular feeling of the nation, by a plurality at least, had demanded the military favorite, Jackson; and through the four years of Adams's respectable but rather colorless administration it still persisted in this demand. The grave, undemonstrative President, not rewarding his friends, if indeed he had friends, had little chance against the popular favorite; his faults hindered him; his very virtues hindered him; and though he was not, like his father, defeated squarely on a clear political issue, he was defeated still. With him we leave behind the trained statesmen-Presidents of the early period, and pass to the untrained, untamed, vigorous personality of Andrew Jackson.

XVIII.

"*OLD HICKORY.*"

DR. VON HOLST, the most philosophic of historians, when he passes from the period of John Quincy Adams to that of his successor, is reluctantly compelled to leave the realm of pure history for that of biography, and to entitle a chapter " The Reign of Andrew Jackson." This change of treatment could, indeed, hardly be helped. Under Adams all was impersonal, methodical, a government of laws and not of men. With an individuality quite as strong as that of Jackson —as the whole nation learned ere his life ended—it had yet been the training of his earlier career to suppress himself and be simply a perfect official. His policy aided the vast progress of the nation, but won for him no credit by the process. Men saw with wonder the westward march of an expanding people, but forgot to notice the sedate, passionless, orderly administration that held the door open and kept the peace for all. In studying the time of Adams, we think of the nation; in observing that of Jackson, we think of Jackson himself. In him we see the first popular favorite of a people now well out of leading-strings, and particularly bent on going alone. By so much as he differed from Adams, by so much the nation liked him better. His conquests had been those of war—always more dazzling than those of peace; his temperament was of fire—always more attractive than one of marble. He was helped by what he had done, and by what he had not done. Even his absence of diplomatic training was almost counted for a virtue, because all this training was then necessarily European, and the demand had ripened for a purely American product.

It had been quite essential to the self-respect of the new republic, at the outset, that it should have at its head men who had as diplomatists coped with European statesmen and not been discomfited. This was the case with each of the early successors of Washington, and in view of Washington's manifest superiority this advantage had not been needed. Perhaps it was in a different way a sign of self-respect that the new republic should at last turn from this tradition, and take boldly from the ranks a strong and ill-trained leader, to whom all European precedent—and, indeed, all other precedent—counted for nothing. In Jackson, moreover, there first appeared upon our national stage the since familiar figure of the self-made man. Other Presidents had sprung from a modest origin, but nobody had made an especial point of it. Nobody had urged Washington for office because he had been a surveyor's lad; nobody had voted for Adams merely because stately old ladies designated him as "that cobbler's son." But when Jackson came into office the people had just had almost a surfeit of regular training in their Chief Magistrates. There was a certain zest in the thought of a change, and the nation had it.

It must be remembered that Jackson was in many ways far above the successive modern imitators who have posed in his image. He was narrow, ignorant, violent, unreasonable; he punished his enemies and rewarded his friends. But he was, on the other hand—and his worst opponents hardly denied it—honest, truthful, and sincere. It was not commonly charged upon him that he enriched himself at the public expense, or that he deliberately invented falsehoods. And as he was for a time more bitterly hated than any one who ever occupied his high office, we may be very sure that these things would have been charged on him, had it been possible. In this respect the contrast was enormous between Jackson and his imitators, and it explains his prolonged influence. He never was found out or exposed before the world, because there was nothing to detect or unveil; his merits and demerits were as visible as his long, narrow, firmly set features, or as the old military stock that encircled his neck. There he was, always fully revealed; everybody could see him; the people might take him or leave him — and they never left him.

Moreover, there was, after the eight years of Monroe and the four years of Adams, an immense popular demand for something piquant and even amusing, and this quality men always found in Jackson. There was nothing in the least melodramatic about him; he never posed or attitudinized — it would have required too much patience; but he was always piquant. There was formerly a good deal of discussion as to who wrote the once famous "Jack Downing" letters, but we might almost say that they wrote themselves. Nobody was ever less of a humorist than Andrew Jackson, and it was therefore the more essential that he should be the cause of humor in others. It was simply inevitable that during his progresses through the country there should be some amusing shadow evoked, some Yankee parody of the man, such as came from two or three quarters under the name of Jack Downing. The various records of Monroe's famous tours are as tame as the speeches which these expeditions brought forth, and John Quincy Adams never made any popular demonstrations to chronicle; but wherever Jackson went there went the other Jack, the crude first-fruits of what is now known through the world as "American humors." Jack Downing was Mark Twain and Hosea Biglow and Artemus Ward in one. The impetuous President enraged many and delighted many, but it is something to know that under him a serious people first found that it knew how to laugh.

The very extreme, the perfectly needless extreme, of political foreboding that marked the advent of Jackson furnished a background of lurid solemnity for all this light comedy. Samuel Breck records in his diary that he conversed with Daniel Webster in Philadelphia, March 24, 1827, upon the prospects of the government. "Sir," said Mr. Webster, "if General Jackson is elected, the government of our country will be overthrown; the judiciary will be destroyed; Mr. Justice Johnson will be made Chief-justice in the room of Mr. Marshall, who must soon retire, and then in half an hour Mr. Justice Washington and Mr. Justice Story will resign. A majority will be left with Mr. Johnson, and every constitutional decision hitherto made will be reversed." As a matter of fact, none of these results followed. Mr. Justice Johnson never became Chief-justice; Mr. Marshall retained that office till his death in 1835; Story and Washington also died in office; the judiciary was not overthrown or the government destroyed. But the very ecstasy of these fears stimulated the excitement of the public mind. No matter how extravagant the supporters of Jackson might be, they could hardly go farther in that direction than did the Websters in the other.

But it was not the fault of the Jackson party if anybody went beyond them in exaggeration. An English traveller, William E. Alexander, going in a stage-coach from Baltimore to Washington in 1831, records the exuberant conversation of six editors, with whom he was shut up for hours. "The gentlemen of the press," he says, "talked of 'going the whole hog' for one another, of being 'up to the hub' (nave) for General Jackson, who was 'all brimstone but the head, and that was aqua-fortis,' and swore if any one abused him he ought to be 'set straddle on an iceberg, and shot through with a streak of lightning.'" Somewhere between the dignified despair of Daniel Webster and the adulatory slang of these gentry we must look for the actual truth about Jackson's administration. The fears of the statesman were not wholly groundless, for it is always hard to count

ANDREW JACKSON.
[Engraved by G. Kruell from the lithograph by La Fosse, copyrighted by M. Knoedler & Co.]

in advance upon the tendency of high office to make men more reasonable. The enthusiasm of the journalists had a certain foundation; at any rate it was a part of their profession to like stirring times, and they had now the promise of them. After twelve years of tolerably monotonous government, any party of editors in America, assembled in a stage-coach, would have showered epithets of endearment on the man who gave such promise in the way of lively items. No acute journalist could help seeing that a man had a career before him who was called " Old Hickory " by three-quarters of the nation; and who made " Hurrah for Jackson !" a cry so potent that it had the force of a popular decree.

There was, indeed, unbounded room for popular enthusiasm in the review of Jackson's early career. Born in such obscurity that it is doubtful to this day whether that event took place in South Carolina, as he himself claimed, or on the North Carolina side of the line, as Mr. Parton thinks, he had a childhood of poverty and ignorance. He was taken prisoner as a mere boy during the Revolution, and could never forget that he had been wounded by a British officer whose boots he had refused to brush. Afterwards, in a frontier community, he was successively farmer, shopkeeper, law student, lawyer, district attorney, judge, and Congressman, being first Representative from Tennessee, and then Senator — and all before the age of thirty-one. In Congress Albert Gallatin describes him as "a tall, lank, uncouth-looking personage, with long locks of hair hanging over his brows and face, and a queue down his back tied in an eel-skin; his dress singular, his manners and deportment those of a backwoodsman." He remained, however, but a year or two in all at Philadelphia—then the seat of national government—and afterwards became a planter in Tennessee, fought duels, subdued Tecumseh and the Creek Indians, winning finally the great opportunity of his life by being made a major-general in the United States army on May 31, 1814. He now had his old captors, the British, with whom to deal, and he entered into the work with a relish. By way of preliminary he took Pensacola, without any definite authority, from the Spaniards, to whom it belonged, and from the English whom they harbored; and then turned, without orders, without support, and without supplies, to undertake the defence of New Orleans.

Important as was this city, and plain as it was that the British threatened it, the national authorities had done nothing to defend it. The impression prevailed at Washington that it must already have been taken, but that the President would not let it be known. The Washington *Republican* of January 17, 1815, said, " That Mr. Madison will find it convenient and will finally determine to abandon the State of Louisiana we have not a doubt." A New York newspaper of January 30th, three weeks after New Orleans had been saved, said, " It is the general opinion here that the city of New Orleans must fall." Apparently but one thing had averted its fall—the energy and will of Andrew Jackson. On his own responsibility he declared martial law, impressed soldiers, seized powder and supplies, built fortifications of cotton bales, if nothing else came to hand. When the news of the battle of New Orleans came to the seat of government it was almost too bewildering for belief. The British veterans of the Peninsula war, whose march wherever they had landed had heretofore seemed a holiday parade, were repulsed in a manner so astounding that their loss, in killed and wounded, was more than two thousand, while that of the Americans was but thirteen (January 8, 1815). By a single stroke the national self-respect was restored; and Henry Clay, at Paris, said, " Now I can go to England without mortification."

All these things must be taken into account in estimating what Dr. Von Holst calls " the reign of Andrew Jackson." After this climax of military success he was for a time employed on frontier service, again went to Florida to fight Englishmen and Spaniards, practically conquering that region in a few months, but this time with an overwhelming force. Already his impetuosity had proved to have a troublesome side to it; he had violated neutral territory, had hung two Indians without justification, and had put to death, with no authority, two Englishmen, Ambrister and Arbuthnot. These irregularities did not harm him in the judgment of his admirers; they seemed in the line of his character, and helped more than they hurt him. In the winter of 1823-24 he was again chosen a Senator from Tennessee. Thenceforth he was in the field as a candidate for the Presidency, with two things to aid him—his own immense popularity and a skilful friend. This friend was one William B. Lewis, a man in whom all the arts of the modern wire-puller seemed to be born full-grown.

There was at that time (1824) no real division in parties. The Federalists had been effectually put down, and every man who aspired to office claimed to be Democratic-Republican. Nominations were irregularly made, sometimes by a Congressional caucus, sometimes by State Legislatures. Tennessee, and afterwards Pennsylvania, nominated Jackson. When it came to the election, he proved to be by all odds the popular candidate. Professor W. G. Sumner, counting up the vote of the people, finds 155,800 votes for Jackson, 105,300 for Adams, 44,200 for Crawford, 46,000 for Clay. Even with this strong popular vote before it, the House of Representatives, balloting by States, elected, as has been seen, John Quincy Adams. Seldom in our history has the cup of power come so near to the lips of a candidate and been dashed away again. Yet nothing is surer in a republic than a certain swing of the pendulum, afterwards, in favor of any candidate to whom a special injustice has been done; and in the case of a popular favorite like Jackson this recoil might have been foreseen to be irresistible. His election four years later was almost a foregone conclusion, but, as if to make it wholly sure, there came up the rumor of a "corrupt bargain" between the successful candidate and Mr. Clay, whose forces had indeed joined with those of Mr. Adams to make a majority. For General Jackson there could be nothing more fortunate. The mere ghost of a corrupt bargain is worth many thousand votes to the lucky man whose supporters conjure up the ghost.

When it came the turn of the Adams party to be defeated, in 1828, they attributed this result partly to the depravity of the human heart, partly to the tricks of Jackson, and partly to the unfortunate temperament of Mr. Adams. The day after a candidate is beaten everybody knows why it was, and says it was just what any one might have foreseen. Ezekiel Webster, writing from New Hampshire, laid the result chiefly on the nominee, whom everybody disliked, and who would persist in leaving his bitter opponents in office. The people, Webster said, "always supported his cause from a cold sense of duty, and not from any liking of the man. We soon satisfy ourselves," he added, "that we have discharged our duty to the cause of any man when we do not entertain for him one personal kind feeling, nor cannot, unless we disembowel ourselves, like a trussed turkey, of all that is human within us." There is, indeed, no doubt that Mr. Adams helped on his own defeat, both by his defects and by what would now be considered his virtues. The trouble, however, lay further back. Ezekiel Webster thought that "if there had been at the head of affairs a man of popular character, like Mr. Clay, or any man whom we were not compelled by our natures, instinct, and fixed fate to dislike, the result would have been different." But we can now see that all this would really have made no difference at all. Had Mr. Adams been personally the most attractive of men, instead of being a conscientious iceberg, the same result would have followed, and the people would have felt that Jackson's turn had come.

Accordingly, the next election, that of 1828, was easily settled. Jackson had 178 electoral votes, Adams but 83;—more than two to one. Adams had not an electoral vote south of the Potomac or west of the Alleghanies, though Daniel Webster, writing to Jeremiah Mason, had predicted that he would carry six Western and Southern States. In Georgia no Adams ticket was even nominated, he being there unpopular for one of his best acts—the protection of the Cherokees. On the other hand, but one Jackson elector was chosen from New England, and he by less than two hundred majority. This was in the Maine district that included Bowdoin College, and I have heard from an old friend of mine the tale how he, being then a student at Bowdoin, tolled the college bell at midnight to express the shame of the students, although the elector thus chosen (Judge Preble) was the own uncle of this volunteer sexton. It would have required many college bells to announce the general wrath of New England, which was not diminished by the fact that Mr. Calhoun, another Southerner, was chosen Vice-president over Richard Rush. To be sure, Mr. Calhoun had filled the same office under John Quincy Adams, but then there was a Northern man for President. For the first time the lines seemed distinctly drawn for the coming sectional antagonism.

But even this important fact was really quite subordinate, for the time being, in men's minds. The opposition to Jackson, like his popularity, was personal. It was not a mere party matter. The older statesmen distrusted him, without much regard to their political opinions. When Monroe asked Jefferson in 1818 if it would not be well to give Jackson the embassy to Russia, Jefferson utterly disapproved it. "He would breed you a quarrel," he said, "before he had been there a month." At a later period Jefferson said to Daniel Webster: "I feel much alarmed at the prospect of seeing General Jackson President. He is one of the most unfit men I know of for such a place. He has had very little respect for laws or constitutions, and is, in fact, an able military chief. His passions are terrible. When I was President of the Senate he was a Senator, and he could never speak on account of the rashness of his feelings. I have seen him attempt it repeatedly, and as often choke with rage.

His passions are no doubt cooler now; he has been much tried since I knew him; but he is a dangerous man." And dangerous indeed the public office-holders soon found him. As has been already seen, a large part of those who held office under Adams were already partisans of Jackson; but the rest soon discovered that a changed policy had come in. Between March 4, 1829, and March 22, 1830, 491 postmasters and 230 other officers were removed, making, as it was thought, with their subordinates, at least two thousand political changes. Mr. Sumner well points out that it is unfair to charge this, as we often do, solely upon Jackson. Crawford, as has already been seen, prepared the way for the practice; it had been perfected in the local politics of New York and Pennsylvania. It was simply a disease which the nation must undergo—must ultimately overthrow, indeed, unless overthrown by it; but it will always be identified, by coincidence of time at least, with the Presidency of Andrew Jackson. If not the father of the evil, he will always stand in history as its godfather.

It is a curious fact in political history that a public man is almost always, to a certain extent, truthfully criticised by the party opposed to him. His opponents may exaggerate, they may distort, but they are rarely altogether wrong; their criticism generally goes to the right point, and finds out the weak spot. Jackson was as vehemently attacked as Jefferson, and by the same class of people, but the points of the criticism were wholly different. Those who had habitually denounced Jefferson for being timid in action were equally hard on Jackson for brimming over with superfluous courage, and being ready to slap every one in the face. The discrimination of charges was just. A merely vague and blundering assailant would have been just as likely to call Jackson a coward and Jefferson a fire-eater, which would have been absurd. The summing up of the Federalist William Sullivan, written in 1834, was not so very far from the sober judgment of posterity. "Andrew Jackson. . . . is a sort of *lusus reipublicæ*, held by no rules or laws, and who honestly believes his sycophants that he was born to command. With a head and heart not better than Thomas Jefferson had, but freed from the inconvenience of that gentleman's constitutional timidity, and familiar with the sword, he has disclosed the real purpose of the American people in fighting the battles of the Revolution and establishing a national republic, viz., that the will of Andrew Jackson shall be the law and only law of the republic."

Really General Jackson himself would not have greatly objected to this estimate, could he have had patience to read it. He was singularly free from hypocrisy or concealment, was not much of a talker, and took very little trouble to invent fine names for what he did. But on another point where he was as sharply criticised he was very vulnerable; like most ignorant and self-willed men, he was easily managed by those who understood him. Here again was an illustration of the discernment of even vehement enemies. Nobody charged Jefferson with being over-influenced by a set of inferior men, though all the opposition charged Jackson with it. The reason was that in this last case it was true; and during the greater part of Jackson's two administrations there was constant talk of what Webster called the "cabinet improper," as distinct from the cabinet proper — what was known in popular phrase as the "kitchen cabinet." Here again came in the felicity of Jack Downing's portraiture. The familiarity with which this imaginary ally pulled off the President's boots or wore his old clothes hardly surpassed the undignified attitudes popularly attributed to Swartwout and Hill and Van Buren.

On the day of his inauguration the President was received in Washington with an ardor that might have turned a more modest head. On the day when the new administration began (March 4, 1829), Daniel Webster wrote to his sister-in-law, with whom he had left his children that winter: "To-day we have had the inauguration. A monstrous crowd of people is in the city. I never saw anything like it before. Persons have come five hundred miles to see General Jackson, and they really seem to think that the country is rescued from some frightful danger." It is difficult now to see what this peril was supposed to be; but we know that the charges of monarchical tendency made against John Adams had been renewed against his son— a renewal that seems needless in case of a man so scrupulously republican that he would not use a seal ring; and so unambitious that he always sighed after the quieter walks of literature. Equally unjust was the charge of extravagance against the younger Adams, who kept the White House in better order than his predecessor on less than half the appropriation—an economy wholly counterbalanced in some minds by the fact that he had put in a billiard-table. But however all this may have been, the fact is certain that no President had yet entered the White House amid such choruses of delight as were called forth by Jackson; nor did it happen again until his pupil, Van Buren, yielded, amid equal popular enthusiasm, to another military hero, Harrison.

For the social life of Washington the President had one advantage which was altogether unexpected, and seemed difficult of explanation by anything in his earlier career. He had at his command the most courteous and agreeable manners. Even before the election of Adams, Daniel Webster had written to his brother: "General Jackson's manners are better than those of any of the candidates. He is grave, mild, and reserved. My wife is for him decidedly." And long after, when the President was to pass in review before those who were perhaps his most implacable opponents, the ladies of Boston, we have the testimony of the late Josiah Quincy, in his "Figures from the Past," that the personal bearing of this obnoxious official was most unwillingly approved. Mr. Quincy was detailed by Governor Lincoln, on whose military staff he was, to attend President Jackson

DANIEL WEBSTER.

From the painting by G. P. A. Healy, now in Faneuil Hall, Boston.

everywhere when visiting Boston in 1833; and this narrator testifies that, with every prejudice against Jackson, he found him essentially "a knightly personage—prejudiced, narrow, mistaken on many points, it might be, but vigorously a gentleman in his high sense of honor and in the natural straightforward courtesies which are easily distinguished from the veneer of policy." Sitting erect on his horse, a thin stiff type of military strength, he carried with him in the streets a bearing of such dignity that staid old Bostonians who had refused even to look upon him from their windows would finally be coaxed into taking one peep, and would then hurriedly bring forward their little daughters to wave their handkerchiefs. He wrought, Mr. Quincy declares, "a mysterious charm upon old and young;" showed, although in feeble health, a great consideration for others; and was in private a really agreeable companion. It appears from these reminiscences that the President was not merely the cause of wit in others, but now and then appreciated it himself, and that he used to listen with delight to the reading of the "Jack Downing" letters, laughing heartily sometimes, and declaring, "The Vice-president must have written that. Depend upon it, Jack Downing is only Van Buren in masquerade." It is a curious fact that the satirist is already the better remembered of the two, although Van Buren was in his day so powerful as to preside over the official patronage of the nation, and to be called the "Little Magician."

But whatever personal attractions of manner President Jackson may have had, he threw away his social leadership at Washington by a single act of what may have been misapplied chivalry. This act was what Mr. Morse has tersely called "the importation of Mrs. Eaton's visiting list into the politics and government of the country." It was the nearest approach yet made under our masculine political institutions to those eminent scandals which constitute the minor material of court historians in Europe. The heroine of the comedy, considered merely as

Peggy O'Neil, daughter of a Washington innkeeper—or as Mrs. Timberlake, the wife of a naval purser who had committed suicide because of strong drink—might have seemed more like a personage out of one of Fielding's novels than as a feature in the history of an administration; but when fate at last made her Mrs. Secretary Eaton she became one who could disturb cabinets and annihilate friendships. It was not merely out of regard for her personal wrongs that all this took place, but there was a long history behind it. There had been a little irregularity about President Jackson's own marriage. He had espoused his wife after a supposed divorce from a previous husband; and when the divorce really took place the ceremony had to be repeated. Moreover, as the divorce itself had originally been based on some scandal about Jackson, he was left in a state of violent sensitiveness on the whole matrimonial question. Mrs. Eaton had nothing in the world to do with all this, but she got the benefit of it. The mere fact that she to whom the President had good-naturedly nodded as Peggy O'Neil had been censured by his own officials, after she had become the wife of one of them, was enough to enrage him, and he doubtless looked across the fireplace at the excellent Mrs. Jackson—a plain, estimable backwoodswoman, who sat smoking her corn-cob pipe in the opposite corner—and swore to himself, and very probably aloud, that Peggy O'Neil should be sustained.

For once he overestimated his powers. He had conquered Indian tribes and checked the army of Great Britain, but the ladies of Washington society were too much for him. Every member of his cabinet expressed the utmost approval of his position, but they said with one accord that those matters must be left to their wives. Mrs. Donelson, his own niece—that is, the wife of his nephew, and the lady who received company for him at the White House—would not receive Mrs. Eaton, and was sent back to Tennessee. Mrs. Calhoun, the wife of the Vice-president, took the same attitude, and ruined thereby her husband's political prospects, Mr. Calhoun being utterly superseded in the President's good graces by Mr. Van Buren, who, being a widower, could pay attention to the offending fair one without let or hinderance. Through his influence Baron Krudener, the Russian Minister, and Mr. Vaughan, the British Minister, both bachelors, gave entertainments at which "Bellona," as the newspapers afterwards called the lady, from her influence in creating strife, was present. It did no good; every dance in which she stood up to take part was, in the words of a Washington letter-writer, "instantly dissolved into its original elements," and though she was placed at the head of the supper-table, every lady present ignored her very existence. Thus the amenities of Van Buren were as powerless as the anger of Jackson; but the astute Secretary won the President's heart, and with it that of his whole immediate circle—cabinet proper and cabinet improper. It was one of the things that turned the scale between Calhoun and Van Buren, putting the New York "magician" in line for the Presidential succession; and in this way Peggy O'Neil had an appreciable influence on the political history of the nation. It was fortunate that she did not also lead to foreign embroilments, for the wife of the Dutch Minister once refused to sit next to her at a public entertainment, upon which the President threatened to demand the Minister's recall. All this time Jackson himself remained utterly free from scandal, nor did his enemies commonly charge him with anything beyond ill-timed quixotism. But it shows how feminine influence creeps inside of all political barriers, and recalls Charles Churchill's couplet—

> "Women, who've oft as sovereigns graced the land,
> But never governed well at second-hand."

The two acts with which the administration of President Jackson will be longest identified are his dealings with South Carolina in respect to nullification, and his long warfare with the United States Bank. The first brought the New England States back to him, and the second took them away again. He perhaps won rather more applause than he merited by the one act, and more condemnation than was just for the other. Let us first consider the matter of nullification. When various Southern States—Georgia at first, not South Carolina, taking the lead—had quarrelled with the tariff of 1828, and openly threatened to set it aside, they evidently hoped for the co-operation of the President; or at least for that silent acquiescence he had shown when Georgia had been almost equally turbulent on the Indian question, and he would not interfere, as his predecessor had done, to protect the treaty rights of the Indian tribes. The whole South was therefore startled when he gave, at a banquet on Jefferson's birthday (April 13, 1830), a toast that now seems commonplace—"The Federal Union; it must be preserved." But this was not all; when the time came he took vigorous, if not altogether consistent, steps to preserve it.

When, in November, 1832, South Carolina for the first time officially voted that certain tariff acts were null and void in that State, the gauntlet of defiance was fairly thrown down, and Jackson picked it up. He sent General Scott to take command at Charleston, with troops near by, and two gun-boats at hand; he issued a dignified proclamation, written by Livingston (December 10, 1832), which pronounced the act of South Carolina contradictory to the Constitution, unauthorized by it, and destructive of its aims. So far, so good; but unfortunately the President had, the week before (December 4, 1832), sent a tariff message to Congress, of which John Quincy Adams wrote, "It goes far to dissolve the Union into its original elements, and is in substance a complete surrender into the hands of the nullifiers of South Carolina." Then came Mr. Clay's compromise tariff of 1833, following in part the line indicated by this message, and achieving, as Mr. Calhoun said, a victory for nullification—leaving the matter a drawn game, at any rate. The action of Jackson, being thus accompanied, settled nothing; it was like valiantly ordering a burglar out of your house with a pistol, and adding the suggestion that he will find a portion of the family silver on the hall table, ready packed for his use, as he goes out.

Nevertheless, the burglar was gone for the moment, and the President had the credit of it. He had already been re-elected by an overwhelming majority in November, 1832, receiving 219 electoral votes, and Clay 49; while Floyd had the 11 votes of South Carolina (which still chose electors by its Legislature—a practice now abandoned), and Wirt the 7 of Vermont. Van Buren was chosen Vice-president, being nominated in place of Calhoun by the Democratic National Convention, which now for the first time came into operation. The President was thus at his high-water mark of popularity—always a dangerous time for a public man. His vehement nature accepted his re-election as a proof that he was right in everything, and he grew more self-confident than ever. More imperiously than ever, he ordered about friends and opponents; and his friends repaid it by guiding his affairs, unconsciously to himself. Meantime he was encountering another enemy of greater power, because more silent, than Southern nullification, and he was drifting on to his final contest with the United States Bank.

Sydney Smith says that every Englishman feels himself able, without instruction, to drive a pony-chaise, conduct a small farm, and edit a newspaper. The average American assumes, in addition to all this, that he is competent to manage a bank. President Jackson claimed for himself in this respect no more than his fellows; the difference was in strength of will and in possession of power. A man so ignorant that a member of his own family, according to Mr. Trist, used to say that the general did not believe the world was round, might easily convince himself that he knew all about banking. As he had, besides all this, very keen observation and great intuitive judgment of character, he was probably right in his point of attack. There is little doubt that the bank of the United States, under Nicholas Biddle, concentrated in itself an enormous power; and it spent in four years, by confession of its directors, $58,000 in what they called "self-defence" against "politicians." When, on July 10, 1832, General Jackson, in a message supposed to have been inspired by Amos Kendall, vetoed the bill renewing the charter of the bank, he performed an act of courage, taking counsel with his instincts. But when in the year following he performed the act known as the "removal of the deposits," or, in other words, caused the public money to be no longer deposited in the National Bank and its twenty-five branches, but in a variety of State banks instead, then he took counsel of his ignorance.

The act originally creating the bank had, indeed, given the Secretary of the Treasury authority to remove these deposits at any time, he afterwards giving to Congress his reasons. The President had in vain urged Congress to order the change; that body declined. He had in vain urged the Secretary of the Treasury to remove them, and on his refusing, had displaced the official himself. The President at last found a Secretary of the Treasury (Roger B. Taney) to order the removal, or rather cessation, of deposits. The consequence, immediate or remote, was an immense galvanizing into existence of State banks, and ultimately a vast increase of paper-money. The Sub-Treasury system had not then been thought of; there was no proper place of deposit for the public funds; their possession was a direct stimulus to speculation; and the President's cure was worse than the disease. All the vast inflation of 1835 and 1836 and the business collapse of 1837 were due to the fact not merely that Andrew Jackson brought all his violent and persistent will to bear against the United States Bank, but that when he got the power into his own hands he did not know what to do with it. Not one of his biographers — hardly even a bigoted admirer, so far as I know — now claims that his course in this respect was anything but a mistake. "No monster bank," says Professor W. G. Sumner, "under the most malicious management, could have produced as much havoc, either political or financial, as this system produced while it lasted." If the bank was, as is now generally admitted, a dangerous institution, Jackson was in the right to resist it; he was right even in disregarding the enormous flood of petitions that poured in to its support. But to oppose a dangerous bank does not necessarily make one an expert in banking. The utmost that can be said in favor of his action is that the calamitous results showed the great power of the institution he overthrew, and that if he had let it alone the final result might have been as bad.

Two new States were added to the Union in President Jackson's time—Arkansas (1836) and Michigan (1837). The population of the United States in 1830 had risen to nearly thirteen millions (12,866,020). There was no foreign war during his administration, although one with France was barely averted, and no domestic contest except the second Seminole war against the Florida Indians—a contest in which these combatants held their ground so well, under the half-breed chief Osceola, that he himself was only captured by the violation of a flag of truce, and that even to this day, as the Indian Commissioners tell us, some three hundred of the tribe remain in Florida. The war being equally carried on against fugitive slaves called Maroons, who had intermarried with the Indians, did something to prepare the public mind for a new agitation which was to remould American political parties, and to modify the Constitution of the nation.

It must be remembered that the very air began to be filled in Jackson's time with rumors of insurrections and uprisings in different parts of the world. The French revolution of the Three Days had roused all the American people to sympathy, and called forth especial enthusiasm in such cities as Baltimore, Richmond, and Charleston. The Polish revolution had excited universal interest, and John Randolph had said, "The Greeks are at your doors." All these things were being discussed at every dinner-table, and the debates in Virginia as to the necessity of restricting the growing intelligence of the slaves had added to the agitation. In the session of 1829–30 a bill had passed the Virginia Assembly by one majority, and had failed in the Senate, prohibiting slaves from being taught to read or write; and the next year it had passed almost unanimously. There had been, about the same time, alarms of insurrection in North Carolina, so that a party of slaves were attacked and killed by the inhabitants of Newbern; alarms in Maryland, so that fifty blacks had been imprisoned on the Eastern Shore; alarms in Louisiana, so that reinforcements of troops had been ordered to Baton Rouge; and a traveller had written even from Richmond, Virginia, on the 12th of February, that there were constant fears of insurrections and special patrols. Then came the insurrection of Nat Turner in Virginia—an uprising described minutely by myself elsewhere; the remarkable inflammatory pamphlet called "Walker's Appeal," by a Northern colored man—a piece of writing surpassed in lurid power by nothing in the literature of the French Revolution; and, more potent than either or both of these, the appearance (January 1, 1831) of the first number of the *Liberator* in Boston. When Garrison wrote, "I am in earnest, I will not equivocate, I will not excuse, I will not retreat a single inch, and I will be heard," Andrew Jackson for once met a will firmer than his own, because more steadfast, and moved by a loftier purpose. Thenceforth, for nearly half a century, the history of the nation was the history of the antislavery contest.

The administration of Jackson will thus be most remarkable, after all, not because of any triumph of his will, but because of something that arose in spite of it—an agitation so far opposed to his wishes, in fact, that he wished for the passage of a law excluding antislavery publications from the mails. It was an agitation destined to draw new lines, establish new standards, and create new reputations; and it is to be remembered that the Democratic President did not abhor it more, on the one side, than did his fiercest Federalist critics on the other. One of the ablest of them, William Sullivan, at the close of his "Familiar Letters on Public Characters," after exhausting language to depict the outrages committed by President Jackson, points out as equally objectionable the rising antislavery movement, and predicts that, if it has its full course, "even an Andrew Jackson may be a blessing." But of the wholly new series of events which were to date from this agitation neither Sullivan nor Jackson had so much as a glimpse. These pages may well close, for the present, with the dawn of that great revolution.

INDEX.

A.

Abbott, Dr. C. C., 26.
Abenaki Indians, 186; their treaty, 187.
Abercrombie, General James, 191.
Acadia, 186, 189.
Act of Navigation, the, 217.
Adams, Abigail, quoted, 252, 254; also, 271, 312, 322, 339, 340, 344.
Adams, Charles Francis, on the Monroe doctrine, 403.
Adams, John: his view of town-meetings, 240; his election as President, 332; his character, 336; his portrait, 337; his wife, 339; his cabinet, 340; his policy towards France, 340; his rupture with his party, 343; his correspondence with Mercy Warren, 351; his old age, 359; also, 240, 253, 254.
Adams, John Quincy, quoted, 393, 402; vote for Missouri Compromise, 393; presidency of, 405; portrait of, 409; internal improvements recommended by, 417; the same accomplished, 418; entertainments of, 424; circumstances of his election, 427, 439; his policy, 428; his defeat, 430, 440; his want of popularity, 440; also, 431, 433, 442.
Adams, Mrs. John Quincy, 396.
"Adams and Liberty," song of, 342.
Adams, Samuel, 254, 293, 304, 335.
Adolphus, Gustavus, 167.
"Adventurer," the word, 146.
Alabama admitted as a State, 393.
Alexander VI., Pope, bulls of, 75, 108.
Alexander, William E., 415, 434.
Algerine pirates, 297.
Algonquins, the, 132.
Aliaco, P. de, 55.
Alien and Sedition Laws, 343, 350.
Allen, Ethan, 251.

Alligators, early descriptions of, 87.
Ambrister, R. C., 390, 439.
American flora, 217; finance, 320; literature, 398; physique, 325; seamen impressed, 366.
Americans, the first, 1.
Ames, Fisher, 300, 319, 398.
Amidas, Philip, 97.
Anderson, Professor B. B., 33.
André, Major John, 291.
Andros, Governor Edmund, and the Boston people (figured), 221; also, 184, 215, 220, 222, 223.
Andros, Lady, 220.
Anghiera, P. M. d' (Peter Martyr), 56, 59, 69, 70, 71, 82, 83, 120.
Anne, Queen, 185.
"Antiquitates Americanæ," 28, 42.
Arbuthnot, A., 390, 439.
Archer, W. S., 424.
Architecture in colonies, 233.
Aristophanes, 194.
Aristotle's narrow sea, 55.
Armistead, Colonel George, 377.
Army, Revolutionary, organization of, 257; condition of, 258; Washington's views of, 259; drilled by Steuben, 286; disbanded, 293; statistics of, 285, 292.
Arnold, Benedict, 43, 251, 263, 291.
Arnold, Matthew, 194.
Asher, Dr., 83.
Asiatics in America, 23, 24.
Astor, John Jacob, 350.
Avalon, colony of, 165.
Aztecs, 2, 4, 17, 19, 24, 63.

B.

Baccalaos, the, 82, 120.
Bache, Mrs. B. F., 424.
Bacon, Lord, 84.

INDEX.

Bacon, Nathaniel, Jr., 180.
Bacourt, M., 423.
Bagot, Sir Charles, 396.
Bahia, alleged column at, 42.
Balboa. (See Nuñez, Vasco.)
Baltimore, Cecil, Lord, portrait of, 166; also, 170, 198.
Baltimore, George, Lord, 165.
Baltimore founded, 165; "horrors of," 372.
Bancroft, George, 28, 46, 109, 225, 272.
Bancroft, H. H., 4.
Bandelier, A. F., 5, 8, 13.
Bank, U. S., 350, 452, 453.
Barclay, Robert, 204.
Barker, Jacob, 376.
Barlow, Arthur, 97, 398.
Barton, Mrs. (See Livingston, Cora.)
Basque fishermen, 120.
Beamish, C. C., 42.
Beaujour, Chevalier de, 325.
Becher, Captain, 62.
Behring Strait, width of, 24.
Belknap, Dr. Jeremy, quoted, 190.
Berkeley, Governor William, 179, 201.
Bernaldez, Andres, 123.
Bimini, island of, 71.
Bingham, Mrs., portrait, 323.
Bingham, William, 424.
Birkbeck, Captain Morris, 414.
"Black Sally," 347.
Blaxton, William, 202.
Block, Adrian, 152.
Bombazen, an Indian chief, 174.
Bonaparte, Napoleon, Federalist sermon against, 370; his decrees, 355, 365; also, 379.
Boone, Daniel, 421.
Boston, settlement of, 162; evacuation of, 260.
Bourbourg, Brasseur de, 18, 19.
Bowdoin, Governor James, 313.
Bowling-alley built by a clergyman, 195.
Braddock, General Edward, 189.
Bradford, Governor William, 152, 155, 158, 195.
Bradley, Thomas, 82.
Bradstreet, Governor Simon, 191, 222.
Brazil, 75, 76.
Brebeuf, Père, 125.
Breck, Samuel, quoted, 424, 427, 434.
Breedon, Captain Thomas, 218.
Brehan, Madame de, 312.
Breton fishermen, the, 84, 120.
Brewster, Elder William, 158, 195.
Brissot de Warville, J. P., 312.
Bristol, R. I., rock at, 44; figured, 46.
British, plans of, in Revolutionary War, 286.

British Yoke, the, 216.
Bromfield, Henry, 349.
Brooks, Rev. C. T., 43.
Brooks, C. W., 24.
Browne, Sir Thomas, 227.
Bryant, W. C., 190, 400.
Buccaneers, 90, 98, 104.
Bumstead, Jeremiah, 174.
Bunker Hill, Battle of, 256, 257.
Burgoyne, General John, 253, 286, 287.
Burke, Edmund, 288, 305, 335.
Burlington, Vt., vase found at (figured), 22, 25.
Burr, Aaron, 343, 344, 355; portrait of, 357.
Burras, Anne, 149.
Buttrick, Major, 246.

C.

Cabeza de Vaca. (See Nuñez, Alvar.)
Cabinet of Washington, 312.
Cabot, George, 372.
Cabot, J. E., 41, 49.
Cabot, John, 77, 80, 81, 82.
Cabot, Sebastian, 64, 77, 78, 79, 80, 81, 82, 83.
Cabot, Zuan (John), 81.
Cabots, the, 78, 104, 120.
Cacafuego, the, captured by Drake, 94.
Calhoun, John C., portrait of, 425; his opinions, 398, 402; Vice-president, 423, 441, 449; quoted, 450.
Calhoun, Miss, 423.
Calhoun, Mrs., 448.
California visited by Drake, 96.
Calvert, Cecil (Lord Baltimore), portrait of, 166.
Calvert, George (Lord Baltimore), 165.
Calvert, Governor Leonard, 165.
Cambridge, Mass., settled, 162; "Tory Row" in, 238.
Canada, derivation of word, 111; attacks on, 186; invasions of, 263, 372; surrender of, by France, 191, 241; influence of this surrender, 227.
Canals, introduction of, 420.
Candidates, nomination of, 429.
Canning, George, 335, 403.
Carleton, Sir Guy, 291.
Carlyle, Thomas, quoted, 152.
Carolina, settlement of, 212; division of, 213.
Carr, Lucien, 176.
Carroll, Mr., 376.
Carter, James, 82.
Carthagena captured by Drake, 100.
Cartier, J., portrait of, 111; setting up a cross (figured), 113; also, 108, 110, 112, 121, 130.
Cartwright, Colonel Thomas, 218.

INDEX.   459

Carver, Jonathan, 158.
Castin, St., 183.
Cathay, 111.
Catholic and Huguenot clergy (figured), 121.
Cavendish, Thomas, 102; his portrait, 102; his capture of the *Santa Anna* (figured), 103.
Chaac-Mol, statue of (figured), 20, 21.
Champigny, M., 184.
Champlain, Samuel de, 16; portrait of, 127; his journals, 128; his residence (figured), 130; his musketry (figured), 132; his campaign with the Iroquois, 134; also, 141, 143, 151, 172, 181, 183, 210.
Champlin, Miss, 290.
Charlemagne, Emperor, 29.
Charles I., 147.
Charles II., 178, 212, 213, 217.
Charlesfort, near Beaufort, S. C., 116.
Charleston, S. C., 263.
Charlestown, Mass., settled, 162.
Charlevoix, P. F. X., 182.
Charlotte, Queen, 339.
Charter of Virginia, 141; of Maryland, 165; of Connecticut, 219; of Massachusetts, 221; colonial charters annulled, 222.
Chastellux, Marquis de, 324, 325.
Chatham, Earl of, 229, 288.
Chesapeake, the, 356.
Chesterton, England, mill at, 43.
Chicago, Ill., 388, 413, 415.
Chichen-Itza, 21.
Choiseul, Duc de, 241.
Cholula, pyramid of, 13.
Chopunish Indians, 11.
Christiana, Del., foundation of, 167.
Christina, Queen, 167.
Christopher, St., 59.
Church, Captain Benjamin, 173, 178.
Cicero, 195.
Cincinnati, O., 388.
Circleville, O., 15.
Circumnavigation of globe by Drake, 96; by Cavendish, 101.
Civil offices, tenure of service in, 402; appointments to, 442; also, 321, 322, 350, 429.
Clark, General William, 350.
Clavigero, Francisco, 11.
Clay, Henry, portrait of, 391; candidate for Presidency, 427, 428, 451; quotation from, 438; compromise tariff of, 450; also, 362, 365, 390, 393, 398, 439, 440.
Clinton, De Witt, 374, 420.
Clinton, George, 355, 358.

Clinton, Sir Henry, 253.
Cobbett, William, 366.
Colden, Governor Cadwallader, 181.
Coleridge, S. T., 73.
Collingwood, Lord, 366.
Colonies, French Protestant, 115, 116, 118, 120; Lane's, Grenville's, White's, 138; Gosnold's, 140; Popham's, 141, 154; Virginia, 141, 146; Dutch, 151; Plymouth, 153; Massachusetts, 161; Connecticut, 164; in 1630, 165, 168; in 1650, 165; Calvert's, 165; Swedish, 167; Penn's, 213; in 1700, 213; union of, 222.
Columbus, Christopher, his voyage as compared with that of the Northmen, 51; his training, 52; portrait of, 53; his reasonings, 54; his voyage, 55; his delusions, 56; his vision (figured, from De Bry), 57; his landing (figured, after Turner), 61; landfall, 62; his treatment of natives, 63; his influence on the Cabots, 78; also, 64, 65, 66, 70, 74, 76, 82, 85, 109, 123.
Columbus, Ferdinand, 55.
Commerce, Jefferson's opposition to, 358, 373; ruin of American, 355, 373.
Commissioners, Royal, in Boston, 217.
Comogre, 69.
Conant, Roger, 161.
Confederacy, New England, 222.
Confederation, experiments at, 222; formation and failure, 295.
Congress, Continental, a single house, 296; manners in, 365; records of, 265; early resolutions, 267; discussions in, 268, 272, 273.
Connecticut: colonies, 164; education in, 201; witchcraft in, 207; charter of, 219; Continental troops in, 292.
Constellation, the frigate, 342.
Constitution, discussion and formation of, 304.
Constitution and *Guerrière*, battle of, 374.
Continental Congress. (See Congress.)
Cooper, J. Fenimore, 400, 421.
Copper-mines, early Indian, 130.
Cornwallis, Earl of, 285, 291.
Coronado, Francisco de, 10.
Cortez, Hernando de, 9, 10, 11, 17, 72, 73.
Costume, changes of, 348.
Coverley, Sir Roger de, an American, 348.
Crawford, William H., 389, 398, 402, 427, 428, 439, 442.
Creasy, Sir Edward, 287.
Creek Indians, 12.
Croatoan, 139.
Cromwell, Oliver, 216.

460 INDEX.

Cromwell, Richard, 217.
Cudraigny, an Indian god, 112.
Cullenden, Rose, 207.
"Cumberland Road" bill, 404.
Custis, Nelly, 328.
Cutler, Dr. Manasseh, 310.
Cutts, Mrs., 376.

D.

Dane, Nathan, 306.
Danes, the, 34.
Danish Society of Antiquarians, 45.
Darby, William, 413, 415.
Dare, Ananias, 139.
Dare, Virginia, 140.
Darien, 68, 69.
Darwin, Charles, 4, 20.
D'Avezac, M., 77.
Davis, Captain Isaac, 245.
Davis, Isaac P., 373.
Davis, John, 344.
Deane, Charles, 77, 82, 219.
De Bry's imaginary monsters, 57.
Decatur, Commodore Stephen, 358.
Declaration of Independence, 273, 274, 289.
Deerfield, Mass., massacre at, 185.
Delaware, Lord, 149, 167.
Delaware settled, 167; connection with Pennsylvania, 213, 225.
Delft Haven, 154.
Democratic party, first called Republican, 336; triumph of, 343; material of, 351; long in power, 360; change in doctrines, 380.
Dennie, T. G., his *Portfolio*, 343; attack on Jefferson, 344.
Denonville, M., 184.
Dexter, F. B., 202.
Diaz, Bernal, 11, 108.
Dickens, Charles, 311.
Dickinson, John, quoted, 226; speech of, 271; also, 268, 270, 272, 277.
Dighton Rock, the, 42; figured, 45.
Diman, Professor, 202.
Donelson, Mrs., 448.
Dorchester Company, the, 161.
Dorchester, Mass., settled, 162.
Doringh, C. H. R., 44.
"Downing, Jack," 433.
Downing, Sir George, 193.
Drake, Sir Francis, portrait of, 91; maps of, 95; attack on San Domingo (figured), 99; also, 90, 92, 94, 96, 98, 100, 101, 104, 138.
Ducket, Lionel, 85.
Duelling at Washington, 364.

Duny, Anne, 207.
Dustin, Hannah, 173.
Dutch in America, the, 151, 168, 211.
Dutch West India Company, 152.
Dwight, Rev. Timothy, 398.

E.

"Eastward, Ho!" quoted, 146.
Eaton, Mrs., 448.
Education in the colonies, 201.
Edwards, Dr. Enoch, 281.
El Dorado, 105.
Elephant Mound, the, 26.
Elephant Pipe, the, 26.
Eliot, Rev. John, 126, 194, 195, 253.
Elizabeth, Queen, Raleigh's tribute to, 107; also, 84, 88, 90, 96, 107.
Ellery, William, quoted, 282; also, 284, 306.
Ellis, Dr. George E., quoted, 126, 171, 174.
Embargo, the, 356; Bryant's poem against it, 356.
Emerson, R. W., quoted, 384.
Emerson, Rev. William, quoted, 257.
Endicott, John, portrait of, 161; also, 162, 164, 195, 218.
England. (See Great Britain.)
English nation, an, predicted by Raleigh, 137.
Englishmen in America, second generation of, 192.
Erik the Red, 36, 41.
Eskimo, 23.
Eustis, Dr. William, 247.
Everett, Edward, 399, 400, 401.
Everett, Dr. William, quoted, 48.
Ewaiponima, an imaginary race, 106.
Excommunication of Fletcher by Drake, 100.

F.

Fauchet, Baron, 331.
Federalists, their inconsistency, 369; their defence of the right of search, 370; their decline, 355, 362; partisanship, 371; their provocations, 372.
Ferdinand, King of Spain, 55, 62, 63, 78.
Fernow, Berthold, 151, 152.
Fersen, Count, 335.
Fielding, Henry, 265.
Finance, American, established by Hamilton, 320.
"First" and "Second" Virginia colonies, 141.
Flag, the American, 291.
Fletcher, Rev. Francis, 93, 100.
Flint, Timothy, 414, 415, 419.
Flora, American, transformed, 217.

INDEX. 461

Florida, mounds of, 15; origin of name of, 71; purchase of, 390.
Floyd, John, 451.
Forrest, Mrs., 149.
Fort Caroline, Florida, 116, 117.
Fort Moultrie, defence of, 263.
Foster, J. W., cited, 14.
Fountain of Youth, search for the, 70.
Fox, Captain, 62.
Fox, Charles James, 288.
France, policy of, towards Indians, 124, 132; discoveries of, 182; activity of, 189; claims surrendered, 191; first treaty with, 287; army of, in America, 289; influence of, on America, 328, 333; X, Y, Z negotiations, 341.
Francis I., 109.
Franklin, Benjamin, quoted, 241, 279, 304; letter to, 294; his political theory, 305; also, 224, 265, 268, 270, 274, 275, 287, 298, 305.
Franks, Rebecca, 323, 324.
Freedom, religious, in Rhode Island and Maryland, 199.
French and Indian wars, 132.
French Revolution: influence upon Americans, 328, 329; influence on party lines, 333.
Freneau, Philip, 329, 398.
Freydis, a Norse woman, 40.
Frobisher, Captain Martin, 97, 98.
Frontenac, Comte de, 124, 184.
Frost, Mr., 234.
Frothingham, Richard, quoted, 243; also, 256, 269.
Fulton, Robert, 420.

G.

Gage, General Thomas, 254, 267.
Gallatin, Albert, 335, 374, 389, 437.
Garnier, Père, 125.
Garrison, W. L., 454.
Gates, General Horatio, 287.
Genet, E. C., 329, 330, 331.
George III., King, 288.
Georgia, mounds of, 15; settlement of, 233; Continental troops of, 292.
Germantown, Pa., battle of, 286.
Gerry, Elbridge, 279, 299, 304, 321, 374.
Gilbert, Raleigh, 142.
Gilbert, Sir Humphrey, 97.
Gilman, D. C., cited, 389, 403.
Gleig, Rev. G. R., 361.
Globe of Schoner (figured), 67.
Gomara, F. L. de, 11, 82.
Goodrich, A., 64.
Goodrich, James, speech of, 388.

Goodrich, S. G., cited, 400.
Gorges, Sir F., 141, 143.
Gorton, Samuel, 199.
Gosnold, Bartholomew, 140, 146, 148, 154.
Gougou, an Indian monster, 131, 210.
Gourgues, Dominique de (figured), 120; also, 119.
Gouverneur, Mrs., 395.
Governor Shirley's War, 187.
Grant, Mrs., of Laggan, 238.
Gravier, M., 49.
Gray, Dr. Asa, 24.
Great Britain: explorations from, 76; seamen of, 84; wars of, with Spain, 88; claims of discovery, 97; early colonies of, 138; wars with France, 169; with Indians, 172; love of colonists for, 216; love changed into hatred, 217; aggressions of, 217; official ignorance in, 223; feeling in, towards colonies, 223; outbreak of war, 241; peace negotiations with, 292; Jay's treaty with, 331; new aggressions of, 355; second war with, 360; treaty of Ghent with, 378.
Greene, George W., 109.
Greene, General Nathaniel, 284, 291.
Greenland, 36, 46, 48, 50, 51.
Grenville, Sir Richard, 138.
Grimalfson, Bjarni, 31.
Griswold, R. W., 324.
Grundy, Lewis, 362, 365.
Guiana, 105.
Gun-boats, Jefferson's, 356, 373.
Gutierrez, Pedro, 61.

H.

Hackit, Thomas, 116.
Hakluyt, Richard, 85, 96, 109, 138.
Hale, John P., 384.
Hale, Sir Matthew, quoted, 207.
Hall, Bishop, quoted, 153, 207.
Halleck, F. G., quoted, 394.
Hallowell, R. P., 204.
Hamilton, Alexander, financial achievements of, 320; quoted, 331; quarrel with Adams, 343; death of, 355; also, 312, 316, 319, 326, 330, 333, 340, 342, 343, 350, 355, 361, 382.
Hamilton, Mrs., 312.
Hancock, John, quoted, 279; letter to, 285; also, 254, 259, 277.
Hannibal, 70.
Harold, King, 30, 34.
Harris, Captain, 254.
Harrison, Benjamin, quoted, 279.
Harrison, General W. H., 375.

Harrisse, H., 62.
Hartford Convention, the, 372.
Hartop, Job, 104, 143.
Harvard, Rev. John, 194.
Haven, S. F., quoted, 22.
Hawkes, Henry, 105.
Hawkins, Sir John, portrait of, 86; arms of, 88; also, 85, 86, 87, 88, 89, 90, 96, 103, 104, 118.
Hawthorne, N., quoted, 192; also, 187, 400.
Hay, Mrs., 395.
Hazard, Isaac Peace, 237.
Hazard, Robert, 237.
Heath, General Benjamin, 249.
"Heimskringla," the, quoted, 30.
Helluland, 38, 50.
Henrietta Maria, Queen, 165.
Henry IV. (of France), 128.
Henry VI. (of England), 88.
Henry VII. (of England), 78, 80, 81, 84.
Henry, Miss, 422.
Henry, Patrick, 229, 231, 298, 300, 304.
Heriulf, 37.
Herrera, T. A., quoted, 58, 59, 60, 61, 72.
Higginson, Rev. Francis, quoted, 162, 163, 197; also, 195.
Hochelaga (Montreal), 111, 112.
Hodenosote (Iroquois house), 12, 14.
Holst, Dr. Von, 299.
Homer, 194, 195.
Hooke, Rev. William, quoted, 216, 231.
Hooker, Rev. Thomas, quoted, 220; also, 195.
Hóp, 39, 48.
Hopkins, Stephen, 227.
Hopkinson, Francis, 266.
Horace, 194.
Howe, Sir William, 253, 256, 281, 282, 285.
Howell, James, 48, 207.
Howells, W. D., 349.
Hubbard, Rev. William, 176.
Hudson, Henry, 143, 151, 152.
Huguenot colonies, French, 115, 116, 118, 120.
Hull, Commodore Isaac, 398.
Hull, General William, 374.
Humboldt, Alexander von, 58, 62.
Humphreys, David, 398.
Hundred Years' War, the, 169.
Hutchinson, Mrs. Anne, 199.
Hutchinson, Governor Thomas, quoted, 158; also, 162, 259.

I.

Iceland, Northmen in, 36; visited by Columbus, 53; also, 50, 51, 52.

Ignorance of English officials, 223.
Illinois admitted as a State, 393; unsettled, 407, 416; settled, 417.
Impressment of seamen (figured), 367.
Independence, American, early feeling about, 266, 267; dawning of, 241; war for, 242; second war for, 360. (See Revolutionary War.)
Indiana admitted as a State, 393; unsettled, 416; settled, 417.
Indians, American, families of, 4; mounds built by, 16; inscriptions made by (figured), 44, 46; ill-treatment of, 109; of Florida (figured), 117, 118; their superstitions, 131; their warfare (figured), 134; found gentle by first explorers, 169; how treated by English, 170, 178; by French and Spanish, 122, 182; by Dutch, 180; purchases from, 170; sentiments of Puritans towards, 171, 175; warfare of, influenced by English, 132, 133, 172; its influence on that of colonists, 173; position of women among, 176; women at first respected by, 177; outbreaks encouraged by French, 184; converted by Rasle, 186; their opinion of colonists, 189; later wars with, 327.
Institutions, American, origin of, 214.
Interglacial period, man in, 25.
Internal improvements, 404, 406, 411, 418, 420.
Intolerance in Maryland, 200; in Virginia, 202; in Massachusetts, 203.
Iroquois Indians, 12, 13, 132, 134, 183.
Irving, Washington, 62, 64, 400, 402.
Isabella, Queen, 55, 62, 78.
Italy, influence of, on American discovery, 76.

J.

Jackson, Andrew: his character, 432; causes of his popularity, 432; Webster's fears of, 434; popular views of, 434; portrait of, 435; early career of, 437; "reign" of, 438; first election of, 440; Jefferson's distrust of, 441; political changes made by, 442; Sullivan's opinion of, 442; inauguration of, 444; manners of, 444; his contest with Washington ladies, 448; his dealing with nullification, 450; his re-election, 451; his contest with the United States Bank, 452; also, 239, 396.
Jackson, Mrs. Helen, description of pueblo, 7.
Jackson, Dr. W. H., 6.
James II., 183.
Japanese and American flora, 24; junks crossing the Pacific, 23, 24.
Jasper, Sergeant, 263.
Jay, Chief-justice John, treaty of, 328, 331; also, 324, 333, 340, 343, 355, 361.

INDEX.

Jay, Mrs. John, 312.
Jefferson, Thomas: his election as Vice-president, 332; his feeling as to French Revolution, 334, 335; his election as President, 343; his portrait, 345; his inauguration, 346; attack on, in *Portfolio*, 347; charges against, 347; his house-keeping, 349; his re-election, 355; his view of townships, 357; his character, 358; his friendship with Adams, 359; his successors, 360; his aversion to commerce, 373; also, 234.
Jeffrey, Lord, 400.
Jemison, Mary, 177.
Jesuit Missions, 122, 125, 127.
Johnson, William, 434.
Johnston, Lady. (See Franks, Rebecca.)
Jones, Captain Paul, 291.
Juvenal, 194.

K.

Kalm, Peter, 224.
Karlsefne, 39, 41.
Kendall, Amos, 452.
Kendall, John, 147.
Kenton, Simon, 421.
Kentucky, resolutions of 1799, 343; admitted as a State, 353; early life in, 327, 421.
Kialarness, 39.
Kieft, Governor Jacob, 167, 180.
King, Clarence, 415.
"King Henry VI.," play of, quoted, 88.
King Philip's War, 176.
King, Rufus, portrait of, 401; also, 306, 355, 380, 383.
King William's War, 183.
Kinglake, A. W., 254.
King's Arms, tearing down of, in Philadelphia (figured), 281.
Kingsley, Charles, 92.
Kinney, Mr., 52.
Kirke, Colonel, 220.
Knox, General, letters from, 297, 304; also, 302, 310, 312, 328, 332, 395.
Knox, Mrs. General, 310, 312, 323.
Kohl, J. G., 77, 143.
Kortwright, Miss, 395.
Krossaness, 39.
Krudener, Baron, 449.
Kuhn, Dr., 424.

L.

Lafayette, G. M. de (Marquis), 283, 286, 287, 334.
La Hontan, Baron, quoted, 172, 183, 185.

Landa, D. de, 19; alphabet, 18.
Lane, Ralph, 138.
Langbourne, Major, 240.
Lapham, I. A., cited, 26.
La Roche, De, 121.
La Salle, Robert C. de, 181.
Laudonnière, Réné de, 88, 116.
Las Casas, Bishop de, his protest against cruelty, 74; also, 123.
Lauzun, Duc de, 289, 335.
Lawrence, Captain James, 375.
Lawyers, rise of, in colonies, 239.
Laydon, John, 149.
League of four colonies, 177.
Le Caron, Père, 123.
Lee, Ann, 199.
Lee family (Marblehead, Mass.), 238.
Lee, General Charles, 257.
Lee, Richard Henry, 227, 267, 268, 305; son of, 267.
Leif the Lucky, 38; his booths, 38, 39.
Leifsbudir, 39.
Leighton, Caroline C., 415.
Leisler, Jacob, 222.
Le Jeune, Père, 125.
Le Moyne, 116, 117, 119.
Leon, Ponce de, portrait of, 71; his voyage, 71; also, 143.
Le Plongeon, Dr., 2.
Lescarbot, 125.
Leverett, Governor John, courageous reply of, 217.
Lewis and Clark's expedition, 11, 350.
Lewis, Meriwether, 350.
Lewis, William B., 439.
Lincoln, Abraham, 327.
Lincoln, Governor Levi, 444.
Livingston, Cora, 422.
Livingston, Edward, 450.
Livingston, Robert R., 268, 274, 275, 308, 407.
Livingston, the brothers, 227.
Locke, John, his singular plan of government, 212.
Lodge, H. C., quoted, 162.
Lodge, Thomas, 85.
Longfellow, H. W., quoted, 97; also, 236, 400.
Long Island, battle of, 284.
Lorges, Roselly de, 64.
Lossing, B. J., 376.
Louis XV., 223.
Louisburg, capture of, 187, 223.
Louisiana, purchase of, 354, 407; admitted as a State, 379.
Loundes, William J., 379.

INDEX.

Lovewell, Captain John, 174.
Lowell, John, 369, 371.
Lubbock, Sir J., 25.
Lundy's Lane, battle at, 377.

M.

Macaulay, Lord, 201.
Macon, Nathaniel, 350.
McDuffie, George, 424.
McKean, Thomas, recollections of, 276; letter from, 277; also, 278, 314.
Madison, James: his election as President, 358; his appearance, 361; his portrait, 363; Federalist charges against, 371; his aversion to war, 371; close of his administration, 379.
Madison, Mrs. James, 361, 362, 365, 395.
Magellan, Ferdinand de, 70.
Magnus, King, 35.
Mail-service, 404, 405.
Maine, forts in, 184; Indian wars in, 186; admitted as a State, 393.
Maine Historical Society, 50.
Major, R. H., 77.
Malbone, Godfrey, 238.
Mammoth on ivory, 25.
Man in Interglacial period, 25.
Mandan Indians, 12, 15.
Manhattan Island, 152, 170.
Manning, Cardinal, 200.
Manufactures, introduction of, 195.
Map showing advance of population, 416.
Maps (figured): Sigurd Stephanius's, 50; Da Vinci's, 66; Schoner's (globe), 67; Cabot's, 79; Drake's, 95; Smith's, 145, 148; Ortelius's, 108.
Marckland, 38, 50.
Marietta, O., 15.
Marion, General Francis, 263.
Marlborough, Duke of, 186.
Marquette, Père, 181.
Marshall, Chief-justice John, 434.
Marston, John, quoted, 146.
Martin, John, 147, 148.
Martyr, Peter. (See Anghiera.)
Maryland founded, 165; religious freedom in, 167, 199; intolerance in, 200; education in, 201; witchcraft in, 208; old institutions of, 215; manners in, 235; insurrections in, 454.
Mason, George, 288.
Mason, Jeremiah, 441.
Mason, Mr., 387.
"Massachusettensis," 242.
Massachusetts Bay Colony founded, 158, 161; relations with Indians, 170; toleration in, 197; education in, 201; intolerance in, 205.
Massachusetts, formed by union with Plymouth, 213; independent spirit of, 217; charter of, vacated, 220; preparations for war in, 144; circular of committee, quoted, 249; services of, in Revolution, 292; Shays's insurrection in, 302; services of, in war of 1812, 379.
Massasoit, 172, 175.
Masts sent by Massachusetts colony to England, 218.
Mather, Rev. Cotton, portrait of, 196; fictitious letter from, 206; quoted, 175, 203, 208, 210; also, 195, 197, 204.
Mather, Rev. Increase, quoted, 171, 219.
Mayas, 2, 4, 17, 19, 63; alphabet of, 18, 19; sculptures of, 22.
Mayflower, agreement on the, 156.
Mechanic arts, introduction of, 195.
Medford, Mass., settled, 162.
Membertou, 126.
Menendez, Pedro, 119.
Mercator's charts, 56.
Mercer, General, 327.
Mermaids, 56.
Merry, Mr., 347, 349.
Merry Mount, 164.
Mexico, ancient, 10, 11, 13, 17; modern, 76.
Miami Indians, the, 327.
Michael, Emperor, 30.
Michigan admitted as a State, 453.
Miller, W. J., 44, 45.
Mills, Elijah H., 398.
Milton, John, quoted, 106.
Minuit, Peter, 152, 167, 170.
Missouri admitted as a State, 393.
Missouri Compromise, 393.
Mitchell, Professor Henry, cited, 49.
Mobile, Ala., settled, 182.
Mohave Indians, 12.
Monocrats, the, 329.
Monroe doctrine, the, 403.
Monroe, James, called "James II." by Josiah Quincy, 360; elected President, 380; his record, 381; importance of his tour, 381; his fear of extended territory, 383; his portrait, 385; his character and physique, 384; his travels, 387; his policy, 389; his re-election all but unanimous, 394; American literature born under him, 398; the Monroe doctrine, 403; his views of the post-office, 404.
Monroe, Mrs. James, 395.
Montcalm, General de, portrait of, 190; also, 189, 191.

INDEX.   465

Montezuma, 4, 11.
"Montezuma," a nickname for Washington, 332.
"Montezuma's Dinner," Morgan's essay on, 4.
Montgomery, General James, 263.
Montreal captured, 191.
Monts, Pierre de, 121, 122, 141.
Moon, Thomas, 92.
Morgan, L. H., 11, 13, 17, 21, 23, 456.
Morris, Gouverneur, 349, 420.
Morris, Robert, 272.
Morse, John T., Jr., quoted, 447.
Morton, Mrs., 291, 326.
Motte, Lieutenant-colonel, 263.
Moultrie, General William, 263.
Mound-builders, the, 2, 15; village of (figured), 14.
Mount Desert first described, 129.
Mount Hope Bay, 48, 49, 50.
Moustier, Comte de, 312.
Mullinger, J. B., 194.

N.

Napoleon. (See Bonaparte.)
Narrowing influence of colonial life, 197.
Navarrete, M. F. de, 62.
Navy, United States, first Secretary of, 342; battles of, 291, 342, 356, 369, 374.
Nechecolee Indians, 12.
Neill, E. D., 200.
Neutral French, the, in Acadia, 189.
Neuville, M. Hyde de, 396.
Neuville, Madame de, 397.
New Amsterdam founded, 152; nationalities in, 153, 211.
New England first named, 144; colonies of, their influence on reviving Virginia colony, 158, 195.
Newfoundland, origin of name of, 83.
New France, Jesuits in, 122; also, 108, 182.
New Hampshire settled, 174, 184; independence of, 213; buildings in, 233.
Newhouse, Sewall, 414.
New Jersey settled, 152; independence of, 213; campaigns in, 284.
New Mexico, pueblos of, 19; Indian inscriptions in, 44, 46.
New Netherlands, name changed, 165; surrender to English, 181, 211.
New Orleans, battle of, 377, 438.
New Plymouth. (See Plymouth.)
Newport, Captain Christopher, 146.
Newport, R. I., old mill at, 42; figured, 43; French in, 289.

New York (city), harbor of, 144; first seat of government, 309; society in, 310; also, see New Amsterdam.
New York, originally New Netherlands, 152, 165, 168, 181; governor of, quoted, 181; transferred to English, 211; revolt of, against Andros, 222; British army in, 260, 263; population of, in 1817, 388.
Nez Percé Indians, 11.
Nicholls, Mr., 81.
Nichols, B. R., 407.
Nicolls, General, 211.
Nixon, John, 280.
Niza, Fray Marco de, 10.
North Carolina colonized, 98; divided from South Carolina, 213; plans a fleet, 300; insurrections in, 454.
North, Lord, 288.
Northern colonies, condition of labor in, 239.
Northmen, their lineage, 28; their habits, 28; their jewellery, 29; their heroism, 30; their ships described, 31; their ships (figured), 27, 32; dress of, 35; precise topography of, unknown, 46; no authentic remains of, 46.
North-west Territory, 306.
Nova Scotia, Northmen in, 48.
Nuñez, Alvar (Cabeza de Vaca), his voyage, 72; also, 10, 181.
Nuñez, Vasco (Balboa), portrait of, 68; his discovery of Pacific Ocean, 69.

O.

Oglethorpe, General James, 225.
Ohio, mounds of, 2, 15, 17, 19; Company, the, 307; admitted as a State, 354.
Ohio River, early life on, 419.
Old English seamen, the, 75.
Old French War, the, 189.
Old mill at Newport, 42; figured, 43; the same at Chesterton, England, 43; figured, 44.
O'Neil, Peggy. (See Eaton, Mrs.)
Onondaga Indians, 16.
"Orders in Council," British, 355, 365.
Ordinance of 1787, 306.
Orinoco, the river, 100.
Ortèlius, maps (figured), 108.
Osceola, 453.
Osgood, J. R., 116.
Ossoli, Margaret Fuller, 415.
Otis, C. P., 128.
Otis, H. G., 388.
Otis, James, quoted, 223; portrait of, 223; also, 229, 352.
Otto, M., 297, 313.

31

Ovid, 195.
Oxenstiern, Chancellor, 167.

P.

Pacific Ocean, seen by Balboa, 69; by Drake, 91.
Page, John, 321.
Paine, Robert Treat, 326, 342.
Paine, Thomas, 270, 271, 399.
Palfrey, J. G., 43.
Parish, Rev. Daniel, 370.
Parker, Captain, 245.
Parker, Professor Joel, 240.
Parkman, Francis, quoted, 121, 125, 181, 198; cited, 119, 126; not quite just to the Puritans, 198.
Parties, enmity between, 371; changes in, 379, 390; disappearance of, 439.
Parton, James, 275, 278, 360, 437.
Pasqualigo, Lorenzo, 80, 81.
Peace of Paris, 169, 191; of Ryswick, 185; of Utrecht, 186.
Penn, William, his arrival, 213; his relations with Indians, 213; also, 174, 213, 222.
Pennsylvania, settlement of, 213; relations of Delaware with, 213, 225; society in, 282, 323; campaigns in, 286; but one legislative body in, 298.
Pentucket (Haverhill) attacked, 185.
Pepperrell, Sir William, 187; portrait of, 188.
Pequot War, the, 169, 175.
Percy, Lord, 247, 248.
Perez, Juan, 71.
Perkins, J. H., 422.
Perry, Commodore O. H., 375.
Peter Martyr, 11, 59.
Peter, Mrs., 422.
Peters, Dr., 202.
Peters, John, 238.
Peyster, Mr. De, 376.
Philadelphia, the seat of government, 230, 322; life in, 323, 324, 325; population of, in 1817, 388.
Philip II. of Spain, 85, 87, 88, 90, 104.
Philip, King (Indian), death of (figured), 179; also, 169, 170, 171, 176, 178, 180, 183, 218.
Philoponus, 57.
Phips, Sir William, 185, 187.
Physique of Americans changed, 217.
Pickering, Timothy, 306, 369.
Pierria, Albert de la, 116.
Pilgrims (Plymouth), landing of, 158; visit to shore (figured), 159.
"Pilgrims of St. Mary's," the, 165.

Pinckney, Charles C., 320, 342, 343, 355, 358.
Pinkney, William, 374.
Pioneers, early frontier, 421.
Pitcairn, General, 245.
Pitt, William, 191, 241, 242.
Pizarro, Francisco, 70, 73.
Plastowe, Josias, 170.
Pliny, 194.
Plutarch, 194.
Plymouth colony founded, 153; compact of, 156; relations of, with Indians, 170, 175; toleration in, 197; merged in Massachusetts, 213.
Pocahontas, 143.
Point Comfort first named, 147.
Polo, Marco, 55.
Pont-Gravé, M. de, 128.
Pontiac, conspiracy of, 191.
Poole, W. F., 207, 209.
Poor, General Enoch, 253.
Popham colony, the, 141, 154.
Popham, George, 142.
Popham, Sir John, 141, 142.
Population: of colonies, 225; of New York in 1787, 309; of cities in 1817, 388; increase in, 406; Madison's estimate of, 322; advance of, 414, 415; of United States in 1830, 453.
Port Bill, Boston, 229.
Port Royal, N. S., taken, 185.
Port Royal Harbor (S. C.) first described, 116.
"Portia." (See Adams, Abigail.)
Portugal and Spain, possessions of, in the New World, 75, 108.
Pott, Dr., 202.
Potter, Elisha, 423.
Powhatan (figured), 144; also, 139, 143.
Preble, Judge, 441.
Prescott, General, 259.
Prescott, W. H., 4.
Prideaux, General John, 191.
Princeton, defeat of Cornwallis at, 285.
Pring, Martin, 140, 141.
Printz, John, 168.
Protestant colonies, French, 115, 116, 118, 120.
Provincial life introduced, 220, 222.
Ptolemy, 66.
Public men usually criticised with justice, 442.
Pueblos, 3, 5, 7, 9, 10, 12. (Special) Acoma, 8; Bonito, 6; Chacos, 19; High Bank, 17; Hungo Pavie (figured), 5, 6; Moqui, 10; Pintado (figured), 2, 3; San Juan, 7; Taos (figured), 8; Zuñi, 8.
Pulaski, Count, 286.
Puritans, numbers of, 164; sacrifices of, 192; ballads concerning, 193; out-door life of, 193;

INDEX.

social and educational character, 194; amusements of, 195; injustice done to, 198; proportion of educated men, 202.
Putnam, F. W., 5, 15.
Putnam, General Israel, 252, 259, 284.
Putnam, General Rufus, 306.

Q.

Quakers, the, in Rhode Island, 199; in Maryland and Virginia, 202; in Massachusetts, 204; objections to, 204; defences of, 204; exhorter (figured), 205.
Quebec, unsuccessful siege of, 185; fall of, 191.
Queen Anne's War, 185.
Quincy, Josiah (Member of Congress), 311, 360, 362, 365, 380.
Quincy, Josiah (junior), recollections of, 422, 444, 447; also, 423.
Quincy, Mrs. Josiah (senior), 234, 288, 291, 349, 361, 362, 373, 402.

R.

Rafn, Professor, 28, 41, 42, 43, 47, 48, 49, 51.
Raleigh, Sir Walter, 97, 98, 101, 104, 105, 106, 137, 138, 140, 141, 143, 158, 168.
Raleigh, Va., 138.
Ramusio, 109.
Randolph, Edmund, 331.
Randolph, Edward, 183, 218, 223.
Randolph, John, picture of, 397; character of, 398; quoted, 454; also, 312, 336, 393, 396, 428.
Randolph, Miss, 398.
Rask, Professor, 48.
Rasle, Père (Father), fac-simile from his glossary, 186; also, 174, 186.
Ratcliffe, John, 146, 148.
Reed, General Joseph, 264, 272, 285.
Republican government, distrust of, 293, 352.
Republican party. (See Democratic party.)
Revere, Paul, 244.
Revolutionary War, battles in, at Lexington, 245; of Concord, 245; taking of Ticonderoga, 251; of Bunker Hill, 256; at Quebec, 263; defence of Fort Moultrie, 263; at Long Island, 284; at Fort Washington, 284; at Trenton, 285; at Princeton, 285; at Brandywine, 286; at Germantown, 286; at Bennington, 287; at Saratoga, 287; at Yorktown, 291; of General Greene, 291; statistics of war, 244, 285, 292, 293.
Rhode Island, purchase of, 171; toleration in, 199; education in, 201; French army in, 289.

Ribaut, Jean, his landing, figured, 115; also, 117, 118, 140, 211.
Richmond, Duke of, 288.
Riedesel, Baroness, 238.
Riedesel, General, 239.
Right of search, British, 355, 366.
Roads and canals, opening of, 411, 417, 420.
Robinson, John, 154, 156.
Robinson, Rowland, 237.
Rochambeau, Comte de, 291, 322.
Rochester, N. Y., 415.
Rodney, Cæsar, 272, 276, 277.
Rogers, Samuel, 62.
Rolfe, John, 149.
Ross, General, 375, 376, 377.
Roxbury, Mass., settled, 162.
Rule, Margaret, 210.
Rupert, Prince, 256.
Rush, Richard, 412, 441.
Russell, Mrs. Jonathan, 397.
Rutledge, Edward, 268, 273.

S.

Sac Indians, 12.
Sagadehoc River (Kennebec), 141.
Saguenay, 111.
St. Asaph's, Bishop of, 283.
St. Augustine, Fla., 119.
St. Castin's War, 183.
St. Clair, General, 327.
St. John, Henry (Viscount Bolingbroke), 186.
St. John's River explored, 116.
St. Lawrence River explored by Cartier, 108, 110.
St. Louis, Mo., 388.
St. Simon's Island, Ga., 1.
Salem, Mass., settlement of, 161; witchcraft at, 208; old usages of, 214.
Sallust, 194.
Sanchez, Roderigo, 61.
Sanctuary, land of the, 167.
San Francisco, Cal., 96.
San Juan de Ulloa, sea-fight at (figured), 89.
Santander, Dr. Pedro, 122.
Saratoga, N. Y., victory at, 287; surrender of Burgoyne at, 287.
Sardinian impressions of Columbus, 52.
Sargasso Sea, the, 58.
Sassafras, trade in, 140.
Savonarola, Girolamo, 199.
Scalps taken by English, 173.
Schenectady, Indian massacre at, 184; also, 413.
Schoner, Johann, globe of, 67.

Schuyler, General Philip, 259.
Schuyler mansion at Albany, 238.
Scientific surveys, 418.
Scott, General Winfield, 450.
Seamen, old English, 75.
Sea of Darkness, the, 56.
Second generation in America, the, 192.
Sedgwick, Catharine, 350.
Sedgwick, Mrs. Theodore, 323.
Selectmen, origin of, 240.
Seminole War, 453.
Seven Bishops, the, 10.
Seven Cities, the, 10, 105.
Sewall, Samuel, portrait of, 208; his share in witchcraft trials, 208.
Shakespeare, William, quoted, 88, 106, 252.
Shays, Daniel, 302, 330.
Shepard, Rev. Thomas, 195.
Sherman, Roger, 268, 274, 275.
Sherwood, Grace, 208.
Shirley, Governor, 187, 259.
Sidney, Sir Philip, 101.
Simpson, Lieutenant J. H., 3, 6, 44.
Skelton, Rev. John, 162, 195.
Skraelings, the, 39, 40; not Indians, 49.
Slafter, E. F., 41, 128, 132.
Slavery first introduced at St. Augustine, 119; in Virginia, 144, 240; influence of, in Northern colonies, 235, 240; in Southern colonies, 239; discussion of, 350, 393, 454, 455.
Slave-trade, the, 85, 87, 88; prohibited, 358.
Smith, Buckingham, 73.
Smith, Chief-justice and Mrs., 291.
Smith, Captain John, portrait of, 142; his romantic spirit, 143; his descriptions, 143; his map, 144, 145, 148; quoted, 138, 147, 150, 172; cited, 153, 154; also, 139, 143, 145, 147, 148, 149, 151, 152, 165, 170.
Smith, Colonel, 244, 247.
Smith, Samuel H., 347.
Smith, Sydney, 400, 451.
Snorri, 40.
Snorri Sturleson, 30.
Society, American, manners in, 309, 310, 313, 314, 349, 361, 362, 395, 396, 397, 422, 423, 448.
Soto, F. de, 73, 122, 182.
South Carolina, separated from North Carolina, 213; old institutions of, 215; State Constitution of, 294; nullification in, 450.
Southcote, Joanna, 199.
Spain and Portugal, possessions of, in the New World, 75, 108.
Spain, exaggerations of chroniclers of, 11; bigotry of, 122, 123; "Requisitions" of, 122; cruelty of, 128.
Spanish Armada, 104.
Sparke, John, 85.
Spring Creek, Tenn., 15.
Squaw sachem, the, 176.
Squier, E. G., 26.
Stackelburg, Baron, 423.
Stadaconé (Quebec), 112.
Stamp Act, the, 228.
Standish, Miles, 157, 158, 173, 195, 197.
Stark, General John, 287.
Starving time, the, 149.
States Rights doctrines, 316, 380, 408.
States, union of, 295.
Steamboats, introduction of, 420.
Stephanius, Sigurd, 50.
Stephens, J. L., 4, 12.
Steuben, Baron, 286.
Stevenson, Mary, 241.
Stiles, Rev. Ezra, quoted, 231, 305.
Stockton, Chief-justice, 269.
Storrs, W. L., 424.
Story, Judge Joseph, 372, 434.
Story, Thomas, defends Quaker nakedness, 205.
Stoughton, Lieutenant-governor, 164.
Strachey, William, 139.
Stuyvesant, Peter, tearing letter (figured), 212.
Succession, War of the Spanish, 185.
Sullivan, General, 263.
Sullivan, William, cited, 311, 312, 344; quoted, 314, 361, 372, 377, 442, 455; also, 349.
Sumner, Charles, 403.
Sumner, Professor W. G., 239, 439, 442, 453.
Swedish colony in Delaware, 167, 171, 211.
Sweinke, his defiance, 35.
Swift, General Joseph G., 387.

T.

Tadoussac, early fur trade at, 121.
Talleyrand-Perigord, Prince de, 324, 341, 342.
Taney, Chief-justice Roger B., 452.
Tariff, the, 350, 379, 389.
Taylor, Jeremy, 216.
Tecumseh, 375.
Temple, Sir John, 313.
Tennessee, mounds of, 15; admitted as a State, 354; emigrants to, 413.
Tennyson, Alfred, quoted, 129.
Terence, 194, 195.
Territory, National, increase of, 354, 383.
Thacher, Oxenbridge, 227, 259.
Thacher, Rev. Peter, bowling-alley of, 195.
Thirkill, Launcelot, 82.

INDEX.

Thomas, General, 252.
Thompson, John, 275.
Thomson, Charles, 277.
Thornton, Colonel Matthew, 277.
Thorwald, 38, 51.
Thorwaldsen, A. B., 40.
Thury, Père, 184.
Ticknor, George, 270.
Ticonderoga, capture of, 191.
Titles of the President, 314.
Tobacco, 154.
Tompkins, Daniel D., 394.
Topila, carved face from (figured), 22.
Torfæus, 41, 48, 50.
Tory Row, Cambridge, Mass., 238.
Town government, origin of, 239.
Tracy, Senator, 324.
Trades, introduction of, 195.
Treat, Robert, 222.
Treaty: of Ryswick, 185; of Utrecht, 186; of Paris, 292; Jay's, 331; with Tripoli, 358; of Ghent, 378.
Trenton, surprise of Hessians at, 285.
Triana, Rodrigo de, 62.
Tripoli, treaty with, 358.
Trist, N. P., 451.
Truxton, Commodore, 342.
Tudor, William, 256.
Tunnachemootoolt, village of (figured), 11.
Turner, J. M. W., 62.
Turner, Nat., 454.
Tylor, E. B., 13, 19.
Tyrker, 38.

U.

Underhill, Captain John, 175.
United States: first organized as a confederation, 296; becomes a nation, 304; Western lands of, 306; inauguration of government of, 308; social condition of, 309; division of parties in, 316, 329, 343; appointment of officials in, 320; adopts Washington as the seat of government, 322; early political violence in, 328, 332, 351, 371; negotiations with France, 329, 331, 340; treaty with England, 331; influence of French Revolution on, 333; great extension of territory of, 354; war with England (1812), 365; era of good feeling in, 381; great Western march of population of, 406; early maps of, 412; centre of population of, 416; wars with Indian tribes of, 453; rise of antislavery agitation in, 453.
Upham, C. W., 193.
Usselinx, William, 167.

Utica, N. Y., 413.
Uxmal, 12, 19.

V.

Valentine, Dr., 19.
Valley Forge, revolutionary army at, 286.
Van Buren, Martin, 398.
Van Rensselaer, Catherine, 422.
Varangian guard, the, 29.
Varnhagen, F. A. de, 64, 65.
Vassall family, 237, 238.
Vaughan, Mr., 449.
Vergennes, M. de, 287, 297.
Vermont admitted as a State, 353.
Verrazzano, his letters, 109; also, 76, 84, 108, 110.
Vespucci, Amerigo, new views concerning, 64, 65; also, 68, 70, 76, 79.
Vikings, visit of the, 27.
Villegagnon, M. de, 115.
Vinci, Leonardo da, 67.
Vinland, 36, 41, 48, 50; not identified, 51.
Virgil, 195.
Virginia, settlement of, 138; starvation in, 149; young women emigrants to (figured), 150; Indian massacres in, 175, 178, 190; education in, 201; intolerance in, 202; witchcraft in, 208; House of Burgesses, 239; resolutions of 1798, 343; insurrections in, 454.
Volney, C. F. C., Count de, 325.
Voltaire, F. M. A. de, 223.
Von Holst, Dr., 431, 438.
Voyageurs, the French, 108, 126, 135.

W.

Wadsworth, William, 219.
Waldsee-Müller, Martin, 65, 66.
Walker, Sir Hovenden, 186.
Wampanoag Indians, 44.
Wamsutta, 176.
War of 1812, opposition to, 372, 373, 374; battles during, 375.
War: the Hundred Years', 169; of the Spanish Succession, 185; of the Austrian Succession, 187; the Revolutionary (see Revolution); the Seminole, 453.
Warbeck, Perkin, 82.
Ward, General A., 253.
Wardwell, Lydia, 204.
Warner, Seth, 252, 253.
Warren, Dr. Joseph, 247, 248, 249, 250, 254, 258.
Warren, General James, 352.
Warren, Mrs. Mercy, spicy correspondence with John Adams, 351; portrait of, 353.

Warville, Brissot de, 322.
Washington City: adopted as the seat of government, 322; British capture of, 376; society in, 313, 314, 349, 361, 362, 395, 396, 397, 422, 423, 448; inhabitants of, 398, 423.
Washington, George, his portrait (frontispiece); his early Western expedition, 189; his report on Indian outrages, 190; takes command of Continental army, 257; his opinion of the army, 257; his views of discipline, 259; forces evacuation of Boston, 260; recognizes need of independence, 266; his promulgation of the Declaration of Independence, 283; his victories, 285; his anxieties, 285; despondent at last, 288; his dancing at Newport, 290; orders cessation of hostilities, 292; his distrust of the Confederation, 296, 301; his breakfast with Jefferson, 298; his release of prisoners from jail, 302; letter of Knox to, quoted, 304; his inauguration as President, 308; his administration, 309; his receptions, 313; his cabinet, 315; his re-election, 326; abuse of him, 331, 332; letter of Jefferson to, 359; his Farewell Address, 371; proposes canals, 420.
Washington, Mrs. George, 310, 313, 326.
Watertown, Mass., settled, 162.
Wayne, Anthony, 327.
Webb, Dr. T. A., 42, 43.
Webster, Daniel, quoted, 274, 434, 443, 444; portrait of, 445; also, 270, 274, 373, 398, 402, 422, 428, 440, 441.
Webster, Mrs. Daniel, 422, 423, 424.
Webster, Ezekiel, 440.
Weetamo, 176.
Welch, Dr., 248.
Welde, Rev. Thomas, 194.
Wellington, Duke of, 396.
Wentworth house in Portsmouth, N. H., 238.
West, Captain, 170.
Western States, early condition of, 407, 413; change in, 413.
Wheatley, Phillis, 326.
Wheeling, Va., 413.
Whiskey Insurrection, 330.
White, Father, 166.
White, John, 138, 139.
White, Mrs. Florida, 422.

White House, early life in, 340, 349, 361, 424.
White Man's Land, 41.
Whitney, Professor J. D., 26.
Whittier, J. G., 204, 205, 400, 402.
Wilkinson, Jemima, 199.
William, King, 183, 222.
Williams, Rev. John, 185.
Williams, Roger, banishment of, 164; purchase of Rhode Island by, 171; toleration of, 198; quoted, 199; also, 195, 202.
Wilson, Deborah, 204.
Wilson, James, 268.
Wingate, Paine, 235.
Wingfield, E. M., 147.
Winslow, Josiah, quoted, 175; also, 170, 176, 195.
Winsor, J., "Narrative and Critical History of America" quoted, 151.
Winthrop, Governor John (of Mass.), arrival of, 162; portrait of, 163, journal of, cited, 207; also, 193, 195, 197.
Winthrop, Governor John (of Connecticut), 185.
Winthrop, Hannah, 245.
Wirt, William, 451.
Wirt, Mrs. William, 422.
Witch, arrest of a (figured), 209.
Witchcraft: in Europe, 206; in Connecticut, 207; in Maryland, Virginia, New York, Massachusetts, 208.
Witherspoon, Dr., 269.
Wolcott, Oliver, 313, 329.
Wolcott, Mrs. Oliver, 323.
Wolfe, General James, portrait of, 191.
Wood's Holl, 48.
Wright, Colonel C. D., 194.
Wyatt, Hant, 202.
Wythe, George, 227.

X.

X, Y, Z correspondence, 341.

Y.

Yeomen of New England described, 239.
Yucatan, 2, 5, 19, 21; sculptures from (figured), 21, 22.

Z.

Zuazo, 11.
Zubly, Rev. J. J., 293.

THE END.